# *The Folklore of* GLOUCESTERSHIRE

— *Roy Palmer* —

WESTCOUNTRY
BOOKS

First published by Westcountry Books 1994



WESTCOUNTRY BOOKS

*Trade sales enquiries:*
Westcountry Books
Halsgrove House
Lower Moor Way
Tiverton. EX16 6SS

Tel: (0884) 243242
Fax: (0884) 243325



**British Library Cataloguing-in-Publication Data.**
A catalogue record for this book is
available from the British Library.

ISBN 1 898386 07 2

Printed by Hillman Printers (Frome) Ltd, U.K.

# CONTENTS

# PICTURE CREDITS

The author and publisher are grateful to the following individuals and organisations which kindly provided illustrations for use in this book. Numbers given are those of plates, unless otherwise indicated.

Blockley Antiquarian Society, 21 (photo: Mayo), 28; Bodleian Library, p.32 (shelfmark Ashm. G.12, 2344); N.R. Braithwaite, 10; Alan Buckwell, p.176; Cheltenham Art Gallery and Museums, p.164 (etching of Owlpen Manor, 1930, by F.M.L. Griggs, 1876-1938); 29 (details from 'The Dixton Harvesters', anon., c. 1725, oil on canvas); *The Citizen*, Gloucester, 6, 7, 27; Cotswold Countryside Collection, Northleach, 11, 12, 13, (photo: Henry Taunt); 20 (photo: F.J. Lawrence); 26,30 (photo: Percy Simms), 32, 34, 35, 37, 38 (photo: Butt of Bourton), 39; Dr J.V. Garrett, 9 (from J.H. Garrett, *From a Cotswold Height*, Cheltenham, 1919); Gloucester Folk Museum, p.145; Gloucestershire Collection, Gloucestershire Library, 3, p.234; *Gloucestershire Countryside*, 5; Gloucestershire Record Office, p.150 (D4923/1), p.180 (D4084 40/7); Haresfield W.I., 31; Hereford and Worcester County Libraries, 25 (photo: Alfred Watkins, 1855-1935); Pat Palmer, 1, 2, 4, 8, 14, 16, 17, 23, 24; Vaughan Williams Memorial Library, Cecil Sharp House, London, 33 (photo: Cecil Sharp); Withington W. I., 19; Yate W. I., 36; Despite extensive enquiries we have been unable to trace the estate of Anton A. van Anrooy (1870-1949), p.260.

## DEDICATION

**For Pat**
with love, to mark our
fortieth wedding anniversary

# INTRODUCTION

What is Gloucestershire, and what is folklore? I have treated the county as it was in 1974, which is how it had been - a few peripheral changes apart - for a thousand years. My stance has been vindicated by the proposal that the county should regain what it lost to Avon, but it would be ironic if the price were to be that no overall authority for Gloucestershire would remain.

Folklore is perhaps best when it is not recognised as such. A pithy saying is simply part of local wisdom. A ghost story gives a first-hand account of a personal experience. A seasonal ritual continues because the participants feel strongly for family or community reasons that it should.

Gloucestershire is extremely rich in historical traditions, stories stemming from river, spring and standing stone, village lore, church legends, superstitions, tales of the supernatural, sporting passion and working wisdom, song, dance, drama and calendar custom. And all these have greater variety through the triple division of 'Forest, vale and high blue hill'.

Many books - histories, reminiscences, essays, poems - mention the folklore of Gloucestershire. Articles and pamphlets describe it - and I am indebted to many of them, as my bibliography shows; but I found to my surprise that no single work of substance was devoted exclusively to it. Hence the present book.

The emphasis is on what people do, say or believe now, or what was the case in living or recent memory, but for perspective information is also given from earlier times. With such a wealth of material choice is inevitable, but precise detail has been preferred to generalisation.

Times change, and folklore with them (to adapt an adage). Elements fall away and cease to live in people's minds and on their lips. In Bibury, for example, I could find no one who knew the classic tale of the Oxford scholar who teaches the landlord of the 'Swan' to draw two different beers from one cask. On the other hand I was able casually to walk into the village pub at Ebrington and to find a man there, Harold Payne, who had a fund of local lore, including that of the 'Yubberton yawnies'. Yet this too - heaven forfend - could be jeopardised by demographic and technological change, which is why a work of record is worthwhile. As Francis Bacon wrote, 'Out of monuments, names, words, traditions, fragments of stories and the like, we do save and recover somewhat from the deluge of time.'

# ACKNOWLEDGEMENTS

I am particularly indebted to F.W. Baty, (for reading part of the typescript and making a number of suggestions), Paul Burgess (information on Harward and Willey), Keith Chandler (for allowing me to see part of his work on the Gloucestershire Morris before publication), Richard Chidlaw (information on wassailing and mumming), Gwilym Davies (information on songs and customs) and Pat Palmer (tune transcriptions and proof reading).

I should also like to thank for advice and information Derek Appleing, Gordon Ashman, Rev. A.C. Berry, Veronica M. Brown, Alan Buckwell, Tracey Caldwell, Mrs M.J. Carrick, E.C. Cawte, Mrs Mollie Davies, Rev. D.F.F. Evans, Mrs A. Fenn, Ron Fletcher, Rev. J.E. Gethyn-Jones, Peter Grierson, Valerie Grosvenor Myer, Bill Hall, Rob Harrison, Glyn and Chris Hoare, Lavender Jones, Richard Mabey, Hilary Mahoney, Hugh Morrison, Iona Opie, Jack Parry, Mrs Dorothy Petrie, Rev. Pat Pinkerton, Bill Pullen, Bill Reece, Leslie Roberts, Miss H. Rouse, Mike Rust, Leslie Shepard, Brian Simmons, Dave Stephenson, Mrs A. Shurmer, Mrs Vic Sutton, Alan Swale, Ron Taylor, James Thompson, Roy Vickery, Jack Watkins and Canon D. Welander.

I am grateful for the help of these institutions: BBC Radio Gloucestershire (Geraldine McCullagh and Bob Sharpe), Bodleian Library (Mike Heaney), Cambridge University Library, Corinium Museum (David Viner), Folklore Society Library (Caroline Oates), Glasgow University Library, Gloucester Folk Museum (Chris Morris), Gloucestershire Collection in Gloucester City Library, Gloucestershire Record Office, Library of Congress, University College London Library and Vaughan Williams Memorial Library at Cecil Sharp House (Malcolm Taylor and Brian Holmshaw).

For permission to reproduce material I should like to thank: Elvin Bloomfield (Draycott May song), Richard Chidlaw (songs, 'Crow-clapping', 'We Shepherds' and 'Late Home came I'), Gwilym Davies (song, 'Buff Blow'), Percy Grainger Estate (song, 'High Germany'), Patrick Harvey (poem, 'Warning', by F.W. Harvey), Ian Russell (transcription of tune of 'High Germany'), Cecil Sharp Estate (tunes, 'Saturday Night', 'Green Sleeves' and 'The Gloucester Hornpipe') and the Society of Authors (story of Newent pear trees from H.J. Massingham's *Shepherd's Country*). I am indebted to the James Madison Carpenter manuscript collection in the Archive of Folk Culture, Library of Congress, for the songs 'Yubberdon Fools' (Sam Bennett), 'An Outlandish Knight' (William Hands), 'The Wager' (Sarah Phelps) and 'Wassail' (George Herbert); and the play texts from Oddington (A. and H. Gorton) and Yanworth (John Philips and William Paish).

1

# BATTLES LONG AGO

Gloucestershire's peaceful landscape conceals a turbulent past which reverberates into the present as tales and traditions. Of these, some are genuine, some false (historically speaking), and others incapable of verification; but all can shed light on those who perpetuated them.

Roman, Saxon and Dane are remembered in place-name and story; so are captains and kings of the Middle Ages. The great cataclysm of the Civil War, some 350 years ago, seems to have made a more lasting mark on the collective memory than many other conflicts, before and since. Its deep fascination is such that at least one of the stories originated over three centuries after the event from which it purports to spring.

The more recent exploits of highwayman and poacher, sheep-stealer and smuggler, still linger in local lore. Peace also hath her victories, and alongside so much violence there are quiet tales of Drake and Ralegh, Dick Whittington and Will Shakespeare.

## Scratch Gloucestershire, find Rome

The old adage has been amply confirmed by archaeology but could also be supported by traditional narratives. In the AD 40s Aulus Plautius conquered Gloucestershire and founded *Corinium* (Cirencester). Among those in the general's circle was Claudia, a British princess of the Dobunni tribe, who married a Roman officer, Rufus Pudens. The couple went to Rome, where their son, Linus, became bishop in succession to St Peter himself. Parents and son were all friends of St Paul, and they persuaded him to visit Britain - and perhaps Gloucestershire. So the story goes.

During Plautius' stay in Britain his wife, Pomponia, is said to have become a Christian. When the couple returned to Rome in AD 47 she was put on trial. There is no evidence that she ever came to Britain at all but Tacitus relates that she was charged with 'foreign superstition', which could have meant Christianity. Offences by Roman women were considered a family matter, and judged by their husbands. Pomponia, acquitted by Plautius, lived another forty years.

By some sixty or seventy years after Plautius left Britain the famous villa at Woodchester may have been in existence. Its great mosaic, the biggest north of the Alps, shows the myth of Orpheus and the beasts. However, Ron Fletcher argues that it is in fact a giant pictogram on the great flood, and closely linked with the River Severn, Woodchester Valley and the circular scar on Rodborough Common above Stroud.

The villa was probably destroyed late in the fourth century when the Romans withdrew from Britain. A local account claims that Marius, Lord of Woodchester, together with his kinsman, Cellus of Selsley, preferred to remain. They defeated a force of invading Danes at a place still called Woeful Danes Bottom (see below), and Cellus, mortally wounded, committed his infant daughter, Mary, to his friend's care. Many years later as Marius in turn lay dying he passed on the charge to his twenty-year-old son, Aco, and a priest, Magnus, asking them to find Mary a husband from her mother's people who were British. Instead Aco, overruling the wishes both of Magnus and of Mary herself, determined to make her his own wife. A band of men burst into the wedding feast. Their leader, a Briton called Leir, killed Aco, and rode off with Mary. The villa, abandoned, fell into ruin - to be rediscovered 1400 years later.

There may be a Roman connection with the village of Aust, close to the present M4 and Severn Bridge. Some argue that its name comes from Legio Augusta, stationed in Gloucestershire until AD 75; others from Traiectus Augusti (the nearby river crossing). Another possible derivation is from St Augustine — not the writer of the celebrated Confessions but St Augustine of Canterbury, Pope Gregory's choice as evangeliser of the Anglo-Saxons. In 603 this Augustine convened a meeting of Welsh bishops to settle differences between the Roman and Celtic churches at a place thereafter called - said the Venerable Bede - St Augustine's Oak, near the border between the Hwiccii and the West Saxons.

The many contenders for the site include five places in Worcestershire and three - Aust, Broadoak and Down Ampney - in Gloucestershire. Of these, two fulfil the criterion of closeness to a tribal border, Aust (the Avon, seven miles distant) and Down Ampney (the Thames, just over a mile away) where an ancient oak stood by the Fairford-Cricklade road at Oak Farm. Aust's claim may be strengthened by the contention that the Welsh bishops, before crossing the Severn for their meeting with Augustine, called at St Tecla's Island off Beachley Point to consult its eponymous virgin and hermit. If Tecla's death occurred in AD 47, as some suggest, they would have been some 550 years too late.

There are traditions that a battle took place in Roman times at the Camp near Rockhampton, and that the Romans sank the local Pennywell. At Alveston, public houses named the 'Cross Hands' are thought to owe their sign to the badge of a Roman legion once stationed there. A feature on Minchinhampton Common called the Bulwarks may have been partially levelled by the Romans because it was the headquarters of a section of the Dobunni tribe which resisted their rule.

The Minchinhampton faction joined Caractacus, whose rebellion ended in defeat - according to local tradition, though there are many other contending places - at the Slaughter, a spot on the east bank of the Wye below Symond's Yat. The same site is claimed for battles between King Arthur's son and the Danes, between Britons and Vikings, and between the two sides in the Civil War. Yet the name may simply derive from sloghtre, a Saxon word meaning 'muddy place', as it does in the villages of Upper and Lower Slaughter.

## Fields of Battle

Several battles of the Dark Ages mistily swim in the collective memory, with some help from place names and landmarks. Mangotsfield is supposed to owe its name to Man, a Saxon general victorious at a place now called the Charnells. A local rhyme runs:

*By Charnocks Mane got his field,*
*And shed his blood on Rodway Hill.*
*They rode, some say, to Standfast Gate,*
*And fought their way from Bridge of Yate.*

Stone coffins have been unearthed at the Charnells, and at Dyrham a few miles away the battle of Deorham was probably fought, in AD 577. During it two Saxon kings killed three British chieftains. This may have given rise to the tradition that at the 'Cross Hands', half a mile south-east of Old Sodbury, two kings met and one was crowned.

Mercians are said to have fought Saxons at Battle Bridge in the hamlet of Barrington near Chipping Campden, and Wiltshire men at Battlefield in the parish of Kempsford. Paganhill near Stroud may take its name from having been used as a base by Danish armies - called pagans in the Anglo-Saxon Chronicle - which had sailed up the Severn.

Woeful Danes Bottom, between Minchinhampton and Avening, means in fact a wooded valley in which a wolf was either fought or caged. Yet tradition holds that Wolfhang the Saxon and a body of Gloucestershire and Wiltshire men routed a big Danish army there. The Long Stone just north of the main road above Gatcombe marks the centre of the struggle, in which blood ran 'as high as the wheels of a cart'. Victory was helped - somewhat unsportingly, perhaps - by women who gave the Danes poisoned pancakes to eat. All the tumps in the neighbourhood are the graves of dead soldiers. Woeful Danes Bottom is a place of ghosts (see Chapter Six), including a dog of which a woman witness said: 'I could see right through him, through his ribs.' Bisley and Sapperton also have their stories of Danes.

Among the reputed Saxon exploits is the capture of Cirencester. Faced with stubborn and protracted resistance their leader, Gormund, had sparrows from the town trapped, then released with wildfire on their feet. The distressed birds flew home to the thatched roofs, multiple fires broke out, and the defenders' morale collapsed. Cirencester was known for many years as *Urbs Passerum*, 'Town of the sparrows'.

Saxon duplicity is also remembered at Cranham. A British priest called Eidel was invited with his retinue to a banquet. They were asked to go unarmed, and at the end of the meal the Saxons produced weapons and set about slaughtering the British. Eidel, a powerful man, tore up a young tree to defend himself. He was the only one to escape alive. Back in Cranham he fell ill. Remarkably, he consulted a Saxon doctor, was given poison instead of medicine, and died. He was buried at the top of the hill behind the present 'Royal William' public house in Eidel's (or Iddell's) Tump, and is said to haunt a lane near Eddell's Mill.

The Dane, Canute (Knut), met Edmund Ironside in single combat to decide who should take possession of the kingdom of England. The result was a draw, so the country was divided; but when Ironside died a year later, in 1017, his share fell to Canute. One tradition places their fight on the Eight (eyot), an island (now gone) in the Severn near Deerhurst. A more likely site is the Isle of Alney close to Gloucester.

Some five hundred years later, only a few miles from Deerhurst, a much less civilised contest took place. During the Wars of the Roses Queen Margaret travelled north with her Lancastrian army, intending to cross the Severn at Gloucester and join Jasper Tudor in Wales. The citizens of Gloucester closed their gates against her so she went on towards Tewkesbury and camped at Gupshill (or Gubshill). The Yorkists, led by King Edward IV and his brother, the Duke of Gloucester and future Richard III, attacked the following morning, 4 May 1471, and routed the queen's men.

Queen Margaret's Camp, Red Piece and Bloody Meadow are still on the maps. The queen herself is said to have spent the two nights before the battle at Owlpen Manor (near Uley) and Gupshill Manor. Red Castle at Tirley took its name from the Red Queen because she sheltered there after the battle. The present house dates from only the seventeenth century but it may stand on the site of an earlier dwelling of the same name. Margaret's son, Prince Edward, was killed in a house close to the abbey church at Tewkesbury, and her ghost has been seen weeping for him in the Bloody Meadow. The last group of Lancastrian supporters was intercepted at Uley as it fled towards Somerset. A field there behind Raglan House where the stragglers were slaughtered is reputed to be the only one in the parish in which poppies grow. Another party of fugitives is said to have been killed at Didbrook in the forerunner of the present church.

## King, Queen, Knave

Perhaps the earliest 'royal' in Gloucestershire was Donwallo Mulmutius, king of the Britons, who built a castle at Tetbury well over 2000 years ago. A later king, Edmund of the West Saxons, died at Pucklechurch in a hunting lodge behind the present 'Star Inn'. His entourage was celebrating the feast of St Augustine of Canterbury on 26 May 946 when he noticed Leolf (or Liofa) whom he had outlawed six years earlier. Edmund ordered his cup-bearer to put the man out. A struggle developed. The king joined in, Leolf fatally wounded him with 'a master dagger', and fled. The rest of the company was too drunk to intervene. Edmund was buried at Glastonbury Abbey.

Roughly a century later Rosamund, mistress of Henry II, faced a choice between dagger and bowl, stabbing or poison. She was born in about 1140, the daughter of Walter de Clifford. She bore the king two sons, one of whom became Earl of Salisbury, the other Bishop of Lincoln. She lodged at the royal palace in Woodstock, and retired to the abbey of Godstow, where she died, probably in 1177.

Tradition holds that Rosamund was born at Frampton-on-Severn, in the manor house (now a farm) on the north side of the green which bears her name. She is reputed to have been so fair that the blood could be seen flowing in her veins. Henry had a house built for her at Woodstock in the centre of a maze so complex that only he and his closest knights could reach her. The jealous queen, Eleanor of Aquitaine, solved the problem by following a silken thread as it unravelled from the king's cloak. She then confronted Rosamund with the fatal ultimatum. The choice was poison.

Another premature death in the reign of Henry II led to the saying 'The Tracys have always the wind in their faces', though this is contradicted by another adage:

*The Lacys, Tracys and Fettiplaces*
*Own all the manors, parks and chases.*

Sir William de Tracy, a Toddington landowner, struck the first blow in the murder of Thomas à Becket. With the other three men closely involved he was ordered by Pope Alexander II to do penance for fourteen years, fighting the infidel in the Holy Land. Tracy tried to comply, but adverse winds always prevented him from reaching his destination. When he died the curse passed to his successors. Even so, the family enjoyed a huge estate at Toddington until the late nineteenth century, when it was sold to an American market gardener. Although the present Toddington Manor dates from the early nineteenth century it has stone carvings by the main door of Becket on one side with mitre in hand looking across to Tracy with upraised axe on the other.

King John frequently visited Gloucestershire. He hunted in the Forest of Dean and stayed at St Briavels Castle, where a room he occupied is still pointed out. His first wife, Avice (later divorced), brought him large tracts of land in the county from her father, the Duke of Gloucester. A great sword thought to have presented to the town of Newnham-on-Severn by John was kept for many years by the lord of the manor at a house called the Haie. It is now in Gloucester Museum, where experts date it only from the fifteenth century.

While staying at Allaston Castle (now gone) near Lydney, John lost his temper during a game of chess with the governor and broke the board over his head. The man was so enraged that, forgetting his allegiance, he retaliated and half killed the king. The outcome is not recorded, but it may well have been violent.

A much milder reaction came from Edward I, who reigned from 1272 to 1307, when he found the streets of Gloucester so muddy that planks had to be laid for his horse to walk on. He merely refused to go there again, thus - allegedly - inspiring the rhyme:

*Doctor Foster went to Gloucester*
*In a shower of rain.*
*He fell into a puddle*

*Right up to his middle*
*And never went there again.*

The text did not appear in print until 1844 but the rhyme implies 'piddle', an old form of the word puddle.

'To dine with Duke Humphrey' means to go without. The saying immortalises one of the Dukes of Gloucester, the youngest son of Henry IV. Humphrey was to have been buried at St Paul's in London, but instead was interred at St Albans. People with no money were directed at dinner time to look for the non-existent monument in St Paul's, and hence to forego their meal.

Duke Humphrey died in 1447 at Bury St Edmunds on the day appointed for his trial before Parliament on a charge of high treason. His death remained an enigma until 1860 when a manuscript preserved in a metal box came to light in the ruins of Bury Abbey.

Humphrey had given orders that a Bury monk, Father Barnard, should be burnt at the stake as a magician. Before taking his vows, Barnard, an alchemist and astrologer, had been Sir Roger Drury. Maud Carew, a nun, secretly loved him, and appealed to Queen Margaret to save his life. Margaret, hating Duke Humphrey and thinking he would be acquitted by Parliament, persuaded Maud that he must die if Barnard's life were to be saved. Following the instructions of Cardinal Beaufort, Maud scattered a few grains of a deadly and undetectable poison on the duke's face as he slept, and was returning to the nuns' chapel when Barnard met her. She told him what she had done, and why, only to be warned that she, too, would die. The poison held in her hand would kill her as it did the duke, if a little more slowly.

Barnard expected Maud's testimony to die with her and prophesied that her spirit would not rest, and would eventually see the downfall of their splendid abbey. He led her back to the chapel, where she fell dead by the altar. The nuns who found her attributed her death to natural causes. The story was written by a monk told by Barnard but sworn to secrecy. He added that Cardinal Beaufort died in great suffering. After the murder of her husband, Henry VI, Queen Margaret spent many years as a prisoner in the Tower of London.

In 1549, during the reign of Edward VI, there were riots against the enclosure of common land. At Painswick the lord of the manor, Sir Anthony Kingston, had a prison built and ordered gallows to be erected at Sheepscombe Green. He also gave three tracts, later called Gallows Land, to provide money respectively for gallows, ladders and halters. In addition a tithingman (a sort of constable) of Sheepscombe was to do the hanging, and have an acre of land for his trouble. As late as the 1930s people remembered the gallows, which stood on a site later occupied by the Coronation Oak. A piece of land at Painswick is still called Hangman's Acre, and plots with similar names and history are to be found at Alveston, Marshfield, Stone and Stowell.

A few miles from Painswick, at Miserden, Hazle House was once owned by Henry VIII. During the reign of his daughter, Mary, a man who played a part in the trial of Bishop Hooper lived there. After Hooper was burned at the stake - his statue in Gloucester marks the place - the man, filled with deep remorse, hanged himself. The nail used for the rope could be pointed out as late as the 1960s, and may be there still.

Another of Henry's daughters, the future Queen Elizabeth, owned Over Court at Bisley. During the nineteenth century workmen digging foundations for a school unearthed a stone coffin with the bones of a girl. The local parson of the time, the Reverend Thomas Keble, invented a story that the little Elizabeth had died suddenly while staying at the Court. Fearing Henry's wrath, the villagers looked for a local child to take her place. They could find only a boy but they dressed him as a girl, and Henry accepted him as Elizabeth. That is why she had to be a virgin queen. This ludicrous fabrication of the 'Bisley Boy' took hold; and many people even today accept it. 'Course she were a man. Never married, did 'er? 'Sides, it do stand to reason a ooman ouldn't a ruled as well.'

## Civil War

In the seventeenth century many skirmishes and struggles took place in Gloucestershire during the Civil War. Local traditions concerning some of the happenings are still current, or were until recently.

Damage at St Mary's Church, Prestbury, is pointed out as the work of iconoclastic parliamentary soldiers. St Michael's at Eastington near Frocester has marks on the tower caused by cannon fire. At Taynton, the ancient church of St Lawrence was destroyed altogether — the village changed hands several times during the fighting — and when it was rebuilt in 1657 Parliament insisted that it should be on a north-south axis instead of the traditional east-west.

At Gloucester, St Mary de Crypt served as a powder magazine, and St Mary de Lode and Holy Trinity as prisons for captured royalists. Parliamentary soldiers were kept prisoner in churches at Cirencester and Painswick, where one man inscribed on a pillar words adapted from Spenser's *Faerie Queen*: 'Be bold, be bold, but not too bold.' Damage to Sir Anthony Kingston's elaborate tomb at Painswick is blamed on parliamentary soldiers but was probably done under cover of war by local people who heartily detested their former lord of the manor.

Other buildings have stories to tell. A house at Box called the Beehive - once an inn which had changed hands over a game of card - had a sign:

*In this Hive we are all alive,*
*Good Liquor makes us funny.*
*If you are dry step in and try*
*The flavour of our Honey.*

King Charles - which one is not specified - heeded the advice, and stayed there.

By contrast, the 'Trouble House', an inn just out of Tetbury on the Cirencester road, has an unhappy history. Early in the nineteenth century a landlord ran out of funds half-way through an ambitious refurbishment programme. The only solution was to hang himself. His successor fell into much the same difficulty, and drowned himself. The inn caught fire during the agricultural disturbances of 1830 after a clash between labourers and soldiers. A skirmish some two hundred years earlier between royalists and Roundheads is shown on the inn sign. A Roundhead marksman posted, ironically, at the 'King's Head' in Coleford shot and killed the royalist, Sir Richard Lawley, in 1643, using a silver bullet. The choice of ammunition is strange, since silver was traditionally used when targetting a witch.

Manor houses and castles, garrisoned by one side or the other during the Civil War, frequently saw action. In 1644 Parliament troops at Littledean negotiated the surrender of a royalist force at Dean Hall but as they moved in a sniper shot one of their men. The infuriated Roundheads stormed the house and killed many of its garrison, including the two most senior officers. The event may account for some of the house's ghosts (see Chapter Six). In the same year Beverstone Castle was captured by Colonel Massey, retaken by royalists, then captured again by Massey. Until the late nineteenth century villagers transmitted tales of terrible hardships, showed the fields occupied by besiegers, and related that 'many of the garrison as well as the assailants were slain.' Berkeley Castle - which claims to be the oldest inhabited house in Gloucestershire - was the last stronghold to surrender to Parliament during the Civil War, in September 1645. The outer bailey was then razed and the keep wall breached.

While pursuing royalists at Newnham-on-Severn some of Massey's men fell into the river, were dragged down by their armour and drowned, though not before cursing the town and praying that its women should not live. For many years afterwards the curse held good: sooner or later every married man in the town became a widower. An even more chilling parallel comes in the story told within living memory at Severn Beach near to where an ancient ferry crossed the 2 1/2 miles of estuary. A party of royalists fleeing to Wales was rowed over by boatmen who returned in very leisurely fashion since they knew they would next have to take the pursuing Roundheads. They embarked the cavalrymen at sword point but instead of rowing them to Portskewett on the Welsh side put them out on the English Stones, a reef some distance short. The tide had just turned. Sixty troopers and their mounts failed to reach the shore, and were drowned. When Cromwell heard he reputedly closed the ferry, which was not used again for a hundred years. Yet one cannot help reflecting that if the story were true the boatmen would have been rewarded, and the ferry restarted, at the Restoration in 1660.

Some five hundred royalist Welshmen, fleeing from the battle of Highnam in 1643, were killed on the west bank of the River Leadon by the present Barber's Bridge (which was locally known as Barbarous Bridge). Legend has it that the Leadon ran red with blood, and that every year from then on a Cranesbill flower bloomed where every Welshman had fallen. A stream which joins the Leadon at the scene is called Red Brook. Evidence of the slaughter came in the 1790s when navvies cutting a canal unearthed large numbers of skeletons. More were found in 1868 when a railway was under construction, and more still in the 1970s during road widening. The commemorative obelisk - made partly of stones from the ancient walls of Gloucester - dates from 1868.

Two fields in Churchdown parish - at Upper Pirton and off Pirton Lane - are called War Close because they saw clashes during the Civil War. Here, too, local tradition was corroborated when fragments of swords and spurs were found. At Great Rissington another battlefield which owed its name to a skirmish between royalists and Roundheads disappeared during the Second World War beneath the tarmac of an aerodrome.

## The Siege of Gloucester

Royalist forces invested Gloucester from 10 August to 5 September 1643. Their failure to take the city marked a turning point in the Civil War. Gloucester's military governor was a man only in his twenties, Colonel Edward Massey (or Massie, as he preferred to spell it). His services had been declined by the king, then accepted by Parliament.

Charles I made his headquarters in Matson House (now part of Selwyn School) on the slopes of Robinswood Hill, while his principal lieutenant, Prince Rupert, lodged at Prinknash Park. On 10 August heralds appeared before the city walls with a demand for the city's surrender. Popular tradition produced this account:

> *King Charles marched to the South Gate with the fife and drum a-playing and his sword drawn in front of the army. The king kicked violently at the door. The guard popped his head over the wall and said, 'Who's there?' 'The king.' 'What do you want?' 'To come in; be sharp and open the door.' 'Don't you wish you might get in,' replied the guard, and retired. King Charles continued to kick at the door for some time, and to demand admittance. The king got tired of waiting, ordered the fife and drum to strike up and commanded his army to retreat, exclaiming in a melancholy tone of voice, 'Never mind, it is little worth.' In consequence of this incident the neighbourhood was called Littleworth.*

There is no such backing for the suggestion that the well known rhyme of Humpty Dumpty refers either to the royalist mortar (the biggest in England) which blew up on 12 August, 1643, or to one of the siege engines built at Llanthony under the direction of William Chillingworth, an Anglican divine turned sapper. John Corbet, rector of St Mary de Crypt and chaplain to the parliamentary garrison, described 'those imperfect and troublesome engines' as running 'upon wheels, with planks musket proof placed on the axel-tree, with holes for musket-shot and a bridge before it, and end whereof (the wheels falling into the ditch) was to rest upon our breast works.' The devices, intended presumably to cross the twelve foot wide trenches on the south side of the city, became bogged down in a marsh and were recovered by the citizens after the siege. The idea that such an engine could be Humpty Dumpty, propounded in 1956 purely as a *jeu d'esprit* by David Daube, was popularised by Richard Rodney Bennett, who suggested in the children's opera, *All the King's Men*, that the bridging of the Severn was intended. There is no record of the rhyme before the early nineteenth century.

The siege was raised on the approach from London of a relieving army. Tradition says that only nine cannon balls and three barrels of powder remained in Gloucester. Food, too, was very low. According to a story set into verse by H.Y.J. Taylor the royalists sent in a spy on 4 September to see how things stood. The citizens - whose counter-intelligence seems to have been remarkably good - were forewarned. Taking their only remaining pig,

*From north to south, from east to west,*
*We marched that pig about,*
*And with a pair of pinchers prest*
*Poor piggy in the snout.*

The animal obligingly squealed its protest all round the city, the last point being in Constitution Walk (which runs behind the present library and museum). The spy returned to report:

*'They are prepared for instant fight,*
*And famine no one fears;*
*For they've killed pigs enough tonight*
*To feed them twenty years.'*

As a consequence:

*King Charles heard all the spy could say,*
*And called his captains liege,*
*And gave command ere dawn of day*
*The camp should raise the siege.*

*The bugles sound, the loud drums rattling beat,*
*And soon against their will*
*The horse, artillery and foot retreat*
*And march up Painswick Hill.*

The prolonged and painful killing of a final pig, intended as a similar ruse, was carried out on the orders of the royalist governor of Nunney Castle in Somerset during a siege by parliamentary forces in 1645. It failed, perhaps because the besiegers knew what had happened at Gloucester.

The day when the Gloucester siege was lifted - 5 September - became a public holiday in the city until the Restoration. During the siege Prince Rupert spent some time at Parton Court, Churchdown, where his room is still pointed out. He was perhaps checking a royalist outpost on the west side of Chosen Hill at a place which has kept the name of Soldiers' Walk. Many houses claim visits by Charles I. Royal Spring (formerly an inn) at Longhope is so called because of the occasion in 1642 when Charles stopped after the battle of Powick to drink from the spring or perhaps to sample some wine made from local grapes. He dined and played a game of bowls at the Old Lodge on Minchinhampton Common. He stayed twice at Coberley and at Abbey House, Cirencester, and his presence at the 'White Hart', Moreton-in-the-Marsh, on 2 July 1644 inspired the couplet: 'When friends were few and dangers near,/King Charles found rest and safety here.'

After leaving Gloucester Charles went to Painswick, where he stayed at the Court House, or possibly the Lodge, and it is claimed he took a bath in the cellar of Kimsbury Farm, near Cud Hill. On the same hill a mounting block on the south side of the Seven Leaze Lane is known as King Charles' Stone. Perhaps this is where he was sitting when one of the royal princes asked when they were going home. 'I have no home to go to, my son,' he replied. Northleach weavers petitioning for the protection of their industry got a similar response: 'Alas, poor people, how can I help you when I cannot help myself?'

The outcome of the Civil War proved happier for others. Massey, increasingly sympathetic to the royal cause, was arrested three times by Parliament, and escaped three times. The last occasion is described by the historian, Samuel Rudder:

> *Colonel Massie, famous for his memorable defence of Gloucester against King Charles the First, being disgusted at some of the parliament's proceedings, deserted their party, and about the year 1659, formed a design of seizing on Gloucester, in which however he was disappointed, and forced to take refuge in a little house near Simonshall. There he was seized by a party of horse, who mounted him before one of the troopers, and carried him towards Gloucester; but in going down the steep part of Nimpsfield-hill, Massie tumbled from his horse, and being a stout man, and his guards a little intoxicated, made his escape under favour of a dark tempestuous night.*

To the anger of soldiers of the garrison, Massey became MP for Gloucester in the Parliament of 1660 which called Charles II to the throne. The king later granted him an estate at Abbeyleix in Ireland, where he died peacefully in 1674.

While Massey was governor of Gloucester one of his opponents was Sir John Wintour, Wyntour or Winter (born in 1600, and knighted while serving as private secretary to Queen Henrietta Maria). Having been granted in 1640 by the Crown the right to fell unlimited timber in the Forest of Dean he used it to such effect that he turned the Foresters from royalist into Roundhead supporters.

The Wintour family home at Lydney - an Elizabethan mansion known as Lydney House, White Cross or White House - stood on the site of the present swimming pool. Sir John garrisoned it for the king in 1643 but burned it down two years later rather than allow it to fall into enemy hands. In 1644 Massey's troops captured Westbury and Newnham from Wintour. In both places the royalists used the church as a strong point. In Newnham the building was stormed; at Westbury the defenders were dislodged by a shower of grenades.

Wintour was not personally involved in these actions but later the same year he commanded a force which re-established a royalist presence near Beachley, to control the Aust crossing. On 14 October a counter-attack by Massey routed Wintour's men. Their leader escaped, most likely riding down the precarious paths of Sedbury Cliffs to reach a boat waiting below on the Severn. Local tradition prefers a more dramatic setting and has moved the escape to the east bank of the Wye more than a mile upstream from Chepstow, where sheer cliffs drop 300 feet to the water. If a man on horseback jumped at that point the only result would be certain death. The place is shown on a map of 1777 as Winless Leap, which makes much more sense; and only since 1830 has it been marked as Wintour's Leap.

Wintour was imprisoned by Parliament for a time but survived the war. At the Restoration he was allowed to resume his tree felling in the Forest until the effects of his rapacity became so disastrous that a law had to be passed to stop him. He died either in 1673 or 1683.

Oliver Cromwell appeared very little in Gloucestershire during the Civil War. He passed through Lechlade in June 1645 and stayed at Gloucester in the summer of 1648 on his way to and from South Wales, but there is no evidence that he took part in any fighting in the county. However, J. Arthur Gibbs wrote in 1898:

> *Oliver Cromwell's memory is still very much respected among the labouring folk. Every possible work is attributed to his hand, and even the names of places are set down to his inventive genius. Thus they tell you that when he passed through Aldsworth he did not think very much of the village (it is certainly a dull little place), so he snapped his fingers and exclaimed, 'That's all 'e's worth!' On arriving at Ready Token, where was an ancient inn, he found it full of guests; he therefore exclaimed, 'It's already taken!'*

Cromwell is supposed to have sat in a chair-shaped box tree at Hailes Abbey, and to have visited Sailwell House at Primrose Hill in the Forest of Dean. He is supposed to have walked out of the inn (now a private house) at Redmarley on the morning of the battle of August 1644, and to have been targetted by a sniper. A local expression, 'Here goes for a fat Minge', is more accurate: it was the parliamentary Colonel Minnie who walked from the inn, to be shot down by 'a country man concealed in a hollow tree with a birding piece in his hand'.

At Naunton tradition has it that Cromwell stayed at Cromwell House, which did belong to parliamentary supporters during the Civil War - the Aylworths. Cromwell is also claimed to have visited Daneway House at Sapperton; and its owner, William Hancox, to have built part of it as guest quarters for his leader.

Until it blew down in 1983 a tree in Daneway Woods bore the inscription: 'His Wood/William Hancox/Captain in O. Cromwel Army.' It was apparently customary for Hancox heirs to carve their names in this way.

Oliver's Cottage at Painswick was once an inn supposedly dubbed the 'Serpent' by Cromwell himself after some of his men got drunk there. If this were true it would show a sense of humour because another inn nearby was called the 'Adam and Eve'. Close to Painswick to the north-east of Haresfield Beacon are Cromwell House and Cromwell Stone. The latter, inscribed with the date of 5 September, 1643, purports to show where Cromwell gave thanks to God for the lifting of the siege of Gloucester.

According to local tradition, both Cromwell and General Ireton visited Chavenage House near Tetbury. Two of its rooms bear their names, and Cromwell's Bath or Well is marked close to the house on maps. The owner of the house was Colonel Nathaniel Stephens, MP for Gloucestershire and supporter of the parliamentary cause. Cromwell and Ireton turned up in 1648 to press him to attend the House and to cast his vote for bringing Charles I to trial. Colonel Stephens' sister, Abigail, urged him not to go, and predicted that his line would become extinct if he were in any way implicated in the king's death. Although he was deeply affected by these remarks he left for London.

Charles was beheaded in January 1649. In May Stephens fell ill with a lingering sickness from which he died in 1660, soon after the monarchy was restored. Relatives assembled for the funeral, their carriages crowding the courtyard at Chavenage. Then a splendid coach appeared, drawn by fine black horses. The shroud-clad spectre of Stephens was seen to glide into the coach, which sped off and disappeared in a great burst of flame as it reached the gateway. The headless driver wore royal vestments and sported the star and garter. The story adds that from then on every lord of Chavenage took his leave in the same way. The ghost of Abigail haunted the house; among those it alarmed was Queen Victoria's daughter, Princess Louise.

In fact, Stephens spoke in Parliament against the 'strange cuer' (cure) which the king's execution would be. He was not in the court that tried Charles, nor among those present when the sentence was passed. In 1654 his oldest surviving son, and heir, Richard, married the daughter of a staunch royalist. The Stephens family or its descendants owned Chavenage until well into the nineteenth century.

A happier - and perhaps truer - tradition concerns the organ at Tewkesbury Abbey. Until 1654 the instrument belonged to Magdalen College, Oxford. Then Cromwell acquired it, and had it installed at Hampton Court where the poet John Milton and others came to make music for Oliver and his family. On the other hand, Cromwell's ghost is said to haunt Starvall Farm, near Stow-on-the-Wold, where the farmer refused him corn for his horse - a very unlikely story.

As with Cromwell, many houses claim a connection with Charles II. In the Cotswolds he stayed at Kineton and nearby Temple Guiting; in the Forest of Dean he planted holly trees at the Speech House - where the King's Walk is called after him - and drank from a well at Portway. He gave a hamlet near Painswick the name it still bears, Paradise. One story is that he drank from a

*Chavenage House, near Tetbury owned by Nathaniel Stephens, a local MP and Cromwell supporter.*

spring at Castle Godwyn and exclaimed, 'This is paradise'; another places the remark at Damsell's Cross. There is a Paradise House and there was an inn called the 'Adam and Eve'. However, the name Paradise - of which there are three instances in Gloucestershire and others elsewhere - derives from a strain of wheat introduced from North Africa in the fifteenth century which gave its name to some of the fields in which it was grown.

Charles II's dubbing of Paradise has been ascribed to the time when he was on the run after his defeat in September 1651 at the battle of Worcester. He spent a draughty night on Painswick Beacon and next morning received such a cordial reception at a farm below that he called it Paradise. There is another claim that Charles slept at Warren House in Stanton after the battle.

Many other stories deal with Charles' flight towards Bristol in the guise of Will Jackson, groom to Mistress Jane Lane. In the Manor House - still called the King's Lodge - at Long Marston, now in Warwickshire, he was loitering in the kitchen when the cook told him to wind the jack. He covered his ignorance of such matters by saying: 'I am but a poor tenant's son of Colonel Lane's. We seldom have roast meat, and when we have we never use a jack.' The cook's response was to hit him, at the very moment when searching troopers entered the kitchen. He was thus absolved of the remotest suspicion of being king. A jack alleged to be the one Charles failed to wind was in the possession of a Mr Tomms of Long Marston over a century later.

From Marston Sicca, as it used to be called, Charles rode on with Jane Lane to Chipping Campden, probably along the ancient trackway which passes Stumps Cross to Coberley, where they stayed in the old parsonage. The present building is Georgian. Next they went to Cirencester and put up at the 'Sun', an inn adjacent to the present 'Fleece Hotel'. Charles slept in a truckle bed in the room of another traveller, a Mr Lascelles. Next morning he was almost recognised but the quick thinking of a servant girl - she must have been in on the secret - who addressed him familiarly again saved him. The following day the fugitives reached Boxwell Court, and asked for shelter. The lady of the house was a Mrs Huntley whose husband had fought under Prince Rupert's command as a cavalry captain. She told them the house had been twice searched within the previous few days; so, fearing another raid, they took her advice and slept nearby at Scrabbetts Farm.

Either on leaving next day or on reaching safety in France, Charles gave Mrs Huntley a turquoise ring which has remained in her family's possession ever since. A path which used to run from a point between Boxwell Court and Scrabbetts Farm through Mill Woods to Ozleworth and Alderley bore the name of King's Walk.

At some stage during his flight Charles also slept in the old coach house at Piers Court, Stinchcombe. The present house dates from the eighteenth century but an older building at the back had connections with Prince Rupert. In the same village, Lamport Court has pollarded trees said to have signalled the Roundhead sympathies of a previous owner; and in the woods above Melksham Court there was an oak tree in which Charles took refuge from his pursuers. As they came near an owl flew out, so they looked no further. The bird, however, was tame, and Charles released it just at the right moment. The story, with its echoes of Charles' more famous escape at Boscobel, is also told of a royalist soldier, an oak tree and a bird he freed at Lydney's Bathurst Park. Back in Stinchcombe they say that Thomas Tyndale hid for three days and nights in a yew tree from the royalist party which burnt his home and those of other parliamentary sympathisers.

The account of a royalist farmer's flight after the battle of Stow in 1646 is more complex. The man hid with his horse in a copse until nightfall but as he rode off he was seen, and followed. His fox-hunter's knowledge of the country enabled him to shake off his pursuers and reach home. Fearful that the lathered sweat of his horse would give him away he slaughtered the animal and frantically covered the carcass with manure. A clatter of hooves told him that he was still not safe. He rushed into the house, ran upstairs and having paused only to throw on nightshirt and cap jumped into bed, leather coat, breeches, boots and all. The searching troopers crashed into the room, only to find what they took to be a sleeping man. His wife, renowned in the neighbourhood for her sharp tongue, started to berate them. They withdrew, and rode off with her hearty maledictions ringing in their ears.

Charles II acceded to the throne in May 1660, and within a month a dissenting congregation at Fairford had its worship violently interrupted by 'a company of Rude People'. Twice they complained to the local magistrate, William Oldisworth, but received no redress. They warned that God would punish the wrong-doers. Next day a man saw near the JP's house, Hydecourt Manor, a multitude of frogs and toads moving 'in two companies, even as Soldiers March in Field'. The creatures swarmed all over the gardens.

Oldisworth - who may have been instrumental in saving the famous Fairford windows (see Chapter Four) during the Civil War - was so deeply impressed by the visitation that after all he rebuked the 'rude multitude'. Then 'the Frogs and Toads were departed and vanished so suddenly and wonderfully as no man can tell how.' So wrote the anonymous author of a contemporary pamphlet, *Strange and True Newes from Glocester.*

It seems that after heavy rainfall on 14 June 1660 there was indeed a plague of frogs at Fairford. The causes were entirely natural but the coincidence with the dissenters' warning proved too much even for the local magistrate.

## Signs of Crime

If great events and personages left their mark on the popular imagination, so did crime and criminals. Tom Long's Post on Minchinhampton Common marked either where the highwayman's body hung in chains to deter others or where he took his own life to avoid capture. A few miles away a much grander monument commemorates another highwayman who was also a pirate and smuggler but, being the fourth son of Lord Chandos of Sudeley, received a pardon from James I. This is the kneeling effigy at Avening of Henry Brydges, who died peacefully in 1615.

A gentleman of the road who escaped with his life has his name on the map at Fletcher's Leap, close to where a brook flows into the Severn at Wainlode. Here he jumped 'a formidable chasm' to reach a different parish, and safety. Jimmy Hind also retired uncaught. His patch included the steep lanes of Saintbury, where his favourite retreat was an ale-house which stood at the crossroads on Willersey Bank where Gunn's Cottages now are.

The 'Bird-in-Hand' (now gone) at Capp's Lodge on the edge of Wychwood Forest was frequented by the Dunsdens, a trio of brothers who went robbing on the Gloucestershire-Oxfordshire borders. Their names were Tom, Dick and Harry, though it is not clear whether this gave rise to the common expression. Among their stratagems was fitting their horses with circular shoes to make the tracks harder to follow. They had a cottage at Icomb with an underground passage leading to a cave in a wood where they hid their booty, including what they obtained by robbing the Oxford-to-Gloucester coach. One day at the 'Bird-in-Hand' they were heard planning an attack on Tangley Manor, between Stow and Burford. Preparations were made to receive them. When one of the brothers opened a little shutter in the door and reached inside for the key a constable dropped a rope noose over his arm and tied it securely. 'Cut,' the highwayman shouted; and one of his brother slashed off the arm. The same raw courage was shown on the scaffold at Gloucester in 1784 when Harry and Tom were to die. Dick - presumably the one who sacrificed his arm - had died earlier, either from the effects of the amputation or shot during another failed robbery. The brothers knew their bodies were to be gibbeted near their father's house. Harry, reported the *Gloucester Journal*, 'endeavoured to keep up his brother's spirits to the last. The brother was lame of one leg, and when they were tying up, he exhorted him to be of good cheer. "Come, Tom," said he. "You have but one leg but you have but a very little time to stand".'

They were executed at Over, just outside Gloucester. The inn there, known until some time in the eighteenth century as the 'Talbot', is now called the 'Dog'. Until perhaps the 1960s Newent children were informed that a statue outside represented the original animal, and told this story. There is a farm on the road from Newent to Huntley called Ploddy House. Many years ago robbers killed every member of the household but a serving maid who managed to hide in a barn. The robbers' dog followed her there but she made friends with it. Perhaps it was unused to affection, for when the thieves called it did not respond, and they left without it. The maid raised the alarm. A group of men wishing to hunt the killers let the dog go, and followed. It led them to the thieves who were either sharing their booty on the bank of the Severn or drinking in the pub close by at Over which from then on was called the 'Dog'.

The Ploddy Farm criminals would have been hanged at Over. So were two members of another gang from Wickwar. Rev. F.E. Witts wrote this comment in 1827:

> *As we went towards Cheltenham, we marvelled at the crowds of people of the lower orders trudging on towards Gloucester, with great eagerness, young and middle aged and many females. We knew not of any Fair or race or merry meeting: at last the truth flashed on my recollection, all these people were hurrying to witness the execution of the wretched brothers Dyer who are to expiate their crimes this morning by their deaths.*

A Forester hanged at Over for sheep stealing in 1818 was later buried in Holy Trinity churchyard at Drybrook. Ozleworth churchyard received the body of the last Englishman to be hanged for highway robbery. Perhaps these men were lucky not to be gibbeted as others were - on Plump Hill near Mitcheldean, for example. Another gibbet in the same area was on Pingery Tump, where the body of an executed murderer, Eli Hatton, was hanged in chains in 1732. Shortly afterwards the body was secretly removed one night because local people believed that flies from it were tainting the meat in Mitcheldean Market, and thus leading to a dearth of customers. Hatton was the last to be gibbeted on Pingery Tump.

Kealey's Hollow near Chipping Campden takes its name from a man who was hanged there in 1744 for robbery and murder. On a fine harvest day a huge crowd gathered, mainly farmers and their men. Rain fell the next day and for a long time afterwards; the corn rotted or sprouted in the ear, and much of the harvest was lost. People called this a judgement on those who had left their work to watch the grim scene.

On the old coaching road to Tetbury a crossroads near Nailsworth called Shipton's Grave takes its name from the hanged sheep-stealer buried at the spot with a stake of elder through the heart. There are several places where sheep-stealers are reputed to have hanged themselves accidently. On Stinchcombe Hill at the top of the Roman track which leads from the village is a mounting block. A sheep-stealer rested his burden there one night as he made his way home. The animal toppled backwards, its hobbled legs tightening round the man's throat to strangle him. The same incident is placed at two Hangman's Stones, one near Northleach and another which no longer exists at Preston, near Cirencester. The story recurs in reminiscences noted by Alfred Williams from a Quenington shepherd, aged 85, whose father too had been a shepherd in the same locality:

> *No, there was no sheep-stealing around Queninton in his time, and if there had been in the days of his father he had never said much about it. He had heard of one or two cases 'towwerds Northleach' of stealing from the pen when men had been 'hard drev' with hunger, but there was more poaching of hares and trouts than assaults made on the fold for sheep. He remembered, however, when a brazen-faced rogue once stole thirty sheep from a fold by night and drove them off and got as far as Woodstock, and was just about to entrain them for London when the farmer galloped up on his nag and gave the thief in charge. At another time, below Fairford, a hungry labourer stole a fat ewe, killed it and carried it for six miles on his back and disposed of the carcass, but was arrested three months afterwards when he tried to sell the skin that bore the private mark of the farmer.*
>
> *A story is told of a Cotswold labourer who stole a sheep and was strangled in the act of carrying it home. He had the sheep slung on his back, secured with a cord which he had put around his neck. At a gate he slipped and as he fell, feet foremost, on one side of the gate the sheep, hanging by the rope around his neck, dropped back on the other side and quickly strangled him.*
>
> *There is, moreover, the tradition of Williamstrip, which lies above the banks of the Coln near Hatherop Castle. In the olden times, when sheep stealing was very commonly practised, the shepherd surprised thieves in the act of carrying off two fat lambs and tried to prevent them, but they set upon him and flayed him alive, and so the field was named Williamstrip.*

Some kinds of crime enjoyed public sympathy. Smugglers who hid contraband spirits on the church roof at Lechlade are still remembered with something akin to admiration. The 'Ship Inn' at Alveston has a cellar known as the Smugglers' Den with a blocked underground passage leading from it. A house at Elmore called the Shark was another smugglers' inn from which contraband was taken across the meadows to what is now No. 1 Spring Lane and hidden beneath the floor. The story was confirmed in the 1980s when a cellar was discovered at the house.

Barcelona Farm at Minchinhampton is supposed to have received from Bristol tobacco which was passed first to the Priory in High Street, then by underground passage to Tobacco Farm (now gone) just off the top of Tetbury Street. A short extension of Friday Street is still called Tobacconist Street - but these names may have come simply through tobacco having been grown there at some time.

These are only faint echoes of the smuggling once widespread in the Bristol Channel and on the lower reaches of the Severn and Wye. These rivers also saw - and still see - poaching. One story comes from Aylburton, where a water bailiff spotted two men making their way home with a fine salmon. They took to their heels, one on either side of a rhine (pronounced reen - a deep, wide ditch), deftly throwing the fish from one to the other so that the bailiff could catch neither in possession.

In 1835, a judge at Gloucester Assizes described poaching as 'the characteristic crime of this as of other counties' - though a Forest of Dean man of the next century pleaded: 'Surry, thic wasn't thievin', thic was survival.' Many violent incidents are remembered. A keeper, William Ingram, was killed at Berkeley in 1816. A painting of the incident, commissioned by Colonel 'Wicked Willie' Berkeley is still kept in Berkeley Castle, though not on public display. The juror who pronounced a guilty verdict on those involved - mostly well-liked local farmers - was in tears. Two men were hanged, and ten others transported. On the other hand, in 1827 a jury acquitted poachers from Hawling who had openly boasted in local pubs after beating up keepers at Turkdean so severely that one died: 'We have let them know we are damned good boys.'

*The Poachers' Contemplation* dating from the 1840s runs:

*'Twas not decreed by the All-bounteous Creator,*
*I take my authority from the Holy Scripture,*
*That the hare or deer, more than the fox or badger,*
*Was allotted to a nabob more than the poor poacher.*
*Then why park-in with Babylonian walls,*
*What in plenty was bestow'd upon us one and all?*
*Nature's beauteous objects man cannot now survey,*
*So true it is he is insnar'd upon the king's highway,*
*I wonder they do not wall in the fishes of the sea,*
*O they'll rue this one day, & sending us to Bastilles.*

On the walls notices such as this (now preserved in the Gloucester Folk Museum) were displayed:

CAUTION!

I give notice that to prevent trespassing dog spikes and engines are set in several parts of these woods. Persons found in pursuit of game, nutting, wood-gathering and otherwise trespassing about the woods and hedgerows in the hamlets of Highnam, Over & Linton, will be prosecuted.

May 1862 T. Gambier Parry

Writing in 1935 a Winchcombe stonemason, John Oakey, recalled:

> *There was plenty of crime locally in my young days, lamb and poultry stealing, wheat, bacon, grocery and the like, while a great deal of poaching was also carried on. It was not unusual to see constables searching for loot stuff, nearly always at the same houses. It seemed there was no need for warrants or any authority for searching in those days.*
>
> *Night poaching for pheasants was common. Two keepers I knew were shot by poachers. One whose name was Pidgeon lost an arm. He was for many years lodge keeper at Southam. Another, John Last, was shot through the arm but just managed to save amputation. A noted poacher from Broadway shot him and served imprisonment. Game was more rigidly preserved then than now.*

Parson Thomas of Tidenham contented himself with shaking his fist in the direction of poachers in his congregation whenever he read the eighth commandment. William Moss, an old poacher at Ampney Crucis, once thanked a magistrate for sending him to gaol, and said it would be his twelfth Christmas inside. When a policeman surprised him with a hare in a trap he claimed: 'I'm only letting the pretty dear go.' The Ampney poachers regularly met to dispose of their game at a public house in Hilcot End which came to be known as the Poachers' House. There must have been many other rendezvous of the kind, up an down the county. Tales would be told like this, from Carter Will of Fairford:

> *Owl' Cleever was the downiest [luckiest] poorcher as ever I know'd, an' in all my time. 'E could allus kip out o' the kipper's claas some'ow or nuther. But a was clawss 'andy bein' nabbed once, though. A was dressed jest like a gippul - sacken smock all ripped an' terred an' tied up in knots, shoes, 'aaf off 'is vit, an' a graacy owl' billicock a-top of 'is yed. One night 'e an' 'is mates 'ad bin round the oods an' set ther wires an' traps an' then went whum to bed for an hour or two. While a was abed a dreamed dree times the kipper was crouched under a tharn bush, an' a felt a bit oneasy. Towwerds mornin' tha got up an' off tha went. Presently, Cleever said to 'is mate - 'Now, thee go my way n' I'll go thine, thas mornin', an' I'll tell tha what for later on', and sure enough, when a got to the bush, ther was the kipper stooped down a-waitin' for 'em, but Cleever 'ed nothin' about un, so the kipper couldn't stop un. When a got to t'other side o' the ood 'is mates was waitin' wi' what thaay'd a picked up, an' tha went back whum wi' that. Thaay sarved the kipper that time, but owl' Cleever was a purty sight more keerful aater that.*

At Henbury a Welsh policeman much disliked locally vowed to catch a poacher known as Chibby. Knowing this, Chibby found a hedgehog, put it in his pocket, and went towards his home when he knew Taffy would be about. The policeman duly pounced: 'What have you got in that pocket? Come on, now. Hand it over.' 'Oh, no. If thee's want it, take it out theeself.' Taffy triumphantly plunged in his hand, only to withdraw it a split second later spurting with blood.

A popular poacher at Box would knock at a door and ask: 'Missus, do ee want one that yent a-running?' If the answer were in the affirmative he would produce a rabbit from a capacious pocket. He was never caught by keeper or policeman.

One encounter is related by Mrs Ethel Smith (who died in 1981):

> *One time when the poacher was walking round Nailsworth Hill with a full sack on his shoulder in the early hours of the morning he was met by a policeman. 'Now, Harry, I have got you,' said the policeman. 'What for?' says Harry. 'For what you have got in that bag,' the policeman replied with a happy grin on his face, taking the sack from the old man's shoulder and diving his hand into it, convinced he would find some rabbits - but what he met with was a bag full of horse manure.*

Another man, caught with rabbits by a landowner, faced him with a question: 'Tell I, how did thee come by thic ground?' 'I inherited it from my father.' 'And how did 'e come by it?' 'He inherited it from his father, and my ancestors fought for it.' 'Right, then, I'll fight thee for my rabbits.'

## Peaceful Victories

A gentler tradition tells us that at Bristol Daniel Defoe first met Alexander Selkirk, his model for Robinson Crusoe.

At Iron Acton, Sir Walter Ralegh smoked a pipe - something worthy of remark because of its novelty at the time. John Aubrey described the incident in his *Brief Lives*: 'Sir W.R. standing in a Stand at Sir Robert Poyntz parke at Acton (which was built by Sir Robert's grandfather to keep his whores in) tooke a pipe of Tobacco, which made the Ladies quitt it till he had donne.' Ralegh is said to have lived at Purton Manor, and taken his bride there. Her initials - DT, for Dorothy Throckmorton - are carved over the fireplace. As well as tobacco Ralegh brought potatoes, and the first of these in England were reputedly grown at Purton - though a counter-claim comes from Churchdown, where the squire of Sandywell grew the first crop from seed supplied by Ralegh.

Ralegh may have been to Purton to visit Sir William Wintour (grandfather of Sir John), vice-admiral of the fleet which defeated the Spanish Armada. Drake came too, perhaps for the same reason, or to buy timber from the Forest. Drake's house (formerly an inn called the 'Sloop') is below the red cliff at Gatcombe. His ghost appears there at dusk, seated in an armchair and gazing westwards down the river. Drake also stayed at Berkeley Castle.

There is a nautical element - the voyage to North Africa - in the adventures of Gloucestershire's best known folk hero, Dick Whittington. Thanks to pantomime his whole story is known to every schoolchild, indeed, every person in the country. Whittington undoubtedly existed, though few things about him can be established with certainty. He died in 1423, having been mayor of London in 1397, 1406 and 1419 - the title of Lord Mayor did not then exist. He had no children, but a collateral branch of the family survives to this day.

Richard, son of Sir William and Joan Whittington, was born at Pauntley Court, near Newent. His mother may have been the widow of Sir Thomas

*Sir Francis Drake's ghost has been seen at dusk at his Gatcombe house, gazing downstream.*

Berkeley of Coberley, whose effigy is in the village church there. A local tradition says that after his own father's early death Richard spent much of his boyhood at Coberley. It is also likely that he visited the Whittingtons' town house in Westgate Street, Gloucester, which is now an inn called 'Dick Whittington's House'.

Further up the same street a stone carving (now in the Folk Museum) of a boy with a cat came to light in 1862. The clever cat which makes its master's fortune is known in the folklore of twenty-six countries, but there was no record of Dick Whittington's until 1605, when his story was the subject of a play entitled *The History of Dick Whittington*. He was certainly not a poor boy when he left Gloucestershire, and he was very wealthy by the time of his death. His many charitable bequests included money to pay for the complete rebuilding of Newgate Gaol in London. During further reconstruction after the Great Fire of 1666 a cat was carved on a column, and this caused first Newgate and later any gaol to be known as 'the Whit'. The expression lasted until the mid-nineteenth century.

A story of Whittington's generosity concerns Henry V, whom he entertained to dinner at the Guildhall in London. The fire burned brightly, and Whittington consigned to the flames bonds for 37 000 gold marks, thus relieving the king of debts to that amount. 'Never had prince such a subject,' said Henry. 'Never subject such a prince,' replied Dick.

The same Henry V - first as Prince Hal, then as the king - appears in three of Shakespeare's plays. In one of these a character called Davy says to Mr Justice Shallow: 'I beseech you, sir, to countenance William Visor of Woncot against Clement Perkes o' th' Hill.' Now Woncot is Woodmancote (pronounced 'Womcot') in the parish of Dursley; and the nearby Stinchcombe Hill is not only known simply as 'the Hill', but it was the site of a house occupied by a family called Perkis or Purchas. Moreover Shakespeare's description in *Richard II* of 'a wild prospect in Gloucestershire' on the way to Berkeley Castle seems to be based on the view from Stinchcombe Hill.

Claims have been made that Shakespeare lived at Dursley, possibly with a branch of his wife's family, during the 'lost years' between Stratford and London. Shakespeares are recorded locally in the sixteenth and seventeenth centuries, and one family at Newington Bagpath claimed kinship with the poet in the nineteenth. A path in the woods near Dursley is known as Shakespeare's Walk. It is exhilarating to think that Shakespeare may have gone to 'coursing matches on Cotswold' (*Merry Wives of Windsor*), seen 'Severn's swift flood' (*Henry IV*, Part I) or viewed from Stinchcombe Hill Berkeley Castle 'by yon tuft of trees' (*Richard II*).

2

# THE LORE OF THE LAND

'Do not forget me quite, O Severn meadows,' wrote the poet, Ivor Gurney. It is not surprising that a county watered not only by the mighty Severn but also the sylvan Wye and infant Thames should be rich in river lore. In addition, lesser streams and many springs are the subject of stories. There are also numbers of wells which once had saintly associations and curative powers.

People find perennial fascination not only in the water which emerges from the ground but also the passages - fictional and otherwise - which run beneath it. Buried treasure strongly appeals to the imagination; so do the graves of our distant forebears and the sometimes spectacular mounds which cover them. Natural hills - including, to quote Gurney again, 'May Hill that Gloucester dwellers/'Gainst every sunset see' - have attracted speculations and stories.

Gloucestershire is particularly rich in standing stones, even though many have disappeared through neglect and vandalism. Some see monoliths as focal points in a network of ley lines - but this is a fairly recent notion which does not feature in traditional lore. Many stones are held in great esteem, and the same is true of certain groups of trees or even individual specimens. Both trees and stones are further links between ourselves and earlier generations who have observed them with affection and even reverence.

## Severn Springs, Severn Stories

Many places in Gloucestershire bear the name of Seven Springs, Waters or Wells. Leonard Stanley has its Seven Waters. Seven Wells can be found at Naunton and also Snowshill; and the Seven Wells of Bisley are the source of the Stroud Frome. At the Seven Springs at Ozleworth the Little Avon rises behind the lugubriously-named Suicide Cottages. Seven Springs at Dodington, near Chipping Sodbury, marks the source of the Frome; at Northleach, close to the church, that of the Leach. The River Windrush rises just above Cutsdean but it can only be guaranteed an all-the-year-round flow from Seven Springs at Bourton-on-the-Water. Finally, Seven Springs in Coberley parish, just off the A435, is not only acknowledged as the source of the River Churn but once claimed to be that of the Thames. In a wooded hollow opposite the 'Seven Springs Inn' a stone still bears the words, *Hic tuus, O Tamesine Pater, septemgeminus fons* ('Here, O Father Thames, is your sevenfold spring'). However, the Thames is generally agreed to rise at Trewsbury Mead in the parish of Coates, some three miles from Cirencester, though some claim that its source is at Culkerton, from where the water flows underground to Kemble.

The river indisputably runs past Lechlade, and a statue representing Father Thames stands there, at St John's Lock.

Both Wye and Severn rise far away in Wales. A legend explains how their respective courses, together with that of the Rheidol, came about:

A great landowner called Plynlimon had three daughters. When they came of age he decided to share his estates among them. They were to leave home on a day appointed, and travel from dawn to dusk. Each would own the land she traversed, provided she reached the sea by nightfall; otherwise she would have nothing.

The night before the journey the strongly-built Severn went to bed early. Next morning she rose with the sun and set out. Though she knew the sea lay in the south she first went eastwards for fifty miles through hilly country. Then a passing swallow told her that Wye had just wakened, so she turned south.

Sweet-natured Wye knew that Severn had made a good start. She, too, knew the way to the sea, and sped southwards through beautiful country. Lively Rheidol, having spent the whole night enjoying herself, did not wake till noon. Anxious to make up for lost time, she rushed towards the sea as fast as she could.

By sunset all three sisters had reached the coast. Severn was muddy after her long journey, Wye as pretty as ever, Rheidol breathless from haste. For his part, Plynlimon sorely missed his daughters and grieved so much that he turned into a mountain. His copious tears made rivers which followed the ways taken by Rheidol, Wye and Severn.

Less poetically, a different story says that three sisters agreed one night to go from their mountain next morning for a bathe in the sea. Severn, in too much of a hurry, set off before daybreak and lost her way, wandering through Shropshire, Worcestershire and Gloucestershire. Wye rose later and saw her way clearly through Radnorshire and Herefordshire; she caught up with her sister near Chepstow, and they went on hand in hand to the sea. Rheidol overslept. Afraid of not reaching the sea at all, she set off by the quickest possible route and arrived at the coast near Aberystwyth. A further version is that the sisters decided on a race to the sea. Wye and Severn went south but Rheidol chose to go west. She won with three weeks to spare.

The name, Severn - one of the oldest still in use - derives from that of Hafren (latinised as Sabrina), who may have been a pre-Celtic river spirit. According to another story she was a virgin drowned in the river on the orders of Queen Gwendoline after the death of her husband, Locrin, because she was his daughter by another woman. John Milton in *Comus* prefers this:

*Sabrina is her name, a virgin pure;*
*Whilome she was the daughter of Locrine.*
*That had the sceptre from his father Brute.*
*She, guiltless damsel, flying the mad pursuit*

*Of her enraged stepdame Guendolen,*
*Commended her fair innocence to the flood,*
*That stay'd her flight with his cross-flowing*
*course.*

She sinks to the bottom. Water nymphs take her to the god, Nereus (normally resident beneath the Aegean Sea), and he makes her goddess of the river.

A further account tells how despairing cries are sometimes heard in the Severn estuary. They come from a woman occasionally seen swimming with the tide but never reaching land - hence her bitter complaints. She is Estrildis, doomed to this fate as long as Severn shall ebb and flow. (If the Severn Barrage ever comes about it will bring an end to her misery.) Locryn, a local prince, married Gwendoline, a Cornish chief's daughter. She was jealous, and not without cause. Locryn relied on wrecking for much of his income. One day he lured a valuable ship to destruction, and took possession not only of the cargo but also a beautiful passenger, Estrildis, daughter of a German king.

Locryn secretly visited her in a great cave beneath the river, where in due course she gave birth to a daughter who was named Avern. Locryn's frequent absences made Gwendoline increasingly suspicious and angry. For a time he claimed to be spending the time in worshipping the gods, but in the end he became so exasperated that he left Gwendoline and lived openly with Estrildis. Gwendoline responded by gathering an army and launching an attack.

Locryn was killed. Estrildis and Avern, taken captive, were cast into the river and doomed, Sisyphus-like, for ever to repeat the same fruitless actions. Avern reaches the shallows but cannot land without her mother's help. Estrildis swims in the mainstream but can never go far enough to assist her daughter. In her distress she calls 'Avern, Avern', and this has given the Severn its name.

Certainly, the Severn is usually regarded as feminine. The saying, 'Severn always gets her man', demonstrates a belief that the river needs at least one victim every year - and a particularly deep place by Wainlode Hill has swallowed many an unwary swimmer. Farm animals also drown in floodwater, and people considered that a winter of many such drownings would bring a good season for elvers. The Severn Bore can also cause casualties, both human and animal. As recently as 1984 people in the Berkeley area believed that locally-bred cattle could sense when the bore was coming, and would move away; foreign livestock stayed too near the river, and might be lost. Cynics held that farmers wishing to dispose of dead livestock might quietly drop them in the river and blame the bore.

The Romans when they first saw the bore believed the world was coming to an end, and even today people in their hundreds marvel at the massive power of the great wall of water which on big occasions sweeps majestically up the Severn. The Broadstone, a monolith over eight feet high, stands by a creek called Horse Pill near the hamlet of Stroat. Of it Brian Waters writes: 'It is the oldest monument on Severn tide and may have witnessed the tragedy of Sabrina... The stone was obviously erected in the river's honour and may at one time have been associated with the cult of the Severn river god, Nodens.'

It may also be that Sabrina was a sacrifice to the bore, or possibly a dispossessed rival of Nodens, god of the Severn Sea and the River Lyd. He was also known as Nodens of the Silver Arm, from an artificial limb made by a son of Aesculapius to replace one lost in battle. The remains of a fourth century Roman temple dedicated to Nodens can be seen in Lydney Park on the top of Camp Hill (otherwise called Dwarfs' Hill). The name Lydney officially means 'sailor's island' but it could be derived via Llud and Nudd from Nodens.

In the Lydney temple a fragment of paving shows a fisherman with a fine salmon which he is offering to Nodens, who looks like a beardless Neptune. An encounter between another fisherman and a huge salmon purports to explain why coracle fishing ended on the lower middle reaches of the Severn. The man netted an enormous fish and hauled it aboard after a tremendous struggle, but his coracle sank beneath the weight.

An episode in the collection of Welsh tales known as the *Mabinogion* relates how a salmon endowed with the power of speech reported that as he approached the walls of Gloucester he sensed such evil as he had never encountered before. He took two of Arthur's knights, Kay and Gwrhyr, up the river on his shoulders, and when they drew level with Gloucester Castle they heard a great wailing. 'Who is lamenting in this house of stone?' called Gwrhyr. The answer came: 'It is I, Mabon, son of Modron.' (Mabon had been snatched from his mother many years earlier when he was only three days old.) On hearing the news Arthur himself with many knights marched to Gloucester and attacked the castle. Meanwhile, Kay and this time Peredur went up-river on the salmon's back and rescued Mabon through a hole in the castle wall. Mabon later became one of Arthur's knights himself.

The knights policed the Severn from source to sea. One day as they watched from Plynlimon, Kay and Peredur saw smoke far to the south in the direction of Gloucester. The Twrch Trwyth, a king punished for his sins by God by being turned into a monstrous wild boar, was raiding the Severn Valley. The knights eventually brought him to bay near the confluence of the Severn and Wye but he escaped to Cornwall, where he was driven into the deep sea, to return no more. The story may be a distant memory of Welsh and Irish raids up the Severn.

## Well Waters

Apart from being a source of clean drinking water - important enough in itself, as even now we are coming once more to realise - wells possessed holy, healing and even predictive powers. 'Woe' wells were supposed to overflow when some calamity was impending. Woeful Lake Farm at Sherborne takes its name from just such a well (now gone).

Holy Well as a name is still widely found - at Haresfield, Highnam, Ozleworth and Sheepscombe, for example - though it may sometimes merely mean 'a spring in a hollow', and have no religious significance. Two hamlets near Wotton-under-Edge, Holywell and Synwell (the latter meaning seven wells), obviously take their names from sources of water. Boxwell combines the trees which flourish locally with the well of St Mary, the water of which was considered good externally for eyes and internally for rheumatism. Until at least the 1920s people used to fill bottles to take away for these purposes. St Mary's may also have been a rag well; that is, one where visitors tied a scrap of cloth to a nearby bush after making a visit so as to leave behind with it some ailment or problem. Similarly, at Drooper's Stream, a spring at the foot of West Hill, Minchinhampton, sufferers used until early this century to fasten a rag to the adjacent wall.

Wells frequently have associations with saints. An eighth century missionary from Malmesbury gave his name to St Aldam's Well (in a field on St Aldam's Farm, Pucklechurch) whose water is both holy and inexhaustible. St Kenelm's Wells at Sudeley and Sapperton are described in Chapter Four. St Chad's Well at Twyning was believed to cure skin diseases, including leprosy. The water of St Tabitha's or Tibby Well in Tibbywell Street at Painswick was mixed with bread and applied as a poultice to sore eyes.

Samuel Rudder says of St Anthony's Well in the Forest of Dean, near Flaxley: 'I have been told by people of merit and judgement in the neighbourhood, that bathing in this water is an infallible cure for the itch, and other cutaneous disorders; and a gentleman of Little Dean assured me that his dogs were cured of the mange by being thrown into it two or three times.' Sceptics maintained that the monks of Flaxley Abbey invented such cures to attract pilgrims, and hence revenue. Nevertheless, centuries after the abbey was gone people believed the well to be good for skin diseases if it were visited on nine successive days in the month of May. For rheumatism twelve visits were needed, with one step taken on the first, two on the second, and so on. T.A. Ryder (1904-1981) remembered picnicking by the well as a child, after which 'we used to fill our lemonade bottles with water and carry them home, for we used to be told by our elders that it was good for everything wrong with the eye such as soreness or styes.' The water flows strongly still, but the well now attracts few visitors.

Many other wells were thought good for the eyes. St Anne's, close to the church at Siston, near Pucklechurch, was one; so, too, St Edward's, now deep in undergrowth some fifty yards off the busy Fosse Way, just south of Stow-on-the-Wold. The latter may derive from a hermit, St Edward the Martyr (a Saxon king of the tenth century), or St Edward the Confessor (who died in 1066). Either way,

*Here those that scarcely could discern the light,*
*Their optics cleared, again receive their sight.*

St Laurence - one of St Augustine's companions on his mission to England - gave his blessing to the holy well at Didmarton and foretold that it would never run dry. It is just up the hill from the old church of Didmarton, and the prediction seems to have held good.

St Cyniburg (or Kineburga) was born at Moreton, near Thornbury. Her family, which was related to the Saxon royal house, wished her to marry a prince. She, preferring to remain a virgin, ran away from home and found work in a baker's shop at Gloucester. The kind-hearted man wanted to adopt her as his daughter but his wife, full of jealousy, killed her and threw her body into a well near the south gate of the city. Miracles began to occur. The body was recovered, and buried in a church built for the purpose on the site. Later a hospital was added. The miracles ceased for a time - supposedly because of the irreverence of the custodian - but resumed after further ceremonies in 1390. When monastic houses were dissolved by Henry VIII the hospital went, too, but Sir Thomas Bell, a wealthy draper and MP for Gloucester, founded an almshouse for six poor people on the site.

A few miles away at Matson is the Red Well, otherwise known as Edith's Spring, whose water was also considered good for sore eyes. It originated, according to tradition, in this way: Edith, a noblewoman from Upton St Leonards marries an earl at the age of eighteen. Shortly after she has given birth to a son her husband dies while fighting for King Harold. Edith decides to kill the child and then herself because she fears what will happen when the Normans arrive. She takes her son to Matson Hill and starts digging a grave. Red water wells up. She takes this as a providential sign and dedicates herself to holy living. Her son becomes an anchorite. The well in its little railed enclosure is now overshadowed by a galvanised tank, and sandwiched between an artificial ski slope and a golf course. It is neglected and dirty, but the water still runs red.

In another Gloucester suburb, Hempsted, is Lady Well (also sometimes called St Anne's Well) with its impressive stone housing. The Virgin Mary in a wildly improbable story is supposed to have climbed the steep slope from the Severn and found the spring. She was on her way to visit Joseph of Arimathea at Glastonbury when her boat was swept upstream by the Severn Bore.

At Kingsdown, Bristol, Mother Pugsley's Well is now lost beneath brick and concrete. Its twin stone basins supplied water respectively for curing eyes and making tea. These virtues were attributed to a maiden-widow's tears. During the siege of Bristol by parliamentary forces in 1645 a young soldier and his bride were married in the cathedral. Straight after the ceremony the groom had to return to his post in the defences, where he was killed. The widow, Mrs Pugsley, built a hut over the place where her husband died and was buried; she gave her name to the field and also a well in it. She wore mourning all her life, but directed that her funeral should celebrate her joyous reunion with her husband. When she died in 1700 at the age of 80, her body was carried to the grave shrouded but uncoffined. Before it a fiddler played a lively air. Two young women strewed flowers and herbs. The bells of St Nicholas' Church rang a merry peal. Even though she left money for charitable doles of bread, some thought Mother Pugsley a witch - and trampled her grave. Nevertheless, the well attracted people for more than a century.

Other curative waters in Gloucestershire include those of the brook at Aylburton; Wanswell, near Berkeley; the Boiling Well (cold, despite the name) at Stapleton, near Bristol; the Cut Well and the World Well at Tetbury; and springs at Coombe (also near Tetbury) and Lower Swell.

An old well on Rose Hill at Bisley was described as 'splendid water for the eyesight; 'tis against the sun rising'. There are similar springs at Avening and on Langley Hill near Gretton. A general tenet was that any water running 'against the sun' had special qualities. This is true of the River Isbourne whose iron-free water makes it suitable for making certain kinds of fine paper. More prosaic, perhaps, than curing eyes but nevertheless useful.

## Underground, Overground

Of the abundant accounts of subterranean passages some are based on fact, some no doubt fictional and some unverifiable. One tunnel in Gloucester long said to run from the cathedral to the 'New Inn' was found when a man fell into it through his cellar floor. Another which purports to link the cathedral with Llanthony Abbey is more dubious. The Monks' Retreat under the 'Fleece Hotel' is on the line such a passage would take but it was probably a cellar in the merchant's house which occupied the site in the twelfth century.

Monks were widely thought to have established escape routes such as the one which ran from the monastery at Standish to a doorway in the cellar of College Farm on the slopes of Haresfield Beacon. A tunnel ran from the priory at Horsley to a point outside what became the east wall of the gaol (now gone). Boseley Court at Westbury-on-Severn is supposed to be linked underground to the significantly named Monk Hill Farm. Flaxley Abbey had a mile-long tunnel of which part was described to me in 1992 by Mrs A. Shurmer of Mitcheldean:

> *There used to be a place in Littledean called the Old Grange. It was a ruin, and courting couples used to light a fire in the old fireplace; and in the winter people thought it was haunted because of the light and sounds of voices. Coming from Cinderford to Littledean by road, there is a bend at the top of the road, where the road goes downhill to Littledean. Opposite that bend behind the hedge was an underground tunnel leading to the Old Grange, and the rumour or legend was that the tunnel was used by monks or royalists. I myself have gone so far down that tunnel before being too frightened to go any farther. I made sure I was the last to enter so that I could always retreat when I felt afraid. I doubt if the tunnel still exists after all this time. I am 76 years old and this was before I left school at 14 years old.*

Perhaps Mrs Shurmer was right to be apprehensive. There is a story that a fiddler set off to trace the course of the tunnel, and invited his friends to follow his music on the surface. They did so, but suddenly the sound of the fiddle ceased - and the man was not seen again.

Berkeley Castle had its underground escape route to Wanswell, known only to successive lords; and a further link to Wotton-under-Edge, six miles away. Barely less improbably, another tunnel in the same area supposedly joined Black Quarr's Caves via Newark Park and Tor Hill with Kingswood Abbey. In

Wotton Manor the false back of a secret cupboard slid aside to reveal a passage leading to an outlying cottage (pulled down in 1893), where it emerged behind a fireplace.

Churches, too, had their tunnels. St James's at Iron Acton had underground links to both Algar's Manor and Aston Court. At Tetbury a passage led from St Mary's - beneath the 'Prince and Princess Inn' (now gone) in the Market Place - to the Priory, a large house in the Chipping. People still talked of it in the 1970s but the tradition may by now have faded.

From St Michael's Church, Mitcheldean, a tunnel ran to an earthwork in a field several hundred yards to the north. At Minchinhampton Holy Trinity and the Lammas (a house some distance away, built on or near the site of a priory) were united by a subterranean corridor which ran red with blood at the time of the battle at Woeful Danes Bottom (see Chapter One), a mile away. Perhaps at the same time, a queen took refuge in another passage leading to the village from an outlying hamlet, Hyde. The entrance was about 100 yards from the Round Tree, a lime tree growing from a knoll where 'they buried soldiers'. Gold was supposed to be hidden there, and the place haunted.

During the Civil War the stained glass of Northleach Church is thought to have been concealed in a tunnel which also contained a golden coffin. The tunnel's whereabouts were unknown, though people said it ran from a house called the Guggle (from gurgle, the noise made by water as it drained) to the church. Then a cave-in revealed the long-abandoned galleries of an old stone mine.

Uley's treasure is a pair of silver gates 'buried up Crawley Hill' - which leaves plenty of room for wild goose chases. The notion may stem from the discovery in 1873 by a man from Crawley Hill of a rubbish pit full of Roman remains on West Hill, near the place known as Money Quarr. Those looking for the rumoured valuables in Pan's Wood at Slad have always been put off by strange noises, or prevented by some mischance from continuing. A hoard buried by monks near Tintern on a path leading to St Briavels is undiscovered. On a certain night the moon shines through one of the windows of the abbey and pin-points the place; but which night, and which window?

Ladbarrows (near Ablington), the largest tumulus in the county, has yet to give up its golden coffins - as has another barrow in the Golden Coffin Field near Oakridge. The Money Tump is another mound near Bisley. When Edith Brill asked an old man to direct her to it in the 1980s, 'He said he wished he could borrow a bulldozer and search for the money that lay hidden inside it and then he would be rich for the rest of his life.' She comments: 'I hesitated to tell him that the legend says it got its name during one of the forays of the Saxons when a wealthy chief fleeing for his life dropped his money as he fled.'

On opposite sides of the road between Minchinhampton and Avening, at Hampton Fields, stand the Longstone and a long barrow known as Gatcombe Tump. This story came from someone who knew its heroine: There was an old woman in Minchinhampton who used to charm ailments; she was called Molly Dreamer because her dreams came true. She dreamed that she would find a pot of gold in Gatcombe Tump, and she and her husband dug here many times.

Once she actually had her hand on the pot and was saying 'Come up! Labour in vain!' when a spirit rose up and frightened her. At another time a spirit appeared to her husband there and asked him to name five parish churches (apparently as a condition of getting the gold), but he could recall only four.

CCXXIV.

A Strange and Wonderful

# DISCOVERY

Newly made of

# Houſes Under Ground,

At *Colton's-Field* in *Glouceſter-Shire.*

THat there is yet a great part of the Earth undiſcovered, is both the Opinion of the moſt famous Geographers (as appears by their vacancies in the Globe) and the Belief of the Learned of this and former Ages; And as *New Iſlands* have been found which were never known to our Anceſtors, ſo ſeveral parts of the Earth which were known, have been loſt, as that Iſland near *Ireland*, which is deſcribed in the Maps, but cannot now be found by all the induſtrious Search made after it, which no doubt hath been ſwallowed up, as ſome Parts of *Zealand* are, by the *Sea*, the tops of whoſe Steeples are yet ſeen by Mariners as they Sail by 'em. Theſe Conſiderations will, I hope, render the following Account more Credible in it ſelf, and give it a better appearance of Truth, and Acceptance in the World, than probable the Strangeneſs and *Novelty* of it would admit of amongſt the ignorant and unlearned part of Mankind. The Relation is thus:

In a piece of Ground within two Miles of *Cirenceſter*, (in the County of *Glouceſter*) commonly known by the Name of *Colton's Field*, as two Labourers were digging a Gravel-Pit at the foot of a Hill (which they had now ſunk four yards deep) they obſerved the Ground on that ſide next the Hill to be looſe, and preſently diſcovered an Entrance into the Belly of the Hill, which appearing very ſtrange to them, and rather the Work of Art than Nature, one of them ventur'd a little way in, and by the Light from the hole, diſcovered a large Cavity; whereupon they got a Lanthorn and Candle to make a further Search into it. By the Advantage of this Light the firſt place they entred appeared to have been a Hall, which was large, and in it two long Tables with Benches on each ſide, which they no ſooner touch'd to feel their ſubſtance, but they crumbled into Duſt; from thence they ſaw a Paſſage into another Room, which by the Furniture had been a Kitchin, ſeveral Utenſils proper to it; as Pots, Kettles, *&c.* being of Braſs or Iron, continued firm, but eaten through with Ruſt and Canker. Beyond the Hall they went into a Parlour, furniſh'd according to the faſhion of thoſe Times, with Carpets richly wrought, and other Furniture agreeable; theſe alſo fell to pieces upon their touching 'em: At one Corner of this Room there appeared to have been a pair of Stairs, but the Earth had fallen in, and ſtopt the Aſcent. Going back, in the Hall, they obſerv'd another

*News-sheet report of the discovery in 1685 of an underground house at Colton's Fields (known today as Tar Barrow, north of Cirencester).*

Another account puts the search near the Longstone itself, where just as Molly was about to lift the treasure there came flash of lightning; and after that she was never the same again. She maintained, though, that she did find the gold.

A great many items, some of them valuable, have been unearthed over the years in barrows by archaeologists and treasure seekers. An amazing discovery made in 1685 was reported in London. Two workmen digging for gravel in Colton's Fields (marked on current maps as Tar Barrow, just off the A429 north of Cirencester) found the entrance to a chamber beneath a hill. They procured a candle and went in. One room had a table and benches which crumbled into dust at their touch. They saw various other rooms, one of which contained urns 'filled with Coyns and Medals of Gold, Silver, and Brass, with Latin Inscriptions, and the Heads of several of the Roman Emperours'. The men were frightened by 'the Image of a Man in full proportion with a Truncheon in his hand, and a light in a glass like a Lamp burning before him'. The figure seemed to strike out. They fled, taking only a few coins to show 'a famous Antiquary'.

The expert returned with them the next day. They encountered the 'Image' a second time and it put the lamp out with a violent blow. They went on with a candle and saw 'two Heads embalm'd': 'the Flesh was shriev'd up and looked like Parchment scorched, of a dark complexion, they had long hair on the Chin, one seem'd to be Red, the other Black.'

The conclusion to the story - which Jennifer Westwood has described as 'a treasure-seeker's version of the one that got away' - is disappointing:

> *Upon further Search, was found several other Passages, leading to other Houses, or different Rooms of the same House; but a hollow Noise like a deep Sigh or Groan prevented any further Discovery, our Adventurers hastily quitting those dark Apartments, which they had no sooner done, than the Hill sunk down and buried all the Rarities, except those Medals and Coyns, taken out the Night before; which are now shewn for the Satisfaction of Curious and Ingenious Persons, who in great numbers flock to see them, and purchase them at great Rates, as the most valuable Relicks of Antiquity.*

A further excavation about a century later revealed nothing of note. A dig in 1935 also proved fruitless.

The theme of treasure in underground chambers recurs in accounts of Crocket's Hole, near Newent. In fact there were two such holes, one on the east side of May Hill, not far from the summit; another 1.5 miles away at Great Cugley Farm. Rudder explains how the name arose:

> *Crocket's Hole [is] so called because one Crocket and his companion Horne used to hide themselves there in the persecuting reign of Queen Mary. Horne was taken and burnt in the yard belonging to the Priory House [now the Old Court], in Newent... His story is briefly thus, as related by Horne's son, who had it from his mother.*

> *Horne was a Papist and a man of parts, and meeting with several Protestants who had assembled near the side of Yartleton Wood [on May Hill] to discourse on religious subjects, at length became a proselyte, and refused to go to Mass; for which he was taken before the Bishop in his Consistory Court at Gloucester, and committed to some prison within the verge of the College. But escaping from it in the night, he returned home, and lay concealed in various manners. At last, his wife being with child was delivered, and entertainment made at the baptising of the child; when the mother desired a cutting of some meat (probably what she knew her husband loved), which having received she laid it by. This being observed by the midwife, created a suspicion, whereupon she procured an officer to search for poor Horne, whom they found concealed in a vessel with the head out. He was immediately carried to his trial, condemned, and led to the place of execution singing the 146th Psalm ['Praise ye the Lord'], where he suffered with great Christian fortitude. Horne was so well beloved by his neighbours, and his execution so much execrated, that when the news was but whispered of Queen Mary's death, the women (men not daring to appear) took the priest that supplied the Church upon a horse, with his face towards the tail, and leading him through the town, sent him away.*

Crocket's fate does not seem to have been recorded, nor that of the informing midwife. Horne's wife was sentenced to be burnt with him but she recanted - perhaps to save her children from becoming orphans - and was reprieved. She later married another man from her husband's old village of Taynton. A curse put on the woman who supplied the wood for Horne's pyre apparently remained on the house where she had lived at Little Cugley. A later owner found it so troublesome that he dismantled the house and rebuilt on another site.

In about 1665 a disbanded soldier called Fairfax travelled from London to explore the hole on May Hill but failed to find the rumoured treasure. A local man, Witcomb, went in drunk and died there, which 'put an end to further investigation'. However, in 1884 a Newent woman aged 71, a widow called Mary Mayo - and there are still Mayos in Newent - told G.H. Piper that she had often gone down the fifteen steps of the cave to play there as a child. Furthermore, both her grandfathers knew there was a passage between May Hill and Cugley with a chest of treasure halfway through. As young men they had crawled along it for several hours, and seen a large box on the far side of a rushing stream. As they wondered how to cross their last candle fell into the water. They found it so hard to get out that they did not repeat the exercise.

May Hill itself is a well-loved landmark visible from twelve counties (at least until the local government reorganisation of 1974). It has been suggested that the name comes from an Admiral May who had the trees planted on the summit as an aid for ships navigating the Severn. There is no record of an Admiral May, and in any case the height was once called Yartleton Hill.

The crowning clump of trees once looked from some angles like a ploughman and his team - John Masefield so describes it in his poem, *The Everlasting Mercy* - but the present shape dates from 1888, when Longhope parish council paid for additional planting with funds raised the previous year to commemorate Queen Victoria's golden jubilee. Local people believe that, like the yews at Painswick, the pines of May Hill can never exceed ninety-nine in number.

On 1 May representatives from local parishes used to meet on the hill to apportion common land during the ensuing year. Earlier on the same day two parties of young people gathered for a symbolic contest between winter and summer (see Chapter Eleven). This custom has died out but in recent years morris men have gathered at the top of the hill on the dawn of each May Day to dance in the summer.

Prince Rupert and a band of soldiers are said to have camped on May Hill during the campaign of 1643 associated with the siege of Gloucester - but there are other hills with far more venerable associations. Earthworks near the Severn at Almondsbury are claimed to be the work of Offa, King of Mercia, who died in 796. 'The common people,' says Rudder, 'think [his coffin] was dug out of a tumulus at Over, in this parish, in the year 1650.' Offa also ordered the construction of the famous dyke, the route of which is followed by a long-distance footpath created in the twentieth century.

A story familiar from a dozen other places tells how the devil came to create Cam Peak, a conical hill near the village of Cam. Infuriated, perhaps, by constantly hearing the expression, 'As sure as God's in Gloucestershire', Satan decided to block the Severn. In the hills above Ulcy he loaded his wheelbarrow with earth and then set off towards the river. On the way he met a cobbler with a sack of shoes on his back and asked how far it was. The crafty cobbler took out a shoe with a great hole in it and said he'd worn it out on his journey from the Severn. 'It must be a devil of a way,' said the devil. He overturned his barrow in disgust, and so created Cam Peak.

The neighbouring hill, Cam Long Down, is associated not with the devil but King Arthur; and it may be the site of the battle of Camlan. Arthur set out from Caerleon in Wales, camped with his men on the Welsh side of the Severn, and crossed next day for the battle. Since the fighting started at noon, as Ron Fletcher points out, Arthur could not have reached either of the usual contenders for its site - Queen Camel in Somerset and Camelford in Cornwall. By contrast, Cam Long Down would have been easily attainable. Fletcher further believes that Arthur was crowned not at Silchester in Berkshire but at Woodchester (which he identifies as the Caerwdi of the chronicles) in Gloucestershire.

A much later figure, Earl Godwin, is remembered at Painswick, where he camped in 1051 on the hill known as Castle Godwin. It has many other names: the Castle, Kimsbury Castle, Kinsborow Hill, Kimsberry Hill, Spoonbed Hill and the Roman Camp.

The name of Robinswood Hill, near Gloucester, has a matter-of-fact origin. It was once owned by the Robins family, of which one member, Henry, has his tombstone opposite the porch of Upton St Leonards Church. For generations of

Gloucester people the hill has been a place of resort. An anonymous balladeer of the late eighteenth century celebrated it under the name of Robin Hood's Hill:

*Ye bards, who extol the gay vallies and glades,*
*The jessamine bowers and amorous shades,*
*Who prospect so rural can boast at your will,*
*Yet never mention sweet Robin Hood's Hill.*

*This spot which of nature displays ev'ry smile,*
*From fam'd Glo'ster city's but distant two mile;*
*Of which you a view may obtain at your will,*
*From the sweet rural summit of Robin Hood's Hill.*

*There clear chrystal springs do incessantly flow,*
*Which refresh and supply all the valley below;*
*No Dog-star's fierce heat e'er diminsh'd the rill,*
*That so sweetly does prattle on Robin Hood's Hill.*

*Here gazing around, you find objects still new,*
*Of Severn's sweet windings how pleasing the view,*
*Whose stream with the fruits of blest commerce does*
*fill*
*The sweet smiling vale beneath Robin Hood's Hill.*

*This hill though so lofty, yet fertile and rare,*
*Few vallies with it can for herbage compare;*
*Some far greater bard should his lyre and quill*
*Attune to the praise of sweet Robin Hood's Hill.*

*Where lads and gay lasses in couples resort,*
*For sweet rural pastime or innocent sport;*
*Such pleasures ne'er flow'd from gay nature or skill*
*As those that are found on sweet Robin Hood's Hill.*

*Had I all the treasures of wealthy Peru,*
*And revel'd in pleasures as emperors do,*
*I'd forfeit the whole, with a hearty good will,*
*To dwell in a cottage on Robin Hood's Hill.*

*Then, poets, record my lov'd theme in your lays,*
*First view, then you'll own it is worthy of praise;*
*Nay, envy herself must acknowledge it still,*
*That no spot's so delightful as Robin Hood's Hill.*

Many of the tumuli which abound in Gloucestershire were popularly thought to be soldiers' graves. Nympsfield Long Barrow was for some reason associated with lepers, and therefore shunned by local people. The many visitors who flock in summer to the National Trust car park only a few yards away would be amazed to hear of such a notion.

Less than a mile away is Uley Long Barrow, known as Hetty Pegler's Tump after the wife of an eighteenth century landowner. Her ghost still haunts the place, some say. H.J. Massingham considered the barrow 'one of the most impressive in England'. In 1992, five thousand years of history was placed by English Heritage on a list for possible 'disposal': the director had an aversion to 'bumps in fields'.

Another barrow with feminine associations is Nan Tow's Tump, just off the A46 1.5 miles north-west of Didmarton. The lady in question, a reputed witch, lived in a house nearby. When she died they buried her upright inside the round barrow - or so it is said.

## Standing (and Moving) Stones

A belief that standing stones could never be moved was based partly on the awe that their presence inspired, partly on the notion of their being like icebergs. People thought that ten feet of the Hoar Stone at Lower Swell was concealed below ground. A ploughman once failed in an attempt to pull out the Longstone east of Minchinhampton, despite the many oxen he set to the task.

Unfortunately, the old belief is belied by the disappearance, among others, of the Cobstone at Minchinhampton (broken up for building material in about 1836) and the Hangman's Stone at Preston, near Cirencester (removed during road widening in 1966). The Caradoc or Longstone near St Briavels was either blown up or broken up by a farmer in 1875. Longstone Field - but not the stone itself - still exists on Closeturf Farm (now a country club) off the road to Bream. The farm takes its name from a remark made to a party of horsemen by King Charles (whether I or II is unclear): 'We shall meet at dawn on the turf close to the Longstone.'

At Lower Swell the Whittle - or Whistlestone - is not on its original site; and at Minchinhampton several monoliths were removed from the Devil's Churchyard (for which, see Chapter Four). The Grey Geese of Adlestrop also took wing, despite a witch's prediction that:

*O never again shall they fly,*
*Till Evenlode flow to the steeple at Stow,*
*And Oddington mount as high.*

The background is that a woman pasturing her geese was confronted by a witch who asked for one of the birds. The woman refused. The witch turned the whole flock into stones on Adlestrop Hill. There they remained until some time before 1808 when Warren Hastings commandeered them for a decorative feature in the grounds of his mansion at Daylesford. He was impeached by the House of Lords, not for this action but for his conduct as governor of Bengal. The stones may still be in the garden of Daylesford House.

Like the Grey Geese, other stones have been ascribed to superhuman agency. The Tibblestone is a monolith by the roadside at Teddington Hands. A giant who lived on Dixton Hill a few miles away amused himself by hurling stones at ships sailing on the Severn. Once he slipped as he threw, leaving a great scar on the hillside and landing his missile off-target, at Teddington. Although ancient maps showed it, the stone came to light again only in 1948 when foundations were being dug for a garage. Although the Tibblestone served as a boundary marker it may well have been in place before that.

Jack of Kent, a mysterious figure from Herefordshire, had a pact with the devil and engaged him in many contests. One of these was a stone throwing match on a stretch of heath called Poors' Allotment, part of Tidenham Chase. The devil managed a mile and a half. His projectile, the Devil's Quoit or the Broad Stone (for which, see also Chapter One), still stands by the railway line in the parish of Stroat. When Jack's turn came he threw clear across the Severn, and won by a margin of three miles. His stone landed between Oldbury-on-Severn and the village of Stone, near Thornbury; and:

*If ever to Stroat you happen to go,*
*The Devil's Quoit there you'll surely see;*
*And beyond the river the good folk show*
*Jack's little pebble at Thornbury.*

Despite the rhyme, Jack's stone cannot be identified. In fury at losing, the devil is supposed to have stamped off to Tintern and set up a great stone on the Gloucestershire bank of the Wye where he could sit overlooking the east window of the abbey and distract the monks from their devotions. This is called the Devil's Pulpit. Another stone - a column left from iron mining by the Romans - has the same name in the Devil's Chapel at Bream. The Devil's Chimney is a tall rock stack left behind when quarrying ceased on part of Leckhampton Hill in about 1830.

People were well aware that standing stones sometimes indicated burial sites. The Drummer Boy's Stone near Blackpool Bridge in the Forest of Dean, the Hoar Stone (Duntisbourne Abbots) and the Whittlestone (Lower Swell) are some of them. A slab of rock on Cleeve Common near Cheltenham takes its name, Huddlestone's Table, from a family which acquired land in the area in the sixteenth century; yet it supposedly marks the place where eight hundred years earlier King Kenulf said farewell to some of the guests who had attended the dedication ceremony of Winchcombe Abbey. At Clearwell Meend in the Forest, Gattles Cross - otherwise known as Cattle Cross, Craddockstone, Milo's Cross and Eleanor's Cross - is thought by some to have been a memorial to Caractacus; by others to commemorate a halt made in 1282 by Queen Eleanor. Earlier in the thirteenth century when King John was hunting nearby - at Staunton - a member of his retinue displeased him so much that the man's death was decreed. Courtiers pleaded, the king relented and pardoned the man provided a buck were killed during the day's sport. A suitable animal appeared, and was shot close to a great rock from then on called the Buckstone.

This is one of several stones near Staunton, close to the Welsh border. Rudder writes:

> *There are various opinions concerning these stones. Some have supposed them to be rude, pagan deities, which the people worshipped on particular occasions; but I rather think the Rocking Stone [another name for the Buckstone] was not the immediate object of worship... Being so nicely adjusted as to move with ease, it seemed calculated to decide any question which might be put, by its motion one way or the other, agreeably to the will of the person officiating; and so of answering the purpose intended by the antient oracles among the Greeks and Romans.*

Because of its associations with magic and divination Oliver Cromwell - it is said - ordered the Buckstone to be dislodged. The attempt failed. So did others, but in 1885 a party of touring actors from London and their host from the Agincourt Inn at Monmouth succeeded in rolling the stone down a steep slope and smashing it. An iron pin inserted during the course of restoration prevented any further movement. The indignity failed to eradicate the belief that a kind of sanctity was conferred on those who touched the stone, and that wishes would be granted to those who walked three times round it. A depression in another stone nearby is called the Maiden's Cup. The water which gathers there confers beauty when applied to those with the necessary qualification.

Another of the Buckstone's uses may have been to convey messages by the vibrations generated in its rocking days. The same applied to the Near and Far Hearkening Rocks: knocking on one could be felt on the other, thus providing early warning of, say, a Welsh incursion. The rock's concave surfaces amplify sounds, and gamekeepers made use of this to detect when poachers were at work.

The Suckstone - at an estimated four thousand tons the biggest rock in England - may have been a meeting place connected with feudal tenure. An outcrop called Toad's Mouth is said to have been a place of execution in early times. Several of the Staunton stones are on a curving ridge, while others seem to be on straight lines. The Longstone is due east of the Buckstone. The destroyed Longstone at St Briavels was due east of the three monoliths of Trelech. The Longstone at Minchinhampton was due east of the lost Cobstone, while the Picked Stone lay south of this. The search for a rationale for such alignments led Alfred Watkins to propound his theory of ley lines, which in recent years has been transformed into the idea of forces running through the earth along such paths. The name of the Tinglestone, near Avening, is unexplained but people dowsing nearby have reported the kind of tingling sensations associated with mild electric shocks. One dowser suggests that ancient monoliths have a north-south magnetic polarity when they are standing but none at all when they have fallen.

Some stones undoubtedly served as markers. The Broad Stone at Stroat could have guided ships on the river. (In addition, a track led from it to Tidenham Chase, then on to the Wye at Brockweir.) On the Severn bank nearby is a line of upright stones called Stone Row which is mentioned in a Saxon charter as part of a manor boundary.

The Speech Stone by Speech House traditionally marks the centre of the Forest of Dean. Near Dursley the Mere Stone shows the boundary between two parishes, Cam and Dursley. The manors of Bisley and Lypiatt met at the Lord's Stone; the Markstone at Eastleach Martin showed the way to Keble's Bridge over the River Leach.

The Four Shires Stone, 1.5 miles east of Moreton-in-the-Marsh on the A44, may occupy the site of a Roman milestone. A tapestry map of the 1580s shows the 'Fowre Sheer Ston', but the current structure dates from the eighteenth century. Its four faces are inscribed respectively Gloucestershire, Warwickshire, Oxfordshire and Worcestershire, though since 1931 only the first three counties have met there.

The Three Shires Stones near Marshfield is even worse off, since all three counties in that area (Gloucestershire, Somerset and Wiltshire) gave way in 1974 to Avon. David Verey tartly comments: 'In their present form they are a sham C.19 megalith, but they are perhaps on or near the site of a destroyed megalithic monument, most likely a chambered long barrow.' This may have stood on the border between ancient Wessex and Mercia.

Even the modest milestones of relatively recent years can be impressive. At Teddington Hands across the road from the Tibblestone is a stone pillar with wooden arms showing directions. Ten generations after its original construction this was restored in 1876 at the expense of Alice Attwood, a relative presumably of the original benefactor:

*Edmund Attwood of the Vine Tree*
*At the first erected me,*
*And freely he did this bestow*
*Strange travellers the way to shew.*

The Long Stone (or Long John), a way marker between Coleford and Staunton, was already ancient on its first recording in 1584. It may also have been a place of sacrifice, dimly recalled in a local belief that the stone bleeds if it is pricked with a pin at midnight on the summer solstice. 'Blood Stone' is another of the many names of Gattle Cross (see above); this, too, supposedly bleeds when pricked at midnight on a particular (but unspecified) day.

Midnight is also significant for the Whisselstone at Lower Swell, which goes to drink from the Lady Well when it hears Stow church clock strike, a mile away. (The word 'when' may be significant.). The Tinglestone at Avening runs round the field when it hears the chimes of midnight; so does the Longstone in Hampton Fields a short distance away - 'as almost every child in the place

[Minchinhampton] will tell you,' wrote Partridge in 1912. When the Hoar Stones at Duntisbourne Rouse hear the same hour strike on Edgeworth church clock they also run round the field, or alternatively, turn over. Further possibilities are that a man springs out of the stones and goes round the field with a rake, or the devil emerges. The field in which the stones stand is called the Devil's Flights.

Similar beliefs have attached themselves to at least two statues. A finial on the gable end of Postlip tithe barn is carved into a naked figure thought to represent the Norman builder of the chapel, Sir William de Postlip. At certain times of the year when he hears midnight strike on the chapel bell he steps down from his perch and goes down to drink at the wishing well at the foot of Cleeve Hill. As a child at Westbury-on-Severn, T.A. Ryder was told that a stone figure thought to be Neptune in the Court water garden left his plinth and took a dip in the pond when he heard the church clock strike midnight. Ryder adds that the Colchester-Wemyss family which owned the Court for many generations maintained that the statue (found on the bank of the Severn) came from the Roman settlement down river at Lydney.

The massive Tyndale Monument (111 feet high) on the hill above North Nibley does not have a story of moving at midnight - that would be too terrifying to contemplate - but it is said that the masonry (completed in 1866) constantly cracked open and needed repair until a Bible which had been built in was removed. The moral is that Tyndale gave his life to make the Bible available to all, and the copy in his monument refused to be hidden. The difficulty is that scholars question whether William Tyndale of North Nibley had any connection with the martyr of the same name who translated the Bible into English. Others contend, though, that Gloucestershire words used in the translation point to local authorship.

Some of the ancient standing stones were thought to have therapeutic powers. Parents wishing to cure babies of rickets passed them through a hole in the Minchinhampton Longstone. (The existing holes would be too small.) Another monolith called the Lang Stone, now gone, stood near the Bulwarks on Minchinhampton Common. Partridge noted a multiplicity of beliefs surrounding it:

> *Still standing is the curious 'Ragged Jonathan' or 'Holey Stone', about 5 ft. high, pitted all over with regular cup-like depressions. It has been used at some time as a milestone; but one old inhabitant says he thinks that children used to be lifted over it to cure whooping cough. I have also been told that the holes in the stone were made by Oliver Cromwell's guns.*

## Tales of Trees

In *Shepherd's Country* H.J. Massingham relates what he calls 'a contemporary Cotswold folk-tale':

*When I was a young mon, I was a kyarter [carter], and in them days there was a smartish bit of kyarrying by road, in waggins and drays, up towards Gloucester. Arter I'd abin a-goin up that road a time or two, I seed five beautiful pear-trees sot in the hedge longside the road just outside Newent; and the first time I seed 'em they was in full blowth, and a prety enough sight they was to be sure. Well, when it come September abouts, there they was loaded, so I whoas up my osses and gets me a pocketful, and they was lovely - not mousey, but as soft as butter and prety moreish.*

*It come to me as it were mortal strange for any mon to plant sich desperate good pear trees in a hedge, and agains the highroad, so I exes a mon as kept a public there about it. This be the tale he telled.*

*'They pear trees was firstly planted in a fine meadow near Pershore, where the land be very kind to pears, and good bearings of capital fruit they had on 'em. But misfortunate for the farmer mon as owned 'em, there was a rookery in some old elms over nights 'em, and as soon as they pears was ripe, they domned old crows ud come and settles on the branches of they pear trees and peck, peck, peck they ud go, till they a-yut all the fruit that there was.*

*'When the next season come round, the farmer mon reckoned as he had 'ad enough of they old crows physic; so just afore the pears were proper ripe, he takes he a gret kyan [can] of bird-lime, and long lother [ladder] and gaums the bird-lime all over they pear tree branches. Next day were warm and sunny and the fruit mellow-ripe. So kyaw! guz one ole crow, then kyaw! guz another, and then flip-flop the whole hustle on 'em guz off and settles in they pear branches.*

*'Prety soon there was heard such a desperate squaking and kraking 'cos they old crows could move ne'er a foot, and was sot as fast as a bussock [rabbit] in a snap-gin. "Lummydays!" says the farmer mon, "I a-got 'em this time. I'll get my old gun and shut the lot on 'em." So off he guz to fetch un. They old crows heered what he said, and set up a-cawing and a-flapping their wings fit to bust; and, as soon as they see the farmer mon come back wi' his muzzle-loader, they made sich a tremenjous desperate flapping that come up all five pear trees by the roots, and whiffley, whiffley, whiffley, off they flies, pear trees and all, over along the river towards Tewkesbury.*

*'Arter they bin a-going for a while, there comes a smartish shower o' rain, and that washed most all of the bird-lime away, and clunk, clunk, clunk, down drops they pear trees into a hedge by the highroad way, towards Newent. Took good root they did too, and there they be to this very day. But domme if I knows what happened to they old crows arterwards.'*

Three birches near Nutterswood on Cleeve Common were known as the Three Sisters (only two now remain). The women concerned - called Faith, Hope and Charity - all had disastrous love affairs, and then devoted the rest of their lives to helping the sick and needy. They were buried at a place from which five counties could be seen, and a birch tree was planted over each of their graves. If the story is not true, at least it is edifying.

Not far away - in the village of Swindon - another burial was marked by Maud's Elm, which well-to-do Cheltonians in the eighteenth century would drive out in their carriages to see. This is how the tree acquired its name. One day a young Swindon woman, Maud Bowen (or Bowing) failed to return home. Searchers soon found her, drowned in Wyman's Brook, a tributary of the River Swillgate. On a bridge close by lay the body of her uncle, Godfrey, an arrow through his heart and a scrap of cloth from Maud's shawl in his fingers.

Although the circumstances were unclear, Maud was declared a suicide, and buried at a crossroads with an elm stake through the heart (which later grew into the tree called Maud's Elm). These events unhinged the mind of Margaret, Maud's mother, who took to wandering the village distractedly. One morning the lord of the manor, Sir Robert de Vere, came across her. He gave orders that she be removed from his sight. A man-at-arms hurried to obey, only to be struck down by an arrow which came from a clump of trees. A search failed to find the assailant. Margaret, having been found guilty of causing the man's death by witchcraft, was sentenced to be burnt by Maud's grave. Sir Robert came to gloat, and a third arrow struck him in the heart. He fell dead on the fire, and with him ended the de Veres.

Many years later the mystery was explained by an aged man who gave his name as Walter Gray. He explained that as a young man he loved Maud, who was desired by both her uncle and Sir Robert de Vere. The uncle, having decided to help his powerful rival, waylaid Maud and began to drag her towards him as he sat his horse, relishing her struggles. Walter, happening on the scene, shot Godfrey and fled, thinking Maud would escape. Instead she fell into the stream, and drowned. Walter later intervened to shoot both the man-at-arms and de Vere before leaving the village. Some say he became a wanderer; others that he went no more than a mile or so away to be the landlord of an obscure inn called 'Hayden's Elm' (a forerunner, perhaps, of the 'House in the Tree', in the hamlet of Hayden). Either way, only as he sensed the approach of his own death did he return to tell the tale.

Church Cottage, a small half-timbered house next to Swindon churchyard, was formerly called Maud's Cottage. Maud's Elm stood at the junction of the present Swindon Road, Richards Road and Malvern Street until it was felled in 1907. Older people in Swindon remember as children being told Maud's story as a true narrative.

Dab's Elm at Alderton marked the grave of a suicide with the odd name of Dab. Emma Dent writes: 'My informant, now a middle-aged man with grown-up children, was bred and born near that mysterious tree, and he described with what awe as a youngster he looked upon it, and how the expectation of seeing Dab or any of his crew would cause his heart to thump, and make him hurry past the dreaded spot.' Unfortunately, there seems to be no record of where this was.

A wych elm which stood on a mound called 'the Bank' in the middle of Broad Campden probably served as a landmark for travellers making their way across the nearby wolds. To the great sorrow of the villagers after centuries of life the tree was destroyed by a gale in 1958. At least this was a natural disaster, but the people of Poole Keynes were dismayed when their beloved tree was felled through sheer malice by a former owner of Lower Farm. The tree, another elm, stood on the village green. On summer evenings people gathered beneath it to sing, play the fiddle, and chat to neighbours. They had a belief that the tree would fall if ever a year passed in which no baby were born in the village. Its wanton destruction parallels that of some standing stones.

Of all trees the native oak is perhaps the most loved. Between Kempsford and Lechlade the fields round Dudgrove are full of oaks. The local explanation is that a miser who owned the land agreed to lease it at a high rent for a single crop. The tenant agreed terms. After the contract was signed he chose to plant acorns.

A Chedworth man claimed that a tree near Woodbarrow known as the Royal Oak broke into leaf 'a fortnight afore the rest'. The famous Lassington Oak, 30 feet in girth, stood for well over 600 years before succumbing to strong winds in 1960. Several famous specimens stood in the Forest of Dean, including Jack of the Yat, the Crad Oak and the Newland Oak. All are now gone. The last, at 44 feet in girth and a thousand years in age, was claimed as the biggest and oldest in England. It collapsed in 1955. Older yews still stand. They are described in Chapter Four.

Another venerable tree survives: the Tortworth Chestnut. Its history is long, though it is not mentioned in the Domesday Book as some have claimed. Tradition holds that King John held a council meeting under the tree, and that by the middle of the thirteenth century it was already called the Great Chestnut. A plaque on the gate in the fence round the tree says - with odd precision - that it was 600 years old on 1 January 1800, and adds this rhyme:

*May Man Still Guard thy Venerable form,*
*From the Rude Blasts and Tempestuous Storm*
*Still mayest thou Flourish through Succeeding time*
*And Last, Long Last, the Wonder of the Clime.*

The tree is now an immense, crumbling ruin, albeit with powerful and vigorous limbs. On the February day I visited, its crusty antiquity vividly contrasted with the delicate and ephemeral beauty of the snowdrops which thickly carpeted the ground beneath. Reflections on King John and his council soon faded as the incessant roar of the M5 motorway a mile distant re-asserted the presence of the twentieth century.

3

# VILLAGE VOICES

Scattered across Gloucestershire's broad acres are hundreds of villages and hamlets whose names alone (together with those of fields, lanes and woods) have inspired a four-volume work and many other monographs. Folk etymology purports to explain some of them. It is sometimes tongue-in-cheek, often fanciful but usually of interest.

The extraordinary richness and variety of field names now face impoverishment. Each year fields disappear beneath concrete or asphalt. Others lose their identity with the removal of walls or hedges. Shifts in population have disrupted the transmission of local wisdom, and few people in certain villages can now rehearse the names of fields, still less the circumstances from which they arose.

The intense rivalry - not to say emnity - which once divided village from village persists mainly in sporting events, if at all. In the past it produced a wide range of traditional jibes and generic nicknames which reflected local pride and also prejudice. At times feeling ran so strongly that it did not stop short of fisticuffs.

The village of Ebrington has long enjoyed the reputation of being full of simpletons, though its people often used this as a smoke-screen behind which they could outwit outsiders: 'Folks be allus a-kyankering about what fools we be. Yes, they thinks what fools we be - but be we?'

Whatever the truth of such things, they provided stories and songs for many a happy hour by the inglenook, under the hedge at bait time, or in the village pub.

## What's in a Name?

Gloucestershire has some splendidly simple names for villages, such as Box, Edge, Ford, Hill, Stone and Syde. Cam (crooked), Slad (valley), Sling (narrow strip), Stroud (overgrown marsh) and Yate (gate) are readily explained. Others have a haunting appeal, like Edward Thomas's Adlestrop or Ivor Gurney's

*Framilode, Frampton, Dymock, Minsterworth...*
*You are the flower of villages in all earth.*

Some names seem to have been so well liked that they came in twos. Eastington, Over, Preston, Staunton, Woodmancote and no doubt others occur twice each in the county. There are many twins, such as Up and Down Hatherley, Up- and Highleadon, and a range of Upper and Lower or Great and

Little: the Slaughters, the Swells, the Badmintons, the Barringtons, the Washbournes, the Witcombes. Triplets include the Shiptons (Moyne, Oliffe and Sollars), the Rissingtons (Great, Little and Wyck) and the Colns (Rogers, St Aldwyns and St Dennis); and for good measure there are the quadruple Ampneys and Duntisbournes.

To confuse the outsider Cold Aston and Cold Ashton are many miles apart, while Taddington, Teddington, Toddington and Tredington are close together. One could compound the difficulty with Alveston and Olveston, Salperton and Sapperton, Tidenham and Todenham, Winson and Winstone, Woolaston and Woolstone.

Pronunciation produces shibboleths for the unwary. One should say Amney, Arpry, Cubberley, Dunsbourne, Nimsfield, Oover, Or or Ah (Awre), Painzick, Prinnidge, Shipscombe, St Brevvles, Twinning and Weston Subbidge. Local people say Rizzington for Rissington, as they have at least since the Domesday Book, where it appears as Risendune (meaning hill covered with brushwood). Bromsberrow is stressed on the first syllable - as it has been since the thirteenth century - and Wotton-under-Edge (oddly) on the third. Equal weight is placed on both parts of Newland, which goes back to when it was new land cleared from the forest seven or more centuries ago. Cirencester, once pronounced as Cissister, now has all its syllables again - unless, of course, it is abbreviated to the homely Ciren.

Hewelsfield is claimed to derive from 'hew and slay' or 'human slay', and Beachley from another battle in which the English cried 'Beat and slay' as they drove their attackers into the River Severn. They come in fact from two proper names, Hygeweald and Betti. Upper and Lower Slaughter might suggest other conflicts but derive from slough (muddy place).

Ready Token reflects insistence at its ancient inn (now gone) on cash instead of credit. There was a belief that one landlord took both money and life from travellers, and many years later an excavation of the inn site is said to have revealed guineas and skeletons. The place also suggests that its name was coined by Cromwell (see Chapter One).

Randwick means 'dairy farm on a ridge' but local tradition provides a different explanation. Fennemore reprints this manuscript in her history of the village:

> *In the days of old, there lived a poor widow in Randwick, who had two sons. She was industrious, honest, and pious, and loved to attend her parish church. One Sunday morning she prepared her dinner before she went to church. She made some apple dumplings, and prepared and dressed a sheep's head. She filled her large pot with water from the spring, suspended it over the fire, and said to her son Tom: 'Now, Tom, I am going to church; as soon as the pot begins to boil, put in the dumplings; and, Dick, if your brother should want some more fire, you go and fetch some thorns from the wood pile.'*
>
> *So saying she put on her gear and departed. Tom kept taking off the lid to see if it boiled. 'Does it boil?' enquired Dick. 'Oh! ah!'*

*replied Tom, 'go and get some thorns to keep it boiling.' Dick went, and soon returned with an armful of thorns, which he flung under the old, huge, black pot. 'Now then,' said Tom, 'the pot begins to boil; bring the dumplings, and put them in.' And one after the other those balls of apples, suet, and flour, were dropped into the pot. The dry thorns began to crackle and bang, and pop and blaze, and soon surrounded the pot with a brilliant flame.*

*The pot began to boil with violence and the lid to heave, as if it were about to jump up the chimney. 'Take off the pot lid,' cried Dick. Tom removed the lid, and both Tom and Dick looked into the pot. The water was bubbling, steaming, and leaping, and jumping, and boiling; the apples dumplings were moving up and down, and were going round and round with the ebullition and gyration of the seething broth.*

*At this critical moment the tongue of the sheep's head began to protrude, and the sheep's head to take part in the gyratory motions, from the violence of the boiling water. The apple dumplings ran round and round the pot, apparently pursued by the sheep's head. 'Look, Dick! Look, Dick!' cried Tom, 'the sheep's head is runnin' round and round with 'is mouth open, and is a-tryin' to swallow all the apple dumplins.' Tom, in a passion, struck the sheep's head with his large wooden spoon, but it did not deter it from its voracity; on the contrary the repeated blows appeared to accelerate its speed, and gyratory motion.*

*Both Tom and Dick began to cry. 'Oh dear! whatever shall we do, the sheep's head will eat up all our dumplins.' Matters appeared to grow worse, for the dumplings apparently disappeared within the capacious mouth of the sheep's head. Tom could stand it no longer, so he said: 'Run, Dick, to the church, and tell mother to make haste home, or the sheep's head will eat all our dumplins.' Dick rushed out of the door, and ran down the road, as fast as his nimble feet could carry him. Tom followed, and, standing in the middle of the road, endeavoured to increased his brother's speed by vociferating, 'Run, Dick! run, Dick! and tell mother to make haste home, or the sheep's head will eat all our dumplins.'*

*The people heard Tom shouting, and thought he was mad. Dick rushed into the church, and to the humiliation and mortification of the mother, and to the utter consternation of the minister, the clerk, and the congregation, bawled, out of breath: 'Be quick, mother! Run home, mother! or the sheep's head will eat all our dumplins.' Now, it happened that there were a great many strangers in the village [most likely it was 'Wap Sunday'], when Tom stood halloing 'Run, Dick,' and from this simple incident the place was nicknamed 'Run Dick'. During the course of centuries this has become Runnick or Randwick.*

In such far-fetched attempts at etymology one can detect a tongue firmly in cheek. In defiance of straightforwardness, Box - which should be simple, because its name comes from the tree which flourishes locally - claims three possible origins: from Lydia Laboxe, a nun from the Lammas in Minchinhampton who came to nurse Flemish weavers when they were ill; from a smugglers' den in the middle of the village known as the Salt Box; and from a shooting box (now called the Beehive; see also Chapter One) used by Henry VIII.

Some names of the past no longer exist. The place Celia Fiennes knew in the late seventeenth century as Morton Hindmost became Moreton-in-the-Marsh. Experts once suggested that the last element was a corruption of 'march', meaning boundary, but Morton in Hennemarsh (recorded in 1253) firmly indicates a marsh frequented by water birds.

Both Pomerton and Kingchester are now no more. According to tradition the former vanished beneath the waters of the Severn, near Awre; the latter, originally a Roman settlement, was near the present hamlet of Kingscot, five miles from Tetbury. In at least one other case the name remains but the village has largely disappeared. Lancaut may have been abandoned when trade on the Wye declined, but the traditional account - still current in the locality - prefers depopulation by plague, adding that the now ruined church was attended by lepers during the Middle Ages.

The tiny settlement of Dorn, near Moreton-in-the-Marsh, for some reason - possibly its Roman past - boasts of having once been a great city. Similarly, Prestbury claims primacy over its enormous neighbour:

*Prestbury was Prestbury*
*When Cheltenham was a pup.*
*Prestbury will be Prestbury*
*When Cheltenham's busted up.*

Valleys, fields and lanes have names numbering many hundreds in total. All had meanings, or explanations or stories - though some of these are now lost. Nanny Farmer's Bottom near Wotton-under-Edge is an example. Bottom is easy for it means valley and has done so at least since the time of Shakespeare; but who was Nanny Farmer? Cut and Fry Green at Yorkley sounds mysterious. Fortunately there is still a local tradition which explains that an old woman who kept pigs there sold bacon, and miners coming up from the pit would buy a few slices and cook them over a fire on the spot.

Potlickers' Lane at Winson is still marked on large-scale maps, but why is it so called? Even the meticulous local historian, Mollie Davis, admits ignorance on the point. Tiny roads avoiding the turnpike bars (and tolls) which existed until the 1880s were collectively known as 'toll dodgers'. One parish with a maze of winding roads round its twelfth century church is Condicote. H.J. Massingham heard this explanation:

*There was four men and a donkey up by Condicote long afore these times, when the roads hadn't been made proper. One Sunday, so as they might have grace, they set out for to gu to church, but not knowing where the church was, they telled the old donkey to find un hisself, so off he guz and they traipsed arter him. Sure to be! that donkey stops to nibble a bit o' clover here, or some keck over there, but at last they comes to the church. When a main Sundays had gone by, a regular path was marked, and 'tis due to that occud old donkey as they roads up on they hills be so desperate twisty.*

A traveller once enquired of the landlord of the 'Old Crown' at Uley the way to Owlpen. He was told: 'You must go along the Green and down the hill by Fairy Lane until you come to Cuckoo Brook; and then a little further on you will pass Horn Knep, after which you will go by Dragon's Den; next you go through Potlid Green; after that it is Marling's End, and that will bring you straight to Owlpen, but you must take care not to miss the road.' The man chose to stay overnight, just ten minutes' ride from his destination. All the names exist, though it appears that Dragon's Den is in fact near the beginning of Fairy Lane.

## Naming the Field

The origin of some names may never come to light. John in the Wood (Churchdown), Olinos (Kempley), the Mork (St Briavels), Maggers Clift (Stinchcombe) and Black Nell (Upper Slaughter) are intriguing examples. Some explanations are obvious. Shape accounts for Harp (Bitton, Hawkesbury, Newent and Westbury-on-Severn), Herring (Upper Slaughter), Leg of Mutton (Lassington), Shoulder of Mutton (Alveston, Barnsley, North Cerney, Woodchester). Natural features supply Orchid Leaze and Sweet Waterings (Alveston), and the Arles (Taynton) or the Orles (Kempley) - both words for alders. A clump of trees gives the widespread Cuckoo Pen (Ampney Crucis, Avening, Cromhall, Didmarton, Lassington, Lechlade, Painswick, Redmarley, Staverton). Flash Stocking (Alveston) may promise erotic delights but merely means a ford (flash) bridged by a tree trunk (stock). Garbling produced Hunt's Hill (Saintbury), from oont (mole), and Merry Heaven (Alveston) from merlin's haven - though a prosaic explanation is that the plot once belonged to a Mary Evans.

Bygone agricultural practice is reflected in Lammas Mead or Meadow (Kemble, Bromsberrow), ground enclosed for hay from 24 June until 1 August (Lammas Day), when it was thrown open for grazing. Draw Acre (Lechlade) and the Lots (Chedworth, Painswick) were allocated by annual ballot. Four Day Math (Dowdeswell) and Seven Men's Mowth (Turkdean) show the amount of work reapers would have needed to put in.

A lengthy list of names points to the difficulty of working certain fields or the meagre returns they produced: Bare Gains (Oxenhall), Break Heart

(Churchdown), Cold Comfort (Churcham, Tetbury), Empty Purse (Boxwell, Hawkesbury), Forlorn Hope (Alveston), Hell's Bottom (Cam), Hungry Park (Oxenhall), Labour in Vain (Thornbury), Littleworth (Brimpsfield, Pucklechurch), Pennyless Pitch (Brimpsfield), Starve Acre (Winchcombe) and Twistgut (Boxwell). Only on a few occasions are favourable conditions shown - in Neednotts (Awre) or Milk and Honey (Kempley), for example. Honey Acre at Coberley might be complimentary, or derogatory (indicating sticky land), or simply literal (meaning a plot on which bee hives were kept).

A long history emerges in some cases. Bearfoot or Barefoot Wood at May Hill seems obvious enough, but it derives from the Saxon, *beofurt*, meaning hellebore. The Thing at Cam may be where a Saxon moot assembled. The Hundred Path and Ground at Hawkesbury is land where the people of the hundred gathered. Plaistow (play place) at Deerhurst, as well as being space for sport was the site for manor and hundred meetings.

Religious connections arise from the Ankerage (Tortworth), meaning land occupied by a hermit or anchorite; and the Bible and Testament Fields at Nailsworth, the rent from which went to Horsley Church to buy copies of the scriptures. Lamplands (Tidenham) is thought to have paid for lamps in the church; Candle Ground (Bibury) and Candlemas Croft (Bisley) provided candles for the festival of Candlemas (2 February). The tithe from Lady's Piece at St Briavels was spent on the Lady Chapel in the church. The darker side of belief may explain the Devil's Dancing Ground (Sherborne) and similar names explored in Chapter Six. At Arlingham a field called the Spurts (formerly the Sprits) may take its name from the ghostly figure of a woman seen there.

A field on Edge Farm in the village of the same name is called Hanging Hill. A labourer wagered that he could mow it in a day. He failed, and hanged himself. An eerie swishing heard there at midnight is the sound of his scythe. Dead Woman Acre above Longtree Bottom near Horsley may simply mean that a female body was once found there. However, the local story is that a woman swore she would reap the field in a day or die. She did both. Deadman's Acre (sometimes shown as Deadman's Copse) at Winson was ploughed in a day by a farmer or labourer, again to win a bet. He, too, succeeded but fell down dead as he completed the task.

Kill Devil Acre on Selsley Hill to the west of Minchinhampton Common boasts a similar tale. A man is promised as much land as he can enclose in a day. He fences (or perhaps walls) the plot, then drops dead from the exertion. An alternative formulation is that the man determined to fence a plot by night and to build on it enough of a house to have a hearth and chimney with a fire burning. Once more, he died immediately after succeeding.

There was certainly a belief in the right to build on the grazing common at Minchinhampton providing that a fire could be lit on the hearth before the proceedings were interrupted. The hayward was plied with drink at appropriate times to make sure that he did not become aware of such ventures until it were too late. Until the eighteenth century in the Forest of Dean it was accepted that a man could claim as much ground as he enclosed in a day with a bank and a ditch, provided he could have a fire burning within. A day was defined as the period from dawn until dusk, and the fire smoke had to go up a flue.

Norman Jewson found the people of Oakridge very independent and attributed this to their having built cottages on the common, 'it being the custom, if not the law, that if anyone could get so far in building as to have smoke coming from his chimney he could not be dispossessed.' Such freeholders looked down on the Sapperton and Frampton Mansell people who either rented their houses or had a three-generation tenure and then became payers of rent.

The enclosure of Oakridge Common, which put an end to further squatting, caused great bitterness:

> *Some of the older men chuckled as they recalled how on dark nights gangs of men collected in the village and demolished many yards of the dry stone walls dividing what had been the common... The chief beneficiary of the enclosure was the then lord of the manor, Sir John Dorington, who had made himself so unpopular by promoting it that, when he put up for parliament, crowds ran beside his carriage shouting 'Who stole the donkey's dinner?'*

A similar report comes from France Lynch and Chalford Hill, where the taunt was varied to: 'Who drove the donkey from the common?' Sir John Dorington of Lypiatt Park, near Bisley, stood unsuccessfully for the Stroud seat on several occasions. He was elected in 1874 only to be defeated later in the same year when Parliament was dissolved.

## Guiding Rhymes

The names of various villages and towns are linked in traditional rhymes which can range from mnemonic to polemic. One collection of neighbours is merely good-humoured:

> *Southrop, Hatherop,*
> *Botherop and Eastleach,*
> *All begins with an A.*

Botherop is the old name for Eastleach Martin. The saying that Hartpury has five ends and no middle is also neutral: the reference is to Corse End, Butters End, Moor End, Blackwells End and Murrels End.

A once-lingering belief that coal measures existed below Down Piece is reflected in: 'When coal shall be found on Alveston Down,/Then Alveston'll be a market town.' 'Bourton-on-the-Water,/That's next door to Slaughter' might seem strange but it simply points to the proximity of the places named. Another rhyme with its hints of vernacular pronunciation is also non-committal:

*Bourton-on-the-Water,*
*Clap'n-on-the-Hill,*
*Th' mightiest way to Gloster's*
*By Frog Mill.*

Frog Mill - a hamlet off the A40 six or seven miles from Cheltenham - comes up again in:

*Dirty Gretton, dingy Greet,*
*Beggarly Winchcombe, Sudeley sweet.*
*Hartshorn, Whittington bell,*
*Andoversford, merry Frog Mill.*

Here, 'Whittington bell' may refer to the church's wooden bell turret, and 'merry Frog Mill' to the public house of that name - though in fact it had the reputation of being haunted.

'Rissington Wyck, where the dirt lies thick' is self-explanatory. Stow-on-the-Wold was said to have plenty of air but to lack the other three elements, water (because it stood high, and had few springs), earth (it had little land) and fire (there was a shortage of wood for fuel). Hence:

*Stow-on-the-Wold*
*Where the wind blows cold,*
*And the cooks have nothing to cook.*

The second line is varied to 'Where the devil caught cold' and the third to 'And the cooks can't roast their dinners'. Some versions added: 'Moreton-in-the-Marsh,/Where the frogs croak harsh.'

Several other places appear in another verse whose variations show it must have been widespread:

*Beggarly Bisley, strutting Stroud;*
*Mincing Hampton, Painswick proud.*

The second line sometimes runs 'Minchinhampton miserable, Painswick proud' or 'Hampton poor and Tetbury proud'. Bisley and Minchinhampton saw a good deal of poverty, especially after the decline of the textile industry there in the late eighteenth century. Painswick and Tetbury were perceived as putting on superior airs. The luckless Stroud features in a further rhyme:

*It is allowed*
*That Stroud*
*Holds nought that's pretty,*
*Wise or witty.*

Such derogatory comments are common. One wonders what scandals lie behind 'Dirty Tredington, wooden steeple,/Funny parson, wicked people' - though the timber-framed belfry is readily visible. Both church and people are again found wanting in:

*St Briavels stands upon a hill.*
*It has a church without a steeple,*
*Looks down on the River Wye,*
*With most deceitful people.*

Unduly compliant women inspired this comment: 'All the maids of Wanswell/May dance on an eggshell'. Diet features in:

*Nympsfield is a pretty place,*
*Set upon a tump;*
*And what the people live upon*
*Is ag-pag dump.*

Evidently the villagers had a great liking for dumplings with wild plums (called heg-pegs or ag-pags), which gave rise to the generic nickname of Nympsfield ag-pags. There are many others. The people of Tintern taunted their Gloucestershire rivals on the other side of the Wye with the rhyme:

*Brockweir toads, big 'n' smull,*
*One abbey cowat [jackdaw] ud beat 'em all.*

The retort would be immediate:

*Abbey cowats, thin 'n' small;*
*Half a loaf ud feed 'em all.*

Animal characterisation is also favoured in Uley moggies (calves), Cam ewes or crows and Painswick bow-bows (see below). Dursley people have two nicknames, baboons and lanterns. The first comes from an obscure rhyme, 'The Dursley baboon/As yut his pap athout a spoon' (pap here means the hasty pudding or 'parritch' which was the standard evening meal for labourers). The second is mentioned in Kilvert's diary for 1873:

*My mother says that at Dursley in Gloucestershire, when ladies and gentlemen used to go out to dinner together on dark nights, the gentlemen pulled out the tails of their shirts and walked before to show the way and light the ladies. These were called 'Dursley Lanterns'.*

The town was also known as 'Drunken Dursley'. To make matters worse, the expression 'a man of Dursley' meant someone unreliable, untrustworthy, or at best apt to drive a hard bargain. Defoe quotes it in his *Tour through the Whole Island of Great Britain*, written in the 1720s. It derives from sharp practice in the textile trade going back to the Middle Ages, such as selling rolls of cloth with good material on the outside and poor within, adding chalk to white cloth to make it weigh heavier (when it was sold by weight per yard) and stretching fabric to make it seem longer than it really was. 'A man of Nailsworth' had a similar meaning.

Tewkesbury mustard had an infusion of horseradish to give it particular pungency. 'As thick as Tewkesbury mustard' meant stupid. 'He looks as if he lives on Tewkesbury mustard' was said of a person who looked sour or ill-tempered. The rationale for 'One at a time, like the men of Maisemore' seems to have been lost. 'Bisley, God help us' may refer to the village's once-proverbial poverty, or to the interdict (see Chapter Four) which once prevented burials in the village.

Bisley also features in a saying about the weather. People at Bussage when the wind blows towards them from the north say: 'Bisley gates are open.' A person who leaves open a door and causes a draught is told in several places: 'You are a man of Cairnscross' or 'You must come from Winchcombe.' At one time, as a man set off for work he left the door open behind him for good luck - or alternatively to leave room for witches to quit the household - and it is possible that this habit persisted longer at the two places indicated than elsewhere.

In the Forest of Dean there are Aylburton shrimpers, a nickname which must have come from Severn fishing. The village is also known as 'duck town', from the large number of birds which used to flock to the brook when pigs' bellies were washed in it. Chalford Hill on the other side of the river owed its name of 'piggy town' to the number of pigs bred there. Back in the Forest the people of Whitecroft are called 'dabdowners', though no one seems to know why. They are reputed to be the wittiest in the Forest (though the claim is disputed by Yorkley) and also the most pronounced in accent (though some say Berry Hill or Broadwell should have this title). Yorkley speech was notoriously hard to understand, to the extent that people from Lydney - three miles away - claimed it was unintelligible, partly because of peculiarities of vocabulary such as 'hummocks and whomzies' (legs and arms). Berry Hill, incidentally, has the reputation of being the last place God made.

Lydbrook was characterised as 'two miles long and two yards wide', which reminds one of the sardonic observation that Northleach in the Cotswolds began at the gaol and ended at the workhouse. Again in Lydbrook, a wag pinned up a railway timetable in the henhouse. To someone who asked the reason he said: 'So the fowls know when there's a train coming.'

At Whiteshill in the Cotswolds and Coalway, Pillowell and Yorkley Slad in the Forest people reputedly put a pig on the wall to see the band go by. The same thing literally happened at Bream in 1937 or '38, and the occasion is still remembered. The pig squeaked so much that the bandsmen collapsed into helpless laughter and had to stop playing.

Such labels are attached to make fun of the villages concerned, but also to assert their identity. In Dymock I saw a lorry driver slow down and bawl to a garage man: 'Which way to the treacle mines?' The immediate reply, accompanied by a broad grin: 'Straight on down there, boss.' Both speakers relished the exchange, each drawing a different satisfaction, one as outsider, one as insider. Some exchanges of this kind were less good-humoured, and even led to violence.

## Feuds and Fools

One definition of a stranger is a person whose grandparents and parents are not buried in the local churchyard. 'Foreigners' were highly suspect in many villages. John Drinkwater tells of Rufus Clay who moved the few miles from Painswick to Oakridge and lived there for over ten years before falling into a canal and drowning. The incident provoked a local comment: 'These foreigners do never learn their way about.'

Some villages were particularly noted for their aversion to outsiders. Anyone moving to Upton St Leonards was a foreigner, especially if he hailed from across the Severn. Yet Upton's keenest foes were the men of neighbouring Brookthorpe and Whaddon who regularly disrupted their Cherry Fair. David Harris, who died in 1904 at the age of 94, recalled: 'We met them with our fists and with sticks, and the blood did flow; it was like Waterloo in Upton.' A similar annual battle was fought between the men of Wotton-under-Edge and North Nibley. When Stroud lads encountered their fellows from Painswick they had only to say 'Here come the bow-wows' for fighting to break out. Laurie Lee remembers fights before the Second World War between gangs of children from Slad, Stroud and Painswick. There was great rivalry between neighbouring pairs of villages such as Bishop's Cleeve and Woodmancote or Woolstone and Gotherington ('Oolstwon be an overcoat warmer nor 'ere,' said a man from the latter, disdainfully.)

The courtship of young women by outsiders, especially from arch-rival villages, was hotly resented. 'A lad from a Forest village couldn't go courting a girl in another village five miles away - he'd be stoned all the way back home for his impudence'; 'I know a Minchinhampton man... who got his nose broken for courting at Avening'; 'If a lad from Painswick tried to go courting a Cranham girl he would be in for a rough time': comments such as these could with suitable changes of name be multiplied.

One of Painswick's claims to superiority was the alleged longevity of its inhabitants, the result of a healthy climate. An old man illustrated the point in the 1920s, but his narrative, far from being unique to Painswick, could be paralleled in Scandinavia, Europe and America:

> *'Twur a nation long toime agone - 'undreds o' years. Afore beer wur brewed, when thur was nubut waater ter drink, yer min' - not but Oi be agun a quilt at toimes, not a pipe o' bacca neither. Well, as Oi wur saayin', 'twur afore these things commed about, yer onderstan'.*

> *Well, some bloke as 'ad a bin hall over the world 'appened ter coom up along this 'ere road one daay, an' 'e ur tired - a pilgrim, thaay called un. Oi dwon't knaaw what a pilgrim be but 'owever 'e wur tired, which caused un to set anunst a yet o' stwons, as might be whur we be now. Agen 'im wur squat a mon as looked like a livin' carpse, all shrivelled up, like, who wur a blubberin' of 'is 'eart hout. This 'ere travellin' pilgrim 'ad sid mony a hold mon in 'is toime, but 'e never commed athurt a cove o' t' likes o' this un. Bein' kind o' neck in 'is 'eart, like, t'pilgrim 'e ups and axes t'bloke what's awry wi' 'e.*
>
> *T'old bloke - a shakin' an' a sobbin' - ses as 'is sheather [father] 'ad bin a yuttin' of un. T'pilgrim axed un whur 's sheather did bide, then ketched olt on t'old bloke an' carried un ter Pains'ick. Aater thaay comed ter t' sheather's 'ouse, another old mon come ter t' door, nation angered, wi' a dazzed girt stick purt nurly as bis as 'issel, seein' as 'e wur bent night double, an' 'ad a girt long white beard, as swep' up 'ground'.*
>
> *T'pilgrim, 'e wur flummuxed wi' seein' of an older mon as 'im as 'e carried on 'is back. But bein' kinder venturesome, like, 'e ups an' ses: 'Elekee, owd mon, dwon ee budge, an' kep thuc stick to theesel'. Then thuc sheather ups an' ses: 'Oi'll gie my son a dazzed girt larropin' if 'e dwon't stop a doin' what 'e 'ave bin a doin'. Cock thi eye up in yon apple tree, guverner, ool't. 'Is gransheather 'ave bin an' rasked 'is old bwones a skinnin' up thuc tree, auter t'fruit, an' this 'ere rascal 'ave bin a dubbin' of un wi' stwons.'*
>
> *When t'pilgrim looked into the tree, 'e wur come all over scared, like, an' 'e cleared off wi' all t'power 'e wur able, a saayin' as folk lived for hever in Pains'ick.*

On the other hand, detractors of Painswick reproached its people with having served puppy dog pie - hence the bow-wow taunt. There are many variations on the theme. Whiteshill quarrymen grew tired of continual thefts of their food by fellow workers from Painswick, so they baked pies with dead puppies in revenge. While the Bath-Cheltenham turnpike was under construction some navvies lodged at the 'Lamb Inn'. They were violent and hard-drinking, so the landlady decided to get rid of them. On Feast Sunday she fed them on pies made of dog flesh, and - no doubt through an intermediary - told them afterwards. They left. Whether they smashed up the 'Lamb' before doing so is not recorded.

Again, hungry travellers arrived unexpectedly at the 'Golden Heart'. The landlord killed a dog to furnish the meat he lacked. Alternatively, some Stroud people ordered meat pie at the 'Falcon'. Either by accident or otherwise this was served to some other customers, and since there was no meat left a dog was slaughtered and cooked. A final variation is that some Stroud people were invited to Painswick to eat venison on Feast Sunday. As no venison could be had, dog meat was substituted. Either before or after eating the visitors discovered the trick. A fight ensued. People from Stroud going to eat at Painswick once invariably asked: 'Oh, dog?' On Feast Sunday Painswickers baked a little china dog in the plum-pie as a commemoration.

Ancient animosities could quickly be sharpened by new disputes. In 1879 a Forest of Dean man called Robert Meredith was employed as a labourer in Dymock on a farm called the Burtons. He became ill. Faced with the prospect of going into the workhouse at Newent (the building later became a grammar school and is now a community centre) for treatment, he hanged himself in a barn from a beam on which dust reputedly never settled afterwards. Another suicide, for the same reason - that of Richard Elliott, shoemaker and turnpike keeper at Nailsworth - was reported in the Gloucester Journal of May 8th 1868.

A coroner's jury at Dymock pronounced a verdict on Meredith of *felo de se* - and a deaf onlooker remarked: 'Damn it to hell, he bloody well hung hisself, he didener fall in the sea.' According to custom, the body was to be buried after dark, on the north side of the churchyard, unshrouded and uncoffined, in a grave aligned north-south instead of the traditional east-west. At the last minute a laundress who lived at the Burtons and worked at Wilton Place nearby provided two sheets in which to wrap the corpse.

When news of the death reached them some Forest miners who were working at Newent came to collect Meredith's body for burial in his native earth; too late. The story of 'the man without a shirt' spread, embroidered by the suggestion that a farmer's sack used as a shroud had been retrieved as the body was lowered into the grave. The laundress's good deed was overlooked, and Dymock people resented so much in the Forest that carters who went down for loads of coal or stone plastered mud or tacked a board over the address painted on their waggons. Recognition might have meant being insulted, pelted or beaten up. In Dymock the house in which Meredith lived has gone but the barn where he hanged himself is still reputed to be haunted.

The case remained contentious for half a century or so but is now largely forgotten. Not so the cry of 'Who killed the bear?' In the 1930s a caravan was attacked and overturned in Ruardean because gypsies leaned out and shouted the question. In the 1950s a stranger discreetly enquiring whether the subject might be raised was answered in the affirmative but told: 'You couldn't have so twenty years ago, and forty years ago you'd have been a hospital case.' However, by 1989 - the centenary of the original incident - from rankling shame the matter had turned into civic pride and a jolly celebration. Some villagers were unhappy about this, and I am told that the old question could still be indelicate, indeed dangerous, if it were provocatively raised in the 'Angel' near to closing time on a Saturday night.

In 1889 four Frenchmen were touring the Forest with two performing bears. On 26 April a completely false rumour began to circulate that the animals had killed a child and mauled a woman at Cinderford. The men were attacked at Ruardean, and the bears killed by a mob. The following month eleven men were heavily fined for their part in the affair - and Ruardean became a laughing stock. F.W. Harvey (1888-1957), who spent much of his life in the Forest, published the poem, 'Warning', in 1926:

*A man there was, a gentle soul,*
*Of mild enquiring mind,*
*Who came into this neighbourhood*
*Its wonders for to find.*

*He sought for vines on Viney Hill,*
*He wondered much to find*
*That Drybrook was reverse of dry*
*It so perplexed his mind*

*That every man he chanced to meet*
*He'd stop to question; and*
*Was answered courteously and fairly*
*By all within this land.*

*They told him who had put the lid*
*On Lydney; who the ale*
*Misspelt in Aylburton. And he*
*Delighted in the tale.*

*And still, like little Oliver,*
*He softly asked for more;*
*And with the utmost courtesy*
*Was answered as before;*

*Until one sleepy summer's eve*
*He came all unaware*
*Unto a place called Ruardean,*
*And asked 'Who killed the bear?'*

*The man arose and punched him flat;*
*Another punched his head,*
*And when the rest had done with him*
*Our gentle friend was dead.*

*The moral of this simple tale*
*Is plain. Dear friend, beware!*
*If you should visit Ruardean*
*Mention of any bear.*

*If you should climb to Yorkley Slad*
*Pause not to question why*
*They put a pig upon the wall*
*To see the band go by.*

*And if your feet so far should stray*
*As Dymock, lest some hurt*
*Befall you, make no mention of*
*The man without a shirt.*

*Nine lives have cats, and you but one:*
*Risk not that gift of God!*
*It's better to be ignorant*
*Than dead beneath the sod.*

Every county has places where the people were considered slow on the uptake. 'Gothamites' was the epithet applied by Painswickers to the inhabitants of Stroud. The men of Drybrook are supposed to have set off to put out the moon, thinking it was a barn or haystack on fire. The Willersey people put a net over their pool to keep the moon in. Gotherington is the place where the wind blew the village pump up and the people thatched the pond so the ducks could swim in the dry.

The inhabitants of Ebrington - locally pronounced Yubber'n, though some say Yabber'n - are known, especially by their neighbours from Chipping Campden, as 'yawnies'. Although Campden has a long standing rivalry with Broadway, just over the Worcestershire border, Ebrington is the traditional butt for its jibes. For example:

*They be a fair-mannered lot on 'em at Yabberton. Only last Campden Market one on 'em was a standin' gaapin' at a pen o' ewes when a gret hullockin' farmer hockles on his foot (not as it were done a-purpose, mind ye). 'I be very sorry to be sure,' says the farmer. 'Oh, you be very welcome, maaster,' says the Yabberton man.*

H.J. Massingham was told that the yawnies periodically mucked their squat church tower to make it grow high, like Campden's; and they let the hedges grow tall - a variant says they fixed hurdles - to keep the cuckoo in, and so prolong the summer. They also put the clock forward to make Christmas come sooner, took the moon's reflection in the pond to be a cheese and tried to rake it out; and like others put a pig on the wall to see the band go by.

In the days when crops were still sown by hand an Ebrington labourer covered a great deal of ground but used no seed, because he forgot to open the shutter of the drill. On noticing what was happening the farmer calmly remarked that it would 'stop they crows from a-picken uv 'em up.' The comment has its own rigorous logic.

An epic liar called Tommy Boots once lived in the village. Among his many tales was one that his dog was carried in a whirlwind, 'yarrapy, yarrapy up to heaven, kow-welping up in they clouds, and never was sin no mwore'; another that 'I was a-minding churries fur my feither when I do see vower and twenty vinches a-setting in a churry tree. So I ketches hold o' my old muzzle-loader and I loads 'e up uv vower and twenty tin-tacks. Then tling, wing, boom! I guz, and I nails they vower and twenty vinches in that churry tree.'

An Ebrington man is supposed to have walked to the 'Eight Bells' at Campden with a wheelbarrow on his back, put it down, and wiped the sweat streaming down his face. To the question why did he not wheel it along the ground he replied: 'I'd nur a-thawt o' that.' Back in the village they decided to have some illuminations rivalling those of London. They took four boltings of straw, tied one to each of the pinnacles of the church tower and set fire to it. Soon, water ran down - as they thought; in fact it was melting lead - so they called for old women to bring buckets to catch it.

Another story of the church was told to me in the 'Ebrington Arms' by Harold Payne in 1991:

> *The church was not quite in the right spot. They thought they'd move it so a gang on 'em got down to the local pub 'ere in Yubberton, and they thought right-o, we'll go up there. They 'ad 'em a drop o' cider, bit o' bread and chaze; they went up there - it was one summer's evening - took their jackets off, chucked 'em down in a pile. They 'ad the foreman of the bell ringers sayin', 'Right-o, chaps. When I says "heave," heave.'*
>
> *So they heaved and they heaved and they heaved, and the sweat was pourin' down their faaces. 'E says, "Right-o, chaps. That's it." Well, in the meantime - 'course, they didn't know - one of the pranksters of the village ud nipped up there and pinched all their jackets. 'Course, when they went to put 'em on there was nothing there. They says, 'Good God, look what we're done. We're moved the tower on to our jackets.'*

I can still hear the delighted chuckle with which he finished the story. Now Harold Payne, who was born in 1921, has spent all his life in Ebrington. When I asked whether the tale might not be construed as unfavourable comment on himself and his fellow villagers he simply launched into a further narrative:

> *During the war [of 1939-45] they removed all the signposts round all the villages and places. There was this fella come down, posh speakin', in a car. 'E stopped in the village there and he said to this young fella, 'e says 'Oh excuse me, young man, could you tell me the way to Moreton-in-the-Marsh?' The fella looks at 'im and 'e says, 'Well, Oi doan't know.' 'Well, what about Chipping Campden, then?' So 'e says, 'Well, Oi doan't know.' 'E says, 'Good gracious man, do you know anything?' 'E looks at 'im and 'e says, 'Oi knows where Oi be - and that's a damn sight more than thee does.'*

In a variation on this story the motorist questions 'old Jim' and goes back to his car, calling him 'all the fools he could think of'. Then, as he sets off again 'down that dommed old rutty lane... he hears some covey a-hollerin' at his back and, a-twistin' round his yud, he sees another old mon a-standin' nigh old Jim. So wobblin' and whimmin', back he guz to the rickyard and shouts out, "Well?"

Old Jim jerks his thumb at the t'other covey and "Jarge", sez he, solemn-like, "Jarge, zur, doan't know neigther".'

Another stranger strolling through Ebrington enthusiastically remarks: 'Quaint village'. A local man replies: 'Aye, an' there be some quaintish uns as comes to it.' A visitor to the 'Ebrington Arms' says: 'Oh Ebrington, that be where all the fools live.' The landlord answers: 'Well, I don't know they all live here. We get plenty passing through.'

Many such stories were encapsulated in a song, 'The Yeverton Maums', issued in the nineteenth century as a street ballad and written (I suspect) by 'Poet' Handy of Ilmington, just over the Warwickshire border from Ebrington, where they take great delight in their neighbours' foibles. To this day people remember snatches of the words. On being asked, Harold Payne immediately quoted:

*Yubberton yawnies went to plough,*
*They 'ad two osses but didn't know how;*
*So they tied their osses to a staake*
*And off they guz to Willsersey Waake.*

He also knew Sam Bennett (1865-1951), of Ilmington, who used to sing, to the tune of 'Dumble Dum Dairy':

*Old Matthew Southam, a man of great power,*
*Lent a horse and cart to muck the tower.*
*They mucked the tower right up to the top,*
*And handed the broom to fetch the muck.*
*(Chorus)*
*Rum-a-dum dairy, flare up, Mary,*
*Whoever did hear of such wonderful times?*

*He mucked the tower to make it higher,*
*But not so lofty as the sky;*
*And when the muck began to sink*
*They swore the tower had growed an inch.*

*Some Yubberton fools to show their power*
*They lit a fire on top of the tower;*
*And lead ran down like blood from a slaughter*
*And old women went runnin' to catch the soft water.*

*There was a blind man and he wanted to see;*
*They bunted him up in a gooseberry tree.*
*He swore it was his heart's desire*
*To see the top of the tower afire.*

*One moonlight night when it did freeze*
*The moon shone in a pool, when they thought it was a cheese.*
*They fetched the rakes to rake it out*
*And swore they couldn't get it out.*

*Old Tommy Abbotts to show he was a fool*
*He built a big hovel over the pool.*
*Some one asked him the reason for why:*
*It was for his ducks to swim in the dry.*

*Old Master Morris got up to brew;*
*There was something amiss with his chimney flue.*
*Old Master Morris went out to see:*
*There was a donkey with his legs down the chimilee.*

*[The donkey was stuck in the chimilee top,*
*And his tail behind went flipperty flop].*
*This donkey belonged to Jonathan Harris*
*They took it to Moreton to swear his parish.*

*Old Charlie Green he learned to play the fiddle;*
*He milked the cow in the calvin' riddle.*
*He kep' on milkin' till that run through,*
*And then they telled him 'That will do'.*

*Some Yubberton fools to Campden went,*
*To take away a barrow was their intent.*
*They carried the barrow from Campden town*
*For fear the wheels should bruise the ground.*

*There was a mad dog went through the town,*
*He bit the side of the barrow all round.*
*They took it to the seaside to have it dipped,*
*And swore the dog he should be whipped.*

Many such songs were sung, tales told and feuds fomented in village inns over glasses of home-brewed ale or rough cider. Some narratives were about inns themselves, their ghosts (Chapter Six) and the famous who slept there (Chapter One). The Swan at Bibury was once notorious for the report that a hard-up undergraduate stayed there on the way to Oxford and thought of a way to avoid paying his bill by offering to teach the landlord how to draw mild ale and strong beer from the same cask. Down in the cellar the student bored a hole in a full barrel and asked the publican to stop it with his finger. That was for the mild ale. Then he drilled a second hole on the other side and asked his host to stop that, too. Then, having removed the bung from the top of the barrel, he ran upstairs and rode off, leaving the landlord still stopping the holes and soon shouting for help. The story of his stupidity soon spread, bringing customers flocking to the Swan, and so turning loss into profit. Oddly enough, a version of the tale is known in the form of a song as far afield as Ireland, and even Canada.

A mnemonic for the pubs at Longhope runs: 'The Farmer's Boy went to the Cross to borrow the Nag to draw the Plough to the Yew Tree.' Of the five, only three now remain. At Ruardean, they said: 'The Bell to toll you in, the Shovel to cover you up, and the Angel to receive you into heaven.'

The 'Severn Bore Inn' was formerly called the 'Bird-in-Hand' (though known as the 'Flat'). In the days of horse-drawn wagons a farmer making his way home from Gloucester Market to Westbury one hot summer's day decided to pull in for a drink or two. While he was inside a couple of local lads thought they'd have a bit of fun with him. They unharnessed his horses and led them round the back, out of sight. When the farmer came out to continue his journey he looked round, pushed back his cap, and scratched his head: 'If Oi be Oi, Oi've lost two osses. And if Oi bent Oi, Oi 'ave found a waggon.'

For two centuries a message painted on a board at the 'Plough Inn ' at Ford has been addressed to those passing at a sensible speed:

*Ye weary travellers that pass by,*
*With dust and scorching sunbeams dry,*
*Or be numb'd with snow and frost,*
*With having these bleak cotswolds crost,*
*Step in and quaff my nut brown ale,*
*Bright as rubys mild and stale,*
*Twill make your laging trotters dance,*
*As nimble as the suns of france,*
*Then ye will own ye men of sense,*
*That neare was better spent sixpence.*

4

# HOLY GROUND

Standing tall in 'God's acre', the church is still prominent in most towns and villages. Like a magnet its venerable pile and little plot attract all kinds of traditions and beliefs, both orthodox and otherwise. Stories of founders reverberate from many centuries past, as they do of conflicts over sites. Through epitaph and anecdote, churchyards conceal or reveal a wealth of popular lore. The bells have their tales to tell, as do ringers, singers and musicians. Within the building (and sometimes without), carved wood and stone, stained glass and painted wall convey messages sacred and profane. Particular customs survive in some churches, as do accounts of unusual parishioners and parsons.

## One Foundation?

'As sure as God's in Gloucestershire', a saying once common, may have stemmed from the existence in the county of large numbers of religious houses, including the six great abbeys (all now gone, save for the churches of the last two) of Flaxley, Hailes, Winchcombe, Cirencester, Tewkesbury and Gloucester. Two wealthy dukes of Mercia, the brothers Odo and Dodo (or Odda and Dodda), were the reputed founders in 715 of a church at Tewkesbury on the site where the abbey was later erected. The former's name survives at Deerhurst in Odda's Chapel, and the latter's at Dodington. Both were commemorated at Gotherington, a few miles from Tewkesbury, where twin stones which stood on Nottingham Hill until the 1860s went by the names of Odo and Dodo.

Flaxley Abbey was built in memory of Milo Fitzwater, Earl of Hereford (himself the founder of St Briavels Castle), at the place where he met his death in 1143. Despite a warning from his wife that 'treachery awaits thee', he went hunting on Christmas Eve and was killed by an arrow which glanced accidentally off a tree. Some said he was murdered by his son-in-law at the instigation of monks of St Peter's, Gloucester, jealous because of Milo's foundation of Llanthony Priory (where he was buried).

The abbey at Hailes owed its origin to the fulfilment of a vow made to the Virgin Mary by Richard, Earl of Cornwall and son of King John, when his life was imperilled at sea off the Scilly Isles. The great church was consecrated in 1251 but its fortunes soared twenty years later when Richard's son, Edmund, deposited a phial purporting to contain some of Christ's blood. This alone may have led to the saying about God in Gloucestershire.

The Tudor antiquarian, John Leland, said the relic wrought 'daily miracles'.

Others were sceptical. Sir John Drury, priest of St Peter's, Windrush, faced a charge of heresy in 1512 for calling the Holy Blood a fabrication and claiming that he had wasted eighteen pence in going to see it. Rumours circulated that the container was regularly topped up with duck's blood; and that pilgrims first told that only those without sin could see the blood, were shown one side with opaque glass; then after confession, absolution and donation were presented with the transparent glass of the other side. Eventually a church commission ruled that the relic consisted of 'an unctuous gum' tinted red by means of the glass, and in 1539 the vessel was solemnly destroyed in London. The following year the dissolution of the monasteries themselves was decreed. Chaucer's Pardoner swore by the Holy Blood of Hailes, and his Nun's Priest knew the story of St Kenelm of Winchcombe which is told later in this chapter.

Less significant churches, too, had their controversies. A Saxon building at Avening was pulled down on the orders of Matilda, William the Conqueror's wife. The present church, which she commissioned, was dedicated in 1080 in her presence. She and William stayed at Avening Court, and the queen gave the builders a feast of boar's head, so giving rise to the village's Pig Face Day which continued to be celebrated for over eight hundred years (see below). History is certainly written (and made) by the victors, and a sad story lies behind the feasting. Before the Norman conquest Avening belonged to Britric, Lord of Gloucester and also owner of land at Tewkesbury. As a young man he went in about 1045 on a mission for Edward the Confessor to the court of Baldwin, Earl of Flanders. Baldwin's daughter, fifteen-year-old Matilda, fell in love with Britric but he rejected her overtures. When she came to England as queen she persuaded William to confiscate Britric's estates and to imprison him at Winchester (where he died). Local tradition says Matilda had him tied to a tail of a horse and made to walk from Avening to Gloucester. Her subsequent remorse caused her to order the building of a new church - though it did not prevent her employing a good deal of slave labour.

Early Christians in some places tried to harness pagan religious feeling by choosing sites for churches which were already considered holy. St Lawrence's at Bourton-on-the-Water replaced a Roman temple. St Mary's, Lower Swell, is built over a Roman crematorium. St Arilda's at Oldbury-on-Severn stands at a place once sacred to Jupiter. St Mary de Crypt at Gloucester has Roman foundations. Nineteenth century excavations at St Mary de Lode revealed a Roman mosaic pavement and a bust which may have been part of a monument to Lucius, whom some have called the first Christian king of England. He reigned and died at Gloucester, where he is said to have founded the first English church on the site now occupied by St Mary de Lode.

The circular churchyards of today may originally have been groves held sacred by the Celts. There are several of these in Gloucestershire - at Frocester (the old churchyard), Hewelsfield, Ozleworth and possibly Dumbleton. But the pagans could hit back, it seems. Church builders at Minchinhampton determined on a site where a stone circle stood, now called the Devil's Churchyard. No doubt they hoped that adherents of the old religion would soon adopt the new, but instead the building work was constantly vandalised -

some said by the devil. A new site - that of the present church - was chosen. Later, a rector ordered stones from the circle to be removed to his house, which is now called Lammas. Nevertheless the Devil's Churchyard retained an evil reputation (see Chapter Six).

At Horsley, church building started in Letchmore (or Ledgemore) Bottom but at the end of each day the devil demolished all the masonry. The hint taken, construction moved successfully to the present site. Of the church then built only the tower remains, the rest having been redone in the nineteenth century.

At Bisley the devil not only knocked down what was built but moved the stones to a different site which was eventually adopted. Here folk memory proves to have an explanation. In 1862 Roman altars were found embedded in the wall of the church tower. They must have come from a villa a mile or so away in a field known as Church Piece, the very spot from which the devil was said to have carried masonry. A similar confirmation exists at Blakeney, even though the church, early eighteenth century, is relatively recent. Foundations discovered at the site - called Churchfields - from which the devil was supposed to have transported materials show that there had indeed been a change of heart.

There is a kind of logic, too, in Churchdown's story of a church re-sited from the plain to the top of Chosen Hill, which presumably owes its name to the choice made; but in fact the village migrated from the church, rather than the reverse. Tradition holds that the devil had the church put on the hill to discourage the faithful from attending. Another story suggests that the monks of a wealthy abbey on the plain became so lax that their patron, St Bartholomew, to whom the church is dedicated, had it moved to the hilltop to make them into more muscular Christians.

It was in the late eleventh or early twelfth century that the Churchdowners deserted their Chosen Hill for life down below. One snag was that they necessarily left behind their well. When they became short of water the Archbishop of York (under whose jurisdiction the place fell at the time - there was no Gloucester Diocese until 1540) agreed that pipes might be laid from the well down the hill. During the work a man named in some accounts as William of Gloucester was buried under a fall of earth estimated at 100 cartloads. St Thomas à Becket - whose martyrdom in 1170 must have been fresh in people's memories - appeared in a dream to a woman of the village and told her the man was still alive. Next morning he was safely dug out, and the sequence of miraculous events later featured in a stained glass window at Canterbury Cathedral. In Churchdown a mural (now gone) at the 'Bat and Ball Inn' showed a different version: William, abandoned to his fate by terrified fellow-workers, thinks of St Thomas and so finds the strength and resolution to save himself.

The church tower at Westbury-on-Severn is detached but bears clear marks on one side of having once been joined to another building. A local tale says that one night, in a fit of rage, the devil moved the tower away from the church. According to another tradition just before the Armada attack in 1588 a Spanish spy used the belfry to look out for the best landing place on the river bank.

When the bells rang he was dislodged from his perch, and fell to his death; or the ringers, having become aware of his presence, deliberately rang with such vigour that he was shaken down.

The only other detached church tower in Gloucestershire is at Berkeley. Here people explain that it was carefully sited to be as far within the churchyard as possible from the castle to prevent anyone's shooting down into it from the top. The present tower dates from the 1750s but stands on the site of a fifteenth century predecessor, to which an earlier church was attached.

At Lydney a young man once climbed the church tower by means of its ivy. At the top he called for an apple to be thrown up. In the effort to catch it he fell to his death, the fruit still clasped in his hand. The effigy in the church with a small round object in the hand is taken to be that of the young man. In fact it probably shows a priest with a chalice, whose end was equally unfortunate. George Prime - the effigy is marked 'GP 13 Aprell 1630' - was either visiting the Wintour family at Whitecross House or acting as chaplain there when he fell from scaffolding round the spire of the parish church, which was under repair at the time.

Church builders at Oldbury-on-Severn started work at Shellard's Green, but at the end of every day what they had done was destroyed by fire. They consulted a wise man - some say woman - who advised that two white heifers should be hobbled in the centre of the village and then be left to wander. Where they stopped, the church should be built. This was done. The place is still called Cowhill.

'St Margaret's Chapel (remains of)' still appears on maps near the hamlet of Stowe in the parish of St Briavels. St Margaret's Well and Grove are to the west of the village, near Lindors. Margaret, daughter of Briavel, king of Gwent - or Cornwall, depending on the account followed - went with him into exile when his subjects, tired of his mis-rule, drove him out. After many wanderings the pair reached the Wye Valley. Briavel, having by this time undergone a change of heart, became a hermit by the Slade brook near Stowe, where he learned to tame the beasts of the forest. Margaret, too, chose a cell in the woods near Lindors. She founded the chapel at Stowe in her father's memory, though its ruins bear her name. St Briavel gave his name to the village of which the first written record dates from 1130.

The church at Sheepscombe has no such venerable traditions; it did not exist until 1820. According to local people, wrote Henry Warren, it 'was mainly built after the men came home at night, by lantern and moonlight.' Whenever the villagers 'looked at that home-made-tower, set so prominently on the rise of the hill... they unconsciously remembered the men who had built it for them.'

At Newington Bagpath the closed and decaying church has been called the loneliest in Gloucestershire. The suggested explanation is that both Newington and Bagpath wanted a church but neither could afford one. A compromise pooled resources to erect a common building half way between the two settlements. Another theory is that neither of the joint patrons wished the church to be nearer the other's mansion, so the two agreed on a mid-way position.

Lancaut might dispute Newington Bagpath's claim to isolation for it stands in a remote loop of the River Wye, its rooflessness bringing to mind Shakespeare's 'bare ruined choirs'. Still current in the area is the tradition that local people shunned the church when lepers attended, and so caused it to fall into disuse. Lancaut must now be one of the most peaceful places in the county.

## God's Acre

The hallowed ground and its contents were thought to be protected from evil influence by a glittering weathercock above (or a flying salmon in the cases of Apperley and Framilode; a dragon at Harnhill) and yew trees below. The extreme longevity of yews symbolises everlasting life, which is why their branches used to be strewn on new graves. In some villages a bough was taken into the church at Whitsuntide and kept there for a year to bring luck. At Winson a tree survives which was planted in 1748 by Drew Larner, husbandman, whose epitaph reads:

*Here lies Drew*
*Who planted this Yew.*
*He lies here*
*Till his Lord and Saviour*
*Doth appear.*

Yet his tree is only a child, compared with some. A specimen at Coln Rogers is reputedly as old as the Saxon church itself. Even Hewelsfield's tree at 1300 years old is left well behind by the yew at Staunton, six miles from Newent, which has a girth of twenty -six feet and was already ancient when it provided bows for soldiers who fought at Agincourt. The tree surgeon who saved it from collapse in 1993 estimated its age at 2000 years. Even so it may be less well known than the group of yews at Painswick where despite counts of over a hundred a stubborn belief persists that they can never exceed ninety-nine in number:

*Painswick maidens shall be true*
*Till there grows the hundredth yew.*

When Wulfstan, Bishop of Worcester (1060-95), went to consecrate a new church at Longney he found a large nut tree growing close by which made the building very dark. He decreed that it should be felled but the local lord, Ailsi, objected: he like to sit in its shade on summer days, dicing and drinking. Wulfstan thereupon cursed the tree which withered and had to be cut down after all. The church was indeed new at Longney in the 1060s (though the present structure is mainly thirteenth century), and it is possible that a tree considered holy by non-Christians had to be felled to make way for it.

*'Painswick maidens shall be true till there grows the hundredth yew.'*
*This exquisite print was engraved by F.L. Griggs (1876-1938).*

At St Mary de Crypt there was once a tree - probably an elder - thought to be descended from the one on which Judas Iscariot hanged himself. This blossomed before coming into leaf but was shunned by birds and insects. More piously, an avenue of lime trees growing six by six in Chipping Campden churchyard and planted in 1770 is said to commemorate the twelve apostles.

A piece of ornate stonework in Bisley churchyard is supposed to cover a well but it is in fact a poor soul's light - the only one of its kind in the open air in

England. (An indoor example once existed at the tiny chapel of St James at Postlip, by a window high in the south wall of the nave.) Candles paid for by the better-off were lit at such places for the souls of the poor; hence the name.

Instead of covering a well the Bisley stonework may have stopped a hole where bones were stored. Nevertheless the saying '"There is one," said Pearse as he fell into the well.' is explained in this way by Abel Wantner in his manuscript history of the county, written in 1714:

> *The Church of Bisley was out of repair, and the officers of the parish set some men to mend what was amiss; amongst those labourers there was one whose name was Pearse, who, with the rest at dinner-time, came into the churchyard, where there was a winch-well, and where they usually sate around whilst they did eat their victuals. Now it fortuned, that as they were waiting for the striking of the clock to go to work, that as the clock struck, Pearse replyed, 'There's one', which word was no sooner spoken, but he fell backwards into the well and was drowned. Whereupon the churchyard was excommunicated, and the parish did bury their dead at Bibury.*

It seems churlish to remark that it would have been unlikely for Bisley Church to have possessed a clock in the thirteenth century, or that a papal interdict would follow the accidental death of a mason.

A tale told by another mason in the 'Eight Bells' at Chipping Campden explains why the death-watch beetle attacks beams in churches and leaves those of barns and houses alone:

> *Well, now, that pesty maggotty beetle thing was once a pretty windsome flutterby - all rainbow-shine like, till he done a most hunkid thing, and for that he was straightway changed into the pesty maggotty beetle he be to this day. 'Tis said as when the Lord Jesus was a-hanging cruel spiked on the cross, this yur ill-souled butterfly flethered and flethered in front of his face and so taysed he in his agony.*
>
> *And now you can't keep the pesty thing out of church. Some says he stays there to get grace - 'cos they found him first in the gret door and chased him out of there, then they found him in the pews and chased he out of there, so now he goes up into the rafters and there lays hid a tidy time afore any mon finds him.*
>
> *Any roads, whether it be for grace or whether it be 'cos the devil be under his hide, he be a tarnation nuisance, and little enough good it be for that man there to say as 'ow paraffin 'ull stop him.*

Graves once occupied only the south side of churchyards, and when the plot was full a start would be made again at the other end. Old bones unearthed - one thinks of the gravedigger's scene in *Hamlet* and 'Alas, poor Yorick' - would be removed to a charnelhouse. Bagendon Church, for example, had a lean-to structure for bones by the tower.

In the two-thirds of an acre making up the old churchyard at Woodchester, between 1563 (when records began there) and 1863 (when the new burial ground was opened) three thousand burials took place. Similar figures elsewhere caused an inexorable rise in the level of churchyards - at Awre, Naunton, Newnham-on-Severn and elsewhere. At Upper Slaughter the path from lychgate to south porch is several feet below the level of the ground on either side. In many places the porch floor is well below the churchyard, and in some the church has a kind of small moat round it because of the upward movement of the earth outside.

The rich and privileged were buried within the church, either beneath the floor or in a tomb raised above it. Lord Coleraine, a Regency rake who lived for a time at Kempsford, arranged for his tomb to be four feet above the floor of the Lady Chapel in the church. People said he was so evil in life that he wished to keep his body above ground, and therefore out of the devil's clutches. Unfortunately for Lord Coleraine, when an organ was installed in the Lady Chapel in 1858 his coffin had to be sunk out of the way below the floor.

The re-use of external burial grounds became impossible from the seventeenth century onwards as more and more people wished to have commemorative gravestones. The south side was still preferred, since those walking into church could read inscriptions and offer prayers for the departed. When the south was full other parts had to be brought into use. The east and west were acceptable at a pinch but until relatively recently the north was avoided. In some cases, geography dictated it - at Standish, for example, where the tombs seem to toss this way and that on the green sward like the sea-chests of shipwrecked sailors rolling on the waves.

'That's the devil's bit, Miss, and don't you be buried there,' said a St Briavels villager of the north side to Margaret Eyre in 1905. Suicides and strangers, vagrants and paupers were interred there - like the six Roundhead soldiers at Yanworth. By the same token, the north door was usually shunned; indeed, physically blocked in some cases - as at Longborough. There are exceptions. At Quenington the south door with its carvings of the coronation of the Virgin is now filled by an organ, so parishioners enter through the harrowing of hell shown on the north. At Miserden, though, it is still called the Devil's Door. Only the dead used it as they left for their last journey after entering from the south. The same is still the case at South Cerney.

Behaviour in churchyards was not always reverent. A ball game - probably a kind of fives - was played against the church wall at Ruardean. One side of the tower at Minchinhampton was whitewashed for the same purpose, and there is a record of church windows having been broken by fives players there in 1775. When Rev. Heathcote Weston-Hicks went to Upton St Leonards in 1831 he found the churchyard used as 'the village recreation-ground, where the boys played at leap-frog and ball. The villagers turned in their horses, sheep, and asses to graze, and the graves were scrambled to pieces.'

Contrasting with such matter-of-factness, the same village has the story of a ghost which haunted the churchyard, appearing to the parson 'as big as a 'oolpack'. A local carpenter was found dead at the bottom of his garden.

Suspicion fell on his wife but the cause of death could not be discovered. Twenty years later the sexton was digging a grave when the parson came to tell him that the ghost had appeared in a dream with the news that a discovery about its death would be made the following day. As the sexton dug he turned up a skull which he pronounced to be 'Bill's' - that of the long-dead carpenter. On close examination it was found to have a long brass pin deeply embedded in the back. Shortly afterwards the carpenter's widow became ill and died, but not before confessing to the murder of her husband.

Ghostly footsteps were once heard in Churchdown churchyard and a will-o'-the-wisp was seen to settle over the grave of a woman drowned in a pond, now filled, at Chapel Hay. Will Crew, a tearaway folk hero, was buried at Wotton-under-Edge where within living memory children ran round the churchyard and dared his ghost to rise. Oddly enough it did; not there, but at Alderley, where it rode round 'wi'out nurn a yud'.

In 1966 people at Salperton Park mansion saw an attractive young woman wandering round the adjacent churchyard and disappearing into a railed tomb. On enquiring they found that a woman of 19 or 20 had been buried there. Salperton Church has an indelible bloodstain on the floor near the pulpit, alleged to be from the victim of a gruesome murder. This person's ghost does not walk, but a grey lady is said to traverse the central aisle of the parish church at Cirencester, and to disappear where the pews make a crossroads.

The architect, Norman Jewson (died 1975), describes in his book, *By Chance I did Rove*, how when he was checking the structure of Chipping Campden Church he went into the Gainsborough vault with the vicar, Lord Gainsborough's agent, and the sexton, Harry Withers. They saw the coffin of Lady Juliana, only daughter and heiress of Sir Baptist Hicks. Withers told Jewson that local people predicted death for one of the party within the week. Next day the agent was taken ill, and died within 48 hours. Tenants of the gatehouse cottages, just beyond the churchyard, reported that Lady Juliana's ghost had been seen walking up and down the drive to the ruins of the great house (burned down by royalists in 1645 to prevent its falling into Roundhead hands) that night and for weeks afterwards, though she had previously been quiet since the re-sealing of her coffin in 1881.

In the early 1940s the old church at Oddington - used for only one service a year - fell into disrepair, and was not entirely weather-proof. The aged sexton did his best to patch the stone tiles of the roof but conceded failure, and removed the great church Bible to his own house for safe keeping. Before the next service came round he was laid to rest in the churchyard in a place he had kept for himself. His son took charge of the Bible, put it away, and forgot it. Then he began to notice, walking towards the churchyard gate and disappearing there, the figure of an old man - which he recognised as that of his father. He told F.W. Baty: 'I fetched the Good Book out of my cupboard and set it back where it came from. It might get wet, but that was of no account so long as it set the old man's mind at rest... I've not set eyes on him since.'

Other terrors were caused by body snatchers who invented stories of ghosts to keep people out of churchyards at night, even when they saw strange lights or heard untoward noises. The resurrectionists - as they were otherwise called - stole fresh corpses for sale to doctors as subjects for dissection. James Maile, sexton at Preston near Dymock, died in the late 1960s. Many years earlier when digging a grave in the churchyard he found an old coffin containing only stones. He believed these had been substituted by resurrectionists for a body, perhaps before interment, a century before.

Some men who put up at the 'Traveller's Rest', Coleford, in December 1830, aroused suspicion by ordering boxes to be made, claiming they were for glass. When they set off on foot towards English Bicknor at 10.30 p.m. they were discreetly followed by three local men who caught them red-handed in the churchyard. The *Monmouthshire Merlin* newspaper reported: 'A grave was open and the corpse of a young woman which had not been interred more than a week was laid upon the ground with the back cut and the body doubled up that it might be more conveniently carried.' What happened subsequently is not given.

H.Y.J. Taylor (1826-1906) met men who had been engaged in body snatching, and told him of experiences such as this:

> *In the parish of — there lived — who were a terrible cripple. He crawled about the earth like a cratish. He waur double jointed. When he died and waur buried, I and siveral more waur offered ten pounds if we would go and dig un up the same night as he waur buried. The doctors wanted to send un to Lunnon. The night were as dark as pitch, not a moon nor a star wuz to be sin. We took our spades and our lanthens; a hoss and cart waited at the bottom of the lane to gallop away with the corpse as soon as we had got un out of the coffin. We muv'd about as quiet as mice. We could not hear a sound. The grave was pinted out, and we begun to dig as hard as we could, and should ha' soon got un out on't, but up kim'd four or five fellers with big sticks and laid into our yuds and ribs. We scampered away, got down to the bottom of the lane, and galloped off as fast as the horse's legs would car' un. The fellers hollered and follered arter us, but we soon got out of their reach. It waur a pity they kum'd, gaffer, for we lost a good job.*

The men with sticks were probably watchers paid by the dead man's relatives, like the man who described this incident to Taylor:

> *I and another were engaged for seven nights in Barnwood churchyard to watch the grave of a young lady. We had a jar of beer and a bottle of brandy to cheer up our spirits and to kip the cold out. It was sad, lonely, miserable work to watch there from sun set to sun rise; but we couldn't grumble, for we had plenty to eat and plenty to drink. Several persons cumd, but they hooked it as soon as they zeed us. They was like enough resurrection men. If they hadn't a-cut fust we should; we was gallus frightened and we had to have a good pull*

*at the brandy bottle to kip up our courage and strength during the rest of the night.*

Two more would-be body snatchers were thwarted in the burying ground of Gloucester Cathedral. Some ladies were walking home through the cathedral grounds one night when they heard voices which seemed to come from beneath their feet. 'High,' said one. 'Low,' answered another. The women took to their heels and ran to the nearest dwelling, which happened to be Cathedral House. They knocked, were let in, and told their tale. The coachman was sent to investigate. When he reached the spot he heard the same litany of 'High' and 'Low'. He, too, was terrified, but then he noticed a newly-dug grave. He peered in and saw two men playing cards by the light of a lantern. He assumed they were resurrection men having a hand of cards on the coffin lid before removing the body. When one again said 'High' and the other answered 'Low,' the coachman interjected 'Jack, and the game,' before jumping into the grave. As he did so, out went the light, and away ran the body snatchers.

The story came from Tony Lebrun, an actor who appeared in the 1780s at Gloucester's Barton Street theatre - but versions can be traced back at least three hundred years before then. Rather more worthy of credence is the account from Lydney of a sexton who worked nights as a factory stoker and sometimes took an hour or two off to dig a grave. Once he was working after midnight at the bottom of a deep grave when he heard footsteps going past in the churchyard. 'Oy,' he called up. 'Couldst tell us the time?' Whoever it was ran off in terror, and for a long time afterwards the rumour went round that Lydney churchyard was haunted.

## Vocal Stones

It is hard to visit a churchyard and read through epitaphs without being interested and indeed moved. Some reproduce time-honoured verses; others have known and even reputed authors. John Dryden wrote the words for John Rogers (died 1683, aged 11) on a tablet in the chancel of St Peter's, Haresfield:

*Of gentle Blood, his Parents' only Treasure,*
*Their lasting Sorrow and their vanished Pleasure:*
*Adorn'd with Features, Virtues, Wit and Grace;*
*A long Provision for so short a Race.*
*More moderate Gifts might have prolong'd his Date,*
*Too early fitted for a better State.*
*But knowing Heaven his Home, to shun delay,*
*He leap'd o'er Age, and took the shortest Way.*

The authorship of most epitaphs is not known. Many are brief. Thomas Bright's 24 years - he died at Longhope in 1708 - take up only two lines:

*His Patience was by long Affliction try'd;*
*In stedfast Faith and Hope he liv'd and dy'd.*

Another laconic statement appears on a table of 1818 near the north-west door of St Mary's, Tetbury: 'In a vault underneath lie several Saunderses late of this parish: particulars the last day will disclose. Amen.'

In the old church of St Catharine (now gone) at Gloucester a tomb was inscribed:

*Here lyeth old Mr Richard Tully,*
*Who lived C [100] and 3 years fully.*
*He did the Sword of the city beare*
*Before the mayor Thirty-one yeare.*
*Four wives he had, and here they lye*
*All waiting Heaven's eternity.*
*He died ... March, 1619.*

The same matter-of-fact faith is displayed in the epitaph at France Lynch to a woman who died at the age of 83:

*This lowly stone doth mark the spot*
*Where Mary Digby's soul is not.*
*She passed in 1924*
*To Jesu's purgatorial store.*

*For 13 years she served the church*
*And never left it in the lurch.*
*No recompense she sought or fee,*
*Save with the sinners' Friend to be.*

*In London, on Cecilia's Day*
*If at St Paul's your eyes should stray*
*And on Cecilia's banner fall,*
*'Twas Mary Digby made it all.*

Much less reverent is the attitude displayed at Great Barrington, where a dedicated angler, Charles Rhys Wingfield, permits himself a mild joke with his maker:

*God grant that I may fish*
*Until my dying day,*
*And when it comes to my last cast*
*I humbly pray*
*When in the Lord's safe landing net*
*I'm peacefully asleep*
*That in his mercy*
*I be judged good enough to keep.*

The puns flow unashamedly in the epitaph in the south aisle of St John the Baptist's Church, Cirencester, to Hodgkinson Paine, who was killed in 1642 during the Civil War:

*The Poore's Supplie his life & calling grac't*
*'till warre's made rent & PAINE from poore*
*displac't.*
*But what made poore unfortunate PAINE blest,*
*by warre they lost their PAINE, yet found noe rest,*
*Hee looseing quiet by Warre yet gained ease,*
*by it PAINE's life began, and paine did cease;*
*And from ye troubles here him did God sever,*
*by death to life, by Warre to peace for ever.*

Jocularity comes to the fore in some inscriptions. This, from Moreton-in-the-Marsh, has often been quoted but no one has seen it in situ:

*Here lie the bones of Richard Lawton,*
*Whose death, alas, was strangely brought on;*
*Trying one day his corns to mow off,*
*The razor slipped and cut his toe off.*

Similarly well known and equally elusive, from Cheltenham:

*Here lie I and my three daughters,*
*Who died from drinking Cheltenham waters.*
*If we'd stuck to Epsom salts,*
*We wouldn't be lying in these 'ere vaults.*

Though I have not been able to find it, I am told by a former rector, Rev. J.E. Gethyn-Jones, that this does exist at Dymock. It is, of course, intended in all seriousness:

*Two sweeter babes youm nare did see*
*Than God amity give to wee,*
*But they were ortaken bee ague fits,*
*And yur they lys as dead as nits.*

Instances of sudden death are often mentioned. William Hinton is remembered at South Cerney:

*As I was riding in the night*
*On a common, for want of light*
*Off my horse I was tossed*
*Into the mill tail, my life I lost.*

Drownings are from time to time recorded in riverside parishes. At Hewelsfield a stone to Richard Bowen (died 1871, aged 31) announces:

*In the cold stream my limbs were chilled*
*My blood with deadly horror thrilled*
*My feeble veins forgot to play*
*I fainted, sank and died away.*

John Yeme of Abenhall was killed at the age of 19 in 1777 by a runaway bull which struck him with a block of wood attached to its horns to prevent it from breaking through hedges:

*As I was riding on the road not knowing what was*
*coming*
*A Bull that was loggered and pursued after me came*
*a running*
*He with his logger did me strike he being sore*
*offended*
*I from my Horse was forced to fall & thus my days*
*were ended.*

In 1799 John Parker, aged 56, of Painswick died of what we should no doubt call a heart attack:

*As through a field he walked alone,*
*By chance he met grim Death,*
*Who with his dart did strike his heart,*
*And robbed him of his breath.*

Trades and professions are frequently given or implied in epitaphs. Peter, butler to Sir William Keyte, is remembered with wry humour at Ebrington:

*Though he had gone to Kingdom come*
*He had left the Keys of the cellar behind him.*

Another retainer, the last private jester in England, died in 1728 at the age of 63, reputedly kicked to death in Berkeley Castle during a drunken brawl. He lies in the churchyard beneath verses written by Jonathan Swift:

*Here lies the Earl of Suffolk's fool,*
*Men call'd him Dicky Pearce;*
*His folly serv'd to make folks laugh*
*When wit and mirth were scarce.*
*Poor Dick alas! is dead and gone,*
*What signifies to cry?*
*Dickys enough are still behind*
*To laugh at by and by.*

In the church tower at Duntisbourne Abbots a memorial is dedicated to Ann Watson, a servant who died in 1812 at the age of 85 after spending 55 years with a single family, the Mesmans:

*If Power and Wealth deserve recorded fame*
*Shall humble Worth no grateful tribute claim?*
*A rare example to the rising age*
*Who in a course of servitude engage,*
*Anxious in childhood's care or manhood's cause*
*She sought the good of all with just applause -*
*E'en to old age her fond affection prove*
*She lived not more to serve than lived to love -*
*But on the fiat of a Heavenly Nod*
*Her earthly service left to serve her God.*

In Newnham churchyard lies Thomas Yerbury, a seafarer who died in 1759 at the age of 67:

*From ev'ry blustrous Storm of Life,*
*And that worst storm, domestick strife,*
*Which shipwrecks all our social Joys,*
*And ev'ry worldly Bliss destroys;*
*I luck'ly am arrived at last,*
*And safe in Port my Anchor's cast;*
*Where shelter'd by the blissful shore,*
*Nought shall disturb, or vex me more;*
*But Joys severe, & calmest Peace,*
*Which Christ bestows, shall never cease.*

Thomas Peirce is commemorated at Berkeley, where he died in 1665 at the age of 77:

*Here Lyeth Thomas Peirce, whom no man taught*
*Yet he in Iron, Brasse, and Silver wrought*
*He Jacks, and Clocks, and watches (with Art) made*
*And mended too when others work did fade*
*Of Berkeley five tymes Major this Artist was*
*And Yet this Major, this Artist was but Grasse*
*When his owne watch was Downe on the last Day,*
*He that made watches had not made a Key*
*To winde it Up, but Uselesse it must lie*
*Untill he Rise Againe no more to die.*

A brass plaque on a stone near the yew arch in Miserden churchyard marks the grave of Samuel Horrell, a shepherd who died in 1807 at the age of 54:

*From youth through life the sheep was all his care*
*And harmless as the flock his manners were*
*On earth he held the faith to Christians given*
*In hopes to join the fold of Christ in Heavn.*

Blacksmiths up and down the country share this verse with James Broadtock (died 1768, aged 'near 50 Yrs') of Upleadon:

*My sledge and hammer he's reclined*
*My bellows too has lost its wind*
*My fire extinct my forge decayed,*
*And in the dust my vice is laid*
*My coal is burnt my Iron's gone,*
*My nails is drove thy work is done.*

Other Gloucestershire examples include verses to Thomas Collier (died 1765) at Rodborough and John Paine (died 1796) at Cheltenham.

Again at Cheltenham a pig killer who died in 1825 at the age of 55 is celebrated:

*Here lies John Higgs,*
*A famous man for killing pigs,*
*For killing pigs was his delight,*
*Both morning, afternoon, and night;*
*Both heat and cold he did endure,*
*Which no physician could ere cure;*
*His knife is laid, his work is done,*
*I hope to Heaven his soul is gone.*

Inscriptions recording the deaths of children can be particularly poignant. A monument still exists in Chipping Campden Church to Thomas Smyth, a sixteenth century lord of the manor, but the plaque bearing these words is now gone:

*Little pretty Betty, Dorothy and Anne,*
*Mary and Moselyn, and Little Gizzey Gamme,*
*Richard and Robert, Geoffrey and John,*
*Edward, William, and little pretty Tom;*
*These are all Mr. Smith's children, every one,*
*Besides two still-born infants,*
*A daughter and a son.*

Strange that Mrs Smith seems not to warrant a mention.

Mary Cox (died 1715, aged eight) is remembered more sententiously at Deerhurst:

*Let Parents strive to be Content*
*What comes from God is only lent*
*In youth & childhood put no trust*
*For all must die and come to dust.*

Grief suffuses these words at Lydney:

*Here a pretty baby lies*
*Sung asleep with lullabies*
*Pray be silent and not stir*
*The easy earth that covers her.*

Wives and husbands mark each other's passing - conventionally, in the case of Albina, wife of James Sansom (died Weston-sub-Edge, 1808, aged 69):

*Within this silent grave lies buried here,*
*A loving wife, a tender mother dear;*
*She is not dead, but sleeping in the dust,*
*In hopes to rise with joy amongst the just.*

Katherine Rowsham (died 1704, aged 28) is made to welcome death at Longborough:

*O Happy change of Heaven that set me free*
*From this base World and all its misery;*
*Fare well dear husband and my babes of love,*
*Till we shall meet again in endless bliss above.*

A monument at Meysey Hampton commemorates both James Vaulx and his two (successive) wives, but has words only for the man:

*Stay, mortall, stay: and looke uppon*
*the language of A speaking stone;*
*Nor wonder is't that he should give*
*Speech to A Stone, who bade men live;*
*When nature bid them dye; 'tis hee*
*By whome I live; not he by mee.*
*This said; I may againe be dumbe*
*I've spoke enough to tell whose Tombe*
*This is: & thou mayest greeting knowe*
*That none but VAULX can lye below.*

Vaulx, a 'famous practitioner in Physicke & Chirurgery', died in 1626. James I once summoned him to court with the intention of making use of his services. When the king asked how he had acquired his knowledge - by reading, observation or practice - Vaulx answered: 'Practice, sire.' James retorted: 'Then by my saul thou hast killed mony a mon; thou shalt never practise upon me.'

At Newnham this epitaph is very much to a couple: 'What needes these many words, all's said is this/A loving pair lodge here, expecting bliss'. The same is true of the inscription at Rodborough to Michael and Joan Stringer:

*One heart we had, one life we led,*
*One death we both desired;*
*One grave we have, our bodies bed;*
*Our souls to God retired.*

Still at Rodborough a traditional epitaph (now gone) showed a less resigned attitude.

*This world's a City full of crooked streets,*
*Death is the Market-place where all men meets.*
*If life were merchandise that men could buy,*
*The Rich would live - the Poor would have to die.*

Essentially the same words appear at Ebrington on a stone to Michael Weston, a blacksmith who made the church clock there. Even more bitter was an epitaph composed at Dursley in 1775 for John Hurlstone, the Poor Overseer, though it was not inscribed on his gravestone:

*Here lies one J...n H...l...ne that pinching Old Dog*
*Why should he lie here, and so much like a Hog?*
*When on Earth not a Soul of him would speak well,*
*The cries of the Poor now reach him in Hell.*
*He got up in the world by practicing Evil*
*Then fulfilled the proverb and rode to the Devil.*

More usually, messages are put in the mouths of the dead which remind the living of their mortality:

*Ye living men, the tomb survey,*
*Where you so soon may dwell;*
*And hark to the awful summons sound*
*In every funeral knell.*

So says Samuel Cadwallader (died 1854, aged 38) at Matson. Opposite the south porch at Tidenham William Humphrey (died 1742, aged 66) is made to observe, slightly ambiguously:

*As you pass by my Grave*
*to see O think that Death*
*Will Come for thee*
*in vain to Live With Christ*
*will be Yur Gain.*

A man called Dyde is much more cheerful at Blockley: 'Live well, die never,/Die well, and live for ever.'

## Tuneful Bells

Over sixty Gloucestershire churches have bells inscribed 'Peace and Good Neighbourhood'. This admirable sentiment is followed in popularity by 'Prosperity to this Place' (or 'Parish') and the stern message of:

*I to the church the living call*
*And to the grave do summon all.*

A variant at St Mary's, Cheltenham, runs: 'I call in prayer the living to combine./The dead must hear a louder sound than mine.'

Arlingham and Teddington have bells marked 'Come when I call: to Serve God All.' At Aston Somerville, Baunton and Beverston a bell says: 'Come away without delay' (or 'make no delay'). Bourton-on-the-Hill is unique in the inscription on its tenor bell: 'That all may com and non may stay at home/I ring to Sermon with a lusty bome.' The melody rather than urgency of bells is emphasised at Chaceley, Elmore, Great Barrington, Painswick, Prestbury (St Mary's), Somerford Keynes, Withington and Wotton-under-Edge, with 'When you me/us ring,/I'le/We'll sweetly sing'. The third bell at Stow-on-the-Wold is marked:

*With merrie note, now God permit*
*That I long time my place do fitt.*

Several churches, including St Laurence's, Stroud, have carillons. At Newnham there is a different tune for each day of the week, secular or sacred: 'Home, sweet Home' (Monday), 'Those endearing young charms' (Tuesday), 'Drink to me Only' (Wednesday), 'The Blue Bells of Scotland' (Thursday), 'Lord, in this thy mercy day' (Friday), 'The Last Rose of Summer' (Saturday) and 'We love the place of God' (Sunday). The bells chime every three hours at Wotton and play Handel's tune, 'Hanover'. At Cirencester the hymn tune, 'O Faith of England', is played at 9 a.m., noon and 3 p.m. daily. Gloucester Cathedral's bells also play a different tune on three occasions through the day. The oldest is 'Chorus Novae Jerusalem', an Easter melody dating from the tenth century. One of the bells, the three-ton Great Peter, is England's only surviving great bell or bourdon.

'The bells are all drunk and quarrelling over beer and 'bacca' was a saying at Upton St Leonards which reflected on the ringers rather than the bells. Another maxim suggested that one could always tell the number of drunkards in a village by counting the ringers. At Standish there was a time when the incumbent, Canon Nash, became concerned at the amount of cider drunk by ringers before, during and after services at a farm near the church. One of them very firmly told him: 'No cider, no bells'.

Rivalry between ringers of different churches led even to the theft of bells, and there was once a belief that if a bell could be removed undetected from one tower and rehung in another no legal process could be brought against those responsible. During the Civil War the church at Slaughterford in Wiltshire was damaged. Two bells were brought down from the tower, and one of them saw service as a drinking vessel for farm cattle. Men from Abson saw their opportunity. They went one night with a horse and cart (hooves and wheels muffled) and loaded up a bell. They avoided detection at a toll gate by telling the keeper they were taking a sick man to Bristol Infirmary. One of their number lent credence to the story by groaning as he lay beneath a tarpaulin which also covered the bell. At Wick the bell was buried in a field near the 'Rose and Crown' until the hue and cry died down. In due course it was retrieved and sent to Whitechapel to be recast. The list of subscribers engraved on the present tenor bell at Abson is said to include the names of those who took part in the theft. Mary Bliss and Frederick Sharpe were told this in 1974 by a relative of the three men involved.

Such validation is lacking in the tale of how some Coaley ringers go to steal a bell from Frocester. They break into the church at night and with great difficulty lower a bell, then pause for a smoke in the churchyard. On returning to their task they find a little old lady sitting on the bell. She ignores them. They try to lift the bell but cannot move it. They panic, and run away. The bell is found next morning, and replaced. The explanation offered is that a local woman who donated jewellery to be cast into the bell metal vowed that her spirit would protect it. In fact one of Frocester's bells was once found half-way down the tower stairs: perhaps some would-be robbers were disturbed or ran out of time. The story of the little old lady may have been tacked on.

Tangible retribution did come to six Avening ringers who in the early 1830s stole a treble bell from Cherington and hung it in their own tower to make the peal up to six. They were sentenced to six months' hard labour. A local song gives the background:

**The Rape of Cherington Bell**

*There was a bell at Cherington,*
*Whose tongue's melodious sound*
*Waked envy in the heart of men*
*Through all the country round.*

*But most of all at Avening*
*Where sons of valour dwell,*
*And made six gallant youths aspire*
*To seize this lovely bell.*

*For Avening had five bells alone*
*So must its ring increase;*

*That these six gallant Avening youths*
*Might have a bell apiece.*

*So on a dark November night,*
*They laid their plans with skill;*
*With ropes and bandages prepared,*
*Climb'd Cherington's high hill.*

*Through gates and doors they burst, and up*
*The winding staircase sped,*
*To the dark chamber where their bell*
*Hung silent on her bed.*

*Her tongue they deftly muffled straight,*
*Bound cords around her waist,*
*And bore her off, and joyed to see*
*Their prize in safety placed.*

*They ranged her with the other five,*
*And bade her join and sing*
*To celebrate their triumph with*
*One merry festal ring.*

*But soon the folks of Cherington*
*The law's strong arm invoke,*
*And make their Avening neighbours pay*
*Right dearly for their joke.*

*The culprits sentenced for six months*
*To fill a convict's cell;*
*And back, behold, to Cherington,*
*Restored the captive bell.*

*Hence, all ye brave, a lesson learn,*
*From fraud and force abstain;*
*Nor ever seek by midnight pranks*
*A beauteous bell to gain.*

*Whate'er ye do, be just and fair,*
*So shall ye live to tell*
*How honest toil and lawful play*
*Bring home the wished for BELLE.*

Within the bell tower discipline among ringers was strictly enforced. 'No drinking, smoking, loud or boisterous talking or jesting, and above all no spitting' was the rule at Ashleworth. A table of fines drawn up in 1785 is still displayed in the ringing chamber at Ashton-under-Hill (transferred to Worcestershire in 1930):

*If first or second Bell you fling,*
*One penny pay, and that's the thing;*
*If third or fourth turn by chance,*
*Pay just the same, there's no advance;*
*But if the fifth you overthrow,*
*Then two pence to the Clerke you owe;*
*And all these forfeits he must have,*
*Before from hence you take your leave.*

The ringers' rules of 1937, still on show at Saintbury, provide for fines of threepence or sixpence for lateness, one shilling for absence without notice, and one penny for bad language.

Verses of the late seventeenth century painted on panels at St Nicholas' Church, Gloucester, simply exhort the ringers to do well:

*He that plyes his Rope aright*
*And guides his Bell by eare, not Sight,*
*He is (be it by day or night)*
*A ringer.*

*Come Boyes cleanely in and out,*
*Keepe true Stroke at every Bout,*
*And then I'll say y'are out of dout*
*True changers.*

Change ringing has a long history. Among the earliest clubs devoted to it were the Marshfield Company of Bellringers (1706) and the Society of Painswick Bell Ringers (1713). Some of the Painswick peals are recorded on tablets in the ringing chamber. At Cirencester 5082 Grandsire Cinques were rung in 1767 by the Ancient Society of College Youths, which travelled from London for the purpose. This was the first ever peal on twelve bells outside London, and took four hours. Precisely two hundred years later there was a commemorative re-run of the feat.

In 1878 the Gloucester and Bristol Diocesan Change-ringing Association was set up with the object of promoting belfry reform and encouraging change ringing. The elaborate rules of the Dymock Ringing Society - set up the following year - have been preserved. Organisation was democratic, and discipline tight:

*12. That any Member, after agreement, being more than ten minutes late, either for practice or ringing, shall be fined 2d; if not more than twenty minutes late 4d; if altogether absent, 6d, unless he send notice, at least the evening previous, to the Leader, to the effect that*

*he cannot attend. And that the following fines be also imposed;-*
*(1) Swearing or quarrelling in the Belfry, for each offence .. .. .. .. .. .. .. .. .. .. .. 3d.*
*(2) Leaving before the Bells are down, without the consent of the majority present .. .. .. .. 3d.*
*(3) Neglecting to oil the Bells .. .. .. .. .. 2d.*
*(4) For entering the Belfry in a state of intoxication .. .. .. .. .. .. .. .. .. 2/6d.*
*The fines to be collected by the Leader.*

Apart from taking turns to oil the bells, attending regular practices and ringing for routine services, members were expected to be available to ring for at least an hour at festivals throughout the year: 'Christmas Day, Feast of the Circumcision [New Year's Day], the Epiphany, Lady-day, Easter Day, Ascension Day, Whitsun Day, and Candlemas. A muffled peal at the close of the year, and on Holy Innocent's [sic] Day, and a full peal on Christmas Eve, and New Year's Eve, at midnight.'

At least Dymock did not have a curfew bell. Others did, even though the legal requirement to signal in this way ended as early as 1100. Lechlade gave up the practice in 1850. Between All Saints' Day (1 November) and the Feast of the Purification of the Blessed Virgin Mary (2 February) under the provisions of a will of 1695 a bell was rung at Haresfield not only at 9 p.m. but also at 5 a.m. The last parish clerk to fulfil this office was John Jones. Kingswood, near Wotton-under-Edge, had an 8 p.m. curfew bell until the outbreak of the Second World War when all ringing ceased, except as a signal of invasion. Winchcombe also continued until 1939, between 24 October and 24 March (the dates respectively of the autumn and spring fairs at Stow) with a bell at 8 p.m. for ten minutes, followed by a tolling of as many times as the number of days which had elapsed in the month. After the war Cirencester alone brought back its curfew, with the tenth of its thirteen bells ringing at 8 p.m. from 8 November until 25 March. It clung on until the 1960s, the last Gloucestershire church to do so.

Cirencester also had, from Michaelmas to Lady Day, a 4 a.m. bell of which the earliest record dates from 1599. The same bell at Lechlade was stopped in 1809 by Churchwarden Gearing because, he claimed, it got people up to be 'wood pullers and hedge tearers'. The day bell at Blockley lasted until 1880. Although its purpose was to wake people for work a new vicar, Canon E.J. Houghton, insisted that it be silenced. Feeling ran high. A churchwarden resigned. Villagers were so incensed that the vicar feared a riot, and sent for the police. He was caricatured 'in small bills, for which there was an immense sale'. One of them read:

*HERE LIES FOR EVER DUMB*
*Until the Day of Disestablishment*
*When it will arise in all its beauty*
*THE 5 O'CLOCK BELL*

*Cruelly murdered by its Guardian and Custodian*
*after 800 years of humble but valued*
*service to the Parish*

*Born September 31st 1066*
*Died April 3rd 1880*

Many of the annual occasions on which bells were rung have also gone, though more perhaps by neglect than suppression. On Shrove Tuesday a bell - originally the signal for confession and shriving - continued at noon until 1881 at Wotton-under-Edge as a reminder for pancakes to be prepared. At Dursley until 1914 one bell at 12.40 p.m. said 'Pan on'; a second at one o'clock added: 'Pan off'. Cirencester still has its Pancake Bell, but children are no longer told - as they were within living memory - that when the town pump hears the sound it rises and walks round the Market Place.

In medieval times a plot of land was donated to the abbot at Cirencester so that its rent could pay for the upkeep of the bells. To prove that they were in good order he instituted a weekly ring, and this still takes place every Saturday morning, when each bell is lifted in turn. Cirencester also holds to its peal at 5 a.m. on 29 May to celebrate the restoration of the monarchy in 1660 - again the sole survivor of many. Willersey used to have a bell at the same time on 21 December to usher in St Thomas's Day and the beginning of the Christmas season. On 28 December, Holy Innocents' Day, a muffled peal was rung in many churches, including Bourton-on-the-Water, Churcham, Churchdown, Dursley, Dymock, Hartpury, Maisemore, Westbury-on-Severn, Woodchester and Wyck Rissington. The custom survived longest (until the 1960s) at Woodchester.

Bourton-on-the-Water had bells at 6 a.m. on Ascension Day, the shortest day of the year, and the sovereign's birthday; at midnight on Christmas Eve; and a muffled peal - called 'buffing the old year out' - on New Year's Eve. After midnight the twelve buffs were removed, and a merry peal rung. At Cirencester a half-muffled peal is still rung for the thirty minutes up to midnight on New Year's Eve, followed by an open touch to welcome New Year's Day.

For the normal church services and religious festivals ringers worked voluntarily. At Marshfield a free barrel of beer was once customarily provided for ringers to drink during and after services, and one remembers the 'no cider, no bells' slogan of their colleagues at Standish. Fees were paid for weddings and funerals, and also various secular celebrations. Over the years churchwardens' accounts record payments 'To the ringers for beer' of five or six shillings on 29 May and 5 November. One entry of 1606 at Deerhurst reads: 'the Ringgers upon the Kings halydaye xij d.' Several royal or national occasions feature at Dursley:

*1689 3/- Thanksgiving Day for the Prince of Orange*
*1707 5/- Duke of Marlborough's victory at Ramillies*
*1716 6/- When the Pretender fled from Scotland*

Such payments continued into more recent times, as can be seen from the accounts at Mangotsfield:

| | | | |
|---|---|---|---|
| *1801* | *October 4* | *Gave Ringers on Coronation Day* | *10.0* |
| | *Ditto,* | *when peace was proclaimed* | *10.0* |
| | *November 5* | *Ringers* | *£1.0.0* |
| *1810* | | *Gave the Ringers towards their Feast* | *£1.8.0* |
| *1819* | *March 11* | *Paid for tolling the bell when the Queen was buried* | *4.0* |
| | *March* | *Candles for singers to practise* | *0.4* |
| *1831* | *November* | *Paid J. Bampton for ringing the bell for the late King* | *16.0* |
| *1838* | | *Gave the ringers at the Coronation* | *£1.0.0* |
| *1839* | | *Ringing the bell on the Queen's Marriage* | *6.0* |
| *1897* | | *Jubilee Day, ringers* | *£ 1.0.0* |
| *1910* | | *Service to late King* | *£1.0.0* |
| *1937* | | *Coronation* | *£2.0.0* |

Ringers at Twyning still receive five shillings for a peal on 5 November, under a benefaction from Charles Hancock, whose wife died on that day in the early eighteenth century.

## The West Gallery

The entry on 'candles for singers' reminds us that ringers are not the only church musicians. At Cam the churchwardens' accounts record the expenditure in 1824 of one shilling for 'fetching the D: Bass', and £1.4.0. for three strings. Repairs to the instrument cost £1 in 1825, and there are further expenses of 5s. the following year; but in 1828 we read: 'Tuning and repairing the organ, 11s. 0d.'

Before it was supplanted by the organ, a band - typically a 'clarionet', fiddle and bass viol or double bass - played in the church's west gallery to accompany the choir. Behaviour there was often not very reverent. The Marshfield churchwarden paid James Long five shillings in 1844, 'for keeping order in the Gallery', but as late as the 1870s 'every sort of missile ... was thrown at the congregation below.'

Like ringers, singers were often independent and sometimes turbulent. A dispute arose at Rodborough in 1748 over the occupation of the 'Singing Seat' in the church. The clergyman, churchwardens, 18 singers and five prominent parishioners met to draw up a lengthy code of practice, which they all signed. Only the stated singers could use the seat, and only they could fill places which became vacant by nominating others. However, 'no person shall sit there unless he understands the rules of musick, and can (with a tolerable voice at least) sing the Psalm tunes.' A single musician was permitted: 'P.-P.-, of Stroud Parish, shall have liberty to sit in the said Pew, and make use of his Bassoon; but ... no instrument of Musick but a Bassoon shall be used there.'

Perhaps the singers made use of the bassoonist as leader. Henry Sale (born 1864) remembered William Lively, the blind fiddler who led the Blockley choir from the gallery. William Smith, who died at 1910 at the age of 90, served for 67 years as parish clerk at Saintbury. As well as being a bellringer he played violin, bass viol, flute and clarinet in church. He was also in demand for musical evenings and servants' balls. At Christmas he joined the waits, on which occasions 'it was a custom often to have a non-player to go round with them to consume superfluous liquor, it not being etiquette to decline any offered.'

Chedworth had a band of 12, made up of woodwind and string players. Such musicians were often village artisans, who enjoyed considerable autonomy. At Bishop's Cleeve the parson once announced 'Who is the King of Glory' as the next hymn. Up in the splendid Jacobean gallery (which still exists) the fiddler responded: "And up th'rosin, Thomus. We'll show 'em who be th'King o' Glory.'

H.Y.J. Taylor (died 1906) remembered when a band of wind and strings played at Brockworth:

> *I think it was called 'The United Choirs of Brock'uth, Witcomb and Badge'uth'. They played a variety of instruments, some of them I have neither seen before nor since. The venerable clerk, with a huge Cromwellian bald head, with a loud voice, shouted from his shabby and worm-eaten reading desk, 'Let us zing to the proys and gloree of God, the long mateur'. As soon as he had delivered this notice to the congregation he vacated his reading-box, and ascended an infirm gallery, and took his position among the musicians. They began to tune their instruments, which operation was more visible than gratifying. At last the old clerk enquired, in a loud and audible voice, 'Be ee all in co-ard (chord)?' 'All right,' was the response. 'Then bust off,' cried the clerk; and bust off they did, and in a fine and vigorous style.*

Clearly fascinated, Taylor returned to the subject on another occasion:

> *The major part of the performers were clothed in smockfrocks. All kinds of musical instruments were used (wind and stringed), from a bassoon to a fiddle. The wave of harmony which rolled up and down and to and fro was most wonderful. The melody of the rustic vocalists, combined with the harmony of the fiddles, flutes, bass viols, 'hosses-legs' [bassoons], serpents, and clarionets, etcetera, produced a most imposing effect upon the minds of the simple worshipper.*

The simple worshipper may have been impressed but not, in general, the clergyman. Thomas Hardy's classic account in *Under the Greenwood Tree* (1872) of the suppression of an old church 'quire' could be paralleled many times over. During the incumbency (1863-77) of Rev. William Burch Gale at Willersey the west gallery was pulled down and the bass viol, flute and singers ejected. Rev. H.D. Cropper banished the band from Sapperton Church in 1887, and aroused a great deal of resentment by doing so. The village musicians continued to be in demand for weddings and harvest celebrations but, as Norman Jewson learned, 'the band met at the corner of the common every Sunday, the estate men fell in behind it... and the procession marched to the churchyard gate, where the band dispersed to put away their instruments before entering the church.'

Bands were replaced by organs, with a barrel organ sometimes providing an intermediate step. Henry White still possessed in 1889 the machine cranked at Bagendon Church some 50 years earlier by his father, the parish clerk, sexton, bellringer and pew-opener. The barrels included 'The Old Hundredth', 'Evening Hymn' and 'While Shepherds'. The gallery 'musicianers' with their 'hitherer and thitherer' (trombone), 'horse's leg', 'sarpint' and fiddle, had downed instruments for good when the rector called in a rival band from North Cerney to play at a garden party: 'If we baint good enough for he on wikdays, zurelie we baint good enough for God on Sundays.'

In the time of Rev. Hicks at Upton St Leonards there were some barrels with sacred and others with secular melodies. 'The story runs that one morning, through some one tampering with this "chest of whistles", the organ groaned out a dance tune instead of a strain more suitable for the new version of the poetry of David.' The barrel organ in Brimpsfield's west gallery had a repertoire of only six tunes, so perhaps some hymns were sung unaccompanied. At Stow a similar instrument was turned by the well-known local figure of Hailes Parrish until as late as 1897, when it finally gave way to a proper organ. North Cerney is among the places which moved from barrel to hand-blown to electric organ.

Tetbury acquired its first organ as early as 1805, bought for the large sum of £300 from Ranelagh Pleasure Gardens in London, no doubt on the principle that the devil should not have all the best tunes. In 1862, by then dilapidated, the instrument was sold for £7 and a new one, built by Nicholson of Worcester, acquired at a cost of £425. This remained in the west gallery until 1900, when it was moved to the south side of the choir. The Blockley organ, bought in 1860, moved from the west gallery to the chancel only in 1924. Most such galleries are now gone, though they remain, with organs, at Buckland, Coln Rogers and perhaps elsewhere. Until its recent removal to Oxford for safe keeping a reminder of the old 'musicianers' was preserved in the church at Ampney Crucis - a case of instruments dating from about 1800.

## Stories in Stone

The church spoke in words, through sermon and scripture, hymn and epitaph. It also conveyed a mute message through aspects of its fabric - inside and out -

and objects in wood, metal, stone, glass. Orthodox religious teachings were propounded, but also many popular traditions and beliefs.

Some churches have many external sculptures. At Fairford these include a dragon, a wyvern and a griffin. Perhaps surprisingly, half of the forty gargoyles at Winchcombe represent dragons. A hideous figure above the east window there is thought to show the devil himself. An almost caricatural helmeted head to the left of the entrance porch purports to represent Sir Ralph Boteler - a curious way of treating the lord of Sudeley Manor who paid for the church's complete rebuilding in the fifteenth century.

On the north wall of the nave at Cirencester above the clerestory windows were carvings (plastered over in a nineteenth century restoration) showing the participants in a Whitsun Ale. This church fund-raiser and general merry-making was once a feature of Cotswold life. The sculptures show the 'lord' and 'lady' (chosen for the occasion), steward, sword-, purse- and mace-bearer, page jester, musicians and dancers. Dover's Games (see Chapter Seven) probably originated as a Whitsun Ale.

Projecting from the west wall at Deerhurst Church are what E.S. Hartland has characterised as 'two rude and unrecognisable animal heads'. Even so they have given rise to the tradition of a local dragon first recorded in 1712 by Sir Robert Atkyns:

> *There goes a story, that a serpent of prodigious bigness was a great grievance to all the country about Deerhurst, by poisoning the inhabitants, and killing their cattle. The inhabitants petitioned the king, and a proclamation was issued out, that whosoever should kill the serpent, should enjoy an estate on Walton hill in the parish, which then belonged to the crown. One John Smith, a labourer, undertook it, and succeeded; for finding the serpent lying in the sun, with his scales ruffled up, he struck between the scales with his axe, and struck off his head.*

In the late eighteenth century a Mr Lane who had married a member of the Smith family claimed to have the axe in his possession. About a hundred years later Rev. George Butterworth wrote that his Deerhurst parishioners still talked 'with bated breath of the "flying addard"'. In 1991 there was still a farmer in the parish called Smith, with a hillock on his land called the Dragon's Tump.

When the porch at St George's, Cam, was restored in the mid-nineteenth century a sculptured boss showing the saint and his dragon was set into the vaulting. A local story tells of a clothier who stole a statue of St George from the same porch and took it in his cart to Colebrook, where he set it up as an inn-sign. What happened subsequently is not related.

More Gloucestershire dragons are shown in carvings over church doors. Moreton Valence's north door tympanum has St Michael spearing a beast more like a water monster than a dragon, probably intended to stand for the devil. The same saint's quarry on the Norman tympanum at Harnhill is undoubtedly a dragon. St Michael's features here are said to have been modelled on those of

William the Conqueror or his son, William Rufus. In 1100, only a few days before his death in the New Forest, Rufus dreamed while visiting the abbot at Tewkesbury that an assassin entered his chamber at night and stabbed him in the chest; and that a stream of blood gushed forth to reach the sky and dim the light of day. He ignored the warning, and rode to his death in the New Forest.

Another Norman tympanum at Dumbleton shows the head of a man with the ears of an ass, and three pieces of foliage springing from his mouth. This again may represent the devil, and it surmounts the north door which was always thought to be his domain. Villagers call it the cat with nine tails, since each piece of foliage divides at the end into three. Instead it may be a Green Man, which symbolises sadness and sacrifice for some, life and renewal for others. The motif - otherwise known as a foliate head - recurs in wood or stone in many churches, including those at Cam, Compton Abdale, Guiting Power, Lechlade and Quenington. A mysterious pig's head is carved on the sanctuary side of the chancel arch at Upleadon. The sculpted toad in Berkeley Church does have an explanation: it is supposed to depict the real toad which grew to a monstrous size by feeding on the bodies of prisoners who died in the castle's *oubliette*.

The outline of two other beasts is cut into the walls of North Cerney Church. They are called manticores. One, over four feet high, has the body and legs of a dog, the hooves of a pony, a thick tail, and the head and upraised arms of a man. The other, also with a man's face, is more leopard-like. The figures, which may be Saxon or pre-Christian in origin, seem to have been intended as guardians for the church.

David with his sling, a Saxon graffito on the north wall of Haresfield Church, may also be offering protection, in this case against the evil eye. The figure cut during the fourteenth century into the north porch at St Bartholomew's, Churchdown, has been interpreted as an emblem of death, with the long hair and breasts of a woman, an hour glass and an asperges (used to sprinkle holy water on a corpse at the graveside); or more simply as a mermaid with her comb and looking glass. If the latter, it might have been brought to mind by the graffito, again at Churchdown, of a whale spouting water into the sky - a metaphor of everlasting life. Finally, there is an aged, bearded and haloed face, perhaps cut by a monk in an idle moment.

Crosses scratched by medieval pilgrims departing for the Holy Land can be seen in the south porch at Tirley. Even travellers facing the few miles to Winchcombe cut crosses in the jambs of the church porch at Hazelton. Some marks on the church walls at Kempsford are said to have been made when weapons were sharpened during a tournament when Edward II and Isabella visited the castle before their marriage. Also at Kempsford a horse shoe fastened to the north door of the church has its own sad tale to tell. Henry, who became the first duke of Lancaster in 1351, was in residence at the castle when his only son drowned at a ford in the nearby River Thames. Henry left Kempsford, vowing never to return. As he rode off his horse cast a shoe which villagers picked up and nailed to the door where it remains. In due course Henry's daughter, Blanche, inherited his estate jointly with her sister, and entertained the poet Chaucer in the castle. On the terrace known as Lady Maud's Walk he is supposed to have written 'The Assembly of Foules', in honour of Blanche's wedding. Her husband, John of Gaunt, had the tower of the church built after her death as a memorial.

Within churches, traditions cling to a host of features. Near the font at Ampney St Peter, set into a wall some six feet above the floor, is the figure of a sheila-na-gig. The church guide piously comments that this is 'perhaps a Saxon fertility goddess converted with her followers in order to give glory to Him who is Lord of all.' Fertility symbol, certainly; but if conversion followed one wonders why the carving has been defaced. Undoubtedly it is because of its frank anatomical display, which caused some people to call the sheila-na-gig a 'witch on the wall'.

The witches' sign, a pentagram, has been scratched on several piers in the nave of Tewkesbury Abbey. This may have been done by puritans intending to mock the high church ceremonies of which they disapproved. The significance, if any, remains obscure of the dog's head incised on a step near the tomb in the abbey of Hugh and Elizabeth Despenser. However, the cat and owl cut into the plaster in the Warwick-Beachamp chapel may allude to the story of a baker's daughter turned into an owl for denying Jesus a fair-sized cake.

Ancient graffiti proliferate in Gloucester Cathedral. Intertwining circles in the eastern cloister may have had mystical meaning. Three fish in a triangle in the Lady Chapel could derive from pre-Christian religion. Upstairs in the singing gallery of the north chantry are to be seen a huntsman, a tree and a church. At the east end of the choir a king fights a great serpent and a winged dragon.

People once thought - as perhaps they still subconsciously feel - that cutting one's name or initials in a church brought grace, healing or simply luck, especially if it could be done on the effigy of one of the founders, a cult figure or a folk hero. I have myself witnessed Italians inscribing their initials on Juliet's supposed tomb in Verona. In Gloucester Cathedral a great magnet for such people was the effigy and ornate tomb of Edward II. During his lifetime Edward was cordially detested. His queen, Isabella, and her lover, Roger Mortimer, deposed him in January 1327 and installed the royal prince as Edward III. The former king was imprisoned in various places before being put to death in September 1327 at Berkeley Castle. Those responsible for the deed were Thomas Gourney, William Ockley and possibly John Maltravers, the brother-in-law of Thomas Berkeley. They were particularly brutal, and a local tradition says that Edward's screams were heard the incredible distance of three miles away:

> *Having suddenly seized him lying in bed and having pressed him down and suffocated him with great pillows..., with a plumber's iron heated red hot, through a horn applied leading to the privy parts of the bowel, they burned out the respiratory organs past the intestines, fearing lest, a wound having been found on the royal body ... his tormentors could be bound to answer for an obvious offence and pay the penalty for it.*

Six years earlier when Edward II was being entertained by the abbot at Gloucester he was shown a series of portraits of previous monarchs. When he enquired about his own the abbot replied that they were keeping a better place for him. The remark proved prophetic. After three other monasteries - St Augustine's, Bristol, St Adhelm's, Malmesbury, and St Mary's, Kingswood - had refused to take Edward's body, Abbot Thokey of Gloucester (probably on orders from the court) agreed to accept it.

A window in the south aisle of the cathedral nave shows the scene when the body arrived in October 1327 but the glass is Victorian and, according to Canon Welander, it 'bristles with anachronisms'. A tomb was built in the cathedral between about 1330 and 1335. Five years later restructuring was done at the expense of Thomas Berkeley. Some said this, together with his payment for the building of St George's Church, Cam, was in expiation for his complicity in Edward's murder (though in 1337 Edward III formally acquitted Berkeley of any blame for the death of his father).

Paintings of stags on the pillars of the tomb led to the belief that Edward's body was drawn to Gloucester by these animals. People flocked to the tomb, which became a kind of shrine. Miracles were claimed for it, and there was even an attempt - by Richard II, Edward II's great-grandson - to have the former king canonised. It failed, but the flow of pilgrims continued unabated, bringing prosperity to abbey and city.

Some historians contend that Edward II was not killed at Berkeley nor buried at Gloucester. Their main evidence is a letter sent by a priest, Manuele de Fieschi, to Edward III. Fieschi claims to have been told in confession by Edward II that a servant warned him of an impending attempt on his life at Berkeley and gave him clothes in which to escape. To obtain keys to the outer door, the king killed a sleeping porter whose body was later passed off as his and solemnly buried at Gloucester. Edward travelled through various countries in the guise of a hermit, and eventually died a natural death in Italy. Others do not accept this thesis; 'few have been convinced by the evidence,' writes Welander. The matter could perhaps have been settled in 1855 when the tomb was opened but the leaden inner coffin was left untouched. The question therefore remains.

Another royal tomb is in St Mary's Chapel at Sudeley. Although it dates only from the 1850s, Queen Katherine Parr lies there. She died some three hundred years earlier (in 1548), seven days after giving birth to a child. She was only thirty-six but had been married four times: to Edward Burghe, John Nevill, Henry VIII (as his sixth and last wife), and finally to Thomas Seymour, Lord of Sudeley and High Admiral of England.

After the slighting of Sudeley Castle during the Civil War the chapel in which Katherine had been buried fell into ruin. Over a century later, however, her leaden coffin was discovered and opened by John Lucas, a gentleman farmer living in or near the castle. The body was found 'wrapp'd in 6 or 7 seer cloths of linnen entire and uncorrupted, although it had lain upward of 230 years'. A cut made in the cloths revealed flesh still 'moist and white' but a further examination the following year showed - not surprisingly - that 'where the incision had been made the flesh was brown and in a state of putrefaction.'

Further ghoulish disturbances of the coffin ensued. In 1792 after a bout of heavy drinking Lucas and some of his friends took out the corpse and made sport of it. 'The details of their work are too dreadful to give or dwell upon,' wrote Emma Dent, a subsequent chatelaine of Sudeley herself, adding 'but the tradition lingers in Winchcombe, that each one of that Baccanalian band met with an untimely and horrible end.' Lucas went mad and in an interval of lucidity told the local doctor, John Phythian, how the queen's ghost had appeared to him one night as he walked by the desecrated grave.

In 1817 when Rev. John Lates had the coffin moved into the Chandos vault all that remained inside was a skeleton, a few scraps of cloth and some ivy. Local people claimed that a berry had fallen into the coffin, taken root and woven a green sepulchral coronet round the dead queen's brow. Dr Phythian recollected that Katherine's hair reached down to her feet. He cut off and preserved a lock of it but this was later destroyed by a superstitious descendant who feared it might be used for casting spells.

Less than a mile from Sudeley chapel are two more royal coffins, those of King Kenulf and St Kenelm, inside the west end of St Peter's Church at Winchcombe. The first extant account of the former occupants' story was produced some three hundred years after it happened by a monk, Florence of Worcester, but the fullest treatment came in the fourteenth century from Richard of Cirencester, a Gloucestershire man writing at Westminster.

When Kenulf of Mercia dies at Winchcombe, Kenelm becomes king but as a child of seven falls under the tutelage of his older sister, Kendrida. She desires power for herself, so prevails on her lover, Askobert, to kill Kenelm. The two go on a hunting expedition which leads them from Winchcombe to the Clent Hills in Worcestershire. Kenelm realises he is to die, perhaps recalling his dream (related by Chaucer in the *Nun's Priest's Tale*) of a great tree standing by his bed, decorated with fruit and flowers. He climbs to the top but his dearest friend chops it down, whereupon he changes into a little bird and flies to heaven. On the Clent Hills Kenelm plants his staff in the ground, where it roots and grows into a thorn tree. Askobert strikes off the boy's head with a long-bladed knife. A dove emerges and flies to Rome with a scroll which it drops on the high altar at St Peter's.

The document is found to carry the words: 'In Clent cow-pasture under a thorn/Of head bereft lies Kenelm, king born.' A party of holy men finds the grave, guided by a ray of light playing on it or a cow standing by which fattens without eating. As the body is exhumed church bells ring of their own accord and a spring gushes forth from the ground.

A dispute arises between the monks of Worcestershire and Gloucestershire over custody of the body. The rival parties agree to spend the night, says the chronicle, at Pyriford (possibly Pershore), with the first to wake on the morrow having priority. The abbot of Winchcombe and his monks wake first and secure an unbeatable lead of several miles before the Worcestershire men, forgetting their agreement, give chase.

The Winchcombe monks bring home Kenelm's body. Nearing the end of their journey they rest their burden on Round Hill near Sudeley, and another spring wells up. As the procession returns Kendrida looks from her window and attempts (for magical purposes) to read the 53rd Psalm ('The fool hath said in his heart, there is no God') backwards. The crowd shouts:'Kenelm is truly God's martyr.' Kendrida answers: 'As truly as my eyes are lying on this book' - and her eyes fall out on the page.

Kenelm was buried at the east end of the abbey church at Winchcombe, near his father. The abbey added the dedication of St Kenelm to that of St Mary, and pilgrims flocked to pay homage. The 'George Inn' (now divided into flats) at Winchcombe was built to accommodate them. A chapel was erected at the Round Hill spring, which came to be called St Kenelm's Well. The chapel is now gone, though one of its windows was built into a neighbouring farmhouse. The spring is still there, supplying water to Sudeley Castle. The well house which stand over it has a modern stone carving of St Kenelm, after a fourteenth century picture.

Two Gloucestershire churches, those at Alderley and Sapperton, are still dedicated to St Kenelm. In a field below the latter is another St Kenelm's Well, with a claim that his body rested there, though it is miles from any possible route between Clent and Winchcombe.

Winchcombe Abbey was demolished in the sixteenth century but an excavation on the site, close to the present church, in 1815 revealed two stone coffins. In the smaller were a skull, a few bones and a long-bladed knife. In the larger, presumed to be that of Kenulf, the body was remarkably preserved, 'even to the fleshy tints on the cheeks'. As the observers, who included Dr Phythian, gazed, 'all returned to dust'. The knife and coffins were presented to the doctor. The knife soon disintegrated but the coffins adorned his garden until eventually they found their way into the parish church.

It is always a shame to spoil a good story but the facts are firmly against this one. Kenelm did exist - he is mentioned in surviving charters dating from between 803 and 811 - but he probably died at the age of fourteen, ten years before his father. At the time Kendrida was a nun, and she went on to become the abbess of Minster in Kent. It is of course possible that Kenelm was murdered. His legend may have been intended as a pendant to the saga of his grandfather, Offa. Then again, the whole thing may have been invented by monks at Winchcombe anxious to compete with prosperous Hailes a few miles down the road.

Others of the dead are easier to document. Dorothy Pauncefoot (died 1568) whose tomb is in the church at Hasfield is supposed to have sacrificed her right hand as a ransom for her lover who had been captured by a rival baron. Similar stories are told of Pauncefoot effigies of different periods at Much Cowarne in Herefordshire and Crickhowell, Powys. When the tomb at Hasfield was opened the right hand was indeed missing.

At Great Barrington, the effigy of Captain Edmund Bray (died 1620) has a sword by the right side. Bray is said to have killed a man and been pardoned by Elizabeth I at Tilbury after swearing never to use his right hand again in anger. A more down-to-earth explanation of the placing of the sword could be that Bray was left-handed. On the level of orthodox theology a tomb of 1685 at Cam purports to show how a farmer called Perrott was killed by a snapping plough chain while working on a Sunday. Such messages were also communicated in two-dimensional form.

## In the Picture

Wall paintings and stained glass reinforced the church's teaching. Murals at St Mary's, Kempley, show the twelve apostles, Christ seated on a rainbow, scenes from the Revelation, the ten stages of life, and St Michael weighing souls. The famous doom painting at Oddington (hidden under whitewash in the seventeenth century and only revealed again in 1913) depicts Christ receiving the righteous into paradise while devils in hell torture sinners with tremendous relish. One sufferer, having scaled the high brick wall which enclosed the damned, is given a helping hand at the top by a kindly angel.

The north wall, where Oddington's doom is painted, often pictured St Christopher, patron of travellers. As people left by the south door on a journey they could turn back for a last comforting look at the saint. In a well-loved episode of the apocryphal gospels St Christopher - his name means Christ-bearer - carries the Christ child over a river, and this scene is portrayed at Baunton (where the watercourse shown looks much like the nearby River Churn) and also in the tiny church at Hailes.

Wheels painted on the walls at Oxenton Church may be associated with St Catherine (martyred by being broken on a wheel and then beheaded) or symbolise the cycle of life. It has been suggested that in a local ceremony - perhaps on 25 November, St Catherine's Day - a wagon wheel, after being bound with straw and covered with grease, was set afire and rolled down the grassy hill behind the church. If it followed a true course to the bottom good luck would accrue for the coming year; if it veered, the reverse would happen.

Scenes from the lives of saints are often shown in stained glass. The east window of Gloucester Cathedral's Lady Chapel shows various holy virgins including Arilda, who was born and also martyred at Kingston-by-Thornbury. Her Saxon beauty attracted the interest of 'one Muncius, a tiraunt, who cut off hir heade becawse she would not consent to lye withe hym.' A well close to where she died bears her name. Its water once possessed miraculous healing powers. Churches at Oldbury-on-the-Hill and Oldbury-on-Severn are still dedicated to St Arilda.

A bishop in a window at Edgeworth is traditionally identified as St Thomas à Becket. A shepherd called Richard Sunieve, who worked for Sir Henry Fitzherbert of Edgeworth Manor, contracted leprosy. He achieved a cure either simply by praying to St Thomas (after which he went to Canterbury to give thanks), or by drinking holy water and a single drop of the saint's blood (for which purpose he had travelled to Canterbury).

Fairford Church, renowned for its stained glass, was built largely at the expense of John Tame, a wool merchant who died in 1500 three years after its consecration. Alfred Williams, who was brought up not far away in Wiltshire, wrote:

> *The people of the countryside for many miles around, though they may not have seen them, have heard of the famous 'Fairfet' windows, and the one item most strongly remembered - usually it is the only fact known - is that upon one of them is depicted the devil trundling a woman off to hell in a wheelbarrow. This I remember to have heard when I was a very young child and I knew nothing more concerning the windows beyond the report that 'owl Oliver Crummel' tried to blow up the church with his cannon and that the inhabitants, anticipating his design, removed the glass and buried it in a field at the back of the town.*

According to another tradition, John Tame captured the glass from a ship taken as a prize as it sailed to Rome. This may be a folk memory of the windows' journey by sea from Flanders, where many of them were made.

Fairford also boasts a set of misericords installed in about 1520 at the expense of John Tame's son, Edmund. These are ledges on the underside of tip-up seats intended to give support to monks or clergy during the long periods of standing for prayers or services. The carvings decorating them seem to have been left to the fantasy of workmen whose vigorous vignettes in wood show scenes from the Bible, popular mythology or everyday life.

At Fairford the subjects include a possible Green Man, two wyverns, and a woman dragging a youth by his long hair while belabouring him with a washing beetle. Among the thirty examples at St Mary Redcliffe, Bristol, is a carving of two foxes in a pulpit addressing a flock of geese - a favourite anti-clerical satire. Many of the medieval misericords in Tewkesbury Abbey have been mutilated but some half-human creatures survive, together with women in fishes' mouths.

Fosbrooke described those at Gloucester Cathedral as 'specimens of licentious carving' and 'gross whims of the workmen'. They nevertheless include such unexceptionable topics as shepherds following the star to Bethlehem, the sacrifice of Isaac, and St Michael once more slaying a dragon. It is true that there are plenty of secular scenes, with wrestling, bear-baiting, fighting, gambling and ball-playing. The fantastic also occupies an important place, with numerous monsters, a mermaid, a wyvern (which may stand for Judas in the jaws of hell) and a pious pelican feeding her young from her own blood. A modern carving, copied from an original in Worcester Cathedral, shows a woman naked but for a net; she rides on a goat, though with one foot on the ground, and holds a rabbit in one hand. The punishment of a promiscuous woman, says one theory; another, that the woman is Disa, commanded by King Frey of Nordic saga to appear before him neither clothed nor unclothed, neither walking nor riding, and bearing a gift that was not a gift. She prays for guidance to the goddess Frigg and meets the king's requirements so wisely and well that he makes her queen. The rabbit is no gift because it can run away.

## High Days

As well as the major religious festivals various other events found a place in the church calendar. Some are very much alive. At St Briavels, Palm Sunday was known as Flowering Sunday because until early this century all the graves were decorated with flowers on that day. Neighbouring villages shared the custom, and there was intense rivalry for the honour of having the best-dressed churchyard.

Among many charitable doles, often under the provisions of bequests, was a distribution of wheat by the parish clerk at Tidenham on Maundy Thursday. The grain was either taken to the mill to be ground into flour or planted in the fields of smallholdings. On the following day - Good Friday - until the 1950s loaves to the value of £1 were distributed to the needy at Woolaston. At Dursley in a very different activity the rector led the churchwardens, followed by the rest of the congregation, up Stinchcombe Hill on a squirrel-hunting expedition. The origin of this now-defunct event remains mysterious.

When Rev J. Burleigh Colvill was vicar at Hewelsfield the churchwardens presented him every Easter Sunday with two bouquets of flowers as he entered the church. One of these he kept, and placed the other on the altar. On the Tuesday after Easter the choirboys of St Michael's, Bristol, are still given large buns which for some reason are called 'twopenny starvers'. On the second Sunday after Easter it was customary at Chipping Sodbury, Hawkesbury and Randwick for the story of Balaam, including the episode of the speaking ass, to be read from *Numbers* (Chapters 22 to 24) to packed congregations. The occasion was therefore known as Balaam's Ass Sunday. Next day Randwick began its 'wap' (for which, see Chapter Eleven).

Forty days after Easter comes Ascension Day. The Sunday, Monday, Tuesday and Wednesday before that make up Rogationtide, the traditional occasion for beating the boundaries of parish or town. Ancient case-law permitted parishioners to go on to private land for this purpose without being guilty of trespass. Participants literally beat stones and the like with willow rods to help fix landmarks in their memories; and children might be given the bumps - more or less gently - with the same end in view.

In the case of ecclesiastical perambulations there were pauses for Bible readings under trees which then came to be known as Gospel Oaks. There was also a Gospel Bush (at Wapley), a Gospel Beech (at Upton St Leonards) and even a Gospel Hill (at Pucklechurch). St Paul's Epistle, a larch-crowned tumulus just off the A436 near the 'Kilkenny Inn', takes it names from a former parson's choice of reading at this point on perambulations. Until the 1930s Chipping Campden had a 'ten o'clock tree', so called because of the time the sun's rays fell on it as the vicar in full canonicals issued from the church door at Rogationtide to bless the crops.

There are, of course, many earlier records, such as this from a church register: 'Memorandum that I, Henry Childe, Vicar of Arlingham, went on perambulation with — of my parishioners, on Rogationtide Monday and

Tuesday, 1606. Upon the Tuesday I went to the uttmost confines of our parish, eastward and from north to south [the western boundary is supplied by the Severn], not for any superstitious sake, but to see the bounds of the parish.'

On the other side of the river, at Westbury, instructions for beating the parish bounds were carefully drawn up in 1833:

> *Commence at Costrel's Brook, between Broad Oak and Hawkin Pill; follow its course to Mosses Grove, which bounds it to the top of the field belonging to Mr Cannock. It then turns to the right, ascending the hill to Mr Bullock's Firs, leaving out a field belonging to the Camp Farm, keeping close round an orchard to the Camp Mill-house, through which it passes, keeping inside the Waste, or Forest land, to a stone in the bank opposite the 'Plough'; crossing the road and along the brook, into the orchard. It then takes a direct line along a bank in the orchard, to a large tree or stone in Mrs Sinderby's hedge, up the road, through her Mill-house, along the path to Gwilliams; across his garden, leaving out the privy, to Mr Cannock's orchard; and then follow an old hedgerow above a spike gate and the next orchard, to the lane east of the stile opposite the T-stone. The Dirty Lane then bounds it to the top of the last field straight to the nursery or garden near the Turnpike Road. It then passes through the middle of the nursery to a Yew Tree, from thence down the road to the old Forge, follow the brook, taking in a nursery and meadow belonging to the Grove, and up the west side of an arable field called the Ten Acres to the road. The road then bounds it to Monk Hill Lane which is left outside, to the Wood. The brook then divides the parishes, to the lower corner of a meadow below Blaisdon Bridge. It then turns short to the left, following another brook to the upper corner of a pasture piece of Mr Gordon's called the Crofts, taking the whole of that into the top gate; then northside a ploughed field to the lane, taking the lane to the left, to the wood, leaving that out till you pass a large pool or marl pit. It then takes a line nearly north, including Major's Grove, Ley Park, Barn Wood and Lady Newburgh's Wood. It then goes outside Mr Probyn's land to the brook, crossing which to a Pollard Oak in the meadow near the mill stream marked W.-H. It then takes in the meadow to the Huntley Road and Wetlow Lane, to the end of Mr Probyn's land, to the brook. It then crosses the road and goes outside a meadow of Mr Parry's to the brook again below the Pidgeon House. [The last-mentioned brook bounds the parish from the Pidgeon House to the point where the said brook falls into the Severn at Denny Bridge. The river itself is then the boundary from Denny Bridge to the point of departure at Broad Oak.].*

W.E. Adams describes a lively occasion of only a dozen years later at Cheltenham:

> *The perambulation in 1845 was largely attended, as was likely to be the case when waggons laden with beer, cider, & penny loaves met the crowd at various points on the route. It was estimated that the followers, when the procession reached the Golden Valley, between Cheltenham & Gloucester, numbered not fewer than 2,000. Practical jokes were supposed to be permissible on these occasions. Boys were given 'something to remember' at disputable corners of the boundary, while young men & old, regardless of age or infirmities, pushed each other into ditches, rivers & horse-ponds. Unhappy (& in some cases even fatal) consequences occasionally resulted from these pranks. Thus in the perambulation of 1845 a retired tradesman who was thrown into the deepest part of the Chelt died from the effects of the immersion. The young fellow who did the mischief was tried for manslaughter, but acquitted. The reason alleged for thrashing boys and larking with elder people was said to be that the parties concerned would recollect the boundaries and the time they were beaten if the facts of the matter in after-years should be called into question. It was alleged to be necessary that the bounds should be traced whatever the obstacles in the way. Agg's House, a conspicuous mansion overlooking the town, was built in two parishes: wherefore a deputation from the crowd had to go through one window in the front and out of another at the back.*

Partly because of the fatality this was the last time the bounds were beaten at Cheltenham. Rev. G.E. Rees tells how he was reproached by the former parish clerk at Bagendon, who had retired in 1880, with no longer making traditional use of the Rogation Days:

> *Why ever dwont ee walk the bounds, same as ee owt ta? Now auld as I be waxed, I do mind every carnder a the parish - for why? There was Trinity Mill, whur Giles wur birched, an end o' Cutem Lane, whur same happened to I - an thur wur No Man's Land, in the burrow by Morwood, whur the dree parishes meet, an dree on us wur betten. Bys wur bys then, an men waz men.*

At Todenham, near Moreton-in-the-Marsh, the Rogation procession continued until at least the 1890s:

> *About 10.30 on the Monday morning, the parishioners are summoned by the ringing of the church bell, and, in obedience to the call, a goodly company of horsemen and footmen muster on the tiny village green. Presently a procession is formed headed by the band. Next come four sturdy yeomen armed with spades, and behind them the mixed multitude, amongst whom the parish clerk and the children hold a very special position. For it would seem that in their presence we may have the modern representatives of the old lay clerks*

*and singing boys, as they are specially invited, and at the close of the day a collection is made of money, which is equally divided among all the children who have made the round. By and by the edge of the parish is reached, and here the interest grows deeper. For now the four spadesmen come forward, and in pairs, facing one another, each casts up four spades' full of earth, which are piled in a heap in the centre, thus forming a deeply cut, well-marked cross. This ceremony is repeated at intervals of from two to three hundred yards (the same spots being chosen year after year) all along the boundary of the parish, and in the centre of each cross the parish clerk plants a sprig of green.*

*By and by a halt is called, when the parish clerk hands round his stock of well-thumbed copies of Tate and Brady, and solemnly, with uncovered head, all join in the quaint version of the 104th Psalm [including the verse, 'Thou hast set a bound that they may not pass over']. This done, refreshment is provided by the squire of the parish, or perhaps at one of the larger farm houses, and then the procession starts again, to repeat the ceremony, until late in the afternoon the task is completed, and weary but happy the villagers return to their homes. Meanwhile the women of the parish have each received from the squire's hand a present of food wherewith to refresh the tired travellers on their return, and the evening is devoted to innocent merry-making.*

Another account adds that the church bells rang to mark the occasion but that only half the boundary was walked each year. The rector led, followed by the squire, then the farmers, with the rest of the villagers bringing up the rear. One of the places where a psalm was sung is called Poors' Ground.

Larger parishes had greater difficulty. T.A. Ryder wrote: 'I can just remember that when I was a small boy before the First World War services were held at various points on the boundary of the very large parish of Westbury-on-Severn where I lived. The perambulation of the entire boundary had long since not been observed - it would have been a very long walk.' Stinchcombe kept up its Rogationtide bound beating until the 1950s, complete with procession, litany and psalms 103 and 104, though here again only part of the circuit was done. Perhaps this was the last parish in Gloucestershire to keep up the old custom, but by the 1980s others - Nailsworth and Tetbury, for example - were reviving it, though not necessarily at Rogationtide.

On Ascension Day some churches reinforced the gospel message by ceremonially hoisting an effigy of Christ to the chancel ceiling. On the same day the seven wells of Bisley are dressed with flowers by local schoolchildren, as they have been since 1863 when Rev. Thomas Keble borrowed what he had seen done in Derbyshire. The event now attracts several hundred onlookers, and in 1989 was extended for the first time to St Anthony's Well - famous since medieval times for its healing powers - at Flaxley. Blockley has a service on the church tower starting at dawn on Ascension Day, which formerly was followed by a local holiday.

The second Sunday after Ascension Day (and the seventh after Easter) is Whit Sunday. Some churches ceremonially renewed their floor covering of grass and rushes then: those at Tirley and South Cerney, for example. The custom continues at St Mary Redcliffe, Bristol. When after over two hundred years' work the building was almost complete, lightning struck the tower in 1446, and falling wreckage shattered the church roof. A wealthy merchant, William Canynges - the owner of ten ships, five times mayor of Bristol and twice its MP - paid not only for rebuilding but great embellishment. After his wife's death he became a priest and celebrated mass in the church for the first time on Whit Sunday 1468. When he died he could not be buried with his wife (already interred in the church in a splendid tomb with both their effigies), but separately (with a second, most modest effigy showing him as a priest). William Spencer, one of Canynges' successors as mayor, left an endowment in 1493 to commemorate that first mass, and since the following year Rush Sunday has been kept at St Mary Redcliffe. The pews are decorated with flowers, the floor is strewn with rushes, and the Lord Mayor (as he is now styled) and Corporation of Bristol attend, always sitting in the second pew on the south side of the nave, behind the churchwardens. The Lord Mayor is met at the church door by the Bishop of Bristol.

On Whit Sunday a bread and cheese dole still held at St Briavels (see Chapter Eleven) was moved from the church because of the boisterous behaviour it occasioned, though the event is now once again sedate. Another charitable distribution takes places at Aylburton Church every year on the first Sunday after 13 August - the sum of £16 to the poor of the parish. The money comes under the provisions of a will made in 1681 by Christopher Willoughby, a Wiltshireman who was travelling through Aylburton when as night was falling he experienced difficulties with the wheel of his coach. The people of the first house at which he asked for help turned him away. Those of the second gave both help and hospitality. It is possible that one member of the household later became his wife, for he did marry an Aylburton woman. His will specifically excludes members of the Andrews and Butcher families from benefit, and provides £1 for the minister to preach a sermon on love and charity.

On the Sunday after 14 September (Holy Rood Day) Pig Face Day was celebrated at Avening. The event is said to date from the time of Queen Matilda and the church's consecration in 1080, though some claim it stems only from the eighteenth century when a wild boar which had been terrorising the neighbourhood was killed in the woods. Pig's head and apple dumplings were eaten, with helpings carried to the ringers as they rang a joyous peal; public houses provided customers with free pig's face sandwiches. The celebrations petered out in the 1950s but in September 1992 the feast was held again with a concert, a service in the church and a meal (including pig's face). Local people hope to repeat the event every other year, thus re-establishing a tradition.

Another feast, at Painswick, was once marred by scenes which 'would have disgraced the most heathen nation'. So wrote Robert Raikes, proponent of Sunday schools, in 1786; and largely as a result of his efforts the event became a pious celebration of the nativity of the Virgin Mary in the form of a 'clipping' (embracing, or encircling) of the church by children on Feast Sunday (September 19th, or the Sunday following). By the 1850s even this ceremony lapsed, to be revived forty years later by Rev. W.H. Seddon. Included in the current service is a clipping hymn, 'Daily, daily sing thy praises'. The children are garlanded with flowers and given buns - though the fare was once puppy dog pie (see Chapter Three). On the Sunday before Michaelmas (29 September) nuts were once traditionally cracked and eaten during church services on what came to be called Nutcracker Sunday.

St Thomas' Day (21 December - see also Chapter Eleven) was often chosen for distributing the proceeds of parish charities. At Ashchurch a loaf of bread was given to those who attended church on Christmas morning, but since 1987 a homemade biscuit has been distributed to each member of the congregation present, at the end of the midnight service on Christmas Eve. The feast of Holy Innocents (28 December), marked by the muffled bell-ringing already mentioned, used to be the occasion preferred for children's parties. Nothing else would be undertaken on what was considered an unlucky day.

## Penitents and Parsons

A touching legacy of past parishioners is to be seen in Stanton Church. At the north-west end of the nave several bench ends are deeply ringed by the chains with which shepherds secured their dogs while attending services. Shepherds' devotions were not very frequent because of their duties, and some were buried with a tuft of wool to give evidence at the last trump of their calling.

A stone still standing outside the north porch of Lechlade Church may mark the spot where the errant stood to do public penance. A case is recorded from Elkstone in 1591 of a man called Cherington who was 'required to come into the church at the beginning of morning praier with a white sheete uppon him, a white rodd in his hand and bare-faced, and then and there standinge on a forme or high place confesse his fault.' By the nineteenth century the practice had become rare enough to warrant the attention of the press. The *Cheltenham Examiner* reported in October 1847:

> *An exhibition, fortunately of rare occurrence in these enlightened days, took place on Saturday, the 17th, at Cheltenham Parish Church. Throughout the week rumours had been afloat that some unlucky wight who had made rather free with the fair fame of his neighbours, had been ordered by the ecclesiastical authorities to expiate his offence by doing penance in a white sheet. It was asserted that the sheet, tapers, and other paraphernalia of the ceremony, had been duly provided by the churchwardens, and the curious in such matters were of course on the tip-toe of expectation. Saturday morning came, and towards ten o'clock some hundreds of persons found their way to the church, where the presence of the curate, the churchwardens, and a proctor from the Consistorial Court, seemed to*

*give colour to the prevailing rumours. A large white cloth, which hung most suspiciously within the vestry door, also gave 'confirmation strong' to the reality of the coming ceremony, and the eager sightseers arranged themselves in the most convenient parts of the building to witness it. The galleries were filled with a motley assemblage of both sexes, every seat and pew in the vicinity of the communion table were crowded with occupants, and the old structure presented more appearance of a theatre, or a cockpit, than of a place of Christian worship. Fortunately for public decorum, all this eager curiosity was doomed to disappointment. About twenty minutes after ten the culprit entered the church, and proceeded to the vestry; but there were no bare feet, no white sheet, no lighted tapers, but a simple form of recantation was read over and subscribed to, and the crowd who thronged the sacred edifice, finding there was no fun to be seen, quietly dispersed.*

One admires the writer's ability to find so much mileage - or lineage - in such a non-event.

Clergymen and their flocks from time to time find themselves at odds. After fifty-five years incumbency at Stow-on-the-Wold, Rev. R.W. Hippisley resigned in 1899 only after townspeople had demonstrated their displeasure by hanging him in effigy. At roughly the same time Rev. Sidney Rimmer was so unpopular at Eastcombe that his effigy was burned in protest. For the same reason the incumbent at Kempley was treated to rough music. For three nights running parishioners marched round the rectory blowing trumpets, beating drums and shaking tin cans and kettles filled with pebbles. The rector left within a few days. Such was the childhood recollection of James Maile, who died in the late 1960s.

By contrast Rev. W.H. Seddon was very popular with his Painswick parishioners. However, he took an old man to task for ceasing to attend services when regular collections were instituted. 'You ought to be glad to give your last penny to Jesus Christ,' said the parson. The reply came as quick as a flash: 'Ah, so I would if I thought he'd get it.'

Finance comes into another story, from the Forest of Dean, where a poor old man desperately needed £10 to buy a cow. He wrote a letter asking for this sum, addressed it to God, and dropped it into the poor box in the church. The parish clerk found it and passed it to the parson, who said: 'I'll take pity on the poor old chap. Here's a fiver. Let him have it from me.' A little later a second note turned up in the poor box: ' Dear God, thank you for the fiver. Please let me have another but not this time through the bloody old parson because he stole half of what you sent last time.'

Canon Harry Cheales was the vicar at Wyck Rissington for thirty-three years from 1947. Shortly after arriving he persistently dreamed of a maze with large numbers of people working their way through it. He set about planting what turned out to be six hundred yards of willow hedge to build the maze in his garden, and opened it to the public in 1953. Sadly, when he retired in 1980 the vicarage was sold and the maze bulldozed. He died four years later, at the age of seventy -three. He is remembered both as an exorcist (see Chapter Six) and a cricketer.

Finally, they tell at Bledington of a parson from Leafield who was visiting a house during Passion Week to tell a woman about the crucifixion. This seemed to be new to her, and she remarked: 'You say, sir, as all this 'appened long since?' 'Why, yes,' he answered. 'Well then, sir, let's 'ope as t'ent true.'

5

# DEATHS AND ENTRANCES

'Death,' said a Forester, is 'one thing we all got to look forward to, if we do live long enough.' If the prospect concentrates the mind it also inspires many beliefs and customs - though attitudes and practices have undoubtedly become more matter-of-fact in recent years. Birth, the first major step we all take, also had its thicket of prescriptions and taboos. These, too, are thinning - not least the stigma attached to child-bearing out of wedlock. In 1992 one baby in four was so born in Gloucestershire; one in three nationwide.

The village wise women who helped at birth and death are gone and with them, to quote Rev. G.E. Rees of Bagendon, their 'true wisdom and immense usefulness'. Those of both sexes who healed by charms have disappeared, too. They operated by a mixture of magic and psychology, and any cures they achieved may have been on the principle that if a patient believes strongly enough in a given treatment it will often work. Warts - as orthodox medical opinion confirms - are especially susceptible to suggestion. Yet it may be worth adding that charmers also cured animals.

One old countrywoman of the past may have led scientists to the discovery of aspirin. She was gathering simples (plants and herbs for medicinal purposes) in the rectory garden at Chipping Campden. The rector asked why she collected willow bark. Her answer - to make an infusion to soothe headaches - led ultimately to the use in aspirin by the German chemical firm, Bayer, of the salicylic acid present in willow (*Salix alba*).

It has to be admitted that some of the effects of folk medicine must have been non-existent at best and absolutely horrific at worst: the reaction of a rabies sufferer to being forcibly ducked in the sea is almost too terrible to contemplate; yet this was the remedy once used. Such a step amounted to pure superstition, and there were literally hundreds of such beliefs, creating a hazardous jungle of obstacles to life and happiness through which people picked their way with the greatest of circumspection.

The mass of vegetation is now heavily cut back, partly because of the generally rationalistic climate of opinion, partly because of technology, with candles, lanthorns and even open fires no longer featuring in people's lives. Yet ancient fears are seldom far distant, despite the paraphernalia of modern life. A newspaper reported in April 1993: 'Tourists all over the world are returning stones illegally taken from Ayers Rock in Australia, in the belief they are cursed by evil spirits. Ian Irvine, acting manager of Uluru National Park, said some people thought the stones brought them bad luck, marriage break-up and ill-health.'

The institution of marriage itself is in decline. The number of first-time marriages is the lowest for a century; and nationally there is one divorce for every two marriages. Attitudes to sexual relationships are much more relaxed (some would say merely lax) than formerly, but we should not be condescending about the past. James Elroy Flecker (1884-1915), best known for *The Golden Journey to Samarkand*, wrote:

*Have I not chased the fluting Pan*
*Through Cranham's sober trees?*
*Have I not sat on Painswick Hill*
*With a nymph upon my knees,*
*And she as rosy as the dawn*
*And naked as the breeze?*

Folk wisdom - and a great deal of this is encapsulated in pithy rhymes and sayings - makes the point less exuberantly but nevertheless effectively, when one remembers that all the year round gorse is in blossom somewhere:

*When goss be out of flower,*
*Kissing be out of favour.*

Nevertheless, many people still derive satisfaction from a wedding with all its rituals and ceremonies, great and small. Rites of passage help us through our deaths and entrances.

## Death Signs and Grave Humour

A robin pecks three times at a window pane, a dog howls at the moon, a hen crows like a cock: these were among the many things taken to warn of an impending death. Other omens include the screech of an owl, the death of any white bird on one's premises, or the fluttering of doves or white pigeons against a window at night. The sudden departure of mice from a house - or for that matter a sudden infestation - pointed to a death in the family.

The people of Soundwell, near Mangotsfield, particularly dreaded the sight of a hob lantern or corpse candle, for its flickering light signalled an imminent death. An unexplained bang on a window pane, the fall of a picture from its hook, the untimely stopping of a clock: these were further signs.

Putting green holly on a fire could even cause a death; so could taking into a house any of these: peacock feathers, May blossom, quaking grass, or flowers removed from a grave. On the other hand the presence of a pigeon - or even simply its feathers - could delay death. In Churchdown (and elsewhere) it was considered that no one could die comfortably on a bed with pigeon's feathers in pillow or mattress, so if any doubt arose on this point a moribund person would be laid on the floor. Conversely, when a dying man at Bourton-on-the-Water sent for an absent child to bid farewell, his friends strove to ensure that he lasted long enough by putting a live pigeon under the bed.

Joe Watkins of May Hill told me how in the spring of 1990 as he was talking to an eighty-year-old neighbour a big black crow flew down and landed on a tree in the garden. The man shouted: 'Yes, and you can bugger off. I ain't ready to come with you awhile yet.' One evening a fortnight later the same crow landed on the road, waddled down the middle and turned into the man's garden. Next day he died.

Two more strange stories concern foxes. Major Gerald Gundry, joint master of the Beaufort hounds, died in the winter of 1989-90. At the very next meeting after his funeral the hounds, which had met miles away, took their own line, ran all the way back to Gundry's house at Shipton Moyne and killed a fox outside the front door.

The Duke of Beaufort himself was out walking early one Sunday morning in 1984, when he was eighty-five, with his fox terrier Ajax. In the churchyard at Badminton they came across three foxes, one sitting on his grandfather's grave, one on his father's, and the third in the open. The duke was unconcerned enough, and Ajax happily scattered the foxes; but a friend thought:'The third was for him.' He died the following Sunday.

A corpse taking too long to cool or go rigid betokened another death in the family. At Stanway they believed that if a burial took place on New Year's Day it could be followed by one in every month of the year (which would have doubled the death rate in the parish). Elsewhere some thought if a woman were the first in a village to die in a given year the greater mortality during the following twelve months would be among women; a man's death betokened a similar fate for his fellows. Some considered that if a corpse lay unburied over a Sunday another death would occur within the week (Churcham), month (Stanway) or merely soon (Bourton-on-the-Water). Because of a similar belief - that if a grave were dug on a Saturday and left open on a Sunday the devil would get in to wait for the soul of the person to be buried - funerals seldom took place in the Forest of Dean on a Monday. At St Briavels the custom of paying a toll of one penny per burial is still remembered. People once thought that anyone keeping watch in that churchyard for two hours from 11 p.m. on New Year's Eve would see the likenesses of all those in the parish who were to die during the ensuing year.

At the moment of death, doors and windows were thrown open to allow the deceased's soul to pass forth. As recently as 1991 a nurse at the Gloucestershire Royal Hospital told me (after first glancing round to make sure she were not overheard) that she always opened a window for this reason as soon as a patient died. The passing bell told others in the community that a soul was taking flight. At Willersey each of the six church bells was tanged once for a child, twice for a woman and three times for a man; then the tenor bell tolled a knell. Miss E.M. Hartland noted in 1892 that Miss Heath, the daughter of the vicar of Hucclecote, told her that if a bell kicked back and repeated the sound while a knell was being rung, there would be another death within three days. An instance of this occurred at Hucclecote. In the 1950s Miss E. Kirby remembered how as a child of ten she climbed the forty-eight steps of Minchinhampton church tower to ring a bell for one hour before and one hour after each funeral - for which she received 3d. When John Byng was passing through Gloucester in 1781 he wondered why the bells were 'ringing merrily at a funeral'. He received the explanation 'that it was usual at the interment of a ringer.' Until at least the First World War a peal followed every funeral, 'to frighten away evil spirits.'

Thunder and lightning at a funeral boded ill for the fate of the deceased in the afterlife, or so they thought at St Briavels. On the other hand, rain augured well: 'Happy the corpse the rain rains on.' 'If it doesn't rain,' said one man, 'then they go to the wrong place.' At Bisley they had strange fish-tailed coffins with a special division for each foot, through this curious practice disappeared by the end of the eighteenth century. One Winchcombe woman had a hole made in each end of her coffin so that when the devil came through one she could creep out of the other.

Bearers took pains to carry a coffin over a stream, since they believed the devil could not cross running water. Their route in general required careful choice because of the notion that to carry a coffin over a piece of land established a right of way. Bier Way Piece at Guiting Power may have been on the path funerals took to a chapel which has now gone. The Funeral Path at Newland is a cobbled lane formerly used when the dead were brought from Coleford for burial. On Cox Hill at St Briavels is a stone where volunteer burying parties set down their burden before handing over to the formal bearers who went on to the church. In the porch of St Peter's at Willersey is a resting place for a coffin. At this point bearers were customarily presented with black gloves. At Great Rissington until the 1950s coffins were always borne on the shoulders of male relatives or friends of the deceased, but now a bier is used.

There is a record at Newent that Jane Mayo (buried in 1705) was 'so fat and large, that she was carried to church by twelve men, not on their shoulders, but by laying hold of small poles, under the coffin, on each side; and the wall of her house was broken, to bring her forth.'

A Saxon chest eight feet long and three deep, known as 'the mortuary', is preserved in Awre Church. Bodies used to be kept in it prior to burial.

At Aylburton it was considered an essential part of a child's education to learn how to stand still by the side of the road with bowed head as a funeral passed; but 'the discipline must have been sorely tried on the occasion when the hearse fell in the brook near the church and there was much ado to retrieve it.' A bier in Deerhurst Church, dating from about 1696, carries this inscription:

REPENT : O MAN : WHILE : THERE : IS BREATH :
THERE'S : NO : REPENTANCE : AFTER : DEATH.

Attitudes were not always so solemn. A Mrs Blocksum of Prestbury died in 1763 at the age of 103. She had previously claimed she would rise again a few days after death, 'and therefore declared that her coffin lid should be taken off when she was interred, which was performed agreeable to her request.' The *Gloucester Journal* tartly commented: 'If the old woman should be as good as her word, our readers may depend upon hearing of it.'

Ethel Smith, who died in 1981, related an apparent resurrection:

> *I well remember my father and mother talking about a man who lived in Box and worked in the Woodchester valley. It was during the winter months and there had been a lot of snow at the time. One night he did not get home during a heavy snowstorm and the next day he was found dead in a snowdrift on Culver Hill. His body was taken to 'Amberley Inn' and he was, it is said, put into his coffin without removing his clothes or boots. Now in those days funerals from Box were always walking funerals. For these a self-appointed man would call around the homes of the people saying something like this. Mr So and So had died and the funeral would be on Saturday afternoon. 'Could you help?' Funerals were always on Saturday afternoon or Sunday afternoon. This was because it was the only time that they could get enough men to carry the coffin the one mile to Minchinhampton, shoulder high, or push the parish bier. Well, when his coffin was brought to his home and his funeral started and the relay of bearers was being changed, they were startled to hear a continuous knocking from inside the coffin. They were quite relieved, on getting to church, to find that it was that rigor mortis had given up, and it was his boots tapping the coffin sides.*

In the Forest of Dean the expression 'gone to oontshire' meant dead - an oont being a mole. F.W. Baty found more macabre humour when asking for directions to the remote farm of a person he calls 'Mr M.':

> *I was given detailed instructions, including references to several trees of various shapes, and a careful description of the dog at the cottage where Mr M. did not live. I moved on, expressing thanks as I went, when my guide called out, 'Thee s'll have to hurry, mind.' I asked if Mr M. was known to be going out, to which the reply came, 'Ay, they'm putting 'e under in 'arf-hour, see.'*

In the Cotswolds, H.J. Massingham was told of the burial of a 'kyantankertus covey ... an ungain mon to look at - sadly out o' shape his kyarkus was to be sure - and the poor mon's voice was like the squaking of a starling.' At the graveside:

> *as soon as they was a-bowsing the coffin, it slips off the webbings, and lands skew-wift into the grave. Old Tad sees this and says out loudish, 'Dang you, Jonas! You was allus a kyantankertus covey when you was alive, and lummydays! if you can help being occud now you be djud.'*

Massingham tells a more decorous story, that of Farmer Stanley of Ebrington, who died one April. He provided in his will that on the anniversary of his death each year boughs of cherry, pear, plum and apple blossom be laid on his grave, and for a fee of ten shillings a sermon be preached by the parson on the excellence of Cotswold orchards. In addition, his three labourers were to be given five shillings apiece every year to drink his health in the 'Ebrington Arms'. It would be interesting to know when this last happened.

No such sweet repose or lasting respect could be accorded to suicides, who at best were buried in unconsecrated ground, and in earlier times at a crossroads with a stake through the body. Dabb's Elm (now gone) near Winchcombe grew from just such a stake; so did Maud's Elm (see Chapter Two) in Swindon Village. Ellis's Cross (Chapter Six) at Four Oaks and Chapman's Cross at Sapperton both take their names from suicides. Charles Meredith, whose death in 1879 led to the taunt of the Dymock man without a shirt (Chapter Three), is reputed to have been buried as a suicide outside the churchyard wall but to have finished in consecrated ground when the plot later expanded.

Uley's Charles Hillier, a wooden-legged veteran of the Peninsular War, died in 1876 at the age of ninety-two. He remembered the discovery in a stream below Grimhill of a skeleton thought to be that of a Scottish pedlar who had disappeared some years earlier. Foul play was suspected, so the skeleton was laid for three successive Sundays in the church porch. Hillier explained: 'If the man as murdered him came by it would bleed.'

Timothy Mountjoy gives an account of another Scottish pedlar killed and robbed near Littledean in 1834. Two men on whom suspicion fell were made to touch the corpse. Mountjoy, who was present in the crowd, reported that the 'nose was as white as before, and no signs of blood.' One presumes the men were released.

A century later when Mr Adlard, the owner of Postlip Mills, died the workers were invited to pay their respects by filing past the corpse. As they did so each man and woman - all local people - touched his hand. When Mr Adlard's daughter asked the foreman why this was done he replied: 'To prevent the spirit from haunting them.'

Until perhaps the 1950s news of any death was usually given to bees. E.A.B. Barnard tells of an Aldsworth woman who had broken her leg. While she was convalescing her husband died, and as soon as she possibly could she hopped down the garden on her crutches to tell the bees. She stood in front of the hives and chanted:

*Bees be said your master's dead,*
*And you must work for me.*

'Otherwise,' she explained, 'they'll all take and die too.'

They believed at Northleach that if bees were not told of a death the honey would go off and they would do no more good. At Great Rissington people thought the bees would desert, so they knocked three times on each hive and said: 'Your master's dead.' As a coffin was raised to begin its journey to the churchyard at St Briavels, hives were lifted; failing this, the bees would die. Rev. G.E. Rees at Bagendon was surprised to hear from his handyman, Richard Townsend, that bees also need to be informed of a birth: 'Bad luck if they byaint tauld.'

## Wise Women, Charmers and Healers

Until two generations ago Forest of Dean women put a knife below the bed during childbirth to 'cut the pain'. At Churcham it was considered very unlucky for a cat to have kittens in a house on the day of a baby's birth, since either kittens or baby would die. On no account was hawthorn brought into a house at Bagendon with a new baby, because this would bring about the child's death within the year.

Village midwives - wise women - would give advice on all such matters. A baby would be carried upstairs before it went down, to ensure it would rise in life. If this were impossible someone would climb on to a box or chair with it. Another pitfall to be avoided was that of the new-born's catching its first sight of the moon through glass.

Until well within living memory it was considered unlucky for women to go out after child-bearing before undergoing the purificatory 'churching'. At Bagendon no woman would allow a new mother into her house before she had been churched; if such a person were so ignorant or insensitive as to call she would be given a chair in the garden.

Nor should a new baby go out before baptism, for fear of various malign influences. At home the unchristened infant might be protected by crossed pins stuck in its clothes, open scissors hung over the cradle, or the father's trousers laid over it.

Whit Sunday was thought an ideal day for baptism, and those within reasonable striking distance would delay until then. For a child to cry out at baptism augured well, since it marked the departure of evil spirits. At Churchdown if several children of both sexes were being baptised at the same ceremony girls invariably took precedence; otherwise they would have been in danger of subsequent marriage to tyrannical husbands. A possible corollary would have condemned boys christened first to effeminacy.

It is a tradition in the Jenner-Fust family at Hill Court, near Berkeley, to give only one Christian name to each child because no one with more has ever inherited the estate. Norman Jewson wrote of an 'exceptionally prolific innkeeper' called Gardiner who fathered a great many children at Oakridge, and although they were mostly born out of wedlock, 'he acknowledged them all as his own, so that they took his name.' Since many also had the same name there were difficulties in distinguishing between them, so it became customary for them to have their father's first name added. Harry Seth Gardiner was not confused with Harry Caleb Gardiner; and in the course of time there was even an Albert George Eli Gardiner. Common surnames also caused difficulty in the Forest of Dean, in which cases families adopted other names for everyday purposes. Another expedient, with first names, was the addition of a nickname: 'Ambulance' Dennis, 'London' Dennis or 'Gloucester' Dennis.

After baptism at Churcham the parish nurse would use any sanctified water remaining to wash out the child's mouth as a safeguard against toothache. The same kind of guidance and advice was offered by healers and charmers such as Ann Townsend, wise woman of Bagendon and wife of Rev. Rees' handyman. She provided for the first Rees baby - whom she called 'the lil' maid' - a charm against teething problems, fits and convulsions, to be hung round the neck: 'a heart-shaped silk bag padded and quilted like a small cushion - the size of a florin, with a secret inside - never to be left off till it wore through of itself.' When it did wear out it was found to contain hairs from a donkey's neck at the cross where the black and white stripes meet. Jesus is supposed to have sat in front of Mary at that place on the flight into Egypt.

Ann Townsend also removed warts, including those of one of the Rees grandchildren. Her method was simply to rub an elder stick on the warts after cutting a notch in it for each of them. She buried the stick, and as it decayed - which could be several months afterwards - the warts disappeared.

There are many accounts of such practitioners, often anonymous, like the Cromhall blacksmith who in 1648 cured scrofula; the old woman living much more recently in Wye Bridge Street, Monmouth, who charmed burns for the Brockweir children whose parents walked them up the riverside footpaths to meet her; or the Saintbury man, still alive in the 1920s, of whom Algernon Gissing wrote that he was 'chiefly in request for cases of erysipelas, but seemed to be called in for any infirmity.'

Alice Mumford of Willersey was famous for predicting the weather. Billy Oakel, a Marshfield hatter, had a wife who told fortunes by means of cards. She could also render people incapable of movement by pointing at them with a stick. One night when Billy arrived home in White Hart Lane he found that he had mislaid his parcel of groceries. His wife said: 'Go back, and just before you get to Oakford you will meet Mr Jones, and he will have your parcel.' She proved to be correct. When Billy died she belaboured his corpse with a broom, remarking that he had thrashed her often enough when he was alive, so she would now treat him in the same way. After she died her ghost was seen in the churchyard.

Some doubted the powers of such people. Benjamin Evans of Box, a cunning man and soothsayer, claimed the ability to tell fortunes and gave a horoscope for a shilling. A failed attempt to trace stolen property led to a year's imprisonment combined with one hour's exposure in Stroud pillory on market day once a quarter for a year, starting in January 1815. He was 'plentifully assailed,' we are told, 'with wordy wit and coarse jest.' Two other Stroud practitioners seem to have avoided such penalties: Sarah Creed of Silver Street, 'the cunning woman who is said to have been the most celebrated fortune teller of her day'; and Philip Wood, a Painswick clothier who set up as astrologer in Stroud and lived near the Greyhound Inn. He died at Whiteshill in 1855.

John Oakey, who was born at Winchcombe in 1847 and published his reminiscences almost ninety years later, remembered a man called Prophecier

William, 'who held forth for hours on the sun, moon and stars, and he knew no more about them than those to whom he was preaching... I can see in my mind's eye the little groups listening intently to him.' Oakey is less sceptical about 'another strange character', who lived in an old, one-roomed, thatched cottage on the Greet Road, Charles Pardington:

> *He had a quarry on Cleeve Hill which he worked all day by himself. He was called the 'cunning man', and by some the 'devil's man' on account of the uncanny things he did, for he professed to find out thieves and evil doers. He was of rather superior education to the ordinary run of the class. In some of these cases he was successful and thus upheld his reputation. He even aspired to conduct an evening class in his cottage during the winter. He was killed in 1864 by a fall of rock in his own quarry.*
>
> *One of his cases occurred almost next door to where I lived. A small shopkeeper, a woman, lost various small sums from her till, so she employed Charles Pardington to find the culprit. Charles secretly questioned her children, of whom she had several, and he also talked to the neighbours and to another shopkeeper. Eventually he fixed it (rightly no doubt) on her eldest daughter. He sought the mother and told her he had found the thief and asked what punishment she wished to inflict on the guilty one.*
>
> *He was to inflict all the curses he was master of, and this he did in his mysterious way with weird signs and mysterious words. He later made known the culprit, who then received a terrible beating. After a day and night's reflection the mother decided that Charles should remove the curses, which he did in the same mysterious manner. Being purged of her sins, the daughter afterwards married and lived to a good age ... Charles also, to my knowledge, found the thief who stole his mate's tools - again enhancing his reputation.*

Margaret Eyres writes enthusiastically of 'a most famous charmer' at St Briavels, 'a man resorted to by the afflicted of villages ten miles distant, both for themselves and for their beasts.' She describes a lesson in charming which he gave her:

> *Old Luke Page is a partial cripple, but a fine handsome old man, with shrewd clear-cut features and a humorous eye. He is an excellent judge of character, intuitively suiting his own methods to the company, but with a real belief in his own gift. In his early days he was a butcher in good standing, and is a man of some education. When I went by appointment to his cottage I was courteously invited to a seat, and it was explained to me that, whatever I said, I was to give no thanks to him. Luke and his old woman - a little shrivelled thing, with the face of a hungry bird - sat on either side of the wood-fire, and a weird black hen sat upright like a penguin in the doorway, and watched me with intelligent eyes whilst the charmer spoke*

*gravely and reverently of his art. That I came from four generations of clergy impressed him greatly, and added much to my fitness to receive the power.*

*'You do want to know how to charm? Well, Missy, 'tis easy; but you must have the love, and you do have to be steadfast. How to do it? Well, 'tis like this. Suppose some one should come to 'ee, an' they have an arm or a shoulder out. You must know the Christian name, and, if it be an animal, you do give him one. You do get hold of the person, and examines the place and handles it over, wherever the place is, and you will know by your own inside what 'tis when they comes to 'ee. You've no need to tell they nothing nor let others know; and see here, Missy, 'ee mustn't never tell a woman the way, because of halving the power. Then you fetches out the complaint. You got to know the Christian name for it to come right.*

*'Rub with the right hand and say: "Father, Son, and Holy Ghost, great God above, send all things right, bone to bone, marrow to marrow, blood to blood, and flesh to flesh, in this right arm of James Reynolds. Send all things right in the name of the Father, Son, and Holy Ghost." Then you do mention the Lord's Prayer. Do this two or three times all to yourself, handling it. Never say them the charm, say it to yourself.*

*'And the same if it was scalds or burns or toothache, or anything. You got to be steadfast, and you got to say the Lord's Prayer. The quicker 'tis done after the injury the sooner 'twill come good. An' you got to take no thanks, but thank the almighty, and keep it to yourself.'*

Luke Page died in December 1904. Other procedures which he or his wife described include the writing of charms on pieces of paper to be carried by sufferers (or the ink washed off and drunk); the burning of salt at midnight to summon a man who had 'wronged' a girl (though ideally this should be avoided as 'the devil's work'); and after turning a key in a copy of the Bible putting it (the key, not the Bible) down the back to stop nose-bleeds.

Another version of the last technique was employed in 1551 by William Newport, vicar of St Owen's, Gloucester. After inserting the key he tied up the book with string, invoked the Father, Son and Holy Ghost, and invited the key to turn when he read out the name of a person guilty of theft. It did turn when he came to the name of Margaret Greenhill, and those involved immediately left the church to look in the woman's bed-straw for the missing property, a handkerchief. Newport was suspended, but claimed a royal pardon on the ground that the sortilege, as it was called, took place 'betwixt Easter and Witsontide was a twelve-moneth'. He was deprived of his post some three years later for being married.

Several formulae for charms have been preserved in a manuscript book compiled at Minsterworth between 1770 and 1796. They include:

*A Charm for a Borne [burn] or a Scold. Mary mild as burned her child and on a Spark of Fier out Fier in Frost in the name of the Father Son and holy Gost Amen amen amen.*

*A Charm for stoping Blood, I Believe Jesus Christ to be Son of god, he was born of the virgin Mary and was Baptised of John the Baptist in the River Jordan the water was wide and red he commanded and it stood so stand ye Blod in the name of the Father Son and Holy Gost Three persons in Trinity & one God Good Lord do this in Charity for they Saarvant Amen, This Charm must be repeated five tims.*

*A Charm for the prick of a Thorn In Bethlehem our Christ was Born they crowned his head with Nails and Thorns Let no flesh corropt in him I tack and the lord heal, pray God prosper my handy works Amen amen amen.*

*A Charm to put in a Horses or Beast shoulder or when they have rested their foot on a stub Thou hast hair to hair skin to skin flesh to flesh Bone to Bone god Bless thou and thy masters and his Estate and all his Cattles an Chattles With hout his gate for Jasus O Christ sake Amen This Charm must be repeated Evry Night and morning 9 times Each time for 9 nights and mornings.*

*for the ague*
*Abracadabra*
*Abracadabr*
*Abracadab*
*Abracada*
*Abracad*
*Abraca*
*Abrac*
*Abra*
*Abr*
*Ab*
*A*
*Gloria Excelsis Deo.*

Such formulae might seem to us pathetic, ridiculous or even ludicrous (with Christ appearing to be an Irishman). Yet they commanded widespread belief, not merely in the eighteenth century, but until the twentieth. Robert Belcher of Withington died in 1911 at the age of ninety. A photograph shows him with the black box in which he carried the wares - cotton, thread, buttons, matches, pins, needles and also herbs - he hawked from village to village. He claimed to be 'in touch with those on the other side,' and styled himself a prophet. He predicted weather, foretold the future, and charmed warts. In his later years he was a well-known figure in Cheltenham, where he travelled every Saturday by train to sell the skins of rabbits he had trapped.

Mrs Ellen Hayward of Cinderford died only a year after Robert Belcher, at the age of seventy-four. She was a wise woman, herbalist and dresser of sores, cuts and wounds. She claimed to have cured eight cases of cancer, while adding: 'You can't cure a cancer when it has spread in more than 13 different directions.'

In 1905 she was asked by John Markey of May Hill village to trace £50 missing from his house which the police had been unable to recover. Within a week of her intervention several members of Markey's family began to show signs of mental illness and one attempted to commit suicide at Blakeney. His wife disappeared for several days, to return distraught, and clutching a hazel stick which she claimed kept witches at bay. People in May Hill and Huntley took to carrying similar sticks.

A question was asked in Parliament about witchcraft at May Hill. A journalist from the *Weekly Dispatch* went to see Mrs Hayward: 'Her hair is tangled and tousled and ragged, grey wisps hanging about her unquestionably dirty, old face. But she is not without a merry twinkle in her eye at times, and her deeply-line cheeks bear wrinkles of good humour and kindliness.'

Mrs Hayward wrote to the *Dean Forest Mercury* to defend herself against accusations of witchcraft:

> *I am widely known through Gloucestershire and the surrounding counties and I wish to emphatically deny that I am a witch (so cruelly called by the press) nor am I a fortune teller or hand reader. I have no knowledge of such pagan ideas. I have no power or ability to bewitch anyone nor do I believe in any such thing. I am only as other of my unfortunate sex - human. I have a knowledge of phrenology, but from this get no portion of my living. I make no charge but leave it entirely to those who have required my services to give me as they please.*

Nevertheless she appeared in court at Littledean in 1906, in connection not with the Markey affair but with James Davis of Pauntley - or rather the pig which he had paid her to cure. The charge (presumably under the Witchcraft Act of 1735, which said that people were not to be prosecuted for witchcraft - because there was no such thing - but for fraudulently pretending to be witches) was that she 'unlawfully did use certain craft or means or device, to wit by pretended witchcraft deceive and impose on one of H.M. subjects.' The case was dismissed.

In 1991 I interviewed in Cinderford a Mrs Lily Mills who had been treated as a small child by Mrs Hayward. She had no recollection of the encounter herself but had been told of it by parents. Mrs Hayward, no doubt embittered by the court case, had greeted them at her door by saying: 'Oh, you be come to th' old witch, are you?' She was wrinkled and bent. Chickens roamed freely round her living room. Little Lily's parents had taken her because doctors said her leg would have to be amputated. Mrs Hayward supplied a homemade salve which did 'the world of good', and Lily still had her legs almost eighty years afterwards. The house in which the Markeys lived (now called 'Counties View') still stands - in Folly Lane.

## Curious Cures

The curative powers of various objects with religious associations were highly prized. Even in the late twentieth century the carving in Lechlade Church of St Agatha - whose martyrdom involved the excision of her breasts (miraculously restored by St Peter) - is a symbol of hope for women who have undergone mastectomy.

Grease from the church bells at Oxenton and Winchcombe was applied for shingles. The practice dates from pre-Reformation times, when bells were blessed, baptised, exorcised and anointed with holy oil. Even older is the use of vervain (*Verbena officinalis*) as an amulet to ward off evil. The Romans called it *herba sacra*, and some said it was used to staunch Christ's wounds on the cross. As a child in the manger at Bethlehem, Christ had protective web woven round him by spiders, which may explain the insect's reputation for healing. Cobwebs were used to staunch bleeding (a practice whose effectiveness modern science has confirmed), and rolled into a pill and swallowed to prevent an attack of ague.

The cross itself was a powerful symbol. To ease a burn one made a cross in spittle on the affected part, then covered it with leaves of mallow (*Malva sylvestris*) - the former having antiseptic, the latter soothing properties. A small cross of 'ellan' (elder wood) grown in a churchyard could be carried to keep rheumatism at bay. Other possibilities were to wear a skein of silk round the waist or to carry a potato, an onion or the fore-foot of a mole. Some believed that confirmation helped, and Emma Dent reports that in an effort to relieve his pain an old servant at Stanton Court went through the ceremony three times.

The elder was viewed with mixed feelings, since it served for the crucifixion of Jesus Christ as well as the hanging of Judas Iscariot. Another candidate for Christ's cross was the poplar, of which one variety - the aspen - has trembled ever since. For that reason a cure for diseases which involved trembling could be obtained by cutting off a lock of the patient's hair and pinning it to the tree.

Silver coins given in church collections were sought to make a ring which cured the wearer of epilepsy. For internal troubles a Good Friday cake was grated into water, and the mixture swallowed. This was not really a cake but a small piece of dough left over from bread making, baked in a flat round shape.

Even without religious associations, some objects had special virtues. The skull of a Roman woman called Julia Casta (chaste Julia) was once kept in a summer house at Cirencester. Eventually all the teeth disappeared, having been stolen for use as amulets against ague. For drunkenness a violet might be worn round the neck. The gall of a wild rose carried in the pocket was thought to prevent toothache. For fits or St Vitus Dance a ring was worn, made by a bachelor silversmith - depending on the area - of three, five, seven or nine sixpences obtained from the same number of bachelors. A necklace fashioned from hairs taken from a grey stallion's tail was believed capable of reducing a wen on the neck.

Certain rituals were also thought to be efficacious. For rickets until at least the 1920s a child was passed through a hole in the Longstone at Minchinhampton (the apertures remaining would not now be big enough), or through a cleft in an elder tree. For whooping cough at Gretton in the 1890s a child was pulled three times on three successive mornings at dawn beneath a briar rooted in the earth at both ends. A variation consisted of passing a child nine times under and over such a briar. Another possibility - and the profusion of would-be cures from whooping cough underlines how common it must have been - was to ask a man leading or riding a piebald horse; and 'whatever him do say will cure the cough.' Someone who often faced the question always replied: 'Patience, and water gruel.'

A sufferer could be passed over and under the back of a donkey - with the cross on his back the animal was seen to be special. A sandwich with twenty hairs from the child's head could be given to the first dog that passed. Valerie Grosvenor Myer, who was brought up in the Forest of Dean, writes: 'In 1937, aged two, I had whooping cough. The doctor recommended rubbing my feet with garlic which they eventually managed when they had subdued me by rolling me in a towel and holding me under the parental arm. His name was Fletcher and he had the usual medical degrees.'

The technique of passing on diseases was also tried with snails. For ague the snail was kept for nine days in a bag worn round the neck, and then thrown into the fire. If it shivered in burning a cure had been effected. For warts, a black snail was pricked as many times as there were warts, then hung on a thorn bush; this was at Upton St Leonards. At Poole Keynes the offending excrescences were rubbed with a broad bean pod which was then buried. This was also done at Nailsworth, where bacon sometimes served the same purpose. Rubbing the patient's warts on a pig's back might also have the desired effect. At Great Rissington the warts were rubbed with a piece of raw meat which was then secretly buried. When the charm was tried in the 1950s it did not work, 'for this generation is lacking in the faith of its forefathers.'

Gravel was rubbed on warts, then wrapped in paper and thrown over the left shoulder. Whoever picked up the package would receive the warts. Alternatively, as many pebbles as there were warts could be put into a bag and thrown over the shoulder, or into water. A pin might be driven into an ash tree with the words: 'Ashy tree, ashy tree,/Pray buy these warts off me.' In the Cotswolds sliced potatoes were placed on the warts; or a potato with a cross cut in it was thrown away, with this formula:

*One, two, three,*
*Warts go away from me.*
*One, two, three, four,*
*Never come back to me no more.*

Water often played a part in these treatments. For boneshave (now better known as sciatica) a sufferer sought out a stream running south, lay beside it and repeated three times:

*Boneshave right, boneshave straight,*
*As the water runs by the stave,*
*So follows boneshave.*

A stream running from Langley Hill, near Gotherington, was thought to give relief for sore eyes because 'the waters run against the sun'. Many holy wells (see Chapter Two) were good for eye troubles; so was rainwater collected on Holy Thursday, Good Friday or St Swithin's Day. A Dymock observer noted in 1900: 'An old woman in Leddington, for many years on Holy Thursday, when it rained, caught the rain in a bottle as it fell. The rainwater thus collected is a certain cure for bad legs and sores. But it must fall direct into the bottle, held in the hand, or it is of no effect.'

One Forester suffered from abscesses round the eyes. He sought advice from an old gypsy woman, who advised him to bathe the places with his own urine. People at Brockweir believed that children bitten by a mad dog should be rushed to Chepstow to be bathed in the sea. There is no record of the cure's having been tried, which is something of a relief.

In the Forest a gypsy's wedding ring was rubbed on a stye to effect a cure. Gypsies also rubbed hedgehog fat into the scalp to keep the hair plentiful and prevent its going grey. The fat from badgers caught on the Good Friday hunt once regularly held at Chedworth was applied to the skin for strains, sprains and rheumatism. Jack Roseblade of Poole Keynes recommended - and used on himself - for boils a concoction largely made of cow dung.

For both external and internal use herbs were very widely used. J. Arthur Gibbs noted this Ablington lore from an 'old gentleman':

*First of all you must know that the elder is good for anything in the world, but especially for swellings. If you put some of the leaves on your face, they will cure toothache in five minutes. Then for the nerves there's nothing like the berries of ivy. Yarrow makes a splendid ointment; and be sure and remember Solomon's seal for bruises, and comfrey for 'hurts' and broken bones. Camomile cures indigestion, and ash-buds make a stout man thin. Soak some ash leaves in hot water, and you will have a drink that is better than any tea, and destroys the 'gravel'. Walnut-tree bark is a splendid emetic; and mountain flax, which grows everywhere on the Cotswolds, is uncommon good for the 'innards'. 'Ettles' [nettles] is good for stings. Damp them and rub them on to a 'wapse' sting, and they will take away the pain directly.*

Rev. Harry Clifford, writing from Bourton-on-the-Water in 1916, adds:

*Sandwiches made of Dandelion, Yarrow, etc., are a splendid medicine; tea made of Yarrow, Coltsfoot, Camomile flowers, Horehound, Nettle, Hops, Agrimony, Dandelion, etc., are all excellent remedies. When stung by a nettle, the first remedy flown to is a Dock leaf. The leaves of Geranium, and of St Joseph's Lilies, draw matter from one side and heal with the other; House Leek or Singreen, Mallow, Comfrey, Solomon's Seal, etc., make excellent remedies; an ointment made of the Pilewort is a certain cure for piles; the young shoots of Hops when cooked cannot be detected from Asparagus; the heart of a roasted onion put into the ear, as hot as can be borne, is a splendid remedy for ear-ache... the juice of Poppies, and water in which eggs have been boiled, are said to cause warts. Tea made from Mistletoe berries is said to be an excellent remedy for St Vitus's Dance. Boiled Violet leaves are a cure for cancer.*

In *A Child in the Forest* Winifred Foley writes: 'Mostly our Dad cured us with his home-made potions. He gathered elderflower, yarrow, camomile, and other wild herbs, dried them and stored them in brown paper bags for his bitter brews. Constipation, coughs, colic sickness, diarrhoea, sores, fever, delirium - whatever we had, out came the dreaded brown jug, and on the hob it went with its infusion of herbs.' Again in the Forest, an infusion of alder leaves or beech buds was taken for boils or piles. A plantain leaf applied to a boil or sore at bedtime would draw out any pus by the following morning. Hot cider with rosemary served as a cold cure. 'Ellum blow' (elderflower) tea provided another possibility, hot at bedtime or cold before breakfast. The flowers were gathered in summer, dried, and saved. An infusion of rue revived the appetite.

Elderflowers mixed with lard made an ointment for chapped hands and sore patches on the skin. A poultice of lily-of-the-valley or ivy leaves served to draw wounds. At Wickwar lily leaves were applied directly to cuts, and dock leaves to stings. An old Dymock man's precept was: 'When you cut yourself always lay some bacca on the wound. It will draw the venomy out.' In the Forest the leaves of 'snompers' (foxgloves) were boiled to make a disinfectant used on dogs and in houses; mullein leaves were used to pad out ill-fitting shoes.

Skin ulcers, boils and swellings responded to a poultice of chickweed or of mallow leaves. Mallow roots, crushed and mixed with unsalted lard, were applied to varicose veins; so was water in which the leaves and flowers of marigolds had been steeped. The bruised leaves of the mallow were laid on sore eyes and also boils. A poultice of hot mashed turnips was also used to treat boils. The juice of red campion squeezed on corns made them shrivel and come out, as did the juice of the greater celandine or an ivy leaf soaked in vinegar.

Tansy tea was recommended at Great Rissington for palpitations; elsewhere it was thought both to aid conception and - if taken in large quantities - to bring on a miscarriage. The mandrake could cure sterility and act as an aphrodisiac. The root of valerian also served as a mild aphrodisiac and stimulant. The plant (*Valeriana officinalis*) has been used in this way at least since the time of the ancient Greeks. Joe Watkins of May Hill knows of a very rare variety (*Valeriana phu*) which he calls God's Hand Leaf - a name apparently not recorded in print. A leaf of this, wrapped overnight around a festering sore on a finger, will draw the poison and effect a cure.

At Wickwar, nettle tea served 'to clear the winter's dirt' from people's digestive systems. Camomile tea relieved indigestion. Vervain (see above), which grows plentifully near Olveston, was used for scrofula or the king's evil - so called because another cure was the touch of a king. No one picked vervain without first crossing himself.

## Good Luck and Bad

A host of actions or signs point to good fortune or the reverse. On a personal level it is lucky to carry a holed stone, to pick up a piece of coal (in the Forest of Dean) or to see a blind man in the street (at Lydney). Some beliefs are confined to a particular place or even family. In Newent there was a saying that 'Whoever drinks the Court pool water will never forsake the town.' The Fletcher family, members of which have run the 'Hobnails Inn' at Little Washbourne since Lady Day 1743, considers that bad luck would follow if a particular settle in the bar ever left the premises.

Actors are noted for their superstitions, and one person's knitting at rehearsals is supposed to have caused a production to fold in 1987 at the Everyman Theatre in Cheltenham. I spoke in the theatre in 1991 to Roger Hendry (technical manager), Carol Ball (actress) and Sheila Mander (play director), who were unanimous that it is unlucky to mention or quote from 'the Scottish play', which is their way of referring to *Macbeth*. When the play is produced incidents and even accidents invariably occur.

Although they relax in a Green Room (which is not necessarily green), actors carefully avoid wearing green on stage. Carol Ball forbids whistling in her dressing room. An inadvertent offender must leave, then turn round three times outside the door, knock for re-admission, then swear: all this to avert ill-luck. Sheila Mander believes that some superstitions are now dying out but when she sends a card to wish a colleague well with a production she always writes 'have fun', lest she offend anyone who still considers that in the theatre it is bad luck to wish good luck.

In pantomime it is universal not to sing the closing couplet at the final dress rehearsal but to replace it by 'da di da' or similar vocables. Many actors have individual rituals in dressing - always right sock first, and so on - very much like professional cricketers and soccer players.

According to Roger Hendry there is never a completely full house at the Everyman. One seat is always apparently empty, since it is occupied by the ghost of a worker who fell to his death from the roof just over a hundred years ago when the theatre was being built.

In private houses, too, there are similar pitfalls and omens. Itching in the right eye points to a surprise; in the nose, to anger; in the right foot, to a journey. Itching in the right hand means money coming in; in the left, it's going out. Signals from sneezing vary with the days of the week:

*Sneeze on Monday, sneeze for danger;*
*Sneeze on Tuesday, kiss a stranger;*
*Sneeze on Wednesday, get a letter;*
*Sneeze on Thursday, something better;*
*Sneeze on Friday, sneeze for sorrow;*
*Saturday, see your true love tomorrow.*

Omens of good luck are to meet a black cat or a frog; to see the new moon over the right shoulder; to see crickets, spiders or ladybirds in the house, or for a swallow to fly down the chimney; to find a double nut, or four-leafed or a two-leafed clover. To find a horseshoe is lucky, and the more nails in it the better the luck. It should be taken home and nailed over the door with the ends uppermost, or the luck will run out.

Signs of impending bad luck include seeing the new moon over the left shoulder or through glass; destroying swallows' nests; putting an umbrella on a bed or opening one in the house; walking under a ladder, unless one spits afterwards; lending a pair of bellows or putting one on a table; transplanting parsley.

It is unlucky to burn bread, old shoes or hair and nail clippings. Although salt is in the same category the taboo is overridden when an evil omen needs to be reversed. For example, it is (or was) 'dreadful bad luck' to put a lanthorn on the table, but the ill can be averted by throwing salt on the fire. Burning elder wood is unlucky, especially in the house (where the devil enters, or sits on the chimney pot, if this is done), though the tree itself provides good shelter in a thunderstorm since it is seldom struck by lightning.

Several flowers are unlucky if they are brought into the house. Until recent times the people of Duntisbourne Leer and Great Rissington thought this the case with Candlemas Bells (snowdrops). Bunches of violets, as well as being unlucky, harboured fleas and stopped hens from laying. May blossom was thought unlucky in the house under any circumstances. At Cheltenham, as well as snowdrops and may, it was considered unlucky to take indoors any flowers used in children's games - daisies (because of daisy chains), for example.

At Northleach people said: 'Never give a bunch of flowers unless you slips a sprig of rosemary in it. It'll bring the receiver good luck, and bad to you if you forgets.' Rosemary is thought to flourish on premises where the mistress is master, which compares with:

*Where the sage is seen in flower,*
*There the good wife hath the power.*

Birds, insects and animals feature in a range of beliefs. The small first egg laid by a pullet should never by brought into the house, but thrown over the roof so that ill-luck would pass over likewise. At Great Rissington a swallow flying into a window pane portended bad luck but the deposit of any bird's droppings on the glass was a sign of good fortune. The sight of a single magpie points to bad luck, which can be averted by several expedients: raising one's hat (which also applies to jackdaws), bowing, reciting the Lord's Prayer, repeating the alphabet backwards, making the sign of the cross, or saying 'Good morning, sir.' The 'magot's' evil reputation stems from the belief that it was the only bird excluded from the ark by Noah. At St Briavels the number of magpies or crows seen had particular meanings: one for ill (with the variation that one seen after dinner brings good fortune), two for good, three for a disappointment, four for a letter, five for something better, six for a wedding, and seven for a burying. On the other hand, the sight of seven rooks at evening is a good omen, as it is for rooks for to build a nest near a house. For them to forsake it is the reverse, and they might do this if they were not informed of a death in the family. If flocks of rooks fly towards their nests at noon it is a sign of rain to come.

It is unlucky to kill a blackbird or 'God Almighty's cock and hen' (the robin and hen). It is lucky to find a hairy caterpillar on one's arm or shoulder, or to hear a cricket sing in the house. Spiders must be carefully preserved from harm. A Bagendon variant of the well-known saying runs:

*If so be you look to thrive,*
*Let a spider bide alive.*

The first butterfly seen in the year is significant: white means good fortune; brown, bad. If the first lamb of the year is seen tail first it is also an unlucky omen.

T.A. Ryder was told as a small boy living in Elton, near Westbury-on-Severn, that pigs could see the wind, which is why they became uneasy during a gale. People could acquire the same ability by running round a church seven times backwards. A horse taken to be sold at Churchdown market always had a new halter, whereas a stray destined for the pound was led by a wisp of straw. In horse dealing this rhyme provided guidance:

*One white stocking, buy me;*
*Two white stockings, try me;*
*Three white stockings, doubt me;*
*Four, be wise, and do without me.*

'Never buy a horse with a curly mane' was a further axiom; another: 'Buy a cow with teats like four Easters' (that is, wide apart).

## More Wisdom - and Weather

Prudent housewives at Churchdown pricked a cross on the dough before putting loaves to bake, lest these fail to turn out well. If butter were slow to form in the churn they stirred it with a sprig of rowan and beat the cow with a spray from the same tree. Both cross and rowan had power against witchcraft, as did the plant variously called silgreen, Jupiter's beard and houseleek. Its Latin name, *Sempervivum tectorum*, points to the practice of its being grown on roofs to afford protection against both evil spirits and lightning. At Minchinhampton the bay tree was thought a good lightning conductor. At May Hill the houseleek was often planted on the pigscot. One of its fleshy leaves would be broken, and the juice applied to remove a wart.

Peonies warded off evil, and their roots were worn by teething babies. As with the mandrake, digging up peony roots could be hazardous lest the devil who lived beneath uttered a shriek which might prove fatal. A piece of meat was therefore hidden very close to the root and a hungry dog was led to it in the hope that he would unearth both meat and root. Parsley, too, had a dark reputation, its notoriously slow germination explained by the belief that it went to hell and back seven times before coming up. Transplanting it (like the lily-of-the-valley) was unlucky, and sowing could be done only by the true head of the household - and this must have given rise to many an argument.

The ideal day for sowing parsley was Good Friday, together with potatoes and broad beans, but nothing else. Other work, too, was severely restricted: 'Cursed is the woman that wash and dry of a Good Friday.' At Avening even cutting nails and turning mattresses were taboo. Baking might be done, as long as one loaf from the batch were kept for a year. Crumbs from it might be taken for various ailments.

Blacksmiths might not use hammer and nails on Good Friday since this was the day Christ was nailed to a cross. Some thought any Friday, by extension, unlucky for changing a bed, taking medicine or starting a new undertaking, including a journey.

The time for runner bean planting varied from one district to another. At Cam 6 May, the day of Dursley Fair, was preferred, and wives insisted that husbands do the planting before going to the fair, lest they return incapable. The villages round Stow-on-the-Wold chose 12 March, the day of Stow Fair; and the same day found favour in distant Dean Forest (where they believed in planting shallots on the shortest day of the year, for harvesting on the longest). Another fair, that of Lechlade on 9 September, dictated when winter cabbage should be planted so that - as George Swinford relates - it would be ready for the following Whitsun.

In general, seeds were set at the waxing of the moon. At Broad Campden corn was always put in 'at the coming up of the moon', up until the 1930s, and it is interesting that experiments by Rudolf Steiner a decade later confirmed the wisdom of the practice. A Chipping Campden farmer said: 'Cut the lambs' tails in the rising moon and a south wind blowing, and never kill a pig when the moon be a-wasting.' It was widely thought that if this were ignored the bacon would not take the salt required for curing, or that it would waste away in the pot while cooking.

Although people thought it unlucky to see the new moon through trees or glass, they considered it lucky to turn money in the pocket on seeing it - a belief recorded in the Forest as early as 1822. Various rhymes gave the predictions afforded by the moon: 'The moon on her back holds water in her lap' (rain); 'In the waning of the moon/A cloudy morning, fair afternoon'; and 'A Saturday's moon and a Sunday's full/Never brought luck and never ull.'

Wood cut at the moon's waxing would last longer on the ground. Different trees attracted particular beliefs. Beating walnut trees - thought to increase their yield - was done at Cranham until within living memory. The merits of alder were stated in rhyme:

*Thatch me well and keep me dry;*
*Hearts of oak I will defy.*

When apples were picked one fruit was always left on each tree. Blossom and mature fruit on a tree at the same time foreboded ill:

*A bloom on the tree when apples are ripe*
*Is sure termination for somebody's life.*

The flowering of apple trees gave a message to cider makers (and drinkers):

*When apple trees blossom in March*
*For your barrels you need not search;*
*When they blossom in April,*
*Some of them you may chance to fill;*
*But when they blossom in May,*
*You may drink cider all day.*

Much weather lore is expressed in traditional rhymes and sayings. Cows lying down, cats playing, rabbits feeding by day, donkeys loudly braying, peacocks screeching, thrushes sheltering by hedges or wagtails by farm buildings, all these were taken to indicate rain. From Bourton-on-the-Water alone one can add:

*Frogs coming into the road; a tight blind cord; flowers such as Scarlet Pimpernel close their petals; cat washing over its ears; the new moon lying on its back; a piece of seaweed hung in the house will be moist; a haze or ring round the moon; a very clear atmosphere, bringing distant objects near; a cloud rising over Clapton; a red sky in the morning; sheep and other cattle restless; if sheep are in a field that is higher at one end than the other, they will keep to the lower end; swallows flying close to the ground; cocks crowing later than their usual time; gnats flying low; wild geese or wild fowl flying over the village predicts rough weather; large black slugs on the roadside.*

Dr Edward Jenner of Berkeley devoted an entire poem to the subject:

**Signs of Rain**

*The hollow winds begin to blow,*
*The clouds look black, the grass is low,*
*The soot falls down, the spaniels sleep,*
*The spiders from their cobwebs creep.*

*Last night the sun went pale to bed,*
*The moon in halo hid her head.*
*The boding shepherd heaves a sigh,*
*For see! a rainbow spans the sky.*

*The walls are damp, the ditches smell,*
*Clos'd is the pink-eyed pimpernel.*
*Hark how the chairs and tables crack,*
*Old Betty's joints are on the rack.*

*Loud quack the ducks, the peacocks cry;*
*The distant hills are looking nigh.*
*How restless are the snorting swine,*
*The busy flies disturb the kine.*

*Low o'er the grass the swallow wings,*
*The cricket too how loud it sings!*
*Puss on the hearth with velvet paws*
*Sits smoothing o'er her whiskered jaws.*

*Through the clear stream the fishes rise.*
*And nimbly catch the incautious flies.*
*The sheep were seen at early light,*
*Cropping the meads with eager bite.*

*Though June, the air is cold and chill,*
*The mellow blackbird's voice is still.*
*The glow worms numerous and bright*
*Illumed the dewy dell last night.*

*At dusk the squalid toad was seen*
*Hopping and crawling o'er the green.*
*The frog has lost his yellow vest,*
*And in a dingy suit is dressed.*

*The leech disturbed is newly risen*
*Quite to the summit of his prison.*
*The whirling winds the dust obeys*
*And in the rapid eddy plays.*

*My dog so altered in his taste*
*Quits marrow bones on grass to feast.*
*And see, yon rooks, how odd their flight,*
*They imitate the gliding kite,*

*Or seem, precipitate, to fall*
*As if they felt the piercing ball.*
*'Twill surely rain, I see with sorrow,*
*Our jaunt must be put off tomorrow.*

Some of the wildlife of the eighteenth century - the leech, for instance - is no longer seen in the Gloucestershire countryside. The ayquil (woodpecker, from the French *aiguille,* needle) is still with us and Upton St Leonards' inhabitants used to say it foretold rain when it 'hollered weet, weet'.

Many sayings about the weather had strictly local application. A Sapperton shepherd, Harry Allen, told Norman Jewson that if an evening mist dispersed next morning down the valley to Chalford the day would be fine, but if it rose to cover the top of Dorvel Wood rain would come instead: 'When the mist climbs up the hill,/It sure will come back with a swill.' A variant of this rhyme is: 'Mist on the hill/Brings water to the mill.'

At Wotton-under-Edge a local landmark features in meteorology:

*When Wotton Hill doth wear a cap,*
*Let Horton Town beware of that.*

Humblebee How is another hill, near Winchcombe (and close to Belas Knap):

*When Umblebee Oo puts on 'is cap,*
*Afore long t' weather ull sure to be wet;*
*But agun t' sun on 'e do shine,*
*Thee's can bord [believe] as t'ull be fine awhile.*

A forecast for Rodborough people is provided by the bells of Woodchester:

*Bring out your sou'westers*
*Say the bells of Woodchester.*
*All right, old thing,*
*Answers Rodborough, ding, ding.*

Not surprisingly, different predictions arise at different times of year. In the following selection several items come from inscriptions on the windows of Toddington Manor, which was built in the early nineteenth century.

**January**
*If grass in January appear,*
*No grass will grow throughout the year.*

*If the first of January be smiling and gay,*
*You'll have wintry weather till the first of May.*
*If St Paul's* [25 January] *be fair and clear,*
*Then betides a happy year.*
*If blustering winds do blow aloft,*
*Then wars will trouble us full oft.*
*But if it chance to snow or rain,*
*Then will be dear all sorts of grain.*

**February**

*February fills the dyke,*
*Whether with black or white.*

*Of all the months of the year,*
*Curse a fair Februeer.*

*Badgers come out of hibernation on Candlemas Day* [2 February].

*When the wind's in the east on Candlemas Day,*
*There it'll stick to the first of May.*

*If it rains at Candlemas it will rain for forty days after.*

*If Candlemas Day be dry and bright,*
*The winter shall have another bite.*

*Crows begin to build on 1 February unless it is a Sunday* [Cold Aston]. *Birds choose their mates on St Valentine's Day* [14 February]. *Housewives should throw out bits of fluff and hair from combs and brushes to help provide nest-building materials.*

**March**

*A dry March never begs its bread.*

*Dust in March is worth a guinea a bushel* [Willersey].

*On March 1st keep your windows shut lest black soldiers* [fleas] *come in* [Minchinhampton].

*There will be as many frosts in May as there are fogs in March.*

*When you can put your foot on ten daisies, spring is here.*

**April**

*When April blows his horn*
*'Tis good for hay and corn.*
*If the first three days of April be foggy there'll be a flood in June.*

**May**
*If you shear a sheep in May*
*You shear it all away* [May Hill].

*Buy brushes in May,*
*Sweep your luck away* [Lydney].

*Two moons in May,*
*Neither fruit nor hay.*

*Who doffs his coat on a winter's day*
*Will gladly put it on in May.*

**June**
*Moist in May, heat in June,*
*Makes the harvest come right soon.*

*If it rains on Midsummer Day the nuts will be spoiled.*

*A dripping June brings all in tune* [Upper Slaughter].

*Rain on 8 June foretells a wet harvest.*

**July**
*If on St Swithin's Day* [15 July] *it rain,*
*For forty days it will remain.*

**August**
*Dry August and warm*
*Doth harvest no harm.*

*A fair and clear St Bartholomew's Day* [24 August] *presages a prosperous harvest.*

**September**
*September blow soft*
*Till fruit be in the loft.*

**October**
*Good October, a good blast*
*To blow the hogs acorns and waste.*

**November**
*November takes flail;*
*Let ships no more sail.*

*If the wind is in the south-west at Martinmas* [11 November],
*There is stays till after Christmas.*

**December**
*A green Christmas (or a hot May) brings a full churchyard.*

*When frosts and snow are both together,*
*Sit by the fire and spare shoe leather.*

Many other saws applied to things other than the weather. These might by wry, as in 'Glaastershire miles be long uns', stern 'Us unt be druv', or self-deprecating:

*Gloucestershire born and Gloucestershire bred,*
*Strong in th' arm and thick in th' head.*

While some sayings were widely known, others circulated only in particular villages, or even families. 'A good year for nuts - a good year for babies' goes back to the times when young men and women went out in September gathering hazel nuts together, and had wide currency. On the other hand, 'Everybody to their liking, as the old lady said when she kissed her cow' may come only from the Dean Forest grandmother of the writer, Valerie Grosvenor Myer. The village of Maisemore offers, among many expressions, 'in Rumble's Meadow' (in the wrong) and 'to cry Bill Tinker' (make a great noise). 'A nimble penny is worth a slow sixpence' comes from Upton St Leonards; and from Kingswood, near Wotton: 'You can always find it on Mary Burden's shelf' (that is, the floor). The Redmarley way of stating that a woman is reliable - 'She's a white hen's chick' - might well be attributed to a potential bride.

## When Shall We Get Married?

One answer to the question posed in a song well known in the county is: 'Not at all'. This was the case with some couples in the Forest of Dean, where a clergyman complained in 1865 that:

*A sort of temporary concubinage was invented, known as a 'lease', binding the parties to live as man and wife for an agreed number of years. Even now there are couples, with no excuse of distance or ignorance, living in this way; and the lawyer is yet living who was most in repute as a drawer of these leases in late years.*

Yet romantic love also flourished in the Forest, where elaborately carved wooden spoons - in a custom borrowed from Wales - were fashioned and offered during courtship. Communities fiercely protected their young women from outside suitors, and this could be as little as a few miles away - from Pillowell to Yorkley, for example. A Ruspidge man who attempted to court a

Ruardean wench (the term was not derogatory) was driven from the village by local men and pelted with stones as he crossed, ironically, a piece of ground called Fair Play. Some villages, though, permitted outsiders to court local women provided they paid their footing - a round of drinks at the local pub.

Winchcombe youths believed that putting the herb Lad's Love (*Artemisia abrotanum*) in their shoes would help them find a partner. A woman attempted to identify a future spouse by several stratagems. She made a cake on Christmas Eve in absolute silence, then scored her initials on it and left it to bake in the dying heat of the oven. She went to bed, leaving the front door of the house ajar so that her lover or his spirit could enter and inscribe his initials next to hers. The compact would be sealed when she ate the 'dumb cake', as it was called. Another ritual required a candle with two pins stuck horizontally through to make a cross, each piercing the wick. As the pins were pushed through the woman intoned:

*It's not the candle I wish to stick,*
*But —'s heart I wish to prick;*
*For whether he's asleep or whether awake,*
*I want him to come to me and speak.*

The man's image would then be seen.

Midsummer's Eve offered two more opportunities. At midnight the woman went into a churchyard and, strewing hempseed behind her without looking back, repeated:

*Hemp seed I scatter,*
*Hemp seed I sow.*
*He that is my true love,*
*Come after me and mow.*

She then ran out and, if she were bold enough, turned to see the vision of her lover, scythe in hand.

The second ritual is for both sister and brother. She lays the table with bread, cheese and cider; he opens all the doors. They sit down at the table, with prayer books open at the marriage service. Both keep silent. At the stroke of midnight two shadowy forms glide in, sit down, eat and drink, and then leave. These will be the future partners of the sister and brother. If instead a coffin appears, neither will see another midsummer.

Many of these ideas are now completely unknown to most young people. Adages such as 'Marry in May, rue for aye', 'Marry in Lent, sure to repent' may be known, but ignored. The story of a lovelorn blacksmith, too shy to propose, also smacks of yesteryear. The object of his affections, a poor spinster in his own village of Cherington, made a modest living by boiling and selling toffee. She was too proud and too modest to seek a husband, but one day she knelt in church and prayed aloud: 'O Lord, please be mindful of me and send me a man to marry.' By chance the blacksmith was aloft in the belfry, mending the church clock. He heard the prayer, and boomed back in what he took to be God's voice: 'Will a blacksmith do?' 'Ern a man's better than nern, dear Lord,' replied the woman. Leaving the church by a back door, the blacksmith ran home, changed into his best suit, and caught the woman as she walked home. He proposed, and was accepted. They married, and lived happily, with toffee making in the forge alongside blacksmithing.

At Cromhall, near Thornbury, it was customary for the congregation to call out 'God speed them well,' after the third reading of the banns. Some thought it unlucky for both partners to hear all three readings. The practice of banns dates from 1139, though it was not rigorously followed until an Act of Parliament which came into force in 1754. Before then, some parsons conducted ceremonies quickly and quietly, with few questions asked. One of these was Rev. Simon Hughes, rector at the tiny church of Hampnett from 1733 until 1771. Before 1754 he married 346 couples; in the next fifty years and more both he and his successor managed only fifty-three between them.

A curious note in the parish register for 1732 at Horsley reads: 'John Pegler and Ann Thomas were half married, 11 August. I proceeded no further, because they paid me but one half, viz. 2s 6d.' What happened to the couple subsequently does not seem to have been recorded. Perhaps they were half married for the rest of their lives. Eight years earlier Rev. Prior of Elkstone complained that he received only *unum tantum solidum* (a mere one shilling) from Joseph Still and Mary Pool, but he did complete their marriage ceremony. It was usual for the fee to be placed on the book with the ring during the service.

At Alveston Joe Nutt, a ragman, proposed living with a woman after his first wife's death, rather than re-marrying, because he could not afford the fee. Then he accepted the ceremony free of charge offered by the vicar, Rev. Langley, but paid later - by means of a load of manure.

A cautionary tale used to be told in the Forest of Dean that if a bride who was not a virgin walked down the aisle in a white dress it would turn to grey before she reached the altar. During Winchcombe weddings the altar was covered with a coarse table-cloth holding two oval glasses and the register. To this day at Upper Slaughter and at Compton Abdale (and probably elsewhere) white ribbons are neatly fastened to the ends of pews in the church on wedding days.

The *Gloucester Journal* reported a minor scandal from Northleach in 1762:

> *A young Girl of about 20 Years of Age having sworn a Child upon an old Man of 60, a warrant was granted for apprehending him, and he was taken into custody, when it was put to his choice, whether he would go to Gaol, or marry the Girl. The poor old Fellow, after a long Deliberation, determined on the latter, and so to Church they went, escorted by the Parish Officers and a numerous Company of Attendants. The Man went through the several Parts of the Ceremony with tolerable Resignation, and the Girl performed her Part with Propriety enough till she came to these Words, Wilt thou*

> *have this Man to be thy wedded Husband? to which she answered, No! and on being asked a Second Time replied I won't! and immediately took to her heels, and ran out of the Church, to the great Joy of the Bridegroom and the Entertainment of the Spectators.*

Such reluctance was far from the thoughts of a Marshfield man, who when the parson asked, 'Robert, wilt thou...?', blurted out: 'Iss, iss. Whoi, that's what oi be cum for.'

Until late in the nineteenth century every married pair at Tetbury was presented with a Bible and prayer book, paid for by two legacies. At Buckland a fine mazer (from the Dutch, *maeser*, maple) bowl preserved in the church is painted green outside and white within. Until perhaps the early nineteenth century, at the end of wedding ceremonies wine and wafers (popularly called sops) in the bowl were blessed by the priest, then consumed by the bride, groom and congregation. (Gremio in *The Taming of the Shrew* (III, ii) relates how Petruchio 'Quaffed off the muscadel,/And threw the sops all in the sexton's face.')

Bride and groom might hasten to rise from their knees after the nuptial blessing if they believed that the first to do so would be master. Leaving the church after the service could also present a dilemma, since the first to do so would be the first to be carried back in a coffin. A Woodchester bride tells this delightful story:

> *When we was starting for the church my mother comed to the door and called arter us, she did: 'Now when you and William do come out of the church, as soon as you be made man and wife, mind, child, as you have a keer which on ee do step furst acrost the threshold of the dure'; but when comed out, that flustered I was, I clean forgot all about what Mother said, and couldn't think nothing about fust or last, but my lad, he hadn't a-forgot, and as we came to the church dure, he up wi' his 'and, and arount my waist it wer in a twinklin,' and, 'My lass,' he said, soft like, 'let's step o'er threshold together, my dear.' And so us did.*

As she left the church, in addition to confetti an onion would be thrown after the bride to ensure that she threw away tears, and bore many children. In the Forest of Dean - there are reports from Aylburton, Coleford and Tidenham - church gates or bridal conveyances were roped until the bridegroom threw handfuls of pennies. The custom continued at least until the 1950s, though by then the roping was done by children rather than adults. Across the Severn, adults at Great Rissington still maintain the tradition that a bride must be lifted over the churchyard gates by the groom - though 'it has been known for the assistance of the best man to be needed.'

After the ceremony the bridesmaid would plant the sprig of myrtle (symbol of fidelity) carried in the bride's bouquet in the newly-weds' garden. She would also make a point of sleeping with a piece of wedding cake under her pillow to ensure that she dreamed of her future husband. It was lucky for the bride to cut the first slice of cake; the reverse if she sampled the cake before her wedding day. The groom had to pass a tiny piece of the cake through the bride's ring - and this was the only occasion when she could remove her ring without risking ill fortune.

Despite all the care taken in choosing a spouse and in carrying out all the ceremonies in due form, marital discord inevitably arose. Wife-beating attracted community disapproval, expressed by the placing of a heap of straw on the offender's doorstep. A wife's beating her husband was regarded as more serious. A case described early this century to Rev. E.C. Scobell by his parishioners at Upton St Leonards involved the depositing of the offending woman's effigy 'under Pinlock' - that is, in the Pound. After she had paid a shilling for its release it was publicly burned.

Scobell also relates how 'tanging' or 'rough music' took place if bells were not rung at weddings or if 'certain offences against the public conscience' were committed. He probably meant adultery or incest. Even so, a vestry resolution passed at Upton in 1858 fulminated not against such offences but the protests at them:

> *The practice of assembling a rough band to the annoyance of individuals and disturbance of the public is an evil which ought no longer to be suffered. This meeting therefore pledges itself to use its utmost power to discourage and put an end to such practice if again attempted.*

Just before the First World War 'a notorious offender against morality was burned in effigy at Nailsworth.' At South Cerney wrong-doers were thrown into the River Churn, or their effigies paraded round the village before being publicly burned. If those so treated ventured out they would be followed by a 'tin band'. The name of Skimmington Hill near Chedworth may derive from the parading there of offenders or their effigies astride a pole.

Such treatment probably made people desist from certain behaviour, become more discreet, or move elsewhere. In about 1910 a married man, Alderman Westerway, proposed to run away with his mistress. At Cinderford railway station he was confronted by his own effigy and a cacophony of saucepans and other vessels. The ceremony shamed him into returning to his wife. In 1973 Katharine Briggs was told by a Mrs Rogers of Painswick how two maiden ladies of the village, the Misses Mason of Beacon House, became so meddlesome and autocratic that their effigies were paraded by torchlight before being burned on Beacon Hill. 'The Misses Mason...walked quietly up and down the street looking at the procession, apparently quite unconcerned, and no one molested them.'

As in the last case, such expressions of communal anger went beyond marital matters. Some industrial instances are given in Chapter Eight. A suspected murderer was burnt in effigy before his own front door at Moreton-in-the-Marsh in 1865.

A punishment which at one time could be ordered by magistrates was that of ducking in water. Originally applied to both sexes for the use of false weights and measures or the sale of adulterated food, this came predominantly to be applied to 'scolding and unquiet females'. Records of the punishment at Tetbury continue until the seventeenth century. The place used was a pool at the bottom of Gumstool Hill. Duck Street at Winchcombe owes its name to the same activity. A building at Northleach now known as the lock-up was used to store both the stocks and the gum-stool, which was probably used in the millpond by the church.

*Ducking in the water was a punishment for 'scolding and unquiet females'. Duck Street in Winchcombe so derived its name.*

To return to marriage, couples who found life together intolerable resorted - though in small numbers - to a form of poor people's unofficial divorce known as wife selling. A handful of cases have been documented in Gloucestershire, dating from 1760 to 1841, and occurring at Bitton, Bristol, Cheltenham, Cirencester, Gloucester and Minchinhampton. In 1902 an eighty-four-year-old woman from Upton St Leonards told Rev. Scobell how she had gone to a Mop with a halter round her neck to sell herself to a new husband. However, the usual form involved the husband's selling his wife, almost invariably with her consent, and often with prior agreement on the new partner.

The occasion in 1838 when a Thomas Barnett sold his wife in Gloucester cattle market to a man called Beard for 1s 6d is described by H.Y.J. Taylor, a schoolboy at the time who even took a minor part in the proceedings:

ACCOUNT OF THE

# SALE of a WIFE, by J. NASH,

## IN THOMAS-STREET MARKET,

On the 29th of May, 1823.

This day another of those disgraceful scenes which of late have so frequently annoyed the public markets in this country took place in St. Thomas's Market, in this city; a man (if he deserves the name) of the name of John Nash, a drover, residing in Rose-mary-street, appeared there leading his wife in a halter, followed by a great concourse of spectators; when arrived opposite the Bell-yard, he publicly announced his intention of disposing of his better half by Public Auction, and stated that the biddings were then open; it was a long while before any one ventured to speak, at length a young man who thought it a pity to let her remain in the hands of her present owner, generously bid 6d.! In vain did the anxious seller look around for another bidding, no one could be found to advance one penny, and after extolling her qualities, and warranting her sound, and free from vice, he was obliged, rather than keep her, to let her go at that price. The lady appeared quite satisfied, but not so the purchaser, he soon repented of his bargain, and again offered her to sale, when being bid nine-pence, he readily accepted it, and handed the lady to her new purchaser, who, not liking the transfer, made off with her mother, but was soon taken by her purchaser, and claimed as his property, to this she would not consent but by order of a magistrate, who dismissed the case. Nash, the husband, was obliged to make a precipitate retreat from the enraged populace.

Copy of Verses written on the Occasion:

COME all you kind husbands who have scolding wives,
Who tho' living together are tired of your lives,
If you cannot persuade her nor good natur'd make her
Place a rope round her neck & to market pray take her

Should any one bid, when she's offer'd for sale,
Let her go for a trifle lest she should get stale,
If six pence be offer'd, & that's all can be had,
Let her go for the same rather than keep a lot bad.

Come all jolly neighbours, come dance sing & play,
Away to the wedding where we intend to drink tea;
All the world assembles, the young and the old,
For to see this fair beauty, as we have been told.

Here's success to this couple to keep up the fun,
May bumpers go round at the birth of a son;
Long life to them both, and in peace & content
May their days and their nights for ever be spent.

Shepherd, Printer, No. 6, on the Broad Weir, *Bristol*.

*If the marriage didn't work out: unofficial divorce, known as wife selling, survived in Gloucestershire until the 1840s.*

*I was standing near the Market, listening to some men who were discussing pigs, horses, and cattle. We saw something approaching along King Street towards the Market, and it was soon apparent that it was a countryman who was leading a fatigued, dust-covered woman by a halter, which was placed round her neck. He would have passed our little garrulous coterie, had not a facetious old pig dealer exclaimed, 'Hallo, old 'un! What's up? What bist a-gwain to do wi' the old ooman, to drown her, hang her, or what?' 'No, I be gwain to sell her,' was the reply. There was a chorus of laughter at this. 'Who be her?' the pig dealer asked. 'Her be my wife,' the countryman answered, soberly, 'and as tidy, sober, industrious, hard-worker a creetur as was ever meyud. Her be as clean and tidy as a pink, and wud skin a flint to save a saxpuns; but her got such a tongue, and kips on nagging from monnin to midnight. I can't have a moment's peace for her tongue, so we have agreed to part, and her have agreed to go to the highest bidder in the market. I wudn't part wi' her for no sort o' money warn't it for her cussed rattle.'*

*'Be you willin' to be sold, missus? enquired one. 'Iss, I be,' she replied very tartly. 'Now then,' said the man, 'how much for her?' There was a pause, when an old cow-banger, with a ground-ash stick, bawled out 'Saxpuns for her!' The husband, holding the halter with one hand and raising the other, cried in the stereotyped style 'Gwain at saxpuns; who ses a shillin'?' There was another prolonged pause, when I, a vivacious youth, with an instinctive love of fun and humour, imprudently exclaimed 'A shilling!' 'Gwain, gwain, at a shilling. Have ee all done?' called the husband. Here was a dilemma for a lad! The bystanders laughed and chaffed, one exclaiming 'Here's a go, youngster! Her'll be knocked down to thee!' I perspired with apprehension of the consequences of my own imprudence.*

*With renewed earnestness the vendor again cried: 'Who'll bid eighteen-pence, vor her be a capital ooman as ever baked a batch o' bread or made a happle dumplin'.' To my intense relief a tidy, respectable-looking man made the bid and the husband striking his hands together exclaimed, 'Her be thine, man. Thee'st got a bargain and a good ooman, all but her tongue. Be good to her.' The vendee took the end of the halter, having paid the eighteen pence and led the woman away.*

Such a story seems incredible, but it is true, and is only one of many similar transactions.

6

# OUT OF THIS WORLD

It is generally felt that we live in an age of rationalism. Yet the 1992 edition of *British Social Attitudes*, a work of careful record, showed that 59 per cent of people believed in life after death, 28 per cent in hell and the devil. Although superstitions now seem to be in decline (see previous chapter) the supernatural retains some of its dread and much of its fascination.

Tales of fairies, now largely addressed to children, were accepted by adults in the early part of this century. Beliefs in the powers of witches also persisted, and by one of the ironies of history these have re-emerged in relation to the activities of certain latter-day Satanists - one of the irrational fringes of our age of reason.

The concept of curses may now seem puerile, but in April 1993 a letter in the *Independent* from a Trevor Mostyn explained how his uncle, cousin, father and brother had successively died after a witch had cursed the family for selling its estate. In the light of such statements it is not difficult to comprehend how a Gloucestershire farmer of a hundred or even fifty years ago might also believe in the power of malediction.

Tales of ghosts seem to be ubiquitous, with barely a village failing to make a contribution to the genre. In some cases they have become merely narratives told for their entertaining frisson; in others the phenomena described continue unabated with a charge of unease or even dread.

## Puck and Satan

Some fairy beliefs of the past are preserved in place names such as Puckpit Lane, between Hailes and Winchcombe, and Puck's Well, below Humblebee Wood at Sudeley. One could add Puck Acre (Daglingworth), Puck Moor (Dymock), Puckpit Meadow (Aston Somerville), Pug's Path (Wotton-under-Edge), Puck Pit (Maisemore), Dobb's Hill (Eldersfield) and Hob's Hole Coppice (Blockley).

When the open fields were enclosed at Upton St Leonards, a space left on Upton Hill for the fairies was called 'No Nation' or 'No Man's Land'. Margaret Eyre was informed that standards - single trees left to grow in hedges - were 'for the fairies to hide in'; and (by a Hewelsfield woman) that the tiny whirlwinds which sometimes carry columns of dust along the lanes were made by fairies riding by. Early this century a Churchdown man, Enos Berry, encountered what he took to be a fairy cortege on Chosen Hill. He remarked: 'You be a bit late for your funeral, bain't ye?' There was no reply but the participants, who seemed to be headless, flew up into the air. One could think of down-to-earth reasons why Berry should have made such a claim, but two or three other people subsequently had the same experience.

An old man at Amberley saw fairies dancing, and from then on was known as 'Cold Water' Jesse because he gave up drinking cider. At Yorkley, before going to bed on Christmas Eve people made up the fire and set before it a bowl of clean water for the fairies' annual bath. Failure to do this would have brought bad luck for the following year.

Early this century, belief in fairies at St Briavels was still strong (and even stronger in witches), though for some time they had not been seen dancing 'like little soldiers' in the Mork. One year John Jones, a farmer, who lived in the Mork decided to sell some cider to help pay his rent. He found a buyer, who said: 'This is what you must do. Carry the hogshead down to the fairy ring in Big Meadow, and pour it out on the grass.' When it came to the point, Jones - although he had been paid good money - thought it a waste to pour away cider, and substituted water. As he stepped out of the ring the man with whom he had struck the bargain appeared, and cursed Jones and his family, adding that the malediction would remain in force until they had lost as much blood as he had poured water. 'And they do say as how a power o' that family did bleed to death.'

In the 1950s Mrs Joyce Rogers, whose parents came from Wickwar and Wotton-under-Edge, recounted a story handed down for many generations in her family. A poor ploughman hears shrill lamentations, and finds a tiny peel (baker's wooden shovel) precariously balanced on the edge of a furrow. He takes it home that evening and by painstaking work manages to replace the minute broken shaft. Next morning he carefully replaces the peel. Later he smells baking, and when he finishes work finds a plum cake, hot from the oven, where he originally found the peel.

Benevolent fairies also helped a traveller benighted and lost in the hills above Dursley, one winter's night. The man finds a friendly inn, where he and his horse are welcomed and fed. Next morning the man gets up to a cheerful fire and a breakfast of cold meat, bread and ale. He calls for his reckoning but there is no reply, so he leaves two guineas. When his friends at Dursley hear his tale they remark that they know of no such inn. He offers to take them to the spot, but when they arrive all they can find is two guineas lying in the snow.

The oldest Gloucestershire fairy story had already been in existence for a least a century when Gervase of Tilbery put it into his book of marvels, *Otia Imperialia*, compiled before 1220. In the county is a forest abounding in boars, stags and every kind of game. If a weary hunter climbs a certain small hill, alone, and says, 'I thirst,' a bearer appears with a jewelled chalice from which a single draught banishes all fatigue. Many have recourse to the fairy vessel until a greedy knight refuses to hand it back after drinking, and keeps it for himself. When the Earl of Gloucester finds out, he has the thief put to death, and - wishing to avoid the retribution which will follow if he, too, holds on to it - presents the chalice to King Henry I. .

The best known fairy tale of the county is related by Beatrix Potter, who was unaware that it had a prosaic explanation. She heard the story of *The Tailor of*

*Gloucester*, her own favourite among all her books, during a visit in the 1890s to her cousin's house, Harescombe Grange. On Saturday evening the tailor leaves a waistcoat uncompleted in his shop, to find it finished first thing on Monday save for one buttonhole. A note pinned to the garment says: 'No more twist'.

Potter wrote down the story in an exercise book and sent it at the Christmas of 1901 to Freda Moore, one of the children of her old companion and German tutor. A covering note said: 'And the queerest thing about it - is that I heard it in Gloucestershire, and it is true! at least about the tailor, the waistcoat, and the "No more twist".'

The tailor, John Samuel Pritchard, took advantage of the publicity - the book was published to immediate acclaim in 1903 - by advertising from his shop at 23 Westgate Street: 'Have your suits made by the Tailor of Gloucester, where the work is done by the fairies.' He moved to Ashley Cottage in Charlton Kings, and died there in 1934. His gravestone bears the words: 'The Tailor of Gloucester'.

He must have been aware of what had really happened. One Saturday night, Pritchard's assistants were out drinking. Feeling much the worse for wear, they decided to spend the night in the shop instead of going home - unknown to their employer, they had a key. When Sunday morning came they were afraid to leave and attract attention, dishevelled and unshaven as they were, so to pass the time they set to work on the waistcoat. They completed it, save for the last buttonhole, and left the famous note. At nightfall they went home, to return to work next morning as though nothing had happened. Not till much later did they confess what they had done.

If the fairies, real or imagined, impinged at times on human affairs, so did the devil - and various features of the landscape (see also Chapter Two) were thought to have been caused by his intervention. Offa's Dyke near St Briavels, known as the Devil's Track, is said to have been cut in a single night with a plough drawn by a fox and goose. A short distance away, the Scowles (from the Celtic, *ceudwll*, cavern) - Roman iron workings at Bream - are called the Devil's Churchyard. One day at dusk a man gathering firewood there heard rustling in a great oak tree above his head, and saw a figure climbing down. Soon it leapt to earth, and there was just enough light for the man to make out horns and cloven hoofs. He did not stay to ask questions. Perhaps in an effort to efface such associations, church services were regularly held there for a time on Sunday evenings. Male voice choirs held competitions. A house opposite is called Heaven's Gate.

Another Devil's Churchyard is the site of a stone circle (see Chapter Two) east of Minchinhampton. Until at least the 1950s local people would avoid it after dark. One story is clearly intended as a deterrent to Sabbath breakers:

> *There was once a man who used to go nutting on Sundays. As he was going down Half-mile Lane that leads to the Devil's Churchyard he stretched out his hand to a fine bunch of nuts, saying, 'Here goes one!' Then to another, saying, 'Here goes two!' And a black hand was stretched out from the other side of the hedge, and it grabbed the*

> *man, with 'Here goes three!' in a terrible voice. So he died, and was buried at the Devil's Churchyard, for the black hand belonged to the devil.*

Holy Rood Day (14 September) was a traditional occasion when families went out nutting together, but if it fell on a Sunday it was better to desist; if not the devil would be an unseen member of the party. A second story about the Devil's Churchyard concerns a tailor who worked on Sundays. A stranger comes to order a suit. The tailor, having recognised him as the devil, runs home to his wife but falls dead before reaching her.

Until the 1930s they told a tale in Aylburton about an encounter between the devil and a tailor, which is paralleled by this narrative from St Briavels:

> *One night there was a shoemaker going up the Gloucester road, very late it was, and there he did meet a stranger, and they two did get a-talking as they went along. And by and by, finding as how he was a shoemaker, the stranger asks will he make him a pair of boots. So down he kneels in the road to take the measure, but when he had done on foot there weren't no other, only a claw. And the poor man makes as though he didn't notice, and the stranger went off, saying meet him there when the boots was done. The shoemaker went home half frighted to death.*
>
> *Early the next morning him did go the parson and told him all about it, and what should he do? And he said, 'Make him the boots, but don't you go for to take no money for them, not on no account.' So when the boots were ready he went to meet the stranger, and the parson, he stayed at the turn of the road, out of sight behind the hedge, him did. So there stood the stranger, and he gave him the boots. But when the money was offered, the shoemaker he wouldn't take it. And there was a great crash in the hedge, and the stranger rose up in the air and fled away, and there's a great big hole in the hedge to this day. Yes, him did take the boots.*

An account of how another cobbler outwitted the devil, who then formed Cam Peak, is given in Chapter Two, as is the story of the contest between Jack of Kent and the devil which is an explanation for monoliths on both sides of the Severn. Perhaps some such encounter led to the naming of the Devil's Lane at Charfield.

J. Arthur Gibbs tells how an old Cotswold labourer wrote a letter to the devil. In response to a question as to where he had posted it, he replied: 'A dug a hole i' the ground, and popped un in there.' He added: 'He got it right enough, for he's left me alone from that day to this.'

Those wishing to see the devil could cause him to appear at the Devil's Well on Painswick Beacon by running round it three times on Hallowe'en (31 October), 'and throw your cap in.' At Mangotsfield the devil made frequent sallies from Overdale House, 'clad in complete armour'. People were

*Painswick Beacon: by running round the Devil's Well three times on Hallowe'en, locals expected to conjure up the Prince of Darkness himself.*

frightened to travel Gangaw Mire Lane after dark: 'Down there by they pigsties, devils or soment else was always about.' Satan's passage through Winchcombe is commemorated more light-heartedly:

*Old Nick went out upon a prowl,*
*An' cumed to Winchcombe, thuck dark 'ole,*
*But A got stuck fast in Sudeley Lane,*
*So swore as 'e'd never cum thur agyain.*

## Weird Sisters

Witches were thought to be connected with the devil, and the oldest Gloucestershire story on the subject could date from as early as 1065. It tells how a Berkeley witch, realising that she is about to die, attempts to prevent the devil from claiming her. She asks her children (a monk and a nun, strangely enough) to wrap her corpse in the skin of a stag and put it in a stone coffin fastened with three iron chains. She hopes to lie secure in the church for three nights, then to be safely buried. On the first night, devils break into the church and burst one chain; on the second, another. On the third night a third devil, bigger and stronger still, smashes the church door to pieces, snaps the last chain, and drags out the protesting corpse. It is impaled on hooks sticking from the back of a black horse which appears at the church door, and vanishes from sight. The scene is shown on a modern kneeler in the church and on an ancient pinnacle outside.

We probably owe the story to monks who invented it as a warning to the faithful. However, the Nine Witches of Gloucester come from the heroic tales of

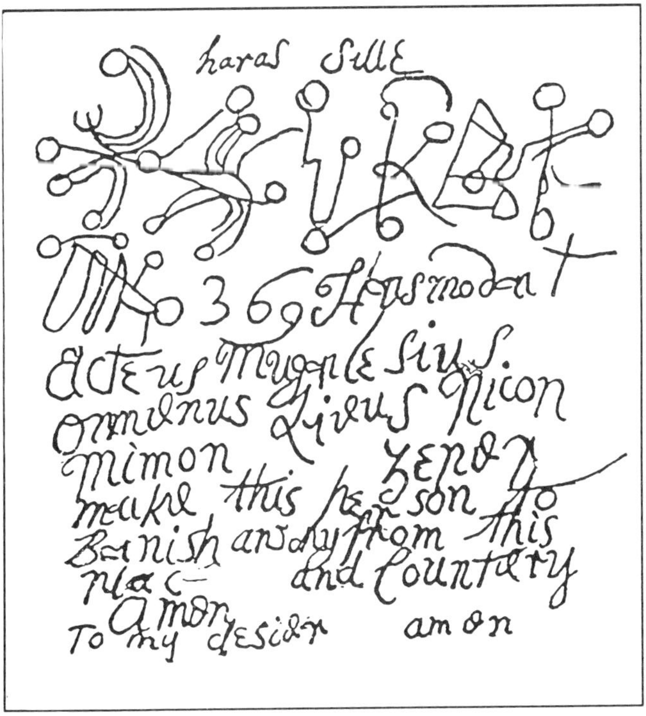


*The 17th century Dymock curse of* haraS sillE *(Sarah Ellis backwards), which came to light at Wilton Place, Dymock, in 1892. The inscribed plaque is now in Gloucester Folk Museum.*

Celtic Britain, and in particular from the Welsh cycle preserved in the early fourteenth century *Mabinogion*. The witches tutor the knight, Peredur, in the martial arts, but he is fated to kill them; and, with King Arthur's help, he does so.

Such things may seem remote, but even ordinary people considered witchcraft a force to be reckoned with. The downfall of the Duke of Buckingham (beheaded on Tower Hill in 1521) was attributed to a curse put on him when he enclosed land at Thornbury. The details have not survived, and it is possible that the idea of a curse emerged as an explanation of Buckingham's death only after it had taken place.

However, the Dymock curse, levelled in the following century has survived in the form of an inscribed lead plaque which came to light at Wilton Place, Dymock, in 1892. It is now kept in Gloucester Folk Museum. The heading, 'haras Sille' (which is Sarah Ellis, backwards), is followed by symbols representing the good and evil influences of the moon, the mystic number 369, then the names of demons - Hasmodat, Acteus, Magalesius, Ormenus, Lieus, Nicon, Mimon and Zeper - who are implored to 'make this person to Banish away from this plac- and Countery Amen To my desidr amen.' Some of the records are missing, but it is possible that Sarah was the wife of Anthony Ellis, who died at Oxenhall in 1669. Local tradition holds that Sarah herself committed suicide as a result of the curse and was buried on the boundary between Oxenhall and Dymock parishes (close to where the M50 now runs, near the hamlet of Four Oaks). Ellis's Cross remained on Ordnance Survey maps until at least 1923.

The Sarah Ellis affair attracted only local attention but a case at Chipping Campden of about the same time became national news. During the year 1660 William Harrison, steward to Lady Juliana, Viscountess Campden (widow of Sir Baptist Hicks), disappeared during a rent-collecting expedition. Suspicion fell on John Perry, Harrison's servant, who eventually confessed that with his help his mother and brother had murdered Harrison. No body could be found but the three Perrys were found guilty and hanged on Broadway Hill. Joan and Richard, the mother and brother, persisted in protesting their innocence; at the last John changed his story and claimed complete ignorance of the whole matter. Two years later Harrison turned up again with a story of having been abducted to Turkey.

One explanation suggested is that Harrison's son arranged his father's abduction (though not necessarily to Turkey) to be sure of succeeding him as steward. However, 'the Campden Wonder', as it came to be called is an enigma which has never been solved. One matter-of-fact suggestion, that Harrison took money from Lady Juliana to her son in Algiers, seems to have attracted little interest, despite a document in the Campden family papers acknowledging the receipt of money 'by hand of Harrison, oure good servant, who retourneth forthwithe.'

The novelist, Hugh Ross Williamson, contends in *The Silver Bowl* (1948) that Sir Baptist Hicks, his natural son, John Perry, and the rest of the Perry family, were all involved in witchcraft. 'Truth brought to Light; or, Wonderful and True

News from Gloucester shire', a ballad issued in 1662 by a London printer, supports the contention that Joan Perry at least was a witch.

After execution the body of John Perry was left hanging, while those of his mother and brother were taken down and buried at the foot of the gallows. Three days later a 'gentlewoman pretending to understand witches' hired a man to unearth the two corpses - probably with a view to cutting off the hands for their highly prized powers of healing - but her horse took fright and 'ran away under the gallows, and her head hitting against John's feet struck her off ... into the grave.' Another bizarre incident was that after Harrison's return his wife hanged herself in their house.

The last witch to be judicially burnt to death in the British Isles died on Dornoch beach in Scotland in 1722. The last woman to be burnt at the stake in Gloucester, Anne Williams, was convicted not of witchcraft but of petty treason - specifically, poisoning her husband. This was in 1753. Eighteen years earlier the death penalty for witchcraft had been abolished in both Scotland and England.

The change of law did not immediately change attitudes, and in the same year Mary Hudd of Thornbury complained of ill-treatment which included the drawing of blood (believed to nullify a witch's powers). Her statement has survived, though not the outcome of the case:

> *This Informant on her Oath saith that on the Thirteenth day of this Instant december she went to the shop of Mr Thomas Webb of Thornbury to Buy half a Pound of Cheese then Mrs Elizabeth Lewis of Rockhampton came into the shop and Layed hold of her and said that She should go up stayrs to Mr Webb's Wife and Haled her into Thomas Webbs House and Forced her into a Chayre and Fastened the doore upon her and Squized her by Both her armes till they were Black and Blew and Swelled and then held her till Mrs Mary Webb Thomas Webbs Wife came down who charged her with Bewitching her and then violently fell upon her and Wounded her Left Arme either with a Knife or her Nailes or some other Weapon and further she Saith that she had in her Pockett about Twelve or Fourteen shillings of her daughters When she went to Mrs Webbs Shop who by her being haled and Tumbled about Lost all the said Money Except Five shillings and further She Saith not.*

Some forty years later and at the other end of the county, similar attitudes are revealed in a letter by Rev. Winterbotham which refers to the Cheltenham of about 1773:

> *The intellect of the inhabitants was low if I may at this time be allowed to form a Judgement from the tales of witchcraft which I well remember and the treatment of two poor women who resided in the Town and had the misfortune of being suspected of that yet too widely imagined crime. These two women and their Cat were*

> *certainly the terror of the neighbourhood. These were sisters and in charity I presume maidens:- tho' very aged they subsisted by means of parochial aid and what they obtained by asking at the hands of their good neighbours who were afraid to refuse them anything while living - but who avenged themselves by refusing Christian interment to their mortal remains. I believe indeed neither of them had even a coffin - at least I recollect seeing one of these innocent victims of folly with her clothes on dragged in a cart followed by a noisy rabble and buried in a piece of boggy ground without the Town with less ceremony than has often attended the burial of a dog.*

Such vigilante action may explain why the burials of some witches fails to be recorded. I have been unable to find any mention in the Poulton parish register of the occupant of Betty's Grave, which is marked on maps - and even signposted at the spot - at a crossroads just outside the village. A clutch of stories cling to it: a gipsy woman was murdered and buried here; this is the grave of a housekeeper who poisoned her employer, or was poisoned by him, or was poisoned herself; a woman called Betty Bastoe made a wager to cut an acre of wheat with her sickle in record time, but after winning the bet dropped dead and was buried at the spot, in 1786. Another suggestion is that she was hanged for sheep-stealing. Finally there is the story that she was a witch, burned and buried where earlier she had been found as a baby and given the name of Betty Bastard.

Alfred Williams wrote:

> *Old Betty was famed for many acts and was a sore trouble to the carters, cowmen, and shepherds round about, bringing the flocks and herds and pregnant mares under her powerful spell and working incalculable mischief upon all and sundry. At one time the lambs, calves, and foals were stillborn. The gates and doors would fall off the hinges; the pumps would not draw water and the cream would not set in the broad pans. The cobbler could not work his wax while she was near, and half the people of the countryside fell sick, while she danced in the streets at midnight and spat up hundreds of pins and young crows, as the villagers confidently believed.*

As late as the 1970s a former Poulton woman told Katharine Briggs that witches at Betty's Grave held up pedlars travelling to Fairford market until it was too late for them to go on to sell their goods. The technique used was probably crossed pins stuck into the signpost.

To the present day flowers are placed from time to time on Betty's Grave and its aura of mystery is still felt. In the late 1980s technical hitches which arose in setting up a nearby factory were attributed by a local electrician to Betty's influence. One morning, hoping perhaps to calm the perturbed spirit, he bought a couple of pot plants and put them on the grave. Later the same day he was thrown across the factory by an electrical shock, and sustained a broken ankle. During his three months of convalescence he had time to reflect that Betty would no doubt have preferred wild flowers.

'Wonderful are the tales they relate of wizards, apparitions and enchanters,' wrote W.S. Wickenden in 1822 of the Dean Forest people. At about the same time William Lygon, the first Earl Beauchamp was riding through Redmarley when he came across a crowd of villagers who were about to duck a woman they suspected of witchcraft in a pond. If she sank she would be innocent (and perhaps dead); if she floated she would be guilty (and suffer the consequences). They assured Lord Beauchamp that all this was quite fair, and sanctioned by tradition, but he ordered them to desist.

Some witches were tolerated, if only out of fear. In the 1890s Emma Dent noted a Winchcombe teacher's account, derived from her mother and dating from some fifty-five years earlier, of a woman at Thornbury known simply as 'The Witch'. After losing the use of her legs the woman went round on hands and knees. The people 'were very much afraid of her, never daring to cross her wishes in any way for fear of being bewitched, so that she went where she chose.' It was firmly believed that in retaliation against two men who offended her, she caused one to break his leg and prevented the other from making candles from his tallow for a whole day.

Mrs Betsy Smith of Minchinhampton, who died in 1919 at the age of ninety-nine, remembered a witch who lived in a cave above Woefuldene. She cooked in a three-legged pot slung over a fire, and could foretell the future. Churchdown people believed that a local witch could enter or leave her house by the chimney. A second witch, Susan Sly (depicted in a mural - now gone - at the 'Bat and Ball' Inn) lived in Buttermilk Lane: 'Neighbours went in terror of her; besides changing into a hare, and in that capacity to be pursued by the hounds, and then changing back into her proper shape when nearly caught, and thus causing much dismay among the dogs, she also had the power of stopping horses, making pigs run round in their styes until they dropped, casting spells, and the like.' Once, closely pursued as a hare, she was bitten on the back leg as she shot into the drain leading to her kitchen. The master of hounds peered through the window and shouted: 'You had a narrow escape that time, Susan.'

Stories abound in which witches metamorphose themselves into cats or hares, and back again. One comes from the Edge Hills in the Forest of Dean, where an old woman practised herbal medicine and befriended miners. The men frequently set their dogs after hares but a particular animal always eluded them, and vanished by a certain holly tree. They consulted a man at Woodside (now part of Cinderford), who advised one miner to hold back his dog until late in the run when the hare was tiring. The ploy worked. The dog managed to sink its teeth in the hare's flank, but the quarry wrenched itself free with a squeal of pain, and disappeared by the tree. Next morning the miners found the old woman dead in her cottage with a wound in her side.

An unusual tale in which a man assumes the shape of a hare was heard by T.A. Ryder as a small boy at Elton, near Westbury-on-Severn. An old man there zealously guarded his pretty daughter from the attentions of suitors. One young man whom he knew to be in love with her went past their house one Sunday morning in his best suit, making for the church at Flaxley. The father thought all was well, but suddenly noticed a hare sitting gazing at the house.

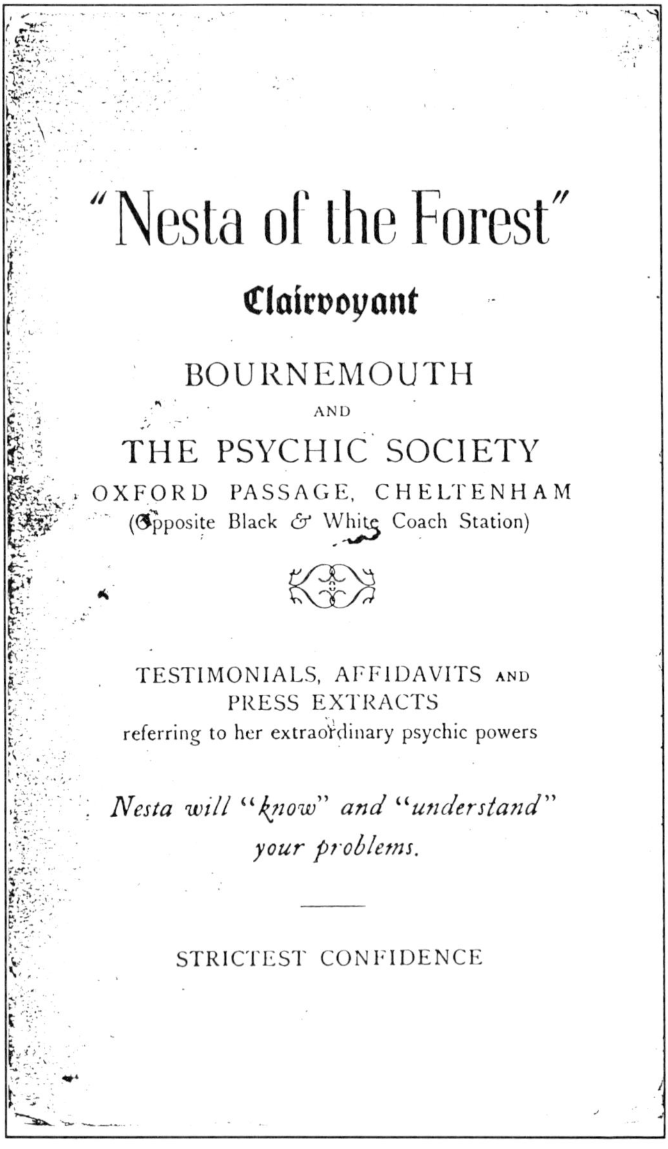

"Nesta of the Forest"

Clairvoyant

BOURNEMOUTH

AND

THE PSYCHIC SOCIETY

OXFORD PASSAGE, CHELTENHAM

(Opposite Black & White Coach Station)

TESTIMONIALS, AFFIDAVITS AND PRESS EXTRACTS

referring to her extraordinary psychic powers

*Nesta will "know" and "understand" your problems.*

STRICTEST CONFIDENCE

*Nesta Lane of Cheltenham could conjure up ghosts, claimed to have predicted Franco's victory in Spain and lost a libel action against Odhams Press.*

He crept in to fetch his gun, took careful aim, and fired. The hare ran off, dragging a wounded right hind leg. When the young man came back across the fields from Flaxley he was limping from an injury to the right leg. Ryder suggests that this is a relic of the Celtic belief that humans can assume animal form, the motivation in this case being the young man's overwhelming desire to see the woman he loved.

Witch stories continue well into the twentieth century. H.J. Massingham heard of Hannah Jervis, the 'fey woman' of Ebrington, who put spells on cows at Broad Campden. He asked Charlie Brotheridge whether he believed her to have been a witch: 'Maybe her were, maybe her weren't, but I uddunt a-liked to have trusted the old bitch.' 'Comfort' Woodhouse lived in a house at Northwoods Green, Westbury, where the mission church now stands. She was reputed to be a witch because of her great skill in making ointments and salves.

The handle-shaped dripstones over the windows of many houses in the Cotswolds were thought to be a kind of broken cross, and therefore to offer protection against witches. A horse shoe on or over the door or a 'quicken' (hawthorn) or yew cross inside it gave it a similar safeguard. So did a glass rolling pin full of salt, since a witch would have to count all the grains before entering.

As late as 1963, when she was in her seventies, Mrs Nesta Lane of Cheltenham claimed to have laid a spell or curse on two people who displeased her. As Nesta of the Forest she was a clairvoyant who claimed to have predicted Franco's victory in Spain, the outbreak of the Second World War, and many other events. At the Old Manse in Cheltenham, on the instructions of a clergyman's ghost which appeared to her, she searched for and found a bundle of ancient manuscripts; the ghost then came a second time to tell her to sell the documents for the benefit of 'the king's armies', which she did, and raised £140. Earlier in her career she lost a libel action against Odhams Press (which had cast doubts on her powers of prediction), and served a three months' prison sentence for failing to pay a fine levied (presumably) for fraud by pretended witchcraft, a case resembling that of Mrs Hayward's (see previous chapter).

When Mrs Lane was living in Oxford Passage at Cheltenham a young couple did odd jobs for her. When they left to live in the Cotswolds they stole - or so she alleged - her spade. Determining on revenge, she wrote three copies of a letter with her name and address, followed by the words: 'They who steal a spade shall dig a grave for one they love best.' Of these she sent one to the couple, buried another in her garden with the new spade she had been obliged to buy, and burnt the third on the fire. Shortly afterwards she found the old spade had been returned to her shed, and she discovered that the couple's baby and the wife's mother had died.

## Restless Spirits

Many apparently eerie phenomena have been explained as natural occurrences: 'Wind in the chimney, bats in the hall,/Mice in the wainscot, cats on the wall.' A phantom in Coaley churchyard in the shape of a thin, misty white pillar some four feet tall turned out to be gas rising from a piece of 'daddocky' (rotten) wood. At Cranham the ghost of a woman revisited the garden where in life she had buried money. One night a man staggering home from the 'Black Horse' was terror-struck on seeing a white shape in a garden. He rushed to friends for help, only to find that it was his own, living, wife in his own garden.

One dark night in Margaret's Stream Hollow, a dip in the road between Gretton and Winchcombe, a woman was terrified by a swaying white apparition. Her companion challenged it - 'Who bist thee?' - and lashed out with his stick. They heard a grunt, then scampering hoofs, and realised that a Hereford cow had been cropping the top of the hedge. At the same place - which is supposedly where a young gipsy girl was murdered or committed suicide - a cyclist once thought his machine enchanted. He could not ride, or even wheel it, and he had to drag the bicycle along the road until it became manageable again.

Some ghostly manifestations were practical jokes or deliberate hoaxes. H.Y.J. Taylor, then a boy at Neville Usher's School in Gloucester, remembered the tremendous sensation caused by an apparition in Asylum Lane until the truth came out: 'a spreeish young gentleman' had used a magic lantern to project it on a wall. A group of boys walking in the dark from Huntley back to Westbury were apprehensive at the prospect of passing a well haunted with much clanking of chains by a woman who had drowned herself in it. On reaching the point they duly heard a lugubrious rattle, and ran off in fright. Later they discovered that a friend had lain in wait with a trace chain.

The state of mind of those involved in these incidents is clearly important. A former landlord of the 'Snowshill Arms', a Mr Biles, saw many times upstairs in an ancient part of the building a strange figure which could open doors and frighten the dog. Yet the present owner dismisses such notions as 'imagination'. Mr Joe Watkins knows of several ghosts in the village of May Hill, including a figure with a red lantern in Folly Lane; a man who on moonlit nights falls in for a time behind people walking up Glasshouse Hill and then disappears; the sound of a rattling chain by the old mill; and the sight of an old white-bearded man wandering as if lost by the chapel. Yet in the poem he has written on the subject of these ghosts he concludes:

*Now if you go out at dead of night,*
*Don't worry, fear or fret.*
*I've wandered this hill for over fifty years*
*And I ain't seen one yet.*

While some may be sceptical, others are anxious to register as many hauntings as possible. Prestbury claims to have more ghosts than any other village in Gloucestershire, though recent sightings seem sparse. The Black Abbot is supposed to appear in the church at Easter, on All Saints' Day and at Christmas. He walks (literally) through the door, visits the site of the monks' burial ground, then approaches Reform Cottage - formerly a tithe barn, and traditionally linked by a secret passage to the church. In some accounts, the abbot enters a house called the Three Queens rather than the cottage. Inside, footsteps in the attic and the sound of things being knocked over are heard - though nothing is in fact disturbed. The abbot may also be the clerical figure seen close to the race-course on the site of the medieval hunting lodge of the bishops of Hereford.

Another ancient spectre at Prestbury is that of a messenger shot as he rode for the camp of Edward II at Tewkesbury in May 1471. Hoofbeats are heard, and the faint outline of a horse and rider seen. In 1901 part of a skeleton came to light during repairs to the road in Shaw Green. It had an arrow in the ribs. It may be that the story of the slain messenger was merely updated in the seventeenth century, with the victim becoming a royalist despatch rider travelling from Sudeley to Gloucester. The man was unhorsed by a rope stretched across the road, and killed on the spot. Hoofbeats are heard in the Burgage, then come to a sudden stop.

In a seventeenth century house at Cleeve Corner visitors occupying a certain bedroom wake - only on moonlight nights - with a feeling of deep dread and the sensation of choking hands round their necks. The background is that a young bride died there, strangled by a burglar who made off with her jewels and wedding presents. Some will ask where the husband was, and an alternative story suggests that he committed the murder for the sake of his young wife's dowry.

Other Prestbury phantoms are less threatening - the spinet playing heard in Sundial Cottage, or the woman's singing first encountered in 1957 at an old house in Ryefield Gardens. At Walnut Cottage, four years later, the ghost of a former inhabitant came to see the renovation work there and remarked amiably: 'Here's Old Moses. You see I likes to look in sometimes.'

In the early 1980s a Bishop's Cleeve man caught sight of a cyclist clad in thirties gear riding down the hill towards Prestbury from Southam. As a result of the publicity the incident attracted, information came to light that an accident had occurred there fifty years earlier. There are still more ghosts in Prestbury, including headless horsemen, phantom shepherds and sheep, an old lady in antique dress, and a misty form, identified as a former Mrs Preece, which drifts across the fields.

Yet even such profusion can be paralleled. In 1962 Kenneth Cooke compiled details of 59 Painswick hauntings, 34 in the parish and 25 nearby. It would be tedious to enumerate them, but Civil War soldiers appeared in the gardens of both Court House and at Castle Godwyn, and there were also a misty woman, a grey lady, an old man and a black dog. St Mary's Acre in Stamages Lane offered weird cries and the sound of shuffling feet, the latter also coming from Chirm Cottage in Kemps Lane. Little Fleece, in Bisley Street, once part of an inn, boasted a former owner searching the cellar for mislaid treasure. Other phantom tradesmen at Painswick include a miller, a Flemish weaver and a cobbler.

Stepping Stone Lane, the old coach route from Painswick to Stroud, takes its name from a mounting block close to where a footpath from the village joins the road. Between this point and a milestone marked '7 miles to Gloster', more black dogs - spectral, of course - have been seen. By the milestone itself a goblin-like figure comes out to dance. On other local roads one might have the pleasure of meeting a headless woman, a figure in white, assorted ghostly highwaymen and at least four different phantom coaches. One of these which Laurie Lee describes in *Cider with Rosie* appears at midnight, especially on New Year's Eve. To the horrific spectacle of careering conveyance and plunging horses are added the crack of splintering wood, the screams of passengers and the coachman's desperate but unavailing cries. Those who see and hear consider themselves cursed.

Close to Bulls Cross, where the phantom coach appears, is Frith Wood. In it lies a stone which once supported the statue of Pan, now standing in the garden of Painswick House. The plinth is all that remains of Pan's Lodge, a house in the wood where a Squire Hyatt lived. Hyatt is said to have invited wealthy pedlars, made them drunk, then killed them for their money and buried the bodies in his cellars. When he learned that Bow Street Runners were investigating he committed suicide, and later haunted the Lodge. When the house was demolished, human bones came to light, and the phenomenon ceased when Pan moved, or perhaps followed him to his new home.

Kempsford in the extreme south of the county also offers a number of ghosts. Eerie sounds of battle coming from near the church may have echoed through a thousand years, since the Gloucestershire Wicci fought the Wiltshire Walsati at what was then called Cynemaeres Ford. An apparition from Saxon times when Oswyn held Kempsford Castle is that of a Norseman, Hengstan. For courting Oswyn's ward, Ina, Hengstan was beaten, then bound with strips of ox-hide to the back of a wild horse which was whipped across the ford into Wiltshire. The horse dropped dead at nightfall but Hengstan survived to lead a successful assault on the castle and win Ina. After death he haunted the river bank.

Kempsford's best-known ghosts are those of the two Lady Mauds. One married Henry, Duke of Lancaster, who came into the possession of the manor of Kempsford in 1355. Their only son drowned in the Thames while still a child. The husband left in despair, never to return (see also Chapter Four). His wife remained, and since her death her spirit has lingered by the river, still seeking the long-lost child.

Another Maud married Henry Plantagenet, third Earl of Lancaster, and grandson of Henry III. Lancaster joined the group of barons struggling against Edward II, and suffered a number of reverses. Although Maud opposed the action against the king she received rebel fugitives at Kempsford Castle, and helped them cross the Thames. One of these, with a price on his head, turned out to be her brother-in-law. In her husband's absence she secretly lodged his brother, and took his meals to him personally. When Lancaster returned another guest - a knight whose advances Maud had rebuffed - told him of her apparent infidelity. He stormed into the chamber, knocked down his brother, and threw Maud from the ramparts into the deep water of the river where she drowned. Then he learned the truth.

Having returned to the wars, he was captured and executed at Pontefract. His brother escaped to France, where he died in poverty. The jealous knight became a penitent monk. He now lies beneath one of the monuments in Kempsford Church but he does not rest, for his spirit haunts the Old Vicarage which occupies part of the castle site. Lady Maud, too, appears on the walk which bears her name in the Old Vicarage grounds - where during the Second World War members of the Home Guard would only patrol in pairs - or she glides over the river in a grey mist.

There are still more ghosts at the Old Vicarage. One must add the foppish 'Blue Boy', thought to be the Regency rake, Lord Coleraine, who sits on a wing-backed armchair in the drawing room; the nursemaid in eighteenth century dress who carries a baby down the servants' stairs, perhaps leaving in disgrace with an illegitimate child; and a tall man with high hat and long cloak who walks through the wall in a back corridor. Some ten years ago the black-clad man was seen by the small son of the present owner, and a former housemaid still living in Kempsford remembers encountering the back-stairs ghost.

## Wayfaring Ghosts

Phantom black dogs are seen at Painswick, on Birdlip Hill and at Woeful Danes Bottom, where carters taking goods to Gloucester Market could only take horses at night if they blindfolded them first, and where in the 1950s a silent figure was seen following people in the gloom. Those walking along the road from Nailsworth to Horsley would sometimes find a black dog padding beside them from the Rockness turn as far as the spring with a stone inscribed 'Be thankful', then vanish. Broad Campden had its running dog, and in Old House Lane at North Nibley there was a spectre which changed from dog to human shape and back again. A black dog leaves Kingswood House at Wotton-under-Edge and crosses to the field opposite. Others at Tresham and Hillesley are thought to be the spectres of animals employed to guard those carrying valuables. By the junction of Broad and High Streets in Chipping Sodbury a cat appears, for which responsibility goes to a local alchemist. He is said to have mixed a potion capable of giving everlasting life and left it in a saucer, from which his pet lapped it up. He was unable to replicate his discovery.

Some phenomena are associated with objects of great antiquity. The Giant Stone between Bisley and Bibury is all that remains of a long barrow. Headless figures have been seen by it, and more at the Money Tump (Chapter Two). A Midland family picnicking by Belas Knap fled in terror when their table-cloth, despite being laden with food and crockery, flew into the air. Two women experienced feelings of sudden dread as they walked past West Tump, off the Birdlip-Foston's Ash road. At Bagendon, Cutham Lane, the scene of a battle, and the Downs, where a chief of ancient time is buried beneath the Whirlstone, were considered haunted. Rev. Rees comments, 'In old days no one would go near these places; both were avoided after dark.'

Roman soldiers have put in an appearance at a camp site on Cooper's Hill. Monks seem to be popular as apparitions, often in connection with Henry VIII's dissolution of the monasteries. Ghostly chants resound at midnight where Winchcombe Abbey stood. At Flaxley one of the monks, Wulfram, spent all of his eighty years in the abbey and was its last sacristan. He refused to leave, and lived in underground passages beneath the building until his death. After that he haunted the lawn which had been the brothers' burial ground. The Cistercian habit is white, as is Wulfram's ghost. The tall form of a murdered monk - struck down, perhaps, as he resisted eviction - haunted the site of Almondsbury's medieval monastery at least until the 1950s. A hooded monk still appears in Leonard Stanley churchyard, and four more are seen on moonlight nights near Cotswold House at North Nibley; they carry a coffin full of treasure which belonged to a rich man who hid it so that no one could find it after his death.

Another classic ghost is that of a mysterious white lady. One appears in Dark Coppice on Aston Hill near Chipping Campden; another at Dumbleton walks round the fish pond near the cricket ground at midnight, then crosses Garden Close. On the great Bledisloe Estate at Lydney the only white-painted gate marks the ride where a white lady walked. Another White Lady's Gate is to be found on Dover's Hill. The name comes from a woman called Beatrice whose white-cloaked figure may be seen the first evening after a full moon. Some details of her melancholy history are known. During the Civil War she and her brothers, John and Maurice, took the side of Parliament. Their neighbour, a royalist called Sir Roger, was ruined by the conflict, and resorted to highway robbery during the Commonwealth. He held up a coach in which Beatrice was travelling. They fell in love, and embarked on a series of clandestine meetings on Dover's Hill. Beatrice would signal that the coast was clear by waving a white cloak. Her brothers found out what was happening. They gave the signal themselves, then lay in wait. When Sir Roger came they jumped from ambush and killed him. Beatrice went mad on hearing the news, and after her death haunted the trysting place.

In December 1937, another white lady frightened the East Compton prize band at Over Court, near Almondsbury. The musicians, who had often visited, knew of the white lady but had never seen her. This time they all came to a halt when, some twenty yards away in a tangle of undergrowth, they saw a bright, white figure with a tall, pointed headdress. It then moved towards a fishpond, by a clock tower (which still stands, though the house was demolished in the early 1980s). The lady is reputed to have been shot by her husband, a former owner of Over Court, for having an affair with another man. After being wounded she staggered from the house to the fishpond, where she drowned.

At Duntisbourne Abbots a holly tree in the wall of the Old Mill House is haunted by a white lady who appears there before proceeding to drive a coach and horses along the meadow opposite. A white, masculine figure haunts the steepest part of the lane between Nailsworth and Box. He is seen sitting quietly on a bench by the roadside. A similar figure encountered in the dark lane between the Weighbridge Inn and Minchinhampton is supposed to emerge where a member of the Playne family met his death - whether by his own hand or otherwise is unclear - some two hundred years ago.

A further hazard of certain roads is a phantom funeral. At Mangotsfield four men bearing a corpse on their shoulders are seen in Middle Pit Lane, but cannot be touched. On a particular (but unspecified) night in the year a cortege appeared on the road at the bottom of Stancombe Pitch near North Nibley. It crossed one of the bridges, with mourners following; the driver of the hearse lifted his head to reveal a familiar face - that of a person, even the watcher himself, who would die within twelve months. Not surprisingly, people avoided that stretch of road but sightings of the ghostly cortege became more scarce after some trees were cut down in the 1950s and made the place much lighter.

At Arlingham Court (of which only the dovecot is now left) a phantom funeral signified that a member of the family was about to die. John Yate, the last male heir to the estate, died twelve months to the day after such a cortege was seen on 24 May 1757.

A different intimation was given to a Mr William Pinching, who lived within recent memory at a house in Cranham called Buckholt. One night he saw the flame of his candle bend. The figure of a little old lady in a rustling silk dress came through the door, crossed the room, and went out of the window. The flame straightened but then bent the other way as the figure returned and retraced its steps through the still-closed door. Next morning Mr Pinching learned by telegram that his heir, while swimming in South Africa, had been killed by a shark.

To return to the roads, it seems that the old-style coach and horse continue to hold the imagination long after their disappearance in reality. The vision is fed by the images on Christmas cards, calendars, films and television advertisements. A coach and six horses driven by John 'Crump' Dutton, a seventeenth century squire, was until recently often seen in Lodge Park, Sherborne. Mothers told their children that they risked meeting the fearsome equipage if they were not home before dark.

At Kingswood House - opposite Lady Katherine Berkeley's School at Wotton-under-Edge - a horse-drawn carriage enters through one of the gates, drives round the house, and leaves by the other. Different phantom coaches are seen on stretches of road at Wickwar, Saddlewood, and Frocester Hill.

In 1972 a Mr W. Jefferies was driving a delivery van towards Cheltenham on the A417. It was about 5.30 p.m., with an early dusk. He had just passed the Highwayman Inn, formerly the Mason's Arms, and was near to the turning for Syde when a white coach drawn by four horses crossed the road in front of him, causing him to brake heavily. At Smith's Cross nearby, the Gifford family waylaid a treasure train belonging to Edward II, and had their castle at Brimpsfield destroyed in retribution.

By the Puesdown Inn on the A40 an eastbound track which diverges from the road was once an alternative route for coaches when the marshy valley below became impassable. A woman driver and her passenger from Charlton Kings have twice seen a coach and four horses emerging from the track and crossing the A40. A short distance away a phantom horse and trap near the Hangman's Stone on the Salt Way have caused accidents as drivers swerved to avoid them. The same is said of a carriage and four horses on the Bream road out of Coleford.

A similar discrepancy between ancient and modern, perceived and real, had tragic consequences on the B4221 between Hall's Barn and the drive to Crookes Farm, just outside Newent. The story, told to me in 1991 by a woman who had lived in the area for twenty years, has since been confirmed in its essentials by several other people. She used to walk home at night to Kilcot after working at the George Inn at Newent. At the place in question on the road she saw nothing but always felt a presence. The feeling was so strong that on one occasion while driving along the road with her mother she wordlessly communicated the whereabouts of the spot. Then the young daughter of the woman's friend was killed there in an accident, while being driven by her boyfriend. He explained that he had seen a cloaked figure on the road, swerved to avoid it, and crashed into a telegraph pole. His evidence was accepted at the inquest. After the death my informant ceased to feel a presence on the road.

Close to the spot is a layby where a gibbet once stood. This is now called Woeful Hill, though in the first record of about 1254, it is referred to as Wolfhameshill, which probably points to an encounter with a wolf. A young man from Newent tells me that a woman was hanged there in the Civil War; a room in a nearby house is never used because it is haunted; a gypsy woman and her baby were knocked down and killed; and his grandfather saw a pig come out of nowhere one night and swiped at it, only to find his stick went right through.

Strange phenomena often seem to be associated with deep grief or suffering. A sixteenth century landowner at Mickleton, Sir Edward Greville, mistook his son for a robber one dark night and shot him. He sold up in 1597 and left for ever, but in Weeping Hollow where the accident took place ghostly yells, moans and screeches continued to be heard for several hundred years. The Mickleton Hooter, as the phenomenon came to be called, ceased in the late nineteenth century as a result, some said, of scientific experiments carried out by a man called Staunton who lived at Hidcote House.

At Wotton-under-Edge the Symn Lane ghost is a woman with her hair on fire who runs along screaming. She was murdered in the nineteenth century by her son who returned from Australia to claim his inheritance and thought himself badly done by. For good measure he set fire to her house on the Chipping and went up Wotton Hill to watch it burn, before being arrested.

One murder was averted by a dream in which a carter saw a woman who said: 'Save me tonight from Benhall's dreary wood.' Next day at midnight he came across the woman on the roadside between Gloucester and Cheltenham. She told him she had to meet a man in the wood but feared to do so. The carter went with her and they surprised a man who was digging a grave under a tree. He fled. The woman fainted as soon as she realised that the grave had been meant for her. The carter carried her back to his waggon, where shortly afterwards she gave birth to a baby.

In the 1930s help came by mysterious means to a portrait painter, Olive Snell, who lost her way in the dark while walking near Cold Ashton. At a house where she stopped, careful directions were given by a man she took to be the butler. She tipped him half a crown, and went on to her friend's. There she was told that the house she described was empty and boarded up. They went to check, and found this to be the case. On the front step they saw half a crown.

Equally strange are cases of a person's meeting someone, only to find he has recently died. This conversation is reported from Yorkley: 'It's terrible about old George.' 'He seems all right to me. He came down the hill as usual and we had a chat a few minutes ago.' 'The milkman found him this morning, hanging from a beam in the kitchen.'

Still in the Forest of Dean, Glyn Hoare told me that as a boy of twelve or thirteen years old he met a distant relative, Tommy Ayrton, with his dog, by a fallen pine in a wood near Five Acres. He stopped for a chat, and arrived home late. His mother asked why, and he explained. She immediately gave him a good hiding. He could not understand her anger, and asked what he had done to deserve the beating. 'Tommy's been dead for three days, and his dog died less than an hour after him,' she said.

Ghosts can be encountered on water as well as land. Some three hundred yards downstream from where a railway bridge once crossed the Severn from Sharpness to Purton is a maelstrom called Fiddlers' Pool. The name comes from a boatload of Welsh fiddlers drowned there as they rowed back from over-enthusiastic celebrations at Berkeley. On stormy nights their music can still be heard in the wind.

A former tug captain, W.H. Savage, places the story elsewhere, which would certainly be more consistent with an attempted crossing to Wales:

> *Between Beachley and Old Passage lie the Benches, a submerged reef, which has the effect of an overfall, causing, particularly on the ebb, about a dozen very nasty short seas. Of the Benches there is a legend that nine jolly fiddlers were returning in a party, and on encountering these troubled seas the boat foundered and drowned them all. Today rough seas on the Benches are described as 'the fiddlers turning up'. I am told that in Aust there is a strongly-held tradition that the ancient landing place was 1 1/4 miles upstream, at the Folly. Such a landing place could avoid the Benches in crossing and provide a more sheltered course.*

On the other side of the Forest, between Redbrook and Newland, lies Swan Pool, in Swanpool Wood. The figure of a tall woman in white, draped with dripping weed, a moaning child in her arms, rises from the water on certain nights. Some say the woman murdered her child; some that both were victims, together with a black dog which appears from a limekiln in the wood, runs round the pool, then returns to cover.

On a disused canal near Newent a phantom boat appears on moonlight nights. Two men jointly owned the vessel. To take the other's share for himself one plied his partner with gin until he became insensible, then stuffed his mouth with hay and pitched the body overboard in Oxenhall Tunnel. It is probable that the murderer was brought to justice, but records are wanting.

## Public Spirits

Inns and hotels seem particularly prone to ghosts which, as sceptics might reflect, seems to do their trade no damage at all. Some, such as the Angel at Coleford and the Ostrich at Newland have a classic cavalier. At the Speech House is a beautiful and mysterious lady who 'does not solace, nor does she affright.' The comment is by John Moore, who lived as a child in what is now the Tudor House Hotel at Tewkesbury, where a lady in white with a black dog appears on a landing - though not very often; a manageress told me: 'Americans are always hoping to see them, but never do.' Visitors know of such things because of guide books and gazetteers, and in 1989 the British Tourist Authority published an information sheet on haunted inns and hotels.

A blue lady (so called from her dress rather than her behaviour) is more forthcoming, and several recent sightings have been reported from the Fleece Hotel in Gloucester. The Manor House at Moreton-in-the-Marsh is haunted by Dame Creswyke, who drowned in a pool in the grounds some two hundred years ago. The ghost which appears on the top landing of the Victoria Hotel at Newnham-on-Severn is a nineteenth century chambermaid, thwarted in love, who hanged herself in an attic.

A former inn, the Weaver's Arms at Nailsworth, stood on the little hill leading from Bristol Road to Arnolds Lane. A traveller murdered there for his money haunted the place, which had 'several of the doors inside reversed, it being the old fashioned idea that if the ghost couldn't find the handle it couldn't walk.' Most of the building was pulled down in 1897 to make way for a new house, but part of the original inn remains in the form of a cottage on the site.

The Ragged Cot Inn at Hyde, near Minchinhampton, still exists. In 1760 the landlord, Bill Clavers, decided to supplement his income by robbing the night coach to London. Well fortified with rum, he picked up his pistols and staggered from the bedroom. On the landing his heavily pregnant wife tried to stop him. He pushed her violently, and she fell down the stairs. He stepped over her and rode off. When he came back with the proceeds of his robbery he found both wife and newly-born child dead at the foot of the stairs. He bundled their bodies into a trunk. By this time the constables arrived, having followed tracks left in the snow. Clavers opened fire from a window but gave up the fight when he saw the ghostly figures of his wife and baby. The constables, too, saw the apparitions. At dawn they searched the house and found the bodies. Clavers was hanged at Gloucester. The ghosts still appear and a young couple recently drove from Holland in the vain hope of seeing the Ragged Cot spectres.

The Puesdown Inn on the A40 near Compton Abdale dates in part from 1236. An eighteenth century landlord once heard three thunderous knocks on the door in the middle of the night and opened to find the tall dark figure of a highwayman (whom some have identified as one of the Dunsdens - see Chapter One). He had an arrow protruding from between the shoulder-blades.

The landlord let him in and did what he could, but the man died at dawn. Ever since, the three knocks have been heard on many occasions, and sometimes a ghostly horseman has been seen galloping towards the inn. A man who lived in a cottage quite near to the inn some thirty-five years ago would never use the road after dark but made a circuit through the fields if he wanted a drink.

In 1992 the *Western Daily Press* reported a new phenomenon at The Puesdown Inn: a lecherous ghost with a patch over one eye who 'watches people while they shower and sneaks into the rooms of young couples in the middle of the night.' The landlord, Nick Wood, said: 'Sometimes when you're in the shower the taps suddenly go on, and sometimes the television suddenly goes up. Pots and pans clatter, and once a bottle of beer flew out of an upright crate and smashed on the floor.'

Some of this activity sounds like the work of the mischievous or malevolent spirit known as a poltergeist. For many decades there has been one, known as Harry, at the Hobnails Inn, Little Washbourne. His exploits include throwing a brass plate and heavy ashtrays across the bar, turning on lights and opening doors. During the rewiring of the pub in 1989 electricians' materials and tools left overnight in an attic were turned into 'a shambles'. The word was carefully chosen by the landlord, Steven Farbrother, who adds that he can find 'no physical or logical explanation' for the continuing phenomena. He refers to Harry with a slightly weary affection like that of a parent whose patience is tried by the behaviour of a wayward child.

The activities of poltergeists at the Kingsholm and Greyfriars Inn at Gloucester have proved more frightening. In the former a series of disturbing occurrences includes the fall of a heavy clock from a secure position, a somersault performed by a football trophy, and the smashing of a large glass jar in a locked cellar. A builder renovating the Greyfriars Inn in Southgate Street told the *Citizen* in 1988:

> *I wasn't happy there even in daylight. I got nervous about the unexplained bumps and noises that were coming from upstairs. Nights were cold but we couldn't see any alternative but to sleep in the building. The atmosphere was spooky, the noises got worse, and doors were cracking eerily; but the final straw was the second evening when I went to shut the outside gate only to see a wheelbarrow thundering towards me even though the courtyard was deserted. I went and slept in my van in the graveyard opposite. I thought the dead would be a better bet than whatever was about at the Greyfriars Inn.*

During the Second World War a mason and his apprentice working on an eighteenth century house at Ford also slept on the site - in the kitchen, to be precise. It was winter, so they kept a fire burning. Even so the apprentice, whose bed was over a great stone slab, complained of cold and sleeplessness. Next night the beds were changed round, and this time the mason could not rest. On the third night they re-arranged again, putting the workbench over the slab, and both slept well. Some days later, when work in the house was finished, the mason, thinking there was perhaps a well beneath it, decided to raise the slab. He found a human skeleton, with fragments of clothing. He replaced the stone. "Twas no affair of mine,' he said to F.W. Baty, who later discovered that many years earlier a farmer returning from Tewkesbury Christmas market with money from the sale of fat cattle never reached home. The skeleton may still lie beneath the kitchen floor in Ford Manor.

For many years at the Berkeley Arms in Tewkesbury heavy footsteps were heard in a large bedroom and strange tappings from the ceiling of a bathroom. In 1969 the landlord's wife felt something 'flit past her' in a corridor. Five years later when a wall was taken down a tiny room came to light, full of rubbish save for two well preserved volumes of a history of England published in the nineteenth century. Perhaps a spirit was striving to keep what in life had been a treasured possession.

Mr Wayne Keane, landlord of the Black Horse at Cirencester, told me in 1991 that he would break into a concealed room - of which he had discovered the existence by making a series of measurements - only on the day he left. I later found out that he did not do so, but I wonder whether there is any connection with the treasure reputedly concealed at the inn (which dates from the fifteenth century) by a rich woman wool merchant. She may also be linked with the ordeal of a young woman, Ruby Bower, who on 13 August 1933 woke in the Black Horse to hear rustling and see 'an apparition in the shape of a stout old lady with an evil face and grim expression, gliding slowly across the floor.' The following morning the letter 'W' and the word 'John' were found inscribed upside down on a small window pane.

A woman medium brought to the inn declined to enter certain rooms but said of the haunted bedroom that there was nothing to fear: 'There was an old man and an old lady. The old lady has a long chin and long beak-like nose. She is earth-bound; she has done the old man some injury and wanders about the house, but the harm she would do or has done is not in this room. It is in one of the rooms I would not enter.' She proceeded to give instructions that the ghost would be laid if at 3 p.m. on the third day of the month three white flowers were laid in Room 3. This seemed to be effective.

However, in the 1970s the landlord found that people sleeping in the haunted room were awakened in the early hours by strange goings-on, including the sound of footsteps. Twenty years later, by which time the inscription on the bedroom window had become 'Jamie', Mr Keane believed he saw the mysterious figure of the lady in the kitchen. In 1993 a new landlady told me there had been no further sightings. The marked pane of glass had been broken and replaced. The inscription should - according to tradition - reappear on the new glass but it has not done so yet.

The 'King's Head' at Gloucester reports three active ghosts, a porter, a cavalier and a monk. The cavalier has been linked with the death of Bulstrode Whitelock in the inn, shot during an affray in 1688 between supporters of William of Orange and those of the House of Stuart. The monk appears in a room dubbed the Monk's Retreat which was the entrance to a passageway leading beneath the market place to the cellars of the abbey on the other side. Guests apparently find these manifestations more intriguing than frightening.

## Ghostly Guests

In some private houses former occupants seem to linger, uninvited and often unwelcome. At two farms in Winson - Pinchpool and Ley Mary - only unexplained footsteps are heard but at Slowwe in Arlingham two old ladies are seen. (The motto of the Slowwe - pronounced slough - family is 'Slowwe is sure'.) Dumbleton Hall has a grey lady on the stairs; so does the Manor House at Stanton. Bet Kebir (Big House in Arabic) at Lydbrook is known as Ghost House because of the figure in riding habit walking down the stairs.

Owlpen Manor near Uley may have been visited by Queen Margaret in 1471 (see Chapter One). F.W. Baty asked the lady of the house about stories that the queen's ghost continued the association. He writes:

> *During the more recent of our Great Wars she had moved into a corner of the house to make room for children evacuated from air-raids. She had no contact with her children, except for a Christmas party each year, and it was clearly understood by those in charge that no ghosts were to be mentioned.*
>
> *Shortly before Christmas 1943 several new evacuees arrived at Owlpen, the mixture as before - with one exception, a boy who was not of the mixture, being unusually quiet and unnaturally well-behaved. The day of the party saw a transformation, created from odds and ends found in the attics, and with the lady of the house in some costume of absolutely no historical inclination.*
>
> *The quiet newcomer approached her, admired her dress, but thought it not as nice as the one she wore on the evening of his arrival. This puzzled Mrs F., for she was not at home that evening, so she went warily to find out who the boy had seen, and what she wore.*
>
> *Very clearly, for a youngster, he described the sort of costume Queen Margaret could have worn; tight up here (bodice), long pointed sleeves with baggy shoulders, pointed shoes, and a high steeple hat with lace down the back.*
>
> *Mrs R. was greatly interested, for she had never worn anything like this; nor had the attics yielded its like. Where had he seen her? If it was in the middle section of the house, popularly regarded as the haunted part, then someone had been telling tales. But no, he saw her at the top of the old stone stairs, and he had not spoken because they had been all told not to disturb her.*
>
> *The lad continued in his way, amenable but strangely detached, until a day came when he insisted upon going home. Three times he was retrieved from the lane, determined to make his way back to Birmingham somehow, though for no reason that he could give. He*

*was finally persuaded to wait until morning, on a promise that his parents would be contacted. With morning came a telegram with the news that his father had died.*

*Owlpen Manor: several appearances of Queen Margaret, the latest as recently as 1991.*

The last reported sighting of anything unusual at Owlpen Manor dates from 1991, when a visitor sleeping in Queen Margaret's room woke to see a light and a female figure bending over a writing table. All three things were phantom, though not frightening.

A housekeeper of a hundred years ago at Sudeley Castle, a Scotswoman called Janet, often sat at the top of the stairs in the servants' quarters to make sure the men stayed away from the women. She re-appears there, especially in the months of August and September, wearing a long grey dress, striped pinafore and mob cap. In 1985 a touring school party saw her, and she shook a feather duster in one child's face. She has also been sighted elsewhere in the castle and grounds.

In the 1950s Mrs Richings of Yate described a personal experience at a farm called The Rocks:

*I was busy cleaning the dining room when I heard the silver of the lunch-laden table rattle. Thinking there was someone there I turned quickly to see a little old-fashioned man with a wrinkled face round as an apple, with merry, laughing eyes, and dressed in a dark green velveteen suit with tarnished brass buttons. He stood by the table, near a chair several hundred years old. At first I felt very frightened and on the point of screaming, when the little man gave me such a friendly smile that the scream died on my lips. There I stood looking at him, feeling now quite unafraid, when he gradually disappeared before my eyes under the table. Thought I, someone is making a fool of me, but on immediately looking under the table I found no one there. On making further enquiries, the daughter of the house fully believed that I had seen this man, as she herself had seen someone very similar; and she thought the chair which was 300 years old had in some way a connection.*

Mrs M. J. Carrick's family lived in Uley Road, Dursley, from 1921 until the late 1960s. In the dead of night an old house is full of noises: the creak of a board, the scuttle of a mouse, the moaning of wind in a chimney. Yet the sound of footsteps coming downstairs and of something heavy being dragged along is something more. Then Mrs Carrick's sister 'suddenly stated that under no circumstances would she sleep in the top bedroom' because of 'being awakened in the small hours to a sense of bitter coldness, and then the silence being broken by the sound of the door latch dropping three times.' Another development was that she arrived from work one evening 'to find every door in the house open, and no one at home.' Then the time came when the house was to be sold:

*A removal firm from over a hundred miles away came to clear it. I left them to start clearing the top floor and coming back down some time later, found a pale faced youth gulping a cup of coffee, and very quiet. Not long after his friend returned from the van and went back up the stairs. Shortly afterwards he came running down and said could he speak to me in the yard. He asked: 'Is this house haunted? I have cleared houses everywhere, and older ones, but never seen a ghost before, and neither has my pal.' Absolutely shattered by this, I did manage to ask what he had seen. He gave me a very clear description, and somehow I managed to get him to go back and finish the work. Later that evening I asked Father if he could remember the person who owned the house before us. He said that the man was stockily built, black hair, and always wore black suits with a white shirt and black tie - just as the man had described to me. No one knew what had happened to his wife.*

Sinister ghosts often appear to stem from incidents of violence and injustice. Bishop John Hooper was burned alive in 1555 where his monument now stands, to the west of Gloucester Cathedral, outside St Mary's Gate. The fire had to be re-lit three times, and his ordeal lasted forty-five minutes, during which he was fully conscious most of the time. One might think his ghost would walk. Not so; but stories persist of a ghostly watcher - perhaps the spirit of Queen Mary herself - looking from a window in the chamber over St Mary's Gate. Dogs have run from the room in terror, or refused to enter it; and people have experienced feelings of sudden dread there.

Littledean Hall vies with Berkeley Castle in claiming to be the county's oldest inhabited house, having been continuously occupied since 1080. Even sceptical visitors have left convinced of the existence of one or other of its many ghosts. During the Civil War two Royalist officers were killed in the dining room (see Chapter One). Their blood is supposed to have marked the floor indelibly ever since, the stains re-appearing even if boards are replaced. Again during the Civil War a member of the Brayne family disguised himself as a gardener and worked at the hall to escape arrest. His ghost haunts the drive, besom in hand, sweeping away leaves.

In the eighteenth century Charles Pyrke, a member of the family which owned the house for 250 years, was killed at the age of 23 by his black servant. It seem that Pyrke had fathered a child with the servant's sister - the baby was later found dead behind panelling in the Rose or Blue Room (accounts vary). It is not Pyrke who walks, but the black youth, patrolling with a candle. There are other ghosts, too. As recently as 1992 a figure in a dark cloak was seen in the tea room, and elsewhere in the building a girl attired in the fashion of a seventeenth century maidservant.

A complicated story of the same period purports to explain the headless horseman who rides round the fifth lake in the thousand-acre Woodchester Park, near Nympsfield. Sir Rupert de Lansigny sought to obtain for himself the estate of his uncle, Sir Charles Harriett, and began by killing Harriett's young son and heir in a grossly unequal duel. On hearing that Sir Charles was about to take on Sir Rupert, John de Tresthaye - who was in love with Sir Charles' niece, Alicia - stepped forward as champion. Sir Rupert, realising that he had met his match, attempted to flee but was cut down by Robert, another friend of the Harriett family.

The decision to sell Spring Park, as the mansion was called in 1846, was attributed to the sighting by an owner, Hamlet-like, of his father's ghost. The owner was Lord Ducie, but it is impossible to say whether he indeed saw his father's ghost. He moved to Tortworth Court, where he died in 1921. The purchaser of Spring Park, William Leigh, had the house pulled down and commissioned a new one, the Woodchester Mansion. At his death in 1908 it was unfinished, and still is, though a trust has set about preserving it. The ghosts of a Roman centurion and a ragged dwarf continue to haunt the park, together with the image of a coffin either floating five feet above the ground or on the surface of one of the lakes (it has been suggested that the original coffin, set adrift on the water, was that of a suicide from Kings Stanley).

Another house, The Ridge at Wotton-under-Edge, is now only ruins, albeit with a new structure within. The family which lived there abandoned the earlier building because of the terrible screams of a murdered ancestress they heard. In addition, strange lights flickered among the trees, and horses refused to pass them. From the 1920s piano playing was heard coming from the empty dwelling. Forty years later builders at work on the house narrowly missed being crushed by a heavy keystone which fell from an arch.

In the same neighbourhood Newark Park was built for Sir Nicholas Poyntz, who obtained Kingswood Abbey when the monasteries were dissolved. Monks attempting to escape were trapped in an underground passage where their bones were subsequently discovered. Their phantoms appeared - perhaps still do - on every saint's day, issuing from a panelled wall, crossing a room and descending a staircase, chanting as they went.

A monk fleeing from the sack of Kingswood also haunts Owlpen Manor, where he was walled up and starved to death. The space came to light when the measurement of certain rooms was found not to tally, but the monk's bones crumbled to dust when it was opened. At Bradley Court in Wotton a phantom pair of bloodstained hands seen protruding from a wall is explained as belonging to a person immured for some crime who, desperately scrabbling at the masonry, managed to force his hands through, and then died.

T.A. Ryder heard from an old lady who lived in St Briavels Castle of three ghosts, a man in armour, a lady in white and another man in centuries-old costume. 'Apparently, I must have looked rather sceptical of her stories,' he writes, 'for she said she would prove to me that the place was haunted.':

> *There was a small dog lying on a rug in front of the fire in the room where we were having tea. The old lady ordered the dog to go into a certain corner of the room but the animal refused to obey her. Then she lifted the dog up and carried him into the corner, but no sooner had she put the dog down on the floor than it darted back to the hearth-rug looking terrified, the hairs along its back literally standing up on end. This was repeated a second time, with the same result. Then my hostess informed me that some while before, during repair work, the wall in the corner had been partly demolished, and that a small chamber had been found in the thickness of the outer wall. In the chamber there was a skeleton, maybe that of some poor unfortunate who had never been released from it.*

Only a short distance from St Briavels Castle stands Cinderhill House, which is said to be haunted by a ghost of Emmeline, a young woman forced in the days of arranged marriages to wed an older man, despite her love for a younger. On the day of the ceremony she rushed out of the church as the time came for her to make her vows. She ran down Cinderhill to the well, jumped in and drowned herself.

Equally unlucky in love was Catharine, daughter of Sir Robert Jenkinson, who lived at Hawkesbury Manor in the early eighteenth century. She, a Protestant, fell in love with a Catholic, Clement Paston of nearby Horton Court. Because of the difference in religion, Sir Robert turned down the young man's request for his daughter's hand. Catharine, having heard this, ran to wave a final goodbye from her balcony as Clement rode away, and then fell - some say deliberately - to her death. Stricken with grief, Sir Robert soon died, too. His spirit haunts the manor grounds, often standing at the edge of a wood from which the fatal balcony can be seen.

An unhappy marriage seems to have produced the ghost of a weeping woman in widow's black at St Anne's, a house in Pittville Circus Road, Cheltenham. Imogen, the second wife of a Mr Swinhoe, lived there with her husband in the 1870s but left because of their violent quarrels. The ghost started to appear only in the 1880s, by which time a Colonel Despard and his family were occupying the house. The black-clad figure was seen many times, day and night, by different people. Indeed it has been suggested that the ghost was in fact flesh and blood, the colonel's mistress whom he wished to conceal from his family and servants. Yet Despard's daughter, Rosina, wrote: 'I attempted to touch her but she always eluded me. It was not that there was nothing to touch but that she always seemed to be beyond me, and if followed into a corner, simply disappeared.' Various odd happenings continued, long after the Despards' departure: the sound of footsteps, the sight of door handles turning of their own volition, a strange chill in places, dogs reduced to abject terror.

Gambier Parry Lodge was a Victorian hospital in Tewkesbury Road, Gloucester. Nuns formerly ran it, and one of them hanged herself after the death of a boy in her care. Later, when that part of the building served as nurses' quarters, several women saw the figure of a young nun carrying a baby; others heard crying, though no babies were patients at the time.

When the building was demolished in the late 1970s workmen preferred to stay in pairs because they felt a presence behind them, especially in the chapel, the mortuary and the corridor where the ghost most often appeared. As the work progressed the presence diminished. Perhaps it is now gone completely. One wonders whether the occupants of the houses now on the site of the hospital have anything untoward to report.

An exorcist might have been brought in; the ritual involved twelve parsons, who were sometimes difficult to recruit because of the belief that one would die within a year of the ceremony. At Northleach a barrel of spirits (alcoholic) also featured, though not to encourage the clergy. The barrel, left in a seldom-used room which was then completely sealed, the door and windows being bricked up, was thought somehow to attract and lay the ghost. Shipton Court and Lodge Park between Northleach and Andoversford are believed to have such rooms.

The sealing of a haunted place was also tried elsewhere. At Winson a young woman who gave birth to a bastard child drowned herself in the well on the green. Then prolonged and piteous cries were heard coming from the cellar of one of the houses nearby. The vicar assembled brother clerics for a ceremony of exorcism, and for good measure arranged for workmen to block the entrance to the cellar whence the cries had come.

At Oakridge, where a son murdered his father at a farm now called Frampton Court, it was the other way round. Despite a plea of provocation - the father had attacked the son's wife - he was found guilty and hanged. 'It was said,' writes Norman Jewson, 'that the ghost of the murdered man haunted one room of the farm, so this was closed and the doorway bricked up. Later the ghost was exorcised by the parish priest.' At Upton St Leonards the bricking up was felt to be unnecessary: 'A certain Miss Nicholls hanged herself, and the ghosts was said to haunt her house. Twelve ghost-layers came and laid the ghost at midnight under the hearthstone.'

Even now the Church of England has an exorcist in every diocese. Canon Harry Cheales (see also Chapter Four) of Wyck Rissington became well known in this role in the 1970s. He began at his rectory, which had a poltergeist he called Geoffrey, who ran up and down stairs, rattling handles and banging doors. In addition he had 'a pet cat which would rub against your legs to be stroked, then walk through the walls.' Canon Cheales simply ordered Geoffrey to 'cut out the rough stuff', and the troubles subsided. Normally his approach was along these lines:

> *No ghost likes to be misunderstood. Often, if there are young children in the house, they will babble something seemingly incoherent, but it will turn out to be the name of the ghost. Sometimes it will write its name on the wall. Only one in ten are evil spirits, and they will never harm children. Exorcism is useless if the ghost is only trying to be friendly. I generally manage to persuade them to stop making mischief by talking to them, although I have one little wretch called Frank, who disappeared from one family only to reappear elsewhere.*

His success was counter-productive in one respect. When he retired in 1980 Canon Cheales hoped to buy a house cheaply because it was haunted, but 'There are none left round here for me,' he said. 'I've cured them all.'

7

# FAIR PLAY

A passion for play seems to be an innate human characteristic, and it has given rise to an enormous range of pastimes, sports and diversions. Some sports involving the baiting of animals have now long disappeared from respectable society, though they were once accepted as part of the normal calendar of events. The pursuit of wild animals for sport is now fiercely contested by some, but supporters of fox-hunting argue that their activities are a traditional part of the fabric of rural life.

With the advent of television horse-racing has increased its already wide appeal, and ranges from village point-to-point meetings to the grand events at Cheltenham which command a national audience. The bustle and excitement of, say, the National Hunt Festival every March have much in common with the atmosphere generated by the great fairs of the past.

Of the three kinds of fair, the 'mop' or hiring is described in Chapter Eight. The wake, formerly a cherished feature of almost every village's life, originated as a church festival but became more and more secular in its pursuit of entertainment. The fair proper, primarily devoted to the sale of goods and livestock, also became increasingly devoted to pleasure.

An almanac of 1794 lists 93 fairs in Gloucestershire held in 38 towns and villages. In 1888, just under a century later, the number of fairs had drastically declined, but 30 places still had at least one. Now only a handful remain, and perhaps only Stow retains its original function of selling horses.

The reasons for change include population decline in some places, the rise of commercialised sport and entertainment, the establishment of new forms of transport, retail selling, and leisure. Yet some fairs and wakes failed not for lack of success but excess of it, with concomitant rowdyism, drunkenness and 'immorality'. Even village events such as Chalford Feast, lasting one week in August each year, aroused such aversion in some that within living memory a temperance organisation arranged outings to Weston-super-Mare to take people away from its unseemly influence.

Nevertheless, some fairs such as Dover's Games have been revived, and others (Cooper's Hill Wake and Gloucester's Barton Fair) have obstinately survived. Many of their rough sports - shin-kicking, for example - have gone, but pugnacity and passion are still there. Few can resist at some time in their lives the lure of the fair.

## Inbred Delight

The name of Stobbal Green near Brockweir recalls a game played in the sixteenth and seventeenth centuries there, and also on Minchinhampton

Common and on the flat top of Stinchcombe Hill. John Smyth, writing in the 1640s, commented:

> *The large and levell playnes of Slimbridge warth and others in the Vale of the Hundred [of Berkeley]; and the downes or hilly playnes of Stintescombe, Westridge, Tickrudydinges, and others in this hilly or Cotteswold part; doe witness to the inbred delight that both gentry, yeomanry, rascality, boyes, and children doe take in a game called stoball.*

This early form of golf also attracted the attention of John Aubrey, some forty years later: 'They smite a ball, stuffed very hard with quills, and covered with scale [sole] leather, with a staffe, commonly made of withy.' He added that the staff was 3.5 feet long, the ball about four inches in diameter, 'and as hard as a stone.'

Another hard ball, an egg-sized piece of elm called a 'nunney', was struck with sticks cut from the hedge in a primitive form of hockey known as 'bandy'. The only rule specified that when a man obstructed the nunney with his feet or body the rest of the players could shout, 'Turn, bumby'. If the man did not immediately do so the others were entitled to set about him. Bandy is one of the games affectionately listed by John Clare in his poem *Remembrances.*

Pastimes could arouse strong feelings. In 1656 Thomas Phipps of Sevenhampton was fined 3s 4d 'for playing att skittells on the Sabath day,' and a similar amount for causing bloodshed. Blood was also spilt at cock fights. A field at Avening called Cockpitts must have been one of the sites. By one account, fights took place at Brockweir where the buttress of the present bridge now stands; by another, where the white-walled chapel was erected in 1831 by Bristol Moravians to counter the ungodliness of local people. The house at St Briavels now called 'Cot by the Castle' once had a cockpit. George Creswick, who died in 1911 at the age of eighty, remembered buying a Duck-winged Grey cock for twenty-five shillings from Newnham-on-Severn, and walking both ways to do so.

Another haunt of cockfighters was in front of Fort Cottage at Rodborough, and in pits at the Falcon Inn, Painswick, the Green Dragon (removed in 1924 when the premises were converted to a private house), and the Hare and Hounds (now the Lygon Arms), both in Chipping Campden. A house at Holcombe, near Edge, has an underground passage leading to a cellar used for clandestine cock fighting after it had become illegal, and another house at Painswick, Yew Tree Mount, had its own pit.

Bull baiting also attracted a devoted following. The Roman amphitheatre at Cirencester, still called the Bull Ring, was used for this purpose. At Tetbury a well-known toast ran: 'To all our friends round Tetbury bull ring.' The place used was on the Lower Chipping, opposite Love Lane. Between 1691 and 1759 there are frequent references in the town's accounts to items such as 'a collar for ye bull, 4/6d' or 'a rope for baiting bulls, 5/-'. The last bulls were baited at Tetbury and Stroud in 1786 and at Minchinhampton in 1817.

Bull baiting and cockfighting were outlawed in 1835. Attempts in recent years to make fox hunting illegal have failed, and the sport has both passionate devotees and determined opponents. In the past gentlemen riders were followed for miles by villagers on foot. In their enthusiasm for the chase working men would forfeit a day's pay, and boys take a caning for truancy. Some sympathised with the quarry. A huntsman reins in and addresses an old man sitting on a fence: 'Tell me, my man, have you seen the fox pass by?' 'Fox? Have 'e got long years [ears]?' 'Yes.' 'An' short legs?' 'That's right. Which way did he go?' 'An' have 'e got a long nose?' 'Yes, yes.' 'An' a big bushy tail?' 'Of course.' 'Ah well, then, I ha'na sid 'en.'

There are still foot followers today, though most who do not ride favour motorised transport; and the social spectrum covered by members of the hunt is undoubtedly much wider than it was fifty or hundred years ago.

J. Arthur Gibbs commented that at the end of the last century in Cirencester alone (he calls the town the 'Melton of the west') over two hundred hunters were stabled, not counting those in the numerous hunting boxes round about. He gives a fine description of a run of that time. Pursuits were often set into song and then sung at hunt suppers. This comes from John Puffet of Lechlade:

**Bold Reynolds**

*Bold Reynolds in Hampshire did dwell,*
*He lived at a plentiful rate,*
*The bones of young lambs he did pick,*
*And the farmers they all did him hate.*

*Then they sent for Lord Badminton's horses,*
*Likewise for his huntsmen and hounds,*
*They searched in the woods and the copses,*
*Until this bold Reynolds they found.*

*'They have chased me full forty-five miles,*
*And I ran it in three hours' space,*
*Till my strength it began for to fail,*
*And the dogs they got forward apace.*

*'They chased me o'er valleys and hills,*
*Where the gamekeeper shot at my bones,*
*I have not had a breathing till now,*
*And I fear I shall never return.*

*'They chased me through Lord Lovelock's park,*
*Where the bloodthirsty hounds they did follow;*
*It made my hair stand on an end*
*To hear how the huntsmen did holloa.*

*'Oh, pardon, dear huntsman, I crave,*
*For the gamekeeper swears I shall die;*
*But I've left my two brothers behind,*
*That love young lambs better than I.'*

*And now this old fox we have killed,*
*We'll go back to Alton and dine,*
*And dip his four feet in the glass,*
*And drink my lord's health in good wine.*

*Here's a health to Lord Badminton's horses,*
*Likewise to his huntsmen and hounds,*
*That have run this bold Reynolds to earth.*
*No better dogs ever trod the ground.*

The Beaufort Hunt is based at Badminton. In the 1760s the fifth Duke of Beaufort gave up hunting the stag and changed to the fox. Two hundred years later the tenth duke (who died in 1984) devoted his long life almost entirely to fox hunting, and when he suffered a heart attack at the age of 83 he was still following the hounds in a car. For four decades master of his own hounds, he was known to his associates, including members of the royal family, only as 'Master'. His death was mysteriously presaged by a fox (see Chapter Five), and after it fanatical opponents were only narrowly thwarted in their attempt to dig up his body and send his head to Princess Anne.

The Beaufort country, the hunter's word for territory, covers two thousand acres of Gloucestershire and Wiltshire, and once boasted as many green-jacketed riders. The Berkeley, whose members wear mustard-coloured coats, also boasts a lengthy tradition. In the late eighteenth century its country ranged through the Cotswolds and Oxfordshire to London. When the fifth earl died in 1810, Colonel Berkeley (later Earl Fitzhardinge) - the man who pursued poachers so ruthlessly (see Chapter One) - became master. Under him the hunt's attentions were confined to the whole of Gloucestershire, save that occupied by the Duke of Beaufort. The southern half was hunted from Berkeley and the northern from Cheltenham (though this was later made over to the North Cotswold). As Fitzhardinge lay dying in 1857 he summoned the huntsman to bring his favourite hounds. 'There are no better ones, Harry,' he said, and died. A later master, the second Baron Berkeley, nicknamed 'the giant' because of his small stature, was renowned for dropping 'h's' in such comments as 'You're riding my 'ounds, to 'ell. Go 'ome with you,' or 'You road-riding, gap-seeking, gate-opening, 'ell-abiding tinker, go 'ome with you.'

As part of their season the hunts have special meetings. For example, on Boxing Day the Berkeley meets at Thornbury, North Cotswold at Willersey and Cotswold Vale at Upton St Leonards. The Berkeley Vale is good hunting country except after prolonged wet weather when the rhines (pronounced reens) and ditches are swollen. At times a fox will make in desperation for the Severn at low water:

One hunt never to be forgotten was on 26 January 1922 when fox and hounds took to the river, chasing over mud and rock, right round the beacon lights a mile from shore and back again, whilst the field had a fine grandstand view from the Severn Bank. On several occasions a fox has been known to cross to the other side at very low tide but the pack, however much tempted, has always obeyed the call of the huntsman.

The hounds were equally well disciplined when a fox went to earth in an old grave in the churchyard at Oldbury-on-Severn. The rector ruled that the quarry had claimed sanctuary, so the hunt was called off. There is a chilling story from Stowell, near Northleach, where Lord Stowell kept a pack of hounds. One night such a frenzied noise was coming from the kennels - it seems that the hounds had not been fed - that a man who lived nearby got up and went to investigate. In their hunger and distress the hounds tore him to pieces, and little was left when a search was made the next morning.

## Sport of Kings

The racing of horses has a natural connection with riding them to hunts. Steeplechasing, as the name implies, was originally a race from one village steeple to another, by any route the riders chose to take. It then became a point-to-point, following a set line over hedges and even walls, sometimes with specially constructed jumps inserted. Several hunts still organise point-to-point meetings, though many steeplechases are now held on race-courses.

Flat races were once traditionally run in places such as the town meadow at Tewkesbury, also the venue for fairs, the common at Minchinhampton until 1827, and Cerney Down, near Cirencester. Eighteenth century meetings on Lansdown Hill, near Dyrham, attracted a mixed bag of spectators: local squires, Bath dandies, Kingswood miners, and criminals such as the notorious Cock Road Gang.

The Bibury Races may have been started by Sir John 'Crump' Dutton, a fanatical sportsman with a passion for deer coursing, who inherited the vast Sherborne estates in 1618. The course - four miles north-east of Bibury, between Ladbarrow and Macaroni Farms - was on Sherborne land. It no longer exists, but the site is shown on Pathfinder maps. In 1681 when Parliament met at Oxford the Newmarket spring meeting was transferred to Bibury. Charles II attended, accompanied by Nell Gwynne. The Prince of Wales, the future George IV, went several times. In 1802 he hacked round the course and stayed for a week. Like other top people he put up at Lord Sherborne's grand house. Humbler visitors rented rooms from Bibury shopkeepers who slept on their shop boards, with the family under the counter.

Some racegoers took the opportunity to indulge in other kinds of sport. George Swinford writes:

> *When the Bibury races were on there was always a lot of fighting there, and Palmer [a Broughton man known to be handy with his*

*fists] was generally amongst it. I heard from a farmer, who worked at Oxleaze Farm and had the half day off to go the races, that as soon as Palmer got there someone came up to him and said: 'They have brought one especially for you today, Palmer.' 'All right, I'll have a bit of dinner first, then you can bring him along,' said Palmer. So they stripped among the caravans and started to fight. After a few minutes sparring Palmer let go, and hit the other fellow a blow on the forehead and the skin fell down over his eyes. This finished the fight, and as Palmer was on his own without friends they tried to mob him. He stood with his back to a caravan wheel and knocked them down as fast as they could come. This was the last fight Palmer had at Bibury. He went to the races as usual, but nobody interfered with him after that.*

Although Bibury races came to an end in the middle of the nineteenth century, training continued in the area until within living memory. Aldsworth has two Derby winners to its credit, 'Coronation' (1840) and 'Dangerous':

*'They be a-comin', they be a-comin',' yelled the watch boy as he rushed forth from his point of vantage on Aldsworth Tower, and hurled himself into the midst of divine service on the Sunday morning after the 1833 Derby. The horses were coming home to Aldsworth from Epsom, with the victorious Dangerous in the line, and there was not a soul left in Aldsworth Church that morning within one minute of the watchboy's cry. Parson and people, out they went pell-mell.*

Training also went on at Northleach, with gallops at Stowell and Puesdown. Isaac Day, landlord of the 'Kings Head', was a trainer known throughout England as the 'Archbishop of Northleach'. From 1800 until 1880, there were stables next door to the inn at Walton House. Bourton Hill was also used for training, as were some areas near Cheltenham.

The Cheltenham races were held on a level tract of land in front of the inn at Andoversford, and on West Down, near Cleeve Hill, which is still used for gallops. Racing now takes place at Prestbury Park, home of the famous Gold Cup Steeplechase and the National Hunt Festival, which owes its origin to a gentleman rider of Prestbury, Fothergill 'Fog' Rowlands. It was at West Down, though, that Gloucestershire's most famous rider won many of his races.

Fred Archer was born at St George's Place, Cheltenham, in 1857, one of thirteen children of a jockey turned innkeeper, William Archer. Soon after Fred's birth the family moved to Cintra House, now called Vine Tree Cottage, at Prestbury. His father was landlord at the Kings Head for seven years until about 1873, then moved to the Rose and Crown in the High Street at Cheltenham.

At the age of eleven Fred was apprenticed to a Newmarket trainer, and won his first race two years later. During a relatively brief career of sixteen years he

*Fred Archer, the legendary Cheltenham jockey who won St. Leger six and the Derby five times. He trained on toast, stomach powder and champagne. After his death, people claimed to see him on a spectral horse leading the field at Newmarket.*

rode in just over 8000 races, of which he won almost 2500, including the St Leger (six times), the Derby and 2000 Guineas (five times each) and the Oaks (four times). His winnings amounted to some £250 000. He was nicknamed 'The Tinman': 'He rides to win,/He rides for the tin.' The catchphrase, 'Archer's up', meant 'everything is all right.'

Despite being six feet in height, Archer reduced his weight during the season to only eight stone seven. His diet was dry toast, stomach powder and champagne. The drastic regime caused him to become seriously ill in 1886, at the age of only twenty-nine. At Newmarket in a fit of depression he shot himself. Of his winnings only £60 000 remained, much of the rest having been spent in gambling.

At the height of his fame, Archer often hunted with the Cotswold, and stayed with his father, whom he had set up there, at the Andoversford Hotel. He is also remembered at the Kings Arms in Prestbury, where this rhyme is displayed:

*At this Prestbury Inn lived*
*FRED ARCHER the jockey,*
*Who trained upon toast,*
*Cheltenham water and coffee.*
*The shoe of his pony*
*hangs in the Bar,*
*Where they drink to his prowess*
*from near and from far,*
*But the man in the street*
*passes by without knowledge*
*That 'twas here Archer*
*swallowed his earliest porridge.*

After his death people claimed they saw him on a spectral horse leading the field at Newmarket, and this inspired more verse:

*Across the heath - along the course*
*'Tis said that now on Phantom horse*
*The greatest horse jockey of our days*
*Rides nightly in the moonlight rays.*

## Wakes and Fairs

'Come, march to wakes and fairs,' says Edgar in *King Lear*; and march country people did, in large numbers, for these were among the few opportunities they had for organised entertainment. A wake was originally a vigil for prayer on the day of a church's patron saint. The religious observance would be followed by merrymaking - originally in the churchyard, later on a convenient space nearby. The prime purpose of fairs was the sale of goods and livestock but they, too, provided refreshment and amusement for those attending. In most places, sooner or later, the pleasure aspect became dominant.

The months favoured for church dedications, and hence wakes (also known as feasts or revels), seem to have been June, August and September. Snowshill commemorated St Barnabas (11 June) with sedate tea parties for children and adults, a procession round the green led by a band playing *Onward, Christian Soldiers*, and a service in the church. More boisterous celebrations on the Saturday after Whitsun attracted so many people that 'you could have walked round on people's heads.' Swings and roundabouts were set up on the green and the adjacent Hall's Piece. Beer and homemade wines, for which the village was famous, were served in a marquee. The venue later moved to a site near the present National Trust car park but the event came to an end in the early 1930s. In 1938 Dick Newman (then aged ninety) looked back in sorrow on 'the Snowshill Wakes on Whit Saturday when the country dances were footed to a capital good band.'

Only a few miles away, Willersey Wake took place on Midsummer Day, 24 June, five days before the main feast of the church's dedicatee, St Peter. Algernon Gissing, who lived close by at Saintbury, has left an affectionate and evocative description of Willersey Wake, published in 1924. He mentions 'roundabouts, swing-boats, cocoa-nut alleys, and shooting galleries, with one or two monstrosities; stalls of sweets and brandy-snap, Birmingham jewellery and what not'. By 7 p.m. everything would be getting into full swing:

> *The discordant organs of two, and sometimes three, roundabouts were in full blast. Men and women bawled or screamed their several attractions. The heavy swing of boats was in the air, or the grating of the board that stopped them, cracks of the rifles, thuds of Aunt Sally missiles against the canvas behind, tremendous blows of the beetle in trials of strength, all blended with the general uproar of voices in almost every conceivable key of raillery and laughter from the throng which was surging to and fro in the roadway or gathered about the greens. Towards nine the first naphtha light would flare out, to be quickly followed by others, and then the peculiar smell of these primitive cressets began to add their part to the general impression of the scene. This was the signal for the younger children and strict propriety to withdraw. Not that I ever saw anything to hurt rational susceptibilities at any hour, and of course two or three policemen were in the crowd, if with no very 'severe regard of control'. But naturally after dark the fun became more fast and furious, youths gave fuller play to facetious humours, delighted in swinging girls to terrifying heights in the boats, squirting scent down their necks, and so on. Even in those days, however, the women seemed quite capable of holding their own and could give quite as good as they got.*

Others, as we shall see, failed to share Gissing's indulgent attitude.

Even small villages enjoyed their celebrations. The feast at France Lynch took place on Whit Tuesday, not too far from the birthday of its church's patron saint, John the Baptist, on 24 June. A modest affair, with a few 'sway boats' and stalls selling gingerbread and cockles, this was nevertheless 'a highlight of village life' until its demise in 1933.

Cold Ashton's Church is dedicated to the Holy Trinity but although Trinity Sunday is the first after Whitsun the village chose Whit Sunday for its revels, at which a favourite dish was whitepot. This was also favoured at Poole Keynes, where the ingredients were four quarts of milk, a pound of flour, a pound of golden syrup, eight eggs, two ounces of butter, two nutmegs, and mixed spice to taste. The flour, eggs, syrup and spice were first beaten in a pan. Next the milk was boiled and stirred into the ingredients to make a paste, and then the butter was dotted in small pieces on the top. At the last moment three quarters of a pint of cold water was poured, without stirring, into the middle. The whole thing was baked in an earthenware vessel in a hot oven for an hour, and then gently for a further seven or eight hours. When cool, the mixture became a kind of jelly. It was popular at Pucklechurch and also at Doynton, where it lingered until the late 1950s.

Several other places had local delicacies. At Nympsfield they ate puddings or dumplings with wild plums ('heg-pegs') and at Painswick apple or other fruit pies with a small china dog inside. Both preferences were reflected in the generic nicknames (see Chapter Three) for the respective inhabitants.

A sheep was roasted whole at Chalford (15 August); leg of mutton and turnips were preferred at Haresfield (third Sunday in September). Several places chose pork. So much pig's cheek was eaten at Woodchester (first Sunday after 8 September) that if you looked from the other side of the valley on the Sunday after the feast, only one chimney would be smoking, and everyone would be converging on that house for dinner.

The Bisley delicacy was pig's cheek with parsnips (Sunday after 12 November). Pig was *de rigueur* at Avening, too, on the Sunday after Holy Cross Day (14 September) in the shape of boar's head - hence Pig's Face Sunday (see Chapter Four). Pork was also eaten with turnips in Gloucester at Barton Feast which followed the fair of the same name at the end of September.

The first day of Coleford Fair (20 and 21 June) was devoted to the sale of horses, sheep, pigs and wool; the second to pleasure, which included roly-poly pudding made in a stocking and retailed at a penny a slice. Traffic problems brought the fair to an end in 1939, and with it the well-loved roly-poly.

Gingerbread horses and other animals were a feature of Minchinhampton Fair, and until the 1870s any householder could obtain a licence to sell beer on fair days. The beverage was advertised by a bush hanging outside the house. A similar custom obtained elsewhere, including Winchcombe, where there might be twenty or thirty 'bush houses' at horse fairs.

The inevitable gingerbread also appeared at Stow, together with homemade rock and Banbury cakes. Oldbury-on-Severn had its sticky gooseberry tarts and also whitepot. The fair was held on the Saturday after Whitsun on the Ship green and along the road as far as the Pound. There was dancing on the green to the music of fiddle and harp, and among the crowds were parties ferried from across the river.

At the big fairs huge quantities of commodities and cattle changed hands. At Marshfield on 24 May and 24 October each year, continuously from 1266, livestock was sold. In 1901 as many as 4000-5000 sheep and 300 cattle changed

*Please bring Catalogue to Sale.*
NEXT THURSDAY & FRIDAY.

# STOW FAIR

THURSDAY, OCT. 23rd,
FRIDAY, OCT. 24th,
1924.

CATALOGUE OF GREAT AUTUMN 2 DAYS SALE
OF

# 240 HORSES

VIZ:
*First day's Sale commencing at 12 o'clock,*

76 VANNERS, HUNTERS, COBS & PONIES.

*Second day's Sale commencing at 10 o'clock,*

164 VALUABLE CART HORSES & COLTS, (Several Shire Breds) including

100 Grand Young Geldings and Fillies,
SUITABLE FOR TOWN WORK, which

## TAYLER & FLETCHER

WILL SELL BY AUCTION IN THE

MOUNT PLEASANT CLOSE,
adjoining the Swell Road, by kind permission of Mr. H. Hollis.

Office: The Square, Stow-on-the-Wold, Glos.
'Phone No. 13. Telegrams "Auctions, Stow-on-the-Wold."

hands at each fair. There was a time at Chipping Campden when as well as Cotswold wool much of the entire Welsh production was sold. During the eighteenth century as many as 20 000 sheep were bought at Stow in a single fair.

Fairs at Stow were traditionally held on 12 May and 24 October. These dates were formerly 1 May and 13 October, the main feast of Edward the Confessor, but when the calendar changed in 1752, eleven days were added so as to keep to the previous timing. The first was for horses and sheep, the second, in

Rudder's words, 'for all sorts of cattle, hops, cheese, Birmingham wares, linen of the manufacture of this part of the country, and other valuable commodities.'

After the First World War the pleasure element predominated but the fairs went on. 'As sure as the fair,' ran a local saying. A Cotswold labourer who emigrated to Australia and told officials that he was 'thirty last Stow Fair' was flabbergasted when they did not understand him. Even today Stow people would know what he meant, for the fairs survive after six and a half centuries.

Many other wakes and fairs have disappeared. Northleach went in the 1880s, Bream some forty years later. Coleford, as we have seen, deemed its fair in 1939 less important than the movement of cars (though in 1993 started to close streets to traffic again for its carnival). The last remnants of Blockley's fair, which had once boasted sixteen days of unbroken festivity, came in the 1970s.

## Fair and Foul

Some events were suppressed or emasculated because parson, squire or magistrate disapproved. As early as 1702 William Blathwayt complained about the lack of progress in building his new house at Dyrham: 'Sunday last was this Town and Cullen [Colerne] Wake or Revell, and between them a great part of the Workmen have been Revelling and drunkening ever since till this Morning, particularly Richard Broad and his Partner.' A further note a few days later mentions that the same two men are missing once more, having gone to Box Revel.

In 1710 similar grievances were expressed, this time at the official level of Gloucestershire's Court of Quarter Sessions:

> *It has been represented to this Court by the ministers and principall inhabitants of the several Parishes of Coaley Frocester and Nympsfield, That there are yearly held in those Parishes aforesaid as in other places in this County unlawfull Wakes and Revells and other disorderly meetings upon several Lords Days and which have been continued on for several days of the week following: vizt (sic) the Sunday after St Bartholomews Day* [24 August] *at Coaley Palm Sunday at Cowleys Pick [Coaley Peak] and Nympsfield and the Sunday after St Peter's Day* [29 June] *at Frocester, and on other particular Sundays in other places in this County, which draw great Concourse of People together, to the great Prophanation of the Lords Day in Contempt of her Majesties Gracious Proclamation against Immorality and Prophaneness, where Rioting and Drunkenness, Lewdness and Debauchery and other immoralities are Committed.*

The effectiveness of such statements seems to have been limited. Similar pronouncements were made in 1718 and 1731, both also referring to 'other disorderly Meetings, for Wrestling and Cudgel-playing for Hats or other Prizes, which are promoted and encouraged by Alehouse-Keepers'. On the subject of

Coaley Peak, Fosbrooke, writing in 1807, quotes John Smyth: 'The wake day of the church is noticed by Mr Smythe, as in his time forming a concourse or fair, where all kinds of country wares were sold; and, he adds, the number of young people ascending and descending the hill called Couley Pike, and boys tumbling down, especially on Communion days, afforded much pleasure to the elder sort.'

The indulgent attitude shown here contrasts with the strong attack made on such events by a cleric from Stow in 1736:

> *What I have now been desiring you to consider as touching the evil and pernicious consequence of Whitsun Ales among us, doth also obtain against Dover's Meeting, and other noted places of public resort of this nature in this country, and also against Midsummer Ales and Mead Mowings; and likewise against the ordinary violations of those festival seasons commonly called Wakes. And these latter, in particular, have been often times the occasions of the profanations of the Lord's Day by the bodily exercise of wrestling and cudgel-playing, where they have been suffered to be practised on that holy day.*

Later in the same century another clergyman, Richard Graves, rector of Mickleton, mentioned Dover's Meeting in his book, *The Spiritual Quixote* (1771), a satire on Methodism. The character, Wildgoose (who is meant to stand for George Whitefield, the Gloucester Methodist) remarks on the 'great irregularities ... practised amongst the common people ... at wakes and revels, and other ungodly meetings; particularly at a heathenish assembly of that kind, on the Cotswold-hills, called Dover's Meeting'. His servant, Tugwell (a local Sancho Panza apparently based on a Mickleton shoemaker), rejoins: 'Ah, I have been many times at Dover's Meeting, and won a hat there at cudgel-playing when I was a young man; and they say there is good sport there this year.' Wildgoose asks: 'Dost thou call that sport where so many poor souls are devoted to destruction, by drinking, swearing, and all kinds of debauchery?'

As the two come on the scene, a race for a Holland shift is announced, 'and six young women began to exhibit themselves before the whole assembly in a dress hardly reconcilable with the rules of decency.' Wildgoose climbs on a hamper to harangue the crowd. At first he is taken for a quack doctor, but when the people realise that he is complaining of their 'anti-Christian recreations' they pelt him, and also poor Tugwell, with orange peel, clods of dirt and pieces of horse-dung.

Dover's Meeting (of which more below) flourished until the middle of the nineteenth century but other events withered in the blasts of reforming zeal. Robert Raikes, the pioneer of Sunday schools, considered the Painswick wakes to be 'a festival that would have disgraced the most heathenish nations,' and lamented the 'drunkenness and every species of clamour, riot and disorder' which 'filled the town upon this occasion.' However, some years later, in 1786, he congratulated himself that 'the usual crowds who attend the feast ... instead of repairing to the alehouses as heretofore ... all hastened to the church.' Raikes attributed the change to the establishment two years earlier of a Sunday school which diverted 'the attention of the vulgar from their former prostitution of the Lord's day, by exhibiting to their view a striking picture of the superior enjoyment to be derived from quietness, good order, and the exercise of that benevolence which Christianity peculiarly recommend' (sic).

This seems rather too good to be true, but it is clear that opposition from the churches - ranging from disapproval through vigorous campaigning to legal action - did much to emasculate or even terminate many fairs and wakes. At Mangotsfield the vestry applied to magistrates in 1806 for an order to ban the local wake. One would have thought the modest stalls, penny shows and Aunt Sally innocuous enough, but there was some rowdyism. Even so, the wake was suppressed, but not until some twenty years later, so its supporters must have put up a fight.

Enclosure helped at Redmarley in 1838, by depriving villagers of the green where the wake had been held on the Sunday before St Bartholomew's Day, 24 August. There was 'much drunkenness and fighting on these occasions, the spectators, they say, climbing some pear trees to watch the fights.'

Fighting also features in the Upton St Leonards Cherry Fairs, which were suppressed by the village's first resident clergyman, Rev. James Henry Parsons (who arrived in 1833). Not only did men from neighbouring Brookthorpe and Whaddon regularly attack the gatherings but Upton villagers settled their own differences there. The fairs, held on the first three Sundays after Old Midsummer Day, 5 July, are described by H Y J. Taylor:

> *The cherry fairs at Upton St Leonards always attracted a multitude of visitors. Boughton of Upton, the Pitts of Gloucester, and the Preedies of Newent, with cake and gingerbread makers from more distant places, usually attended, and drove a lively trade. The poor villagers who could not rise to the dignity of stalls placed their scales and weights on the stones and their cherries and gooseberries in traps by the roadside ... The field opposite the inn [the 'Kings Head'] was called 'Cider mead', and there at the cherry fairs the belligerents and malcontents of the village usually assembled not only to drink cider but to settle the year's accumulation of disputes by pugilistic conflict ... Much heavy drinking prevailed at the fairs; the Sunday evening was systematically profaned; immorality, drunkenness and profanity were in the ascendant. I could give you from my notebook stories ad nauseam of still-remembered encounters in which village bullies were brought to their knees, to the unbounded delight of the spectators. But I refrain. It should, however, be remembered that these pagan orgies were held at a time when the parish was without a resident clergyman ... The good and gentle Mr Parsons came at an opportune time as an apostle and missionary in a heathen land, and his light shone in the surrounding darkness.*

It is hard to remember that Taylor is talking about a small village a few miles from Gloucester, in the third decade of the nineteenth century. The strength of his language is all the more remarkable in that he is normally a tolerant commentator on popular traditions. He seems to reserve a particular animus for wakes. He writes that 'the ancient history of Littleworth [a district of Gloucester just outside the old South Gate] was graphically described to me by an old toper as follows: "Why, in those there dees you could ha' got a pint of eel [ale], a pipe o' bacca and a fust-reet pair o' black eyes at any public house in the pleece for threpuns [threepence]".' Taylor, rejoicing that 'these annual wakes and orgies are defunct,' warms to his theme:

> *Many years ago a lady of education, taste and refinement visited Gloucester. She still remembers the day. Her impression was that it was the most heathenish town in England. She had to pass through Littleworth and Sudbrook. Ropes were hung across the streets upon which were suspended shifts, trimmed with gaudy ribbons, &c. She could not avoid witnessing some of the orgies of the neighbourhood. Everybody, men, women and children appeared to be drunk and furious, lewd and obscene. Young women were racing like mad creatures for shifts; old women, who shook with the palsy, were being galvanised by gin and cider into a run for bladders of snuff; men were fighting and wrestling, and some were scrambling like Hottentots for a pig with a greasy tail; some were climbing a greasy pole for a huge leg of mutton; boys were ducking their heads into tubs of water for apples and oranges; and some were jumping up for treacle rolls.*

This is a view from outside. The memories of those involved have a different perspective. John Oakey writes with great affection of the Winchcombe horse fairs, pointing out that 'one of the best farmers in the district,' Richard James of Hailes, was responsible for 'a splendid team of horses, arrayed in their best, who with their harness polished and a new waggon beautifully painted, paraded the streets.' He also makes clear that among the livelier participants in Whitsuntide revels were numbers of 'swells'.

On Whit Monday the church bells rang from 6 a.m. At 10 a.m. the three or four hundred members of the Winchcombe clubs moved off in procession behind the local band to the church. After a service there came sports and games:

> *In the street several tubs (shallow ones) were placed, and the men and lads with their hands tied behind them used to dip their heads into these for coins thrown in by those standing round. A cord would be thrown across the road, six feet high, with penny loaves dipped in treacle hanging from it, and men and boys with hands tied would compete in eating them. The swells would throw hot coins from the upstairs window of the George Hotel to be scrambled for by*

*the crowd, many of whom with their faces blackened would be dancing about. Half a crown would be offered for a sparring bout, the men pottering about until one just scratched the face of the other, drawing blood and so winning the prize. Foot and wheelbarrow races were held in the streets, and men blindfolded and often drunk would engage in them, with queer results.*

Apparently no orgies; but Oakey mentions other fights which were rather more fierce, often between the rival villagers of Alderton and Gretton. Vincent Perkins (1830-1921) relates how the men of Wotton-under-Edge and North Nibley met for an annual fight on Whit Monday at the Cockshoot Fair - so called because it was held in the Cockshoot Ride of Westridge Wood, between the two places. This seems to have been unofficial, since Wotton's charter fair, dating from 1252, is held in September.

The Cockshoot, with the usual shows and stalls, was presided over by a master weaver called Abbott, from Bear Lane. At dusk waggons laden with barrels of beer would arrive, and later the great fight would start - to resume next day on Ley Hill, and perhaps to continue into a third at North Nibley itself. A combination of strenuous opposition from the local clergy, Rev. Rowland Hill in particular, and unemployment which curtailed expenditure on feasting, brought Cockshoot Fairs to an end.

Among the warmest - and perhaps idealistic - accounts of fairs are those contributed to the *Wilts and Gloucestershire Standard* by Alfred Williams in 1914. Of Fairford he writes that 'the old rule of ducking pickpockets, cheats and all sharpers in the millpool was faithfully observed.' He undoubtedly witnessed the scene he described at Lechlade's September Fair:

*Now the busiest time of the fair is fast drawing on, for it is evening in the great Thames Valley ... Down the road from Inglesham and Highworth, a stream of pleasure seekers continues to arrive, while through the trees and above the house-tops the sound of the organ and shriek of the siren, mingled with the shouts and cries of the children, are heard.*

*A great crowd has gathered in the Market-place and along the street in front of the inns. This is chiefly composed of Cotswold people, with a few from the Wiltshire and Berkshire side of the river. The cheerful shepherds from the downs, the carters and cowmen with their wives from the farms, the ploughboys with their sweethearts, and all the youth of the town are there. What matters now the long labours of the field in burning heat and rain, the dark hours of winter approaching, the hardships of the every day life? All these are forgotten amid the noise of the street and the pleasure of meeting with acquaintances once more. And tonight everyone is cheerful. The harvest money has been paid; the pockets of all are jingling. Everyone is equipped with means to take his pleasure or to make purchases of some kind or other, either for use at home or to adorn the walls of the cottage.*

*The strangest things are offered for sale at the stalls and by the cheap-jacks, those who dispose their goods on the ground and stand in the centre with smoky, flaring paraffin lamps. Here are gaudy coloured pictures and painted glass ornaments, green and blue umbrellas large enough to cover a summer rick, bright gay handkerchiefs, mufflers and ties, preposterous jewellery, with hundreds of alarm clocks and cheap, foreign made watches, all warranted to be the finest obtainable. You might think that no one would purchase these articles, but John and William, Jane and Mary are out to buy and will not go empty away from the fair. The boys try their luck with the spinning wheel to get a brand new Sheffield blade, or obey the proprietor's injunctions to 'roll, bowl or pitch at the milky cocoanuts' and bring them crashing to the ground, while others buy crackers or leaden water-squirts of the beautiful dark gipsy girl and pelt or otherwise annoy the more sober of their companions. Donkey rides please some, and others amuse themselves by taking three balls and pelting at the top-hat worn by a juvenile who walks to and fro along a low platform with a stout lattice and is as cool as a cucumber under the showers of balls hurled at the top hat upon his head.*

*Naturally the inns are full tonight and there is more than the usual good feeling evident among the ploughmen and farm hands who beam at each other across the rooms of the 'Red Lion', or sit very close together and engage in a long confidential chat on the year's happenings, the crops and harvest, lambs and foals, and draw comparisons between this and that time and season.*

Still no orgies; yet many such occasions for simple pleasure came to an end with the First World War - though Lechlade continues. However, if many fairs and wakes died, other survived or were revived.

## From Shin-kicking to Nude Dancing

The lawyer, Robert Dover, moved to Saintbury in 1611. The following year he plunged into helping to organise the traditional Whitsuntide festivities held nearby on open land above Chipping Campden. Such was the dominance of his personality that soon the meeting took his name. An engraving of 1636 shows him as an impressive figure sitting on a white horse in fine clothes, which include a hat and ruff formerly worn by James I, and obtained through the good offices of Endymion Porter of Aston Subedge, groom of the royal bedchamber.

The events of Dover's Meeting (later called Games) were varied. Contests of skill and chance such as chess and cards took place in tents. Dancing competitions catered both for mixed groups and for women only. Ample supplies of food and drink were available from booths. The main attraction

1. *The Trouble House Inn near Tetbury: two landlords committed suicide here, and the inn was fired during civil unrest in 1830.*

2. *Beverstone Castle, taken and retaken by the Parliamentary troops of Colonel Edward Massey* [3.](below ) *during the Civil War.*

4. *Gateway to Llanthony Abbey, has an unlikely link with the Humpty Dumpty nursery rhyme*

5. *The Robber's Door at Tangley Manor, where a highwayman sacrifice an arm to avoid arrest.*

*6. The Severn Bore. On first seeing this phenomenon, the Romans thought the world was ending.*

*7. Our Lady's Well, Hampstead. The Virgin Mary stumbled across it when she lost her way on a visit to Joseph of Arimathea at Glastonbury in Somerset.*

8. *The Longstone near Minchinhampton which played its part in Alfred Watkins's ley line theory.*

9. *The three sisters near Nutterswood on Cleeve Common reputed to mark the bur of three sisters Faith, Hope and Charity, from a photograph published in 1919. Only two of the trees now remain.*

10. *The legend of Maud's Elm, in the village of Swindon, near Cheltenham, survived its felling in 1907.*

11. *A classic country inn scene; sitting by the fire in the Ebrington Arms, Ebrington.*

12. *Dymock: famous for its treacle mines and its curse.*

13. *An astonishingly (to modern eyes) unbusy Bibury with the Swan Hotel in 1901.*

14. *The ruined church at Lancaut, isolated in a remote loop of the River Wye.*

15. *Cirencester Church retains several peals, including its Pancake Bell which is rung on Shrove Tuesday.*

16. Above and [18.] below. *Stories in stone and wood: a shiela-na-gig at Ampney St. Peter; the mermaid misericord at Gloucester Cathedral.*

17. *This horseshoe has been nailed to th door at Kempsford Church since 1351, a relic of Henry, the first Duke of Lancaste who left the area in remorse at the death his only son in the nearby Thames.*

19. *Last of the old charmers? Robert Belcher of Withington with his black box of cotton, thread, buttons, pins and herbs. He predicted weather, told the future and charmed warts.*

20. *The wedding of Eva Lawrence and Will Smith at Chedworth (date unknown).*

21. *Funeral at Blockley of bus accident victims, 1924.*

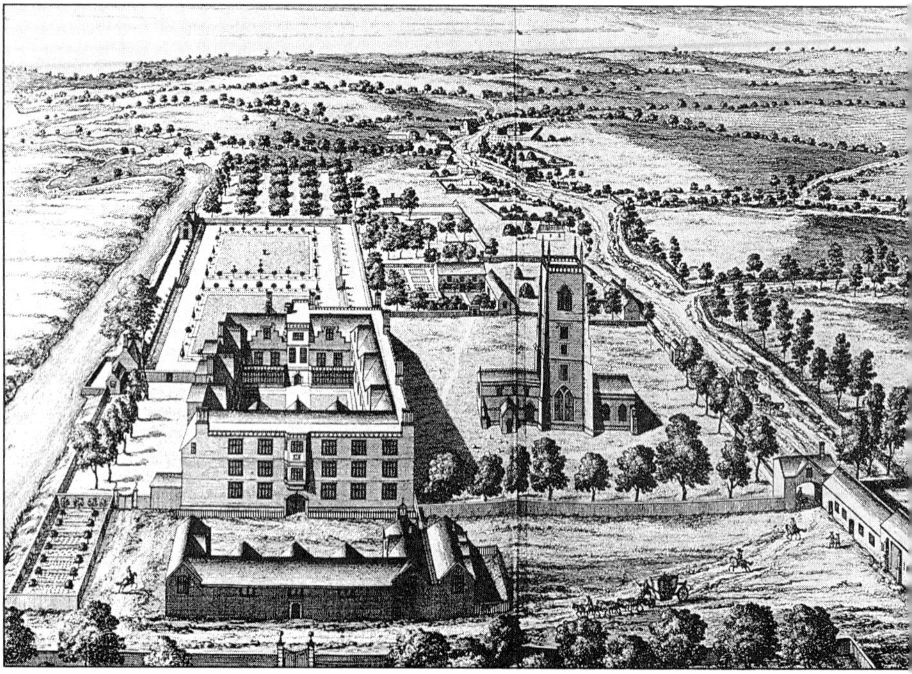

22. *Kempsford, after the Kip engraving of 1712, with the River Thames* (left). *The mansion* (to the left of the church), *which grew out of the former castle, is now gone. The haunted Old Vicarage* (foreground), *though much altered, remains.*

*Ghostly sightings at the Puesdown Inn,* (above) *the A40 near Compton Abdale and at the Ragged t Inn at Hyde* [24.] (right) *near Minchinhampton.*

*St. Briavel's Castle boasts ghosts of a man in armour, ıdy in white and another man in antique dress.*

26. *Stow Fair, one of the several markets held in Cotswold towns since the Middle Ages. Originally a sheep fair, Stow became better known as a market for horses.*

27. *Cheese rolling on Cooper's Hill in 1989.*

28. *The gleaners: 'Trotty' Eastbury of Rose Row, Blockley, with helpers, c. 1905.*

29. *The Dixton Harvesters c. 1725.*

30. *Ploughing with oxen, Fyfield, Eastleach.*

31. *Farm workers at Haresfield, 190*

32. *Thomas Pitts, photographed at Eastleach in 1935 at the age of 80, was a dancer and musician at Sherborne, and also danced at Longborough.*

33. *William Hathaway, Lower Swell musician and shoemaker.*

34. *Chipping Campden Floral Festival in 1896.*

35. *Northleach morris dancers on the cricket field in 1923.*

36. *Yate village band - everyone with a bowler.*

37. *The Sherborne Mummers in action.*

38. *Maypole dancing at Upper Slaughter in 1933.*

39. *Chedworth band on club day, 1905.*

*From* Annalia Dubrensia *(1636), a collection of poems 'upon the yeerely celebration of Mr Robert Dovers Olimpick Games upon Cotswold Hills'*

consisted of horse races, keenly contested over a distance of several miles. Dover himself had a pack of hounds and a huntsman who wore yellow (the colour of today's North Cotswold Hunt).

It is possible that Dover knew Shakespeare - they certainly had a number of friends and acquaintances in common - and that Shakespeare attended the Games. The wrestling match in *As You Like It* may have been based on his knowledge of the sports on Dover's Hill, which is only 12 miles away from Stratford.

Like wrestling - the shin-kicking element of which later became a separate contest - various forms of fighting with staffs or cudgels remained popular in Gloucestershire for many years. The advertisement which appeared in the *Gloucester Journal* on 15 June, 1778 is typical of many:

> *On Friday the 19th. of June will be played for at Backsword, at Stow-on-the-Wold, Gloucestershire, a Purse of TEN GUINEAS, by nine or eleven a Side, to appear on the Stage in the Market Place, in Stow aforesaid, by Eleven o'Clock in the Forenoon; and in case no side by Twelve o'Clock. Half a Guinea will be given to each Man breaking a Head, and Half a Crown to each Man having his Head broken.*

The pursuit continued into the nineteenth century, and Thomas Hughes provided a detailed and enthusiastic description in *Tom Brown's Schooldays* (1856). Late in the same century old countrymen gave H.Y.J. Taylor memories both of backstick and of shin kicking:

> *We tawks a deal about futball matches ... There be zummut savage about the game, and they reminds I o' so many wild beasts a-trying to yut one ship at a time. But I don't think as futball be half so brutal or dangerous as the wrestling matches as took place when I woz a kid at village feasts, wakes, and fagaries. I ha sin two vine young fellers stand up, figure away, and hug and tug and pull awoy, and twist and bend and drow one another down like bullocks in a slaughter-house. Tav mayud the very erth shuk wi the termengus weight o' thur carcusses. Why, I ha sin um kick one another's shins until the blood has run down in strames into their shoes. The ring as stood an zeed was men, women, children, gentlemen, squires, doctors, tradesmen, labourers, with zuntimes a pazun among um.*
>
> *Lar, how they did clap and shout and roar, while they kicked one another's bleeding shins and drowed one another down like sacks o' sawdust. Zum on um suffered awful aterwards. I zeed old Jack a-walkin' like a vrog on two sticks. I said to un, 'Wot be the matter w'ee, Jack?' 'Oh, I be awvool bod. I be never vree from payin' [pain]. 'Wot's yer age, Jack?' 'Oytee-dree next birthdoy comes a wik.' 'Well, Jack, I ha zeed thee mainy a bout o' wrestling, mainy, mainy year agone.' 'Hiss, you ha, mon. I be a-sufferin' vromt now, ond I con tell ee, if I had my woy agen I'd never stond up to ha my precious limbs kicked to pieces to plese a crowd o' yokels and tomvools.'*
>
> *My old friend said, 'When I woz a boy I was at a wrestling match, and I stood oz near to um as I be to you. How thoy did maul*

*one another. All of a zudden I yurd summut snop loike a stick. I thought it waur a stick. One on um fell down like a hos, ond thur waur a cry thot his leg waur bro-ock, ond a vot lot thoy cared about it.*

*'There waur another great game - vighting with back sticks - quarter staffs. The sticks woz hazle wood, wi wicker baskets for handles. My feether waur a don at it. There waur not mony as could get nigh him. He attended all the wakes, and woz always the best mon, and broke many hood yuds. He went to Oxenton wake. Thur waur a ring formed, and a mon as know'd feethur took off his hat ond drowd un in the air. Up went another, and in ten minutes feethur had broke his henemny's yud in dree or vour places, and had pocked his stick droo his ribs. Feethur nearly killed un, and muther gid feethur a bit o' tongue pie, wi plenty o' pepper, and wound up her chattering machine by soying, "Thee leave off this nonsense afore it be too late and thee bist had up for manslaughter." I wuz but a little un, but I remembers it well. I woz a kid in petticoats ond muther woz in our horchud. Muther had yurd as feethur hod bin at it agen and hod bin b'yut by a boy - a lad of about ateen. He didn't come whoam all night. In the morning, how-zumdever, oz I ond muther wuz in the horchud, down comes feethur wi his yud bound up in a tablecloth, a black eye, his face covered wi sticking-plaster, and his arm in a sling. He said, "Mary, I ha had my poor yud broke." "I knows thee hast; I yurd ont, ond I shud be ashamed to be b'yut by a boy. Be off wi thu," zed mother in a tanterum, "thee shotunt stoy yur"; ond while I waur a-crying, "Oh dontee, muther; dontee, muther," her raised her fut and kicked his behind awl droo thu horchud into the road. This cured feethur, and he gid it up, and joined the Methodies. All those old wakes, develrus wonderments, ond Sayton's abominations be all done away wi, and in the main we ha to thank the Methodies for't.'*

As late as the 1930s, H.J. Massingham, who lived for a time near Chipping Campden, heard stories of shin-kickers. He learned of a seventy-year-old stone-breaker whose shins were like corrugated iron from the times when 'Broddy fowt Kyanden' (Broadway fought Campden). At Ebrington he was told of 'an old warrior, dead some years, [who] used to sit in the pub and have his shins beaten by a deal plank as a form of training.' Another man, at Campden, 'thraped' his shins with a hammer to prepare for contests. After Dover's Games ended groups of men would go from their village to another, and challenge the men in the inn there.

Robert Dover died in 1652 at Barton-on-the-Heath, Warwickshire. Dover's Games, interrupted at the time because of the Civil War, resumed after the Restoration and lasted until the mid-nineteenth century. Their end came not for lack of popularity but excess of it, coupled with rowdyism.

As late as 1826 a newspaper reported: 'It is still a great holiday for all the lads and lasses within 10 or 15 miles of the place, and is attended by numbers of gentry and people of respectability in the neighbourhood.' Yet within twenty years, according to E.R. Vyvyan of Cheltenham, the games had become 'the trysting place of all the lowest scum of the population which lived in the districts lying between Birmingham and Oxford.' At about that time Mrs Ann Stratton, landlady of the Plough and Harrow at Evesham, regularly supplied refreshments to people attending. Her son later wrote:

> *My mother used to go to Dover's Hill each year, taking a large tent, a good supply of ale, cider, wine, spirits, and eatables to sell during the gaming week. She made a good sum of money, and the surroundings were so alarming that as far as her silver changed into gold she would drop the sovereigns into the large barrels of ale or cider through the bung-hole (this was her safety bank). She also had a couple of loaded revolvers under her serving table ready for use. She never left the tent day or night until the festivities were over, and no one was safe from the lawlessness of the card sharpers, thimble-riggers, pick-pockets, thieves, confidence-men, vagrants, and criminals of the deepest dye, the riff-raff of society. During the daytime the turmoil was terrible, but all night long it was a perfect pandemonium. Cries of murder were often heard, and disorder and rapine held full sway. If the shadow of a person showed through the sheeting of the tent at night he would almost sure to be struck with a heavy bludgeon from without, and the miscreant would crawl underneath and rob his victim. One year every stall and tent (except my mother's) was levelled to the ground and their contents pillaged. Scores of persons, nut sellers and others, found a safe asylum in my mother's tent. The scenes, she said, were indeed terrible. Yet my mother went there every year with her serving-maids and her men, and with eatables and drinkables for sale, and was never molested or robbed.*

Mrs Stratton later found out the reason for her immunity: her husband once helped a man who subsequently 'proved to be a sort of leader of the lawless band who attended Dover's Hill.' It was he who quietly organised protection.

Canon G.D. Bourne, Justice of the Peace and rector of Weston Subedge, determined to bring the games to an end by having the land enclosed. He successfully arranged for it to be included in an Act of Parliament which came into force from 1853. The last games, held in 1852, attracted an attendance of 30 000 people. The final entertainment included a backsword fight between Spyres of Mickleton and Prestage (known as Nezzy Plested) of Campden, which lasted an hour. Plested won, despite losing an eye. His opponent died a fortnight later of the injuries he had sustained. The same kind of stoic ferocity recurs in a story told to Massingham of a Winchcombe man who came home from Gretton Wake with his head 'all bloodied' from a backsword fight. Without a word, his father reached up to the shelf, took down a cudgel and strode out. Later, having walked to Gretton and back, he returned, replaced the cudgel, and said: 'I've broke his arm.'

In 1951, a century after their demise, Dover's Games were resurrected as part of the nationwide Festival of Britain. From the early 1960s they were held annually, and now take place on the Friday evening after Spring Bank Holiday Monday. Chipping Campden's Scuttlebrook Wake follows on the Saturday. The wide-ranging programme of events on Dover's Hill includes throwing the hammer, putting the shot, tossing the caber and hauling on the rope in a tug of war. Backsword fighting and shin-kicking still feature, though now as an exhibition rather than in earnest. After the games at 10.15 p.m. a torchlit procession winds down the hill to Campden, where on the following day the activities include a fancy-dress parade, the crowning of a May Queen and dancing round a maypole. This is a sanitised form of the Saturnalia of the past but it nevertheless draws a crowd of several thousands.

One of Gloucester's ancient fairs also continues to attract large numbers, though its billing as 'historic street fayre and pageant' betrays a self-conscious would-be gentility far removed from the vigorous vulgarity of the past.

Under a charter originally granted in 1227 Barton Fair was the focus of the great sheep and wool trade of the Cotswolds. Horses, many of them from Wales, also changed hands in large numbers. The fair opened in late September, and was followed by hirings (see Chapter Eight) on the three succeeding Mondays. The serious business was supplemented by an ample provision of side-shows and entertainments, including booths where 'the appreciative public could have a sanguinary tragedy with seven dreadful murders, a laughable farce, a comic song, a fairy dance, a sailor's hornpipe, and the brass band for the low charge of threepence.' Edmund Kean, one of the greatest tragic actors in the history of the English stage, is said to have played several times at Barton Fair beneath a canvas roof. 'I can remember,' wrote H.Y.J. Taylor, 'when at our Barton Fairs the travelling theatre was permitted to remain in the street from the afternoon of the day preceding the first Fair day until the expiration of the Runaway Mop. It had full houses. They performed plays which the working men and the boys and girls of the period could understand.'

In a letter of 1889 to the *Gloucester Standard* G. Armstrong Hewitt, a contemporary of Taylor's, expressed the opinion that the fair would soon be lost, together with 'all its history of theatrical performers, clowns, harlequins, giants, fat ladies, conjurors, tumblers, menageries, sights, sayings, and doings.' Yet almost half a century later it still flourished, too much so for a group of Grundyish ladies who discovered booths in which scantily clad women posed.

The tableaux, accompanied by a suggestive commentary, had themes like 'Midnight Madness', 'Brazen', 'Eve tempting Adam', and (with a dubious sense of chronology) 'Where Queen Victoria wore her furs in 1904'. 'In the first scene,' runs one complaint, 'the girl was covered by some clothing and in each succeeding scene more was removed until nothing remained except the slightest piece of material across the breasts and round the hips something similar to the scantiest bathing drawers.' Another dates from 1937:

> *We visited the Fair on Saturday evening and found everything in full swing. We went into several shows, but although all were suggestive, we found nothing to which exception could really be taken until the last two. The first was called 'Blonde in the Barrel' and there was a strip-tease act, and a fan dance and the audience were assured that on the last night the fans would be dropped altogether.*
>
> *The other was called 'Mrs Barrett's Superior Blackbirds' and there was an utterly revolting and disgusting 'wedding night' dance between a coloured girl and man, after the girl had already worked her audience well up by a solo dance; and this show concluded with an act in which we were told that what the showman said would be better than what we actually saw. His remarks were all ambiguous, and in one case a girl was shown holding a muff in front of the lower part of her body, and this he entitled 'Where Eve wears her furs when it's cold'. This was presumably precisely similar to the scene called 'Where Queen Victoria wore her furs in 1904' which was shown and objected to at Barton Fair in 1934.*

Having said all this, the writer, Miss E.M. Hartland (sister of the folklorist, E.S. Hartland) adds: 'I have made arrangements to go to the Fair again tomorrow Monday evening, and shall probably try to go on Tuesday evening too, as I saw in the *Citizen* that the Pleasure Fair which commenced yesterday was well in advance of the Fair proper.' Such prurient concentration on a seamy side of the fair contrasts with the picture painted at much the same time by C. Henry Warren in his book, *A Cotswold Year*:

> *Of all the fairs that are held hereabouts none is quite so important as Barton Fair at Gloucester ... For a week or ten days the fun goes on, but it is the first day that really counts. On that day few farmers for miles around fail to go into Gloucester either to watch or take part in the great annual sale of sheep and horses. Old men, who perhaps do not go near the town all the rest of the year, turn up on Barton Fair day and may be seen lounging about in their best corduroys and black felt hats. If you want to hear Gloucestershire dialect at its best and ripest, go to Barton Fair: a 'foreigner' will be lucky to understand one word in two...*
>
> *After the first day, the Fair degenerates into a mere amusement park, where the Gloucester children can spend their pence and the lads from nearby villages take their girls for a spree. Last year it rained almost continuously throughout the Fair; and by the end of the week, since the fair-ground lies by the margin of the river, the place was little better than a swamp. This year, the Fair has opened*

*just as inauspiciously. But the naphtha flares blaze on the roundabouts churning out their dismal tunes.*

Some sixty years on, the fair is still held - on the last Saturday in September. In 1993, with scant regard for tradition, it was moved to the first Saturday so as to fall within the period of the 350th anniversary celebrations of the Siege of Gloucester. One recalls, though, that at the end of the siege the citizens were enjoined ever more to eat pork and turnips at Barton Fair in remembrance of the pig whose squeals betokened plenty of meat for the town, and caused the Royalists to withdraw.

## Mock Mayors and Maypoles

Barton Street in Gloucester had its own self-appointed 'court' which met every year in the 'Bell Inn' to elect a mock mayor. To be eligible for the office a man had to be a native of 'the Barton' or to have lived there for twenty-one years. An essential qualification was to have been guilty of some spectacular piece of nonsense or error of judgement. One year two brothers were elected jointly. They put a pot on the fire to make mutton broth, returned to find only water, and came to blows after accusing each other of taking the meat. Neighbours who intervened found the joint still hanging from a hook in the pantry.

The Island, a district to the west of the city, had its own elected king, an office filled by a Harry Hudman. He 'kept the throne for many years, but was at length outvoted; but resolving to retain by stratagem what he could not by free choice, invited his competitor to a glass; and whilst the latter was taking his draught, Harry jumped into his seat, was chaired through the island, and was thus king another year.'

Barton's 'mayor' survives another is chaired at Randwick (see Chapter Eleven) during ceremonies involving the rolling of cheeses. These feature prominently in Cooper's Hill Wake, for which a Saxon pedigree has been claimed. Even more extravagant is the notion that rolling the cheese is a relic of the discs of withies ignited and allowed to run downhill in honour of Baal by the Phoenicians (and introduced by them to Gloucestershire when they sailed up the Bristol Channel). More likely is the belief once held by participants that their action perpetuated certain ancient grazing rights. During Cranham Feast on the second Monday in August (revived in 1950) villagers also assert the right to common land by roasting a deer on it in the presence of the lord of the manor, and a similar practice (revived in 1965) applies at Frampton-on-Severn.

There are no early records of Cooper's Hill Wake. A document of 1680 on the subject of wakes mentions Cranham and Coaley but not Cooper's Hill. The classic local histories of the eighteenth and nineteenth centuries ignore it, thought it certainly existed by the early 1800s. A paper sent to the Gloucester town crier in 1836 with a request to proclaim 'the annual sports of Whitsuntide' sheds light not only on the event but on local pronunciation:

> *Cooper's Hill Weke to commence on Wits Monday per sisly at 3 o'clock. 2 cheeses to be ron for. 1 Plain Cake to be green* [grinned] *for. 1 do. do. to be jumpt in the bag for. Horings* [oranges] *to be Dipt in the toob for. Set of ribbons to be dansed for. Belt to be rosled for. A bladder of snuff to be chatred* [chattered] *for by hold wimming* [old women].

H.Y.J. Taylor left his own description of the event, written in 1890:

> *Some of my earliest recollections are associated with Cooper's Hill wake, which, in old days, was a festivity of some magnitude. Old John Jones, of Cooper's Hill, and the late Sir William Hicks, of Witcomb Park, were great patrons of the annual saturnalia. I can recollect Organ, the master of ceremonies, who was a fine, tall, handsome fellow. He used to appear upon the summit of the hill, dressed in a white linen chemise [smock], adorned with ribbons of all the colours of the rainbow. His hat was also decked with ribbons, and around his waist he wore the belt for which the wrestlers were to struggle, the winner claiming honour as champion wrestler for the year...*
>
> *The wrestling was not a pleasant spectacle, despite its ardent admirers and votaries. A man of pugilistic build and character formed a human circle by beating the turf, and alternately the toes of the crowd, with a long ground-ash stick and shouted 'A ring!/ A ring!' When the arena was formed, the struggle commenced. I have seen a couple of stalwart fellows, with sinew and tendon of iron, struggle fiercely, not to say ferociously for the mastery. What a shout of exultation went up when the victor landed his opponent fairly on his back on the sward! It was surprising how human limbs could be strained and kicked without the thews cracking and the bones breaking.*
>
> *These brutal trials of strength may have made the race hardy, tough, and valiant. To me, however, the spectacle was brutal and inhuman. I once met an aged athlete, who had been the champion on Cooper's Hill, but had become a cripple. 'John,' I asked, 'what is the matter?' 'Why, Mayster Harry, I ha' got a nashun bod leg.' 'How is that, John?' 'Mayster Harry, the follies o' my youth. If I had my days to go over agen, I'd never stond up to ha' my legs kicked to pieces at Cooper's Hill wake. I ha' larned this, thot our blessed Meeker nivver made our precious limbs to be kicked at vor other volks' amusement.'*
>
> *The grinning through 'hosses' collards' was a grand amusement. Some of the faces distorted to produce the 'best grin' would have puzzled Lavater and delighted Hogarth. Dipping in a tub of water for oranges and apples, and bobbing for penny loaves smeared with treacle, need no description.*

*The grand climax to the annual revel was running down the frightful declivity of a hill after a cheese. It was a perilous feat; but young fellows were ever willing to risk the danger. An old man described the cheese as being 'hard as Fayrur's* [Pharaoh's] *heart or the nether millstone.' I have seen the cheese bound down the hill and over a stone wall into the ground beyond. I have seen it in the hands of the winner without the symptom of a crack in it or the sign of an abrasion. To have run down the descent was perilous; to have eaten the trophy must have been a more dangerous feat than its capture.*

*Racing for the prize chemise was to me the most degrading part of the revel; but there were plenty of girls eager for the contest until a sad catastrophe occurred. On one occasion a young woman outpaced her competitors and reached the goal first - and there dropped dead.*

*After the wake was over ruffianism commenced. The village feuds, grudges and personal quarrels were then settled. Hats were thrown into the air, rings were formed, and sanguinary and prolonged fights followed... Happily, the schoolmaster has been abroad among our rural as well as our town populations; the village flower-show has superseded the bouts at wrestling and grinning; and Cooper's Hill wake is numbered among the things that have been, and is now only a memory to those who have crossed the summit of life's journey.*

Taylor's prediction proved ill-founded. The efforts of people like William Brookes ensured that the wake went on. When he died in 1934 at the age of eighty-three - he is buried in Brockworth churchyard - he had served fifty continuous years as master of ceremonies of the Cheese Roll (as it is called locally). The event did shed its wrestling but the maypole - periodically renewed - still crowns the hill. During the Second World War wooden mock-ups replaced the cheeses but the sport continued. In 1967, keeping up with changing times, the event moved from Whit Monday to the new Spring Bank Holiday. It now starts at 5 p.m.

The Double Gloucester cheeses, made by the Smart family from between Birdwood and Churcham, are neatly packed in round cases to give them some protection as they hurtle at 70 m.p.h. down the hill. Tumbling headlong after them remains a dangerous pursuit. In 1993, of those negotiating the one-in-three gradient fifteen were injured, four seriously. Two cheeses were won by Rob Preece, a roofer from Quedgeley. The record holder, though, is Stephen Gyde of Brockworth, who has won twenty-four times in fifteen years.

In the past, spectators have been injured by mis-directed cheeses, and at least one was killed. The epitaph may be apocryphal:

*Here lies Billy if you please,*
*Hit in the stomach with a cheese;*
*Cheese is wholesome fare, they say -*
*It turned poor Billy into clay.*

Something of the raw courage, the passion and pugnacity of shin-kickers and fair-goers of the past undoubtedly survives at Cooper's Hill. The same spirit is to be found in rugby players such as those at Berry Hill, who regularly beat teams from much bigger places. It is illustrated by an anecdote which recalls the laconic, vengeful ferocity of the Winchcombe man whose son was injured at shin-kicking. An ex-miner, Jim Hale, said: 'The last time I played for Berry Hill in Wales thoy finished up wi' fower of their players on the touchline. Nor they couldn't walk whum as easily as we could.' He explained to Dennis Potter, who relates the conversation in *The Changing Forest*, that one opponent was put out of action for some time. 'Half-heartedly I remonstrated,' said Potter, 'that surely that would have been going a bit too far? but sank back, grimacing and defeated, when he brought out a phrase which justified everything: "Well, mind, him had the ball".'

8

# WORKING WAYS

There is ample evidence in Gloucestershire of masons' work, some of it now several hundred years old, and those who produced their materials, the quarrymen. Yet the lore of their craft has received relatively little attention.

By contrast, the work of miners is largely invisible, but at least some parts of their culture would be familiar to outsiders. Even so, their beliefs, stories, superstitions, and even vocabulary await the greater attention they deserve.

The task is now more urgent since the mining communities of Gloucestershire are largely gone. The same might be said of the boatmen of canal and river, and of the deep-sea sailors who ventured forth from Bristol and Gloucester, Lydney and tiny Brockweir. As for soldiers, the Gloucestershire Regiment has now lost its independent existence, after three hundred years. The textile trade is also greatly reduced, and although agriculture continues to be of major importance its techniques and technologies would be unrecognisable to a farm worker of fifty years ago, let alone a hundred.

To record the rich lore, customs and indeed culture of the men and women from these trades and occupations could be seen as a form of rescue archaeology: twenty years from now, even ten, could be too late, and the loss would be irreparable. New ways may in due course generate new wisdom, but in the meantime we can treasure the heritage which comes from Gloucestershire working people of the immediate past. We may not see their like again.

## Masons and Miners

The mason is preceded by the quarryman. The high limestone cliffs beetling over the Wye near Tidenham were hand-drilled by men wearing red neckerchiefs and cord trousers tied below the knee. The great blocks of stone dislodged - some of which can still be seen lying abandoned on the bank - were wheeled in barrows over precarious planks to barges on the river or, earlier, to sailing trows (see below) with names like *Spry* and *Sunbeam, Emily* and *Priscilla.*

At Little Barrington the quarry was in fact a stone mine, with underground levels running towards the Oxford road. One of these passed beneath the New Inn (now called the Inn for All Seasons), and the story goes that the landlady used to summon the men for their dinner by banging on the floor.

Another tale comes from the 1920s:

> *When Bourton-on-the-Hill quars was working regular, Jimmy Malin used to gu all the way from Kyamdin to work there, and sure enough there he was every marning at half-past six on the clock ready on the*

*job. But I go day if Tom Bagnal as lived only about three chain up the road could ever get there until nigh enough seven. One morning the yudmon stops Tom and says to he, 'How the hell is it as Jimmy Malin can get here at the proper time and got to come from Kyamdin at that, and you as lives over the bank be allus later?' 'Well,' says Tommy, 'if Jimmy finds himself a bit behind, he have got plenty of time and road to run and make up for it.'*

In 1958 Henry Warren wrote of another quarryman at Coln St Aldwyns:

*It seems he was one day engaged on splitting a great slab of stone with his 'jad' or pickaxe, when suddenly the stone fell apart and there, in the middle, sat a toad, complete and whole. 'How that got there I dunno,' he said, 'but there 'twas. I shouted to my mates to come and hev a look; but at that minute - pouff! - the owd toad fell away, all to dust. And if that ent the truth, may beer never agen touch my lips.'*

Masons, too, had their stories, one of which suggested that their ancestors went on strike during the building of Solomon's temple. As a result Solomon imposed a curse which caused them to wander for ever in search of work. Masons certainly walked a good deal, as for that matter did other workers. John Oakey, who left school in 1859 at the age of twelve, tells us that as a journeyman mason he set off every morning at 4.45 from Winchcombe to walk the 2.5 miles to Toddington. Three evenings a week, after returning home, he did a further five miles to Cheltenham for an engagement. The bicycle, which turned up late in the nineteenth century, was the best friend the workers ever had. So said the old journeymen to George Swinford (born 1887) who, like his father before him, was a mason at Filkins in Oxfordshire.

In much the same area lived another family of masons, the Strongs. Timothy leased quarries at Barrington and Taynton in 1617. Of his six sons, Thomas laid the foundation stone of St Paul's in London, and in 1708 Edward set the last stone in its lantern. Thomas also built Strong's Causeway, which still links Great and Little Barrington. Valentine died in 1662 while working on a house in Fairford, where he was buried. His epitaph (now lost) ran:

*Here's one that was an able workman long*
*Who divers houses built, both fair and Strong;*
*Though Strong he was, a stronger came than he*
*And robbed him of his Fame and Life, we see;*
*Moving an old house a new one for to rear*
*Death met him by the way and laid him here.*

Another stone inscribed to a mason, this time at Chipping Campden, has also disappeared: 'Here lies the body of John Bower/Built Gloucester Cathedral and Campden tower'.

A surviving custom in the trade is that of capping. Katharine Briggs writes: 'When the masonry work is finished and the chimneys are put on, a flag is run up from one chimney and everyone downs tools and gathers round for a drink. A master builder suggests that the flag was originally run up to summon the farm hands and other voluntary labourers to help in lifting the heavy roof-tree to the ridge.'

Many Cotswold houses are roofed with stone slates, as they have been for some three hundred years. Indeed, the practice is said to go back to Roman times. The slates are graded into twenty-six sizes, each with its own name though this varied from place to place. For example, whippets (fourteen inches long) at Bisley were wivutts in the North Cotswolds. Among the many other names remembered are bachelors, becks, countesses, duchesses, muffeties, short days, long days and movedays. Cussoms went over the eaves, bottomers (paradoxically) in the centre of the roof, and those on either side were called lye-byes. The even more exotic names of earlier times included haghatter, rogue-why-winkest-thou and Jenny-why-gettest-thou.

A century ago, masons were paid 6d an hour. Dry stone wallers also claimed Roman ancestry for their skill. A good worker could do three yards in a day, and his work was reckoned to last a hundred years. An old craftsman boasted to Kenneth Hare: 'There be more art, look, goes to th' making of a dry wall than there goes to a wet 'un.'

Miners, too, claimed a venerable pedigree. Although they used charcoal for smelting, the Romans mined both iron ore and coal in the Forest of Dean. Free Miners' rights date from the thirteenth century, probably not, as has been suggested, as a reward for tunnelling to deliver King John from imprisonment in St Briavels Castle, but for helping later monarchs from Henry III onwards. Twelve Forest miners were at the siege of Berwick-on-Tweed in 1319, and this is generally held to be the time when their privileges were established by a grateful king, Edward II - though the earliest document on the subject dates from 1610.

To qualify as a Free Miner a man must have been born in the hundred of St Briavels and to have reached the age of twenty-one. He was also required to have worked a year and a day in a Forest mine, and to be registered with the gaveller. After fulfilling certain other conditions he had the right to cut timber for props, to pass over other people's land to reach his workings, and to take disputes to a special mine court (though this last met in 1777). A mid-fifteenth-century font at Abenhall has incised shields with smiths' and Free Miners' emblems; a brass, possibly of similar date, at Newland shows a miner with hod on back, pickaxe in hand and wooden candle-holder gripped in his teeth.

The Foresters' reputation for uncompromising defence of their rights was reinforced by resistance to enclosure. In 1632 an outbreak of fence smashing led to the imprisonment in Newgate Gaol of John Williams, a miners' leader who styled himself Lady Skimmington. (Female dress was often adopted by protesters to conceal their identity.) In 1831, two centuries later, miners were to the fore in another bout of fence breaking, after which they took refuge in their pits or in the woods. Several men, including the leader Warren James, were

*Forest of Dean iron-miners in the mid nineteenth century.*

tried at Gloucester Assizes and sentenced to terms of transportation to Australia. Others escaped punishment. 'An old miner has told me,' wrote Brian Waters in 1951, 'how his grandfather as a young man had to hide for three months in a pit at Coalway, where the only light that he saw was at the top of the shaft.'

In 1763 in protest at a newly-introduced tax on cider, Forest miners forcibly detained an exciseman underground. A Bristol newspaper reported: 'The Colliers, it is said, use him well, and he lives as they do; but they swear the Day of his Resurrection shall not come to pass till the Cyder-act is repealed.' The man was still there four days later. His fate is not recorded, but the act was indeed repealed, in 1776.

At about the same time the miners of Kingswood on the other side of the Severn were described by the Methodist, George Whitefield, as 'little better than heathens'. In 1795 these men, objecting to the levying of tithes by the local landowner, William Blathwayt, burnt him in effigy and advised him by anonymous letter to leave for Bath if he valued his skin.

No miners are left now at Kingswood. In the Forest only a few remain in tiny pits, though many remember the days before 1960, and the closure of Cannop, the last mine of any consequence. James Thompson's story could be repeated in its essentials many times over. He started work in 1921 as a boy of thirteen. His wage was £1.19.11 a week for pushing carts on the pit head at Park Gutter, near Bream. Three years later he went underground as a pony driver, first at the Deep Navigation, Parkend, then back at Park Gutter, where he became a face worker, cutting coal by hand. A group of six men worked together as a 'company', two on each of the shifts: morning (7 a.m. to 2 p.m.), afternoon (2 p.m. to 10 p.m.) and night (10 p.m. to 6 a.m.). The combined earnings were shared out at the pit head on a Friday.

(The house at Elton now called The Gardens was formerly an inn where the butty man paid wages to colliers who spent the greater part on drink, and then went round on boisterous pranks such as removing farm gates from their hinges. As a result the area became locally known as Hell's Corner.)

For Mr Thompson the butty system was superseded by individual piece-work which paid 2s 3d per ton (perhaps rising to 2s 9d if the coal were particularly hard to get), with a guaranteed minimum wage of 7s 9d a week. The highest weekly wage which he ever received was £20. He had to leave the mine in 1952, suffering from 50 per cent pneumonoconiosis.

Work might be interrupted by accidents, strikes (in 1921 and 1926, for example) or lack of demand for coal. Miners knew that if the pit hooter sounded at 5 p.m. it signalled that there would be no work the following day. During strikes and lay-offs Bream miners would congregate for a chat at an oak tree (now gone) by the crossroads known as the 'Hard-up Tree'. There was no sick pay before nationalisation, so after six weeks of illness, miners would organise a smoking concert in the pub. Anyone available and able would be pressed to perform. The sale of tickets at 3d or 6d a time would usually raise about £2 for the sick man, the equivalent of a week's pay at the time.

On Sundays miners typically wore a grey or blue three-piece suit, shirt with collar and tie, watch and chain across the chest, and trousers hitched high over sturdy boots. A flower in the lapel and a cloth cap or bowler on the head completed the outfit.

For work, corduroy or moleskin trousers were held up by a broad leather belt and tied below the knee with yorks (pronounced yarks). New moleskin was a dirty white in colour, prompting such cries as 'Who stole the donkey?' or 'There's bin a vire somewhere.' Protection was provided by knee pads and in later years a pit helmet with carbide lamp. A tommy or bread bag - customarily made of black and white check material - was carefully hung out of reach of the rats which pullulated underground.

Mr Granville Giles (born 1908) remembered the typical pit meal as bread, cheese and pickles, followed by an apple or a homemade cake, washed down by cold tea or water from a bottle or tin. He also recalled the miner's usual conversational gambit:: 'How's gwain on, ould butty?', ''Ow bist thee today, zurry?' or 'Nice day for weather, yun it, ould un?' Responses might be: 'Oh, I be pretty good in 'ealth but bloody low in pockut,' or 'Well, owl butt, when I zall my vissog in the glass this morning, zurry, it were white and pecked; I thought I uddent zee tha day out, be buggered.'

Mining was, and is, taxing work. When one old collier appeared before St Peter and stated his name and occupation in due form, the immediate reaction was: 'Come in and take a harp. This is the place for you. You've had your share of hell.' In this life, humour provided a means of coping with adversity, and it came out even in the names of pits. The Strip and At It (at Brierley) had a twenty-inch seam which required ten to fifteen hours work a day for a miner to make a living; the Trafalgar in the same village was the scene of the first Forest pit strike, in July 1871, when colliers sang (to the tune of 'The Jovial Foresters' - see Chapter Nine):

*A better time is coming, boys,*
*Than we have ever seen,*
*For working men of every class,*
*Throughout our ancient Dean;*
*Seventy thousand have our union joined,*
*I hope they are all of one mind;*
*You Foresters with them combine,*
*But don't you duffers be.*
(Chorus)
*Come all you jovial Foresters,*
*Who cut and mine and coal,*
*And workmen all both great and small*
*And swell the union roll.*

The Duck and the Leg of Mutton were called after their respective owners' Christmas boxes to the miners. The Ready Penny near Christchurch acquired the name from its first customer's having arrived with coin in hand. The Old Stay and Drink had a pond near the pit where horses regularly stopped to slake their thirst. Like those of fields (see Chapter Three) the names of pits could be sardonic (Pluckpenny, Work or Hang, Gentlemen Colliers), optimistic (Never Fear, Long Looked For) or merely homely (Bread and Candles, Arthur and Edward - after the owner's sons).

Forest miners were famed for their powers of repartee. One man, teased that he had become Welsh on returning from a spell in Wales, replied: 'Then as I aim as thou wud zoy as if a cot were to go into a fish shop and have kittens as they ud be bloaters.' Humour is often based on a kind of perverse logic. Two men converse. 'Dist thee knoaw owd Tom so and so was judd?' 'No. When did a die, then?' Well, butty, if a 'ad lived till termorral im oud a bin dudd a vornight.' Two miners arrange to meet in the woods. 'If tha gits thur fust, butty, tha puts a stone on thic wall, and if I gits thur fust I knocks un off.'

Miners also had a thirst for sport. Mr Thompson remembers that on a Saturday when work finished at 2 p.m., the men would go straight off in their dirty clothes to play football. He says: 'All miners had gardens; some had orchards, and a pig in the cot.' Others became sheep badgers, and ran flocks in the woodlands and on the commons. Some drank to excess: 'Surry, I 'ad a dream las' night, dreamt I 'ad drunk all tha beer and cider in tha pub; and woust thou believe it my dream was zo real I 'ad to get out o' bed a dozen times and more.' The passion for male voice choirs and brass bands (see Chapter Ten) remains strong.

One holiday for the miners and their families was the annual demonstration at the Speech House in June. A trade union speaker aired grievances and expressed hopes, then drinks and refreshments were served. Roundabouts and the fun of the fair were also available. Colliers from Cinderford and Littledean customarily took Good Friday off and walked to Newnham to see the Severn Bore. The tradition reputedly dated from 1819, when four young men were killed in an accident in the Old Bilson Pit near Cinderford as they worked on a Good Friday.

Mondays were unpopular because after a pit had lain idle the previous day things were more likely to go wrong - or such was the rationale. In September 1873 the *Forest of Dean Examiner* reported that on a Monday a group of men went into the pit 'and on reaching the bottom tossed up to see whether they should work or return to bank' (the surface). The process continued 'until it was decided to return to bank.'

Miners, like many in dangerous trades, are often superstitious. H.G. Nicholls wrote in 1858 of the Forest men:

> *Many superstitions... linger amongst them, such as the use of charms and incantations, a belief in witchcraft and an evil eye, a resort to 'wise men', and even to the minster of the parish [Nicholls was a parson himself] as being a 'Master of Arts', or for some of the offertory money, out of which to have a charm-ring made. They are likewise inclined to give credence to tales of apparitions, and to regard sickness and accident as fated and inevitable.*

A century later Dennis Potter, whose father worked at Waterloo Pit and Cannop, observed that the 'older Foresters ... use a hundred-fold country and coal-mining superstitions and prejudices.' He gave no examples, but the sort of thing he had in mind was probably the belief that Ralph Anstis illustrated in his short story, *Late for the Shift*. It arose, he says, 'following the flooding of the Union pit in 1902. It is said that two of the men who died in the disaster did so because after the alarm had been given they went back to their work face to collect clothing and a watch. Afterwards no collier ever returned for something he forgot.'

Timothy Mountjoy relates in his autobiography, *The Life, Labours and Deliverances of a Forest of Dean Collier*, how a stone mason known as 'Get-it-to-go' disappeared from Ruardean Hill after being struck 'an unlucky blow' in a fight. A year later noises 'like a man boring a hole with a hammer and drill' were heard coming from a disused pit shaft. A search was made, fruitlessly. However, the noises redoubled and a more thorough investigation proved successful: 'The stone-cutter's body was found, and his clothes helped to keep the body together to shovel it into the coffin. I saw the coffin landed and took out into the green for people to see, which ought not to have been done. The wonder was that scores did not die from the horrid stench.' According to a more recent writer, Sue Law, the man's plaintive cries are heard even now, on certain nights.

Miners have reported strange experiences between the Forest Church and Steam Mills. One man says he was intercepted by a ghost: 'He used my own voice to speak to me. I could feel myself choking. I fought against it and told the spirit: "In the name of God, let me be." It disappeared immediately, and I slumped to the ground.'

The mining of iron ore at Clearwell Caves has a history of some 2500 years, and a ghost is often reported there. This is the 'old man' who made helpful suggestions to a television crew filming in the caverns in the 1960s. The technicians, pleased that his advice had saved them hours of work with their cables, asked at lunchtime who he was. The mine owner, Mr Ray Wright, could only tell them that he was a benevolent spirit. Mrs Rita Miles, who works at the caves, explained to me that she had not seen the man, but that in the Barbecue Churn 'the hairs on the back of your neck stands up, so we know he's there.' For this reason she avoids going down alone, though she knows him to be kind and helpful. It might be suggested that Mrs Miles is being influenced by what she has heard rather than by what she in fact experiences. Yet I have been told by a visitor to the caves who knew nothing of these stories that an old man helped her with her child's pushchair. On returning to the surface she enquired about him, only to be informed that no one else was there at the time.

## Sailors and Soldiers

'Shipshape and Bristol fashion': the saying echoes from the days when Bristol was a major port, and its shipping maintained in first class condition. Much of its trade was in wool, and looms were set up as early as 1337 by a man whose name is still a household word, Thomas Blanket.

Bristol merchants can claim some of the credit for the discovery in 1497 of Newfoundland, since they chartered the ship, *Matthew*, which carried John Cabot there (though he thought he had arrived in China). They were also the first - in the seventeenth century - to export shoes, but their involvement in the slave trade was much less creditable, to say the least.

It was in Bristol that Alexander Selkirk, the original Robinson Crusoe, landed in 1711, and it is possible that Daniel Defoe met him there before writing his best-selling book, published eight years later. Thomas Dover, son of Robert (see Chapter Seven), while serving as ship's surgeon under the command of Captain Woodes Rogers, found Selkirk on the island of Juan Fernandez where he had been marooned.

Though Bristol declined as a port during the nineteenth century it continued to shelter many deep-sea sailors who held it in great affection:

*When we gets back to old Bristol town,*
*'Tis there we will drink and sorrow drown.*

Men would 'swallow the anchor' (retire) to Bristol, bringing with them a store of songs. Thomas Ginovan, who first sailed in 1883, found himself forty-five years later in the Merchant Venturers' Almshouses at Bristol. He recalled both forebitters and shanties (recreational and work songs respectively) with titles such as 'Paddy West', 'The Mermaid', 'Mains'l Haul' and 'Haul away Joe'.

When Ginovan was at sea, Stanley Slade wandered Bristol docks as a boy of eight, hearing seamen singing, to fiddle and accordion accompaniment, 'Aboard the Kangaroo':

*Once I was a waterman and lived at home at ease,*
*But now I am a mariner, ploughing the angry seas.*
(Chorus)
*Oh I never thought she would be false or ever prove untrue,*
*As we sailed away from Bristol quay on board the Kangaroo.*

The expectations of fidelity proved to be unfounded.

Some sea-going vessels could navigate the lower reaches of the Severn and Wye but a great deal of river traffic took the form of barges or trows crewed by fresh water sailors. Barges were towed by bow-hauliers - men pulling on a rope. For every ton of cargo, one man was required. When in the early 1800s a tow path was established on the Severn as far down as Gloucester to permit the use of horses, the men protested because they lost their jobs, hard as they were. The first steam tug appeared in 1830.

Horses needed only one man (or boy) to lead, while another steered aboard the boat. At Ashleworth the tow-path changed from one side of the river to the other, so horse and driver were ferried across, thus providing an opportunity for refreshment at the 'Boat Inn'. Bargemen would tie up for the night at any convenient cider or beer house, according to taste. They are reputed to have had a different name for every stretch of a hundred yards or so of river but these were never written down, and many are now lost. Stave All, Golden Point and Poppies Parlour are remembered near Sandhurst.

W.H. Savage became master of the steam tug, *Resolute*, in 1903. In the 1920s he reflected on fifty-two years' experience of the Severn Sea during which he had made 2000 passages between Sharpness Docks and Avonmouth or Portishead, assisting or towing barges and sailing craft. 'I am just beginning to get familiar with the river,' he said, 'but I have not yet dared to reach that stage of familiarity that breeds contempt.'

As a young man he worked on barges: 'They were miserable, cranky craft at best, as nearly as I can recollect 70 feet long, 12 to 14 feet beam, and between 3 and 4 feet draught.' They carried pottery down the Severn from Ironbridge, and withies down the Wye and on to Bristol from Brockweir and Bigsweir.

The word, trow, comes from *trog* (early English for trough). The vessels were flat-bottomed, up to 80 tons displacement, with a big sail on a single mast almost 80 feet in height. They were often built of Forest oak, though later some were made of iron. A detachable keel enabled them to sail the more open waters of the estuaries.

They navigated the Wye to Brockweir, often to collect timber for Bristol. The Severn was a much more difficult prospect: it could take anything from a week to a fortnight to sail from Sharpness to Gloucester, depending on wind and tide. This is why the Gloucester and Berkeley Canal was opened in 1827, though to avoid tolls skippers still used the river when conditions were favourable.

One ballad underlines the hazards of Severn navigation:

> *The seventh day of February from Bristol we sail'd out;*
> *Our trow was richly loaded and bound for Worcester port.*
> *At half-past six that very night it was a dismal sound,*
> *Our gallant ship struck on the sand and four of her crew were drown'd.*

'The Trowman's Fall' goes on to relate how one of the corpses is robbed by two watchmen at Oldbury after being dragged up the mud at the end of a rope - a telling detail which suggests that the incident is authentic.

Captain Savage complained about similar behaviour on the other side of the Severn:

> *The people of the right bank had peculiar ideas about the property and lives of the people on the left bank, and they certainly harassed the shipping industry. Apart from seizing vessels at anchor, casting crews adrift, spiriting the cargo inland, and breaking up their vessels; they had another trick of blackmail on coming out armed and insisting on transfer of cargo at rather heavy rates to their own smaller vessels for the upriver ports.*

The trowmen themselves had a reputation for stealing, fighting and drinking. They organised poaching expeditions for game or deer, and even stole horses before making their escape - by water, of course. They pilfered from the cargoes they carried. They loved coarse and boisterous practical jokes. At Oldbury-on-Severn, where the local cider had a justified reputation, they drank in the Ship, the Anchor, the Salmon and the Star (Cowhill). Then they fought each other and all comers in a field called Little Wharth Paddock or Bloody Acre.

Another of their favourite haunts was a little further upriver: the New Inn at Shepperdine, better known as the Windbound or the Blow. The prevailing wind often blew up the river, thus holding back outward bound sailing vessels, whose crews took full advantage in the Windbound of their enforced leisure. Much further upriver, at Deerhurst there was a small island called Deerhurst Tail (now gone) and in summer when the water was low or the wind adverse sailors would camp there and hold wakes.

The river trade eventually collapsed under competition from the railways. By 1946 only about fifty trows were left; now there are none. No more shall we see the *Dabchick, Good Hope, Mary Jane, William and Sarah, George and Mary* and their like, nor the rough old men who sailed them. A few trows are decaying, high and dry on the Severn shore at Purton, together with a dozen iron and concrete barges. Some pictures remain, and the name of the occasional pub, like the Landoger Trow in Bristol. Apart from Fred Larkham's undertakings, based at Newnham and Westbury, there is no commercial river traffic between Sharpness and Gloucester. North of the city, only pleasure craft cruise the Severn.

In 1994, more traditions were lost with the merger of the Gloucestershire Regiment and the Duke of Edinburgh's Royal Regiment. The famous back badge, showing a sphinx and the word 'Egypt', dated from the battle of Alexandria in 1801. The honour of wearing it commemorated a stage in the conflict when the Gloucesters simultaneously fought off French attacks to the front, the rear and both sides. Until 1993 the regiment - the only one in the British army to wear two badges - celebrated Back Badge Day with an annual parade through Gloucester on 21 March.

The unofficial regimental song, 'We are the Gloster boys', may live on. The original version runs:

*We are the Gloster boys, we are the Gloster boys.*
*We know our manners, we pay our tanners,*
*We are respected wherever we may be.*
*When we're marching down the Hotwells Road,*
*Doors and windows open wide.*
*It's there you'll hear the sergeant shout:*
*'Put those bloody Woodbines out'.*
*We are the Gloster boys.*

In Gloucester singers marched 'down the Bristol Road', and a North Cotswold version mentioned the 'Campden men' who were 'marching down the Aston Road' - the reference being to Aston Subedge. In a different context Cheltenham Town supporters sing 'We are the Cheltenham boys', and they march 'down the Whaddon road'. In the early 1990s, before Mike Teague left the club, Gloucester rugby fans preferred:

*Maggie dear, a pint of beer, a Woodbine and a match,*
*A twopenny halfpenny stick of rock and we're off to the football match*
*To see old Teaguey score a try, the best try in the land,*
*For we are the Gloucester boys.*
*We are the Gloucester boys, we are the Gloucester boys.*
*We know our manners, we spend our tanners,*
*We are respected wherever we go,*
*And when we're walking down the Kingsholm Road*
*Doors and windows open wide, open wide.*
*You can hear the captain shout,*
*'Put that bloody Woodbine out',*
*For we are the Gloucester boys.*

## Factory and Farm Workers

The once great textile trade of the Cotswolds is epitomised by names which recall lengths of cloth stretched out to dry after fulling or dyeing: Racknap (Windrush), Rack Close (Bagendon), Rack Isle (Bibury) and Rack Hill (Fairford, France Lynch, Painswick, Rodborough, Stroud and Woodchester). As Edith Brill says: 'In the old days the army went to war in Stroudwater scarlet; in peace huntsmen wore it chasing the fox, and the Red Maids of Bristol wore it to school, keeping warm in their fine red cloaks; county squires went to church in a coat of Uley blue, and coarse blue cloth was supplied to the navy and many a Blue Coat school.'

The raw material comes to mind when one sees the signs of the Woolpack (Painswick and Stroud) or the Fleece Inn (Cirencester, Dursley, Stroud). A melancholy story is attached to the Old Fleece at Rooksmoor. Early in the nineteenth century a Woodchester weaver was hanged at Gloucester for damaging cloth during a strike at Rooksmoor Mills. His body was borne twelve miles home on men's shoulders, to receive a hero's welcome. One account says that a robin alighted on the corpse at Gloucester and stayed perched there for the whole of the journey; another that the bird came down when the bearers left the body outside while they took refreshment at the Old Fleece.

Until the 1970s or even later, many villages - Chalford, France Lynch, Nailsworth and Painswick, for example - had houses with a large living room known as 'the shop' which had originally been used for hand weaving. Well within living memory wool gathering continued. At Leckhampton one mother with a large family used to collect sheep's wool from the hedges and send it to Stroud to be woven into cloth for home tailoring. Until the 1880s a cloth mill at Cam sent carts round the village to collect blood, urine and pig manure from houses and farms. The mixture was used in soaking cloth to remove wool grease and loom stains, and the material so treated was described as 'segged'.

The weavers had a strong sense of natural justice. As early as 1726 they rioted over wage cuts, truck (payment in goods instead of cash) and 'illegal' workers, that is, those not having been properly apprenticed in the trade. Thirty years later there was a strike at Stroud because weavers were having to work between fifteen and sixteen hours a day to earn sixpence a week. Troops called in to keep order were led by General Wolfe, who privately sympathised with the strikers. The clothiers tried to persuade workers to sign a document which declared them satisfied with the rates of pay. The response was an uncompromising circular: 'This is to give notice to all weavers not to put their hands to any paper made by Mr Roberts or any other clothier. If you do, we the weavers of each parish are fully resolved to meet in a body and car him on the wooden horse, and then throw him into his master's mill pound where he sign'd the wrighting.'

In 1802 the croppers - brawny men who trimmed the nap on cloth with heavy hand shears - protested at being put out of work by new machines. They sent an anonymous letter to Paul Wathen, a wealthy and arrogant clothier who owned a mill at Woodchester and lived at Upper Lydiatt Park near Bisley:

> *Wee Here in Form you get Sheer in mee sheens and if you dont pull them down in a fortnights time Wee will pull them down for you, Damned infernal Dog. And before Almighty God we will pull down all your mills that have Meany Sheer in me Sheens in. We will cut out your Damned Hearts and will make the rest Heat them.*

During another strike of five thousand weavers in 1825 feelings were expressed in a ballad issued by Bonner and Henson, two Bristol printers.

**The Weavers' Turn-out**

*O, hark my lads, and give an ear, to listen unto me,*
*A story unto you I'll relate which happen'd the other day*
*It's concerning of weavers, who for their rights maintain,*
*We have been laboring many a year, but still it was all in vain.*
*(Chorus)*
*So let us all, while in our bloom,*
*Drink success to the weaver's loom.*

*In Dursley town in Gloucestershire, for wages we stood out,*
*It was for 3 pence per yard on a chain of broad cloth.*
*Our clubs we have to support our wives and children dear,*
*We live in hopes of better times while we drink a jug of beer.*

*Look all around the neighbourhood and you will quickly hear,*
*We are in hopes our employers our wages will ensure*
*For provisions they are plentiful, they are so rich and good,*
*And so my boys we'll never fear our clubs they will stand good.*

*Behold Stroudwater and Wotton-under-Hedge too,*
*The weavers they are all combin'd to their colours will stand true,*
*The towns of Trowbridge as you hear, and not leave Milsom out,*
*And all round the neighbourhood for wages will stand out.*

*All round the neighbourhood the trade it has been good*
*For all mechanics in the trade do support themselves with food,*
*But the weavers they are valiant men as you will understand,*
*Then for our wages we stand out and no more be at command.*

*So to conclude my ditty and finish up my song,*
*We'll drink success to the weavers, may the trade be carried on,*
*Likewise to our employers wherever they may dwell,*
*May the trade be in a flourishing state, and never for to fail.*

Anyone persisting in working received short shrift: 'The usual procedure was to take the beam out of the offender's loom and, mounting the poor weaver astride it, to take him to the nearest canal and tumble him in.' This 'coolstaffing' or 'riding', like rough music (see Chapter Five), was a time-honoured way of expressing collective disapproval. In 1892 the *Gloucester Standard* reported that the 'Dead March' was played during the rough musicking of blacklegs during a strike of boot and shoe makers.

If industrial life had its grim aspects, there were also traditional festivals and recreations. Tetbury records show a payment of ten shillings in 1705 for combers to have a drink on the 'morrow after Bishop Blaize'. The day of Bishop Blaize - patron saint of woolcombers and by extension of others in the trade - was 3 February. Evidently celebrations were so enthusiastic that the workers needed another drink the following day to relieve a hangover. There is a strong possibility that the expression, 'drunk as blazes', derives from 'drunk as blaiziers' - that is, those keeping St Blaize's festival.

A local tradition suggests that St Blaize (died 289), having landed at St Blazy in Cornwall, spent the night at the Bishop Blaize Inn in Cirencester, before travelling on to Gloucester. Further celebrations included the lighting of hilltop bonfires on 3 February, and a chapel was dedicated to the saint in the grounds of Blaise Castle, near Bristol.

Young men starting work in factories were initiated by being given assignments such as collecting a long stand or three pennyworth of 'oily strap 'em'. Laurie Parker, a Whiteshill boy who started work shortly before the First World War in the button department of a clothing factory in Stroud, was asked if he would like to see the mantrap. 'I was taken into the cellar and upon reaching the far end the gas lights were suddenly extinguished and I found myself being showered with bundles of wrappers which had been round bales of cloth when delivered.' He could consider himself lucky, since these practical jokes were often coarse, and sometimes hazardous.

The same might be said of the rites of passage undergone by apprentices coming out of their time. Printers were 'banged out', tied up, and doused in flour and water. The ordeal has now disappeared, along with apprenticeships in the printing trade. Something of the old treatment continues in engineering. A Newent man, Bill Hall, told me how a black apprentice became completely covered in white paste, save for the lustrous brown eyes looking out.

Bill's son, John, received another kind of treatment on the eve of his wedding in 1972. A cutting from the *Citizen* still treasured in the family shows John, aged twenty-one, with hands and neck in a wooden yoke being paraded through Gloucester city centre by workmates from Severn Joinery. Hanging by a string from his neck is a placard with the words 'I'm getting married in the morning'.

The classic way of starting work on the land was to frighten birds from the crops. To keep up their spirits the boys would sing little songs like this 'crow-clapping' verse from Mr N.H.K. Pilsworth of Woodfield. It was taught to him by his father Bill, who sang it endlessly in the fields of Petty France and Badminton - his first job:

*Shee auver, birds, shee auver, birds,*
*Out of the cornfields and clover.*
*Powder and shot shall be your lot,*
*Shee auver, birds.*

Henry White of Bagendon began 'crow-keeping' in 1832 at the age of ten. His wage for a twelve hour day was threepence. Half a century later George Nobes of Blockley left school for the same working day. He scared birds from the beans in Colonel's Piece, then chased them from young wheat in Keeley's Hollow. So that he did not eat his meal of bread and cheese too early he made himself a little sundial from a stick and some stones to keep in touch with the passage of time. Within living memory 'rook starving' still went on, at 6d a day. At Winchcombe the rate was 1d or 2d, plus a swede.

At Haresfield in 1902 a man's wage was 15s per week, or 13s plus a tied cottage. Typical prices at the time were 1s 1d per pound for butter, 1s for 18 eggs, 3s 6d for a bottle of whisky, and 18s or £1 for a ton of coal. A boy who graduated to being a half-man earned between 6s 6d and 8s a week at Sherborne in 1911. A full man received between 16s and 18s; a shepherd, 14s together with a house.

'The life of a shepherd,' wrote Alfred Williams (an ex-birdscarer himself) in 1914, 'is attended with many hardships and privations, and especially so in the winter-time and lambing season, when the earth may be covered with snow several feet deep.' He met a shepherd at Quenington who was both 'partially disabled with rheumatics' and 'minus an eye as the result of a kick received from a ewe while he was attending to the lambs in the field.'

Shepherds expressed in song the pride they took in their calling. 'We shepherds' was known all over the county; this version comes from Mr William Chappell of Tresham:

*We shepherds be the best of men that e'er trod English ground.*
*When we come to an alehouse we value not a crown,*
*We spend our money freely, and pays before we goes.*
*There's no ale in the vale where the cold winter winds do blow.*

*A man that is a shepherd does need a valiant heart,*
*He must not be vaint-hearted, but boldly do his part.*
*He must not be vaint-hearted, be it raain or vrost or snow,*
*With no ale in the vale where the cold winter winds do blow.*

*When I kept ship on Tres'am Hill it made my heart to ache*
*To see the ewes hang out their tongues and hear the lambs to bleat,*
*And I rose up with courage and o'er the hills did go,*
*And penned 'em there in the vold while the cold winter winds did blow.*

*As soon as I had penned 'em there I turned me back in haste*
*Unto a jovial company good liquor vor to taste,*
*Vor drink and jovial company they are me heart's delight,*
*While me ship lie aslip all the vorepart of the night.*

Shepherds believed that if most of the new lambs they first saw faced towards them, food for the coming season would be plentiful; a preponderance of animals seen tails first signified poor pastures. Counting lambs was considered unlucky, even after weaning, and many Cotswold shepherds waited until they were tailed. Rev. G.E. Rees of Bagendon explained this reluctance as 'fear of the unknown power that is on the watch to mortify pride, the vengeance that punished David for numbering his people and the rich fool for counting up his crops.'

The carter or horseman had a standing and a wage similar to those of the shepherd. The working horse lasted until the 1950s in Gloucestershire, and it is curious to reflect that oxen were used as draught animals until only a few years before then. Mr Belcher, the ox man of Chedworth, was remembered singing at village parties the song he used to encourage his beasts, though only a fragment was noted: 'With a yup, yup, yup, yup and a holler.'

During the Second World War oxen ploughed some of the ancient sheep pastures at Blockley which were too steep for tractors. In 1945 they hauled timber and pulled harrows in Lord Bathurst's Cirencester Park, though by this time they were more of a picturesque survival than a basic source of motive power. Some forty years earlier, Norman Jewson marvelled at them in their classic role:

*After tea I had a most unexpected and, to me, thrilling experience, for taking a look round from the highest part of the ground [between Perrott's Brook and North Cerney], I saw silhouetted against the skyline a man ploughing with two yoke of oxen... For a moment I had a feeling that it was a vision from the time of Virgil and half-forgotten lines from the Eclogues came crowding into my mind.*

'Good horses, good farm', was a Gloucestershire saying. Carters took immense pride in their charges, which were typically named Blackbird, Boxer, Briton, Captain, Douglas, Duke, Jerry, Jolly, Major, Nancy, Ploughboy, Polly,

Prince or Violet. They would scour gardens, fields and woods for helpful plants. Bearsfoot (*Helleborus foetidus*) was favoured round Chipping Campden for conditioning both horses and sheep. Walnut leaves, dried and rubbed to a powder, were widely added to horses' bait as a cure for worms. The mandrake - in fact, bryony (*Bryonia dioica*) - was also greatly prized. A pinch of the dried root helped to stimulate horses and to make their coats glossy. H.J. Massingham tells how Jimmy Teapot of Broad Campden said that old-fashioned carters dosed their teams with it when they were to do the particularly demanding work of dragging felled trees out of the woods. He thought it best to pull up the root on a dark night because it 'bled like blood when you drawed it up in the daytime, but it hollers like a child if you draws it up on a moonshiny night.'

Alfred Williams described a typical carter and his wife, from Fairford:

> *He is a strong-made man, with large limbs, broad shoulders, short, thick neck, massive head and square face, and he has a loud, deep voice; just the kind to terrify the carter boys when they have been guilty of any misdemeanour. His wife is a portly dame, robust-looking, honest and homely, whose chief pride is in keeping a clean house and having everything ready for her 'man' when he comes home at meal times and in the evening. As a girl she went to work in the fields with twenty other young women and earned an honest shilling, but there are scarcely any females employed now [1914] except at threshing time, when the farmer may be glad of one or two women to cut the bonds of the sheaves and help feed the machine.*

At Willersey women dragged twenty-two- feet-wide wooden rakes with iron tines to collect any hay left behind when the men had finished carting. They also tied and packed asparagus, onions and other crops. Only one generation before living memory, women at Stone took a pail to the cow, milked in the field, and carried buckets back on yokes. In the 1890s a Birdlip woman did turnip-hoeing and stone-picking; children helped, and were paid a penny an hour. She also remembered gleaning or leasing: 'Each child wore a bag-apron into which the corn could be stuck. We made little bundles of gleaned corn, twisted a bit of straw round it and laid it on the wall till it was time to go home. Next day we took the corn to the mill to be ground.'

Leasing began at Stinchcombe as soon as the last load was carried. Elsewhere, a single stook or 'policeman' left in a field signalled that gleaners might not enter. Even with this gone, gleaning could only start when one of the church bells rang for the occasion, usually at 8 a.m. There is a story, once told in the Plough at Ford, that some women went to Oak Piece at Temple Guiting after the bell, only to find some women from Stow already there. A fight ensued, with bags, sticks and fists, before the interlopers were driven out.

Corn from gleaning provided a useful addition to that grown on allotments in order to provide bread for the winter. By the late 1930s, though, it might be fed to fowls or used to make wheat wine.

*Country skills from the lithographs of J.B. Pyne.*

Before women could rake hay or glean corn, men had to do the cutting. Hay was cut by scythe with a line or 'flight' of mowers spread in echelon across the field. The famous picture of Dixton (see also Chapter Ten) shows just such a scene, with twenty-three men mowing, while women and boys rake. A piper provides music as they work. Such encouragement must have been welcome in a day which might run from 4 a.m. until 10 p.m., with breaks at 6 a.m., 10 (mid-morning), 12.30 or 1 p.m. (dinner) and 4.30 or 5 p.m. (tea).

Mowers also sang as they worked, a monotonous chant which no doubt helped them keep the pace set by the leader: 'Mow high, mow low, mow levelly, O.' The leader announced pauses for sharpening, in fulfilment of the saying: 'The mower mows ill who ne'er whets his scythe.' There might also be a stop for a different kind of wet - a drink of beer or cider:

*Wit to wet the scythe do cut,*
*The mowers be so lazy.*
*A pint will make 'em drunk,*
*And a quart will drive 'em crazy.*

Crazy or no, a man was expected to cut an acre a day on the flat; rather less on some of the steep Cotswold slopes.

Gangs of scythe men continued to operate until well into the twentieth century. On 18 June when sideshows and the Waterloo Races took place on Aust Wharf, labourers ground their scythes in the morning and went to the fair in the afternoon. It was customary at Newnham-on-Severn, too, to start haymaking on the morning of Fair Day, 11 June - St Barnabas: 'Lord bless you, the old farmers, rain or shine, 'ould burst their guts to start mowin' on fair day.' After finishing the last field of the season hay-makers flung off their caps and said: 'Thank God. Now send rain.'

As late as 1867 a report on Gloucestershire commented that only a quarter of wheat was cut by machine, a quarter by sickle and half by scythe. Hand reaping continued on smaller farms until the 1920s and even later. Before the introduction of mechanical reaper-binders sheaves were bound by women and boys, as they had been since biblical times. One binder was expected to tie for three reapers. A good man, his scythe fitted by the village blacksmith with a reaping cradle, could cut an acre a day. For this he earned between 7s 6d and 10s, out of which he had to pay his boy.

William Creswick of St Briavels remembered:

*... the gangs of reapers and boys that tied the sheaves with about twenty pieces of straw still containing the ears of corn. The all-in cost of this was ten shilling an acre, ten to twelve sheaves being in a stook. The reapers had between them 8/6 per acre and the binders 1/6 per acre. My eldest brother John was quite the most adept I ever saw. He regularly tied after three reapers, my brother Foskett tied after two and at my first venture I tied after my father at the age of ten. My father who had for some years headed a reaping gang, arranged with local farmers the date of commencing work on their particular farm... Work commenced at 5 a.m. and went on until about 9 p.m., with three breaks for food during this time. Cider in those days being the chief drink in the harvest field some farmers did give cider free gratis, but generally the reapers preferred beer. This was delivered by Burgoynes Brewery, Redbrook, the cost in those days for their best beer being 10d per gallon. On the completion of reaping on a farm the last sheaf was bound up as a dolly by each reaper and binder.*

Brian Waters writes of a band of harvesters from Tetbury who came each year to reap at Arlingham:

> *As the Severnside harvest began a fortnight earlier, the Cotswold men were able to do their reaping in Arlingham and return in time for their commitments on the hills. A band of nine or ten of them would give up the best part of a day to walk a score of miles to Arlingham. Their only implements were a reaper's hook and a stick. Their leader, the eldest of them, was lord of the harvest and the best reaper of them all. He would open the field with his sickle and his followers would work in a line behind him. They received seven shillings an acre, and reaping from dawn to sundown a man averaged an acre a day. At this price they earned double and more than double their daily wage at other times of the year.*

The end of harvest was joyfully celebrated (see below) but the work of threshing remained. This was also done by hand, using a flail, known as a 'poverty stick'. Sid Knight wrote in 1960 that he remembered seeing his grandfather's discarded flail hanging in the woodshed:

> *This ... was simply a handle of well-seasoned ground ash, secured to the swingle, a short wooden bar shaped like a sword, with a band of strong leather. The flail was swung over the head, and then brought down swingle first with a resounding thwack on the corn laid out on the barn floor... I have been told by my father and grandfather that flailing corn was a much sought after job in winter time years ago, when many farming and building operations were held up by bad weather.*

Even after the mechanisation of threshing some hand work continued. A Westbury-on-Severn woman commented in the 1950s: 'When I was a child I well remember peas and beans being threshed by flail, or nile, as it was then called.' She added: 'The little wooden barrel of cider, always called a bottle, which was the worker's perquisite, held about two quarts and appeared to provide the driving power for this arduous task.'

It is true that cider once played an important part in farm work. A supply stood in lieu of part of the wage paid by farmers, but was given free after 1887 when the practice became illegal. The daily allowance seems to have varied. The Saintbury parish clerk told Algernon Gissing that 'eight quarts a day was a common allowance for one man in the hay or harvest field.' A Westbury man remembers labourers queuing with their bottles (which carters hung from their horses' hames) at the entrance to his father's cellar before starting work; he suggests a gallon. This quantity was certainly allowed to the fifteen men who, one day early this century, cut with scythes the fifteen acres of a field at Frowens Farm, Westbury. Each had a costrel holding two quarts, which he drank from a horn cup, and was then replenished.

A Cotswold farmer's daughter suggests a gallon for the foreman and half for the rest, but adds: 'if they needed more they could always come to the cider house for a refill.' In 1954 John Moore met a seventy-six-year-old labourer, still working, who claimed he had never drunk less than eight pints a day since his twenties. Clem Hignell of Henbury remembered 'a real old timer' who drank '4 1/2 gallons of cider between daylight and dark, day after day,' and another who would 'drink two quarts of cider from a wooden bottle without taking it from his mouth.'

Another farmer's daughter, without specifying exact quantities, testifies to large volumes:

> *What jars of cider used to be drunk during harvesting and haymaking by the men. One could imagine they had hollow legs judging by the quantities consumed. Then at supper time in the kitchen, after quantities of bread and cheese and more cider, there would be a grand sing-song accompanied on an accordion, and another happy summer day would end.*

In the early years of this century cider began to be replaced by a bottle of cold tea, with a consequent loss in both savour and nutrition. The old farm cider 'very nigh took the skin off your throat,' or 'was sharp enough to cut the throat of a graveyard ghost.' Some kept up cider-making until the 1950s - at Gastrells Farm, Upon St Leonards, for example - while at Flat Farm between Tirley and Staunton the Hartland family do so to this day, but they supply the general public, not merely their own workers.

Cider makers were renowned for adding meat 'to give body'. Bernard Kear mentions pieces of bacon put in at Yorkley 'to feed the yeast'. He also recalls the use of elderberries or beetroot to give a rosy colour. Ron Pickford lists beef steak, brown sugar and raisins; Harry Howell of Blockley remembers a chine of beef. John Moore reports this conversation with a ciderman:

> *'Rats is as good as steaks for cider. I once saw a score of rats drowned in father's big hogsyud, and that was the best cider I ever tasted. And when we come to the bottom of it, Lor' bless you, there wan't a trace of rat left. It had yut 'em, see?' 'You'd drunk 'em,' I observed. 'It had yut 'em and we had drunk 'em,' he said. 'Comes to the same thing.'*

Farmers unable or unwilling to make their own cider could use the services of a travelling ciderman. The farmer would supply press, accessories, apples and horse (for the mill). The ciderman contributed his skill. Later a portable machine known as a 'scratter' came in. At France Lynch the arrival of such a machine was an annual event. It was set up on the bank behind Orchard Cottage to grind apples for all comers.

Different places had their own preferences for species of cider apple. In the Forest of Dean, where the famous styre apple was unaccountably allowed to die out in the mid-nineteenth century, they favoured Lady's Finger, Sheep Snout and Underleaf. One Forester, asked how much he drank in an evening replied: 'Well, I haves me six or eight quarts, but sometimes I have me a tiny drop.'

Near Oldbury-on-Severn the soil is particularly well suited to the Kingston Black. Buyers came from miles around to sales at which cider was brought out for tasting in buckets called wooden decanters. Small pieces of cheese were handed out, too. On occasions 10 000 gallons of cider (at 1s 6d a gallon) were sold in a day, and the drink was still available at fairs until the 1950s. A teetotal rector at Oldbury tried hard to reform one cider-addict. He was walking from Cowhill and saw the man, who had been to the Star and was resting on his way home, under the hedge. 'Drunk again, William!' the rector thundered. 'Be you, sir?' the man innocently enquired. 'So be I.'

There were more local ciders round Chipping Campden, where one day a carter drank seventeen pints in three hours, then remarked: 'This be doen I no good. I'll try a pint of beer.' In the same area farmers also made large quantities of their own wine. Cowslip, dandelion and elderberry were considered women's drinks. Men favoured plum jerkum, made from a dark, damson-like plum. Different recipes produced a colour varying from deep purple to claret, and a taste from sticky sweet to potent dry. The latter goes to both head and feet 'so you knows what you wants to do but can't do it.' Having preached against the evils of such wines the Ebrington parson was cornered a few days later by a runaway bull and forced to take refuge for four hours on top of a hayrick. Villagers said it was a judgement on him.

## Masters and Men

Working relationships find expression in many stories, some concerned with particular incidents, some recurring with variations in different parts of the country. Two workers, drowsy with the noontide heat, sit down in the shade of the wall they are re-building, and fall asleep. Later the farmer arrives, sees no work being done, and calls: 'Adam! Adam!' Adam fails to stir but his companion awakens and responds: 'Hallo. What's up?' 'Where be Adam?' 'I doan't know.' 'What be he a-doing?' 'Nothin'.' 'And what bist thee a-doing?' 'Why, I be a-helpin' on him, to be sure.'

A stingy nobleman, 'a crochety old codger so mean as he'd skin a stwun,' is outwitted by a labourer:

> *T'other day he ketchud up with old Willium as works on his estate, a-mombling across the dairy ground, come day, go day, God send Sunday, like. 'Can't yer walk faster than that, my man?' snaps he to Willium. 'Sir Lord,' says Willium, 'I be walkin' at twelve bob a wik rate.'*

In another encounter a young farmer is worsted at Blockley:

> *Old Jeremy Gillet was a-scything the meddar and maaking hard goin on it when the young gaffer, as thought a lot of hisself, comes up and*

*takes the scythe off of he. 'What's the good o' nickeling about wi' that for? It wants sharping.' He gets hold o' the whetsun as was lying on the ground, and gives he a good whetting. He hands back the scythe to old Jeremy an' says, 'There. It'll gu by hisself now.' Jeremy drops the scythe and up the nearest tree he guz like a little squirrel. 'Hey,' shouts the young gaffer. 'What be you up there for? By you mazed or summat?' 'No, I byunt,' says Jeremy 'but you said he ud gu by hisself, and how the hell were I to tell which way the creatur were going?'*

Another farmer greets a labourer, one cold winter's morning. 'Mornin', James! Fine mornin', James!' He receives the reply: 'Fine marnin's no good wi' no bren cheese in the cupboard, maaster.' At Oldbury a furious farmer sacks a man and says: 'Min' thee dissent ever come back.' He answers: 'Mind thee dissent ever zend for I.' At Moreton-in-the-Marsh a labourer is regularly dismissed and then reinstated. Eventually the farmer dies. The man does not attend the funeral but arrives at the churchyard afterwards as the sexton is filling the grave. 'Wouldn't you like to stamp it down a bit, Will?' he asks. With great glee, Will jumps on the grave, shakes his clenched fist in the air, and shouts: 'Ah, y'owld bugger. You wunt never sack I no mwore.'

At Stow Mop a farmer talks to a shepherd, finds him acceptable, and says: 'I'll get your reference and see you later on.' When the two meet again shortly afterwards the farmer remarks: 'Well, my man, I've heard your character and it's quite satisfactory. You can consider yourself hired.' The shepherd replies: 'Aye, and I've heard thine, and I be'ant a-comin'.'

Hiring fairs were held at Cheltenham (first and second Thursdays after Michaelmas Day), Chipping Sodbury (Fridays before Lady Day and Michaelmas Day), Cirencester (Mondays before and after Michaelmas), Dursley (near Old May Day and Michaelmas), Gloucester (first three Mondays in October, the last known as Runaway Mop), Moreton-in-the-Marsh (Tuesdays before and after 11 October), Northleach (second and third Wednesdays in October), Stow (Thursdays before and after 11 October), Tewkesbury (Wednesdays before and after 10 October), Thornbury (Tuesdays before Lady Day and Michaelmas) and at Winchcombe (Saturday before Michaelmas and the two Saturdays following, the last known as Runaway Mop). There were twenty-five hirings or 'mops' in all, and workers if they wished could also travel beyond the county boundaries to other such fairs.

Those wishing to find work or change employer attended in a clean smock, and sported an emblem of their calling. The term 'mop' is said to have come from the tiny mops carried by maids, though at Cirencester girls wore a blue ribbon if they wished to work in the dairy, red if they preferred the land. A shepherd pinned a tuft of wool in his hat. A carter carried a whip or wore a bunch of horsehair in his lapel; at Gloucester he would wear two parallel strips of green ribbon. A general sign of availability for hire was a leaf or twig in the buttonhole for men and a greenish ribbon in the hat for women.

Potential employers and employees bargained over conditions. At Winchcombe one man asked when he would have to turn up for work in the mornings: 'Thee mights come as early as thee hast a mind, but not later than half past four.' Details of the arrangements made were often entered in the farm account books. 'Hired at Sodbury Mop Thomas Bailey at £7 10 0d for one year' (Meredith family, Shipcombe Farm, Tockington, 1876). Similar entries continued until the late 1880s. In 1893 G. Hyatt of Snowshill hired Daniel Nurden to work from Michaelmas for 13s a week, for 7s extra for haymaking and £1 for harvest.

When a bargain was struck the farmer would offer a shilling to seal it. The agreement was legally binding, except where a runaway mop provided a way out. Thus when John Bear absented himself from John Carter's farm at Puckpool, Arlingham, having been hired at Gloucester Mop in 1836, he was arrested and brought to court. 'I did not like attending two blind horses. I could not eat fat bacon,' he said. It is not recorded whether his excuses were accepted or not, but servants hiring to work at Severnside farms did sometimes stipulate that they should not eat salmon more than twice a week.

The local press made frequent references to the hirings. In 1859 the *Gloucester Standard* reported: 'The Dursley Mop has at last expired. On Thursday last a few of the votaries of this antiquated and slave-like system attended, but the business done was nil.' On the other hand, three years later the *Bristol Mercury* commented that the second mop at Moreton-in-the-Marsh was 'visited by a large number of agricultural servants from the neighbourhood, a great many of whom met with new engagements.' At Tewkesbury in 1871, wrote the *Gloucester Journal*, there was 'a large attendance of pleasure seekers, servants requiring places, and masters and mistresses seeking servants.' The following year a lengthy account appeared in the *Western Daily News*:

> *The appearance of Gloucester on Monday would have been a decided puzzle to any new-comer. Why such a crowd about the Cross? - men and women, boys and girls, are gazing inanely into space, as only the country rustic can gaze; and stranger still, in each man's buttonhole, there is a leaf or twig; the women's hats and bonnets all bear a ribbon of greenish tinge. This is the servant market, and here Hodges, male and female, are on sale. For one year from this date labourers, and carters, milkmaids and house servants will bind themselves to serve. Stout jovial looking men are moving among the crowd, and eyeing with a tender care the smock-dressed twig-bearer while homely dames view with a searching eye the girls who want a place. These are the employers looking for the finest goods. From Stroud and Tewkesbury, from Stow-on-the-Wold and Cheltenham, the meeting has gathered. But we have not seen all; the Town Hall still remains, and there the thoughtful care of certain Gloucester ladies has provided a refuge for the day for female servants.*
>
> *Into such a melee I at once plunged. It was such a stolid crowd, but Gloucester is always stolid, the words of each seem few and far*

*between, and 'yes, oigh be,' and 'Nau, oigh bain't,' are heard on this side and that. A conversation is going on beside me: it was as follows:- Farmer (loquitur): 'A carter, are you?' 'Yes, oigh be.' 'Willing to go to Cheltenham?' 'Yes, oigh be.' 'Not engaged with anyone else?' 'Nau, oigh bain't.' And master and servant depart to settle further preliminaries. I saw that Hodge some two hours afterwards, and there could be no doubt that he was not sober.*

*The variety of faces and dresses among the female servants strikes one unpleasantly. There is a young girl of fourteen or fifteen whose first 'mop' this is, who with blushing cheeks and downcast eyes, looks the picture of innocence itself; of these the Town Hall audience is largely composed. Outside the picture is darker, the dress more gaudy, the faces themselves coarser, the language far too free. Passing through any of the small turnings which lead from Northgate stationwards, the low beer shops are full of guests, both male and female, old and young. Few still retain the symbol of being for hire, and, for the most part, they are 'wettin' their new commissions. Strong as may be the temptations held out to female servants to rendezvous at the Town Hall, let them know as much as you will that the best employer will pick them there, the vagrant spirit will be too strong, and the Cross will be preferred. Huddled together in a crowd, scarcely yielding for the passage of a cart or carriage, the older hands will stand, the performance being varied by a trip for something 'short'.*

Against this narrative one could set the picture from an insider in the form of a song which Alfred Williams noted from Joseph Iles of Poulton:

**Tetbury Mop**

*You young men and maidens, come listen to me,*
*I'll tell you a sight you never did see.*
*Oh, helter skelter, off you trot,*
*On the road to Tetbury mop.*

*Oh, Michaelmas is drawing round,*
*And we poor slaves draw off the ground;*
*There's many a farmer, I'll be bound,*
*Will try to pull your wages down.*

*They'll say they cannot sell their grain,*
*To get the wages down again;*
*But of these men, if you remark,*
*There's good and bad of every sort.*

*Now, when you come into the mop,*
*There's fine fat sheep in every spot;*

*There's pigs upon crutches without any legs,*
*And two or three turkeys keep laying of eggs.*

*There are soldiers and sailors and boys from the plough,*
*A four-headed ox and a two-headed cow;*
*I'll tell you the truth, and I don't care a pin,*
*There's a lot of old women get drunk with the gin.*

*There's old farmer Waddle, so stout and so fat,*
*The nasty old rats ate the rim of his hat;*
*He's a nice little wife, as smart as a queen,*
*She has two wooden legs and a hooped crinoline.*

*The dames of the town get up for a spree,*
*They all get as lushy [tipsy], as lushy could be;*
*They met an old smudge [blacksmith] and made him so drunk*
*That he went for to light his short pipe at the pump.*

Gradually the hiring element of such fairs declined. Maidservants were increasingly engaged through register offices set up for the purpose. From the 1870s onwards farmers began to advertise in the press for workers. Nevertheless in 1885 the *Stroud Journal* reported that 'Ciziter' Mop was 'dying hard, even if it be dying at all; and ... the much invaded townsfolk may well and easily conclude there is life in the fixture yet.' 'Few servants,' it went on, 'are foolish enough to perform the risky feat of "standing mop", and the number of men and youths who thus get situations is decreasing yearly,' though 'at the pleasure part of the fair ... catchpenny, twopenny and threepenny attractions were as plentiful as blackberries even in this prolific fall.' By the 1920s John Drinkwater's mason, Thesiger Crowne, still counted his years by the event: 'If I live I shall be 77 come Ciceter Mop,' but hiring by then was long finished. Like Tewkesbury Mop it is still held every October, though purely as a pleasure fair.

The annual mop was not the only high point in country life. Festivities involving the whole community are considered in chapter eleven but some events catered particularly for farm workers. On New Year's Day the ploughmen came back from the fields at noon and stabled their horses. The head carter marched into the farm kitchen, followed by the under-ploughmen and boys, and placed a rough spanner and a wooden wedge on the table in front of the mistress. 'Now for the owl cock, Missus,' he announced, or 'Rain or shine, the cock's mine.' Then he and his mates went outside and chased the cockerel round the farmyard for ten or fifteen minutes before returning for a substantial meal of meat and vegetables. The afternoon was spent in cleaning harness.

A few days later, on the eve of Twelfth Day, one large and twelve small fires were lit to represent Christ and the twelve apostles. The fire standing for Judas Iscariot was put out immediately but the rest were allowed to burn for as long as possible. Various predictions were made about the ensuing year from the way they burned or the time they went out. As many as sixty such fires could sometimes be seen burning, and the custom was kept up until perhaps a hundred years ago. Some areas were more enthusiastic than others:

> *At Pauntley and the surrounding neighbourhood the servants of each farmer used formerly to assemble in one of the fields that had been sown with grain. Twelve fires with straw were made in a row, around one of which, much larger than the rest, the servants drank a cheerful glass of cider to their master's health, and success to the future harvest. Afterwards, on their return home, they feasted on cakes soaked in cider, which they claimed as their reward for sowing the grain.*

Until the beginning of this century a similar ceremony took place at St Briavels, though on Christmas Eve.

Plough Monday - the second Monday in January - does not seem to have been kept up in the Cotswolds. However, at Elberton (and no doubt elsewhere) ploughs were blessed in church the previous day. Rev. John Thornton revived this custom at St Peter's, Bentham, in 1973, and it is remembered at Huntley. The Monday was taken as a holiday in Elberton and some of the surrounding villages. Bands of men toured, singing and collecting money:

> *Tip a poor old plough boy,*
> *Tip a poor old plough boy.*
> *We are poor labourers out of work,*
> *We have no job to do.*
> *So set us a job and give us a bob.*
> *We've no baccy to chew.*

The occasion was also called Black Button Day, named after the sweets made of black treacle, butter and ginger, which some women specially prepared to give to the ploughmen.

'Fifty year ago,' J. Arthur Gibbs was told in the late 1890s, "twere all mirth and jollity. There were four feasts in the year for us folk. First of all there was the sowers' feast - that would be about the end of April; then came the sheep-shearers' feast - ther'd be about fifteen of us would sit down after sheep-shearing, and we'd be singing best part of the night, and plenty to eat and drink; next came the feast for the reapers, when the corn was cut about August; and, last of all, the harvest home in September.' Alfred Williams said that the seed feast - also called 'sidcyek' (seed cake) - was held in the barn or brew house, and was attended only by those who worked on the farm. At Upton St Leonards it took place after planting beans, and was called a bean feast or 'whip-cat'. A supper would be followed by games such as hunting the slipper. At Aldsworth the favourite dish for the occasion was a 'good big fore-chine, sometimes called the christening chine, with large suet puddings.' At Hatherop the last Sunday in April was preferred, provided the weather had been favourable for planting.

The shearing feast followed in late June or early July. 'Much beef and ale were consumed,' said one participant. According to Williams:

> *A select body of shearers was chosen from a village. They took the farms around one by one, and when they had finished all the flocks they were entertained at a public feast provided by the farmers collectively, who invited as many others to attend as they thought fit. Games and songs followed the feast, and appropriate toasts were made by the shepherds and responded to by the farmers.*

At harvest time the cutting of the last few stalks in the last field was a special task which the men's leader, the lord (as he was called), would often delegate to the prettiest girl present. The stalks were then fashioned into a corn dolly and taken back to the farm on the last load. 'There byunt the time to do it now. The quickest be the best,' lamented one labourer to H.J. Massingham in the 1930s. He remembered the last corn dolly on Hill Farm at Buckle Street, near Bourton-on-the-Water. However, T.A. Ryder, who died in 1981, knew of an old farmer at Coaley who continued to keep one year's harvest dolly until the next year's spring. Dollies are now made purely as a decorative craft. The old unspoken belief is gone that they carried the corn spirit safely through the winter and ensured fertility for the next season's crops.

To return, though, to the last load of corn: the horses would be decked with ribbons or flowers, and everyone who could find a place crowded on to the waggon, which might also bear a green bough. Bystanders 'whooped it home'. Early in the nineteenth century an observer wrote that in Gloucestershire when the last load arrived at the farm:

> *he who has the loudest and the clearest voice, mounts upon a neighbouring shed, and with a voice which would do credit to your city crier, shouts aloud -*
>
> *We have ploughed, we have sowed,*
> *We have reaped, we have mowed.*
> *Hip, hip, hip, harvest home!*
>
> *and thus, sir, the whole assembly shouts 'huzza'. The strong ale is then put round, and the cake which Miss made with her own hands; the load is then driven round to the stack-yard or barn, and the horses put into the stable.*

A century later the custom was still strong, as Miss M.K. Ashby's account from Bledington shows:

> *The last load from the last farm to finish was escorted home by a cheering crowd. One year, recalled by one young at the time, the wagon came home over the little town bridge, into the gateway of Home Farm. It was late and the men*

*leading the horses carried modern 'hurricane' lanterns, with oil lamps inside: others in the crowd had in their hands little old horn lanterns, with candles. Safely through the gate-posts, the horses stopped. Farmer Hawker and his wife stood beside a barrel of their own cider, handing horn tumblers to everyone who came. Our farming was somewhat backward, but it was life, not a mere specialism.*

Harvest feasts are of great antiquity. In the thirteenth century the prior of Leonard Stanley used to give one for the harvesters of Frocester, Cam and Coaley who had worked on the priory lands. Unfortunately, gatecrashers spoiled the fun and the harvesters' reward was commuted to small payments of money. Nevertheless, harvest homes were to continue until modern times.

The feast took place on trestle tables in a specially cleaned barn. All the farm hands were invited, and their wives and children. The farmer would also invite blacksmith and wheelwright, village constable and parson. He and his guests sat at the top table, the workers on the others in order of importance - foreman, head carter, shepherd, and so on down to the farm boys at the bottom.

The fare was typically beef or mutton with plenty of vegetables. Then came apple dumpling or plum duff, followed by bread and cheese and salads. There were ample supplies of beer or cider. Churchwarden pipes and tobacco jars circulated at the end of the meal, and this gave the signal for toasts to the master:

*Here's a health unto our master, the founder of the feast.*
*I hope to God with all my heart his soul in heaven may rest,*
*And all his works may prosper, whatever he takes in hand,*
*For we are all his servants and are at his command.*
*Then drink, boys, drink, and see you do not spill,*
*For if you do you shall drink two, it is our master's will.*

And to the mistress:

*Here's a health unto our master, our mistress shan't go free,*
*For she's a good provider, provides as well as he;*
*For she's a good provider and bids us all to come,*
*So take this cup and sip it up, for it is our harvest home.*

Then there were songs: 'The Farmer's Boy', 'O Shepherd, O Shepherd', 'Dame Durden', 'Our Captain Calls' and 'Let genelmen foine/Set down to their woine/But feyther ull stick to 'is beer, 'e ull.' After a time, 'the ladies withdrew' - those in the farmer's party, that is, not the men's wives - and the songs grew more and more free. This, says Williams, was 'the most important and best-loved festival.'

In 1870 the report in the *Vale of Evesham News* was by no means unusual:

*The farmers in this neighbourhood [Chipping Campden] have gathered their friends and employees together to rejoice with them at the ingathering of harvest. The good roast beef of Old England, the foaming home-brewed, and the smoke of the fragrant weed were most liberally supplied and the jovial toast and song went round, which made the very walls resound with the mirth of those within.*

Twenty years later harvest homes had begun to disappear. They were gone at Kingswood, near Wotton, by 1891; from Broad Campden by 1910 - though one farmer there, Leonard Potter, tried to revive the event in 1934. T.A. Ryder could just remember as a child before the First World War how at Westbury-on-Severn 'All sat down to the meal, farmer and wife and children, together with men and women helpers. There were toasts to master and his wife and to the harvesting implements. The farmer would give bonus gifts of money and tobacco to his men, and laces, ribbons and pins to the girls. There would be harvest songs and dancing.'

This is part of a world we have lost.

9

# GOING FOR A SONG

From the late sixteenth century one can begin to find ballads printed in London but making reference to Gloucestershire. The county supported its own ballad printers from the mid-eighteenth century for perhaps a hundred years, and the 'dolorous chant' of the hawker is only just beyond the reach of living memory. The scores of sheets which have survived - a fraction of those produced - give a good idea of what ordinary people were singing. They range from sentimental songs such as 'The Mistletoe Bough', written by Thomas H. Bayly of Cheltenham, to the classic ballads of Robin Hood, with social protest in between.

Penny ballads were predominantly sold at fairs, markets and public merrymakings, though a few of the better-off sort of people might also take an interest. The philanthropic Dr Edward Jenner (1749-1823) wrote some of his own. He also played the fiddle and flute, and sang in a catch club which met at Cam. 'I have seen him in his latter years,' wrote his biographer, 'after his renown filled the world, and after the many cares attendant upon vaccination had often weighed heavy upon him, shake them entirely off; he would then take up a humorous strain, and sing one of his own ballads with all the mirth and gaiety of his youthful days.'

Alongside the printed ballad, and inter-reacting with it, was a rich oral tradition, again largely the preserve of working men and women. 'When one listens to these traditional singers and players,' wrote H.H. Albino in the late 1930s, 'it becomes clear what an important part of their lives it all was. Singing at their work, playing for their dancing, carols and wassailing at Christmas, Morris dancing at Whitsun, harvest suppers where singing especially was indulged in; they did indeed make their own amusements.'

Almost by a kind of osmosis people absorbed songs by hearing them at family gatherings, at village celebrations, in public houses, and even at work. H.J. Massingham heard cherry pickers from Chipping Campden singing as they 'dandled their lothers [ladders]' against the trees:

*My feither died and I cannot tell how;*
*He did lave me two hosses for to follow the plough.*
*With my wim wom wommle, O.*
*Jack sold the saddle.*
*Blossie boy, bubble O,*
*Under the moon.*

Dennis Potter writes poignantly of the Forest miners 'singing their yearning hymns through the dark, wet woods on their way home from work.' In more lively mood, tree fellers working at Woolaston camped in the woods and entertained themselves by singing to the accompaniment of tin whistles, piccolo and accordion.

What did they sing? A whole series of song hunters including such people as Cecil Sharp, Percy Grainger and the American James M. Carpenter, have between them noted or recorded very large numbers of items, while nevertheless failing to rescue hundreds more. Even so, the heritage is very rich.

## Flying Stationers

The sellers of street ballads had an unsavoury reputation. In the 1750s applicants for public house licences in Gloucester were required to declare to the mayor and aldermen: 'That we will not Entertain in our houses any Pedlars who travel about without a licence, Ballad Singers, Beggars, or any other Persons whatsoever who by the Laws are declared Vagrants.'

The wares of ballad vendors - or flying stationers, as they were called - came from printers established in Gloucestershire from the mid-eighteenth century onwards. Before then London printers issued the occasional sheet dealing with people and events (fictional or otherwise) in the county. Bristol features strongly, starting in 1590 with 'The joyfull Entertainment of the Wherry and iij Wherrymen, viz. Richard Fferrys, Andrewe Hilles, and William Thomas, by the Maiour, Aldermen and Citizens of Bristol.' Five years later there was 'The Merchant's Daughter of Bristol', which became well enough known to be mentioned in one of John Fletcher's plays, *Monsieur Thomas*. In 68 verses it relates how the heroine dresses in 'ship-boyes garments' to follow her true love to Padua, where she saves him from death so that they can return to Bristol and marry.

The nautical context continues in 'The Honour of Bristol', celebrating the fame of a privateer, the Angel Gabriel, which sailed out of the port in the 1620s; 'The Bristol Tragedy', published in the 1690s, the story of a man press-ganged to sea on his wedding day, and the death of his bride from a broken heart; and 'Molly's Lamentation for her Sailor' (1781), later re-issued as a sixpenny music sheet, 'As I walked through Bristol City. A Favorite Ballad Sung by Mr Huttley at the Convivial Societies of Bath and Bristol.' The original words are:

*As I walked thro' Bristol city I heard a woman sing,*
*In behalf of her sailor and in praising the King,*
*She did sing pleasing and sweetly sung she,*
*Of all the men in the world a sailor's the man for me.*

*You may know my jolly sailor wherever he goes,*
*He's so neat in his behaviour as so kind to his love,*
*His teeth are white as ivory, his eyes black as sloes,*
*You may know my jolly wherever he goes.*

*God preserve my jolly sailor when he lies on the raging main,*
*May the heavens direct him to his Molly safe again.*
*Could I but see my honey, in my arm I'd him enfold,*
*And I'd drink to my jolly sailor with a fully flowing bowl.*

*For sailors are men of honour, and men of courage bold,*
*[If they go to fight their enemies they will] not be controuled.*
*When they get on board a man of war where thundering cannons roar,*
*They'll venture their lives for yellow boys* [guineas] *and spend*
*it on the shore.*

Rather more earthy is 'The Skilfull Doctor of Glocester-shire', of which various editions - one of them preserved in the collection of Samuel Pepys - appeared between 1656 and 1692. When a farmer makes his maidservant pregnant the doctor manages to persuade the man's wife that her husband is expecting to give birth to a child himself, and must pass it to a woman by sleeping with her. The wife falls for the story and approaches the maid who after a show of reluctance agrees to sleep with the farmer and 'take on' the child, thus regularising the position. The reader (or singer) of the ballad presumably made the assumption that only in a rural area like Gloucestershire could anyone believe such a farrago, and it has no connection with the county other than the name. At least one sheet is more specific. 'The Truth brought to Light; or, Wonderful strange and true News from Gloucester shire', printed probably in 1662 for 'Charles Tyus at the three Bibles on London-bridge', deals with the extraordinary sequence of events known as the Campden Wonder (see Chapter Six).

Between the 1760s and the 1860s some forty ballad printers worked locally, almost two-thirds of them in Bristol. The rest were spread over five other towns: Cheltenham, Cirencester, Gloucester, Tewkesbury and Wotton-under-Edge. One dynasty, the Bonners, worked in Bristol for the whole period. W. Collard printed in the same city from 1807 until 1846. Samuel Harward set up the first printing press at Tewkesbury in 1760 and produced chapbooks (8 or 16 page booklets with ballads or prose narratives) which he sold in his shops both at Tewkesbury and Gloucester. In 1772 he set up as printer, stationer and bookseller at 162 High Street in Cheltenham, and five years later opened a circulating library there. He died at Charlton Kings in 1809 of an 'apoplectic fit'. The family fortunes continued to prosper with the construction of Harward's Buildings in Cheltenham by his son in the 1820s.

Other printers came and went, struggling with rudimentary equipment in poor premises at back-street addresses. Robert Raikes of Southgate Street, Gloucester (printing 1758-1802) is something of an exception, for he owned the *Gloucester Journal* for a time, and ballad production was only a marginal part of his work. When the prolific song writer, Charles Dibdin, was passing through Gloucester he is supposed to have called on Raikes and left 'A Gloucester Ballad' as a memento of his visit (to the tune of 'Yankee Doodle'):

THE

# FARMER'S

BOY.

The sun went down beyond yon hills,
Across yon dreary moor,
Weary and lame a boy there came,
Up to a farmer's door;
Will you tell me if any be,
That gill give me employ.
To plough and sow, ann reop and mow,
And be a farmer's boy.

Ey father's dead and mother's left.
With her five children large and small,
And what is werse for moteer still,
I am the biggest of them all;
Tho' little I be I fear uot work.
If you will me employ,
To plough and sow, and reap and mow,
And be a farmer's boy.

And if that yos won't me employ,
One favour I have to ask,
Will you shelter me till break of day.
From shis cold winter's blast;
At break of day I'll trudge away,
Elseghere to seek employ,
To plough and sow, and reap & mow,
And be a farmer's boy.

Lre farmer said prhy jake the lad,
No farther let him see7,
O yes dear father tne daughter cries.
While tears ran down her cheeks:
For those that will work its hard to want.
And wander for employ.
To plough and sog aud reap and mow,
And be a farmer's boy.

In course of time he wrew a man,
The good old farmer died.
And left the lad the farm he had.
And the daughter for his jbride:
Now the boy that was, now farmer is,
Oft smiles and thinks with joy,
The lucky day he came that way,
To be a farmer's boy.

W. Clift, Printer, Cirencester.

*The sheet, issued when "The Farmer's Boy' was still a new song, shows some of the printing errors common in the ballad trade.*

*Come, my very merry gentle people, only list a minute,*
*For tho' my song may not be long there's something comic in it;*
*A stranger I, yet, by the bye, I've ventured in my ditty*
*To say a word at parting, just in praise of Glo'ster city.*

*The Romans they this city built, and many folks came down here,*
*Kings Richard, Henry, John, and Ned, did visit Glo'ster town here;*
*King William dined each Christmas here, and Glo'ster folks it pleases,*
*To know the food he relished most was double Berkeley cheeses.*

*The ladies, Heaven bless 'em all! as sure as I've a nose on,*
*In former times had only thorns and skewers to stick their clothes on;*
*No damsel then was worth a pin, whate'er it might have cost her,*
*Till gentle Johnny Tilsby came, and invented pins in Glo'ster.*

*Your fine cathedral when I saw, tho' much I was delighted,*
*Yet in the whisp'ring gallery I got most sadly frighted;*
*Some question there I asked myself, when not a soul was near me,*
*And suddenly an answer came, as if the walls could hear me.*

*The Severn, full of salmon fine, enriches low and high land,*
*And then, for more variety, you've got a little island;*
*Of which I've read a Taylor's Tale, a dozen verses long, sirs,*
*And may I go to Old Harry, if it's not a clever song, sirs.*

*George Ridler's Oven, I've been told, contains some curious jokes, sirs,*
*And very much of it is said by many Glo'ster folks, sirs;*
*But ovens now are serious things, and from my soul I wish, sirs,*
*Your ovens here may ne'er want bread to fill the poor man's dish, sirs.*

*Now if you will but all forgive this slight attempt at rhyme, sirs,*
*I'll promise, like the little boys, to mend another time, sirs;*
*May health with every blessing join this company to foster,*
*Till, with your leave, some future time I come again to Glo'ster.*

The considerable local knowledge deployed here casts doubt on the supposedly casual origin of the piece. Johnny Tilsby (verse three) was a Bristol man who set up a pin-making factory in Gloucester in 1626. A 'Taylor's Tale' (verse four) is a lost ballad on the manners and customs of the Island, a district to the west of Gloucester, which had its own church (St Bartholomew's), four pubs (Angel, Boot, Nags Head and Royal Oak) and mock king (Harry Hudman; see also Chapter Seven). 'George Ridler's Oven' (verse six) is another ballad, sometimes rendered in dialect:

*Thus stwons as built Jarge Ridler's hoven,*
*An' thauy keum vrom t'Blacknest quaar;*

*An' Jarge 'e wur a jolly aud mon,*
*An' 'is yead it graw'd above 'is yare.*

However, early printings use standard English.

*The stones that built George Ridler's oven,*
*And they came from Blakeny's quar;*
*And George he was a jolly old man,*
*And his head did grow above his hair.*

*One thing of George Ridler I must commend,*
*And that was for a notable thing,*
*He made his brags before he died,*
*With any three brothers his sons shall sing.*

*There was Dick the treble and Jack the mean,*
*Let every man sing in his own place,*
*And George he was the elder brother,*
*And therefore he would sing the bass.*

*My hostess's maid, her name was Nell,*
*A pretty wench and I loved her well.*
*I loved her well and the reason why,*
*Because she loved my dog and I.*

*My dog has got him such a trick*
*To visit maids when they are sick;*
*When they are sick and like to die*
*O thither go my dog and I.*

*My dog is good to catch a hen;*
*A duck or goose is meat for men,*
*And where good company I spy,*
*O thither go my dog and I.*

*My mother told me when I was young*
*If I did follow the good ale pot*
*That ale would prove my overthrow,*
*And I would wear a threadbare coat.*

*When I have three sixpences under my thumb,*
*O then I am welcome wherever I come;*
*But when I have none O then I pass by,*
*'Tis poverty parts good company.*

*If I should die, as it may hap,*

*My grave shall be under the strong beer tap;*
*In folded arms there will I lie,*
*Cheek by jowl by dog and I.*

This text, of which the original is in gothic or black-letter type, is a broadside without imprint which may date from the seventeenth century. The song was associated with the Gloucestershire Society (founded in Bristol in 1657) which had various branches, including one in London. Its object was charitable, to pay apprenticeship premiums for poor boys and to contribute to the expenses 'at the Time of their Lying-in' of women 'whose Husband or themselves, are Natives of the County'. Broadsheets issued annually in Bristol during the 1770s had a list of beneficiaries on one side and a copy of the song on the other.

Charity and conviviality (at least for the donors) go together, and the song celebrates in homespun manner singing, drinking, good fellowship and even amorous dalliance. The London branch of the society had an elaborate model on castors which was wheeled round during meetings to stimulate members to dip into their pockets. George Ridler appeared, 'reclining upon a barrel with pipe and jug, emblematical of his conviviality', surrounded by an oven, a dog with a fowl in its mouth, two boys holding indentures, and a pelican (symbol of benevolence). The song (but not the model) also featured at meetings of the Cirencester Society in London, which was in existence by 1701 and still thriving in 1899.

Perhaps the earliest recorded reaction to 'George Ridler's Oven' is that of a Mrs Thomas of Newbold in Warwickshire, who wrote in 1774: 'I have heard it sung extreamly well by Mr. Blackwell; & another Gentleman sang the Bass, 'tis really musical in a kind of Tune not unlike a psalm-Tune.' The first publication of the tune seems to have been at Cirencester in 1836, and two or three years later a handsome sheet music copy appeared in Cheltenham. The song became widely known in Gloucestershire, and in parts of Wiltshire and Oxfordshire. By 1812 an anonymous writer commented: 'The lessened popularity of that fine old Gloucestershire dialect song, 'Gaarge Ridler's Oven', is a regrettable fact, yet within the recollection of the writer the programme of remote village festive gatherings - particularly in the neighbourhood of Cirencester - was incomplete did it not include that patriotic song.'

The various versions - give or take the addition of a chorus and lighter or heavier dialect pronunciation - are remarkably consistent in text. There are nine verses of which four are borrowed from earlier songs (4, 7 and 9 from 'My Dog and I' and 8 from 'Todlen Hame'). A single phrase varies: 'Blakeney's Quar' in some cases becomes 'Blacknest Quar'. The former has led to suggestions that the song comes from the Forest of Dean, and the Cheltenham sheet music has the note: 'The words are collected from an M.S. found several centuries ago in a place called the Speech House.' Others argue that a more convincing reading is that 'Blacknest Quar' refers to Blackness, between Stroud and Chalford, of which the stone was particularly suitable for ovens. Furthermore, the Ridleys, a family of farmers and clothiers, lived in the late seventeenth and early eighteenth centuries at Quarhouse, a hamlet close to Blackness, and also on the packhorse road from Stroud to Chalford.

At some stage - 1835 by one account - a theory was propounded that the song was in fact a kind of Royalist anthem, coded because it was sung before the restoration of the monarchy in 1660. An elaborate key revealed that George Ridler stood for Charles I and his oven for the cavalier party. The stones which built the oven were the followers of the Marquis of Worcester, who held out for the king at Raglan Castle until 1646. The head growing above the hair signified the crown which the king wore 'above his hair'. The explanations run in similar vein through the remaining verses, becoming more and more fanciful.

Mention of the key is strangely absent from the writings of earlier commentators such as Fosbrooke (1807) and Thomas Hughes (1854) but is constantly repeated, more or less verbatim, in later books including those of J. Arthur Gibbs (1898) and Reginald Nettel (1969). Yet the theory simply does not stand scrutiny. There is no evidence to support it. If the secret code had existed it would surely have been triumphantly revealed at the Restoration. Instead it had to wait 200 years. And why did the Gloucestershire Society - the originator of the song and presumably therefore of the code - show literal depictions of Ridler, his dog and oven as late as 1803, and possibly later? A careful examination of the text reveals no hidden meaning. George Ridler's head grew above his hair because he was bald, not for some cryptic reason.

Many printers combined the sale of ballads with other items such as primers, children's books, patters, battledores, memorandum books and all kinds of stationery. Harward stocked a large number of patent medicines, from Attenuating Tincture for the Rheumatism to Walker's Patent Jesuit Drops and Specific Purging Remedy, together with corn plasters, perfume and 'Andrews' Powder for cleaning Ladies Riding Habits, Gentlemens Cloaths &c'. His chapbooks included notices like this:

> *Printed and Sold by S. Harward: at No. 20 in the West-Gate-Street, GLOCESTER, where Travellers and Country Shopkeepers (to sell again) may be supplied with the greatest variety of new and old Songs, Patters, Christmas Carols, Histories, two Sheet Maps and Prints, Copper and Wood Royals, Lotteries for Children, Copy Book Covers, Bibles, Common Prayer Books, Testaments, Spelling Books, Psalters, all Sorts of School Books, &c. &c. on the most reasonable Terms. Likewise the True Original Daffy's Elixir, Bateman's Drops, Scotch Pills, and all other Medicines of established Reputation, that are advertised in the Weekly Papers. BOOKS neatly bound, gilt, and letter'd.*

His stock of well over a hundred garlands (eight-page booklets of ballads) drew heavily on nationally known traditional material such as 'The Blind Beggar of Bethnal Green', 'The Bloody Gardener', 'Chevy Chase', 'The Children in the Wood', 'The Death of Andrew Barton', 'The Famous Flower of Serving Men', 'Jane Shore', 'King Edward IV and the Tanner of Tamworth', 'The Lady's Fall', 'Little Musgrove' and 'Robin Hood and Little John'. His customers were evidently fond of ballads of unhappy love, called 'tragedies', and he published examples from Carmarthen, Kent, Leeds, Northamptonshire, Oxfordshire, Plymouth, Woodstock (Rosamund and Henry II) and Yarmouth. His edition of 'The Gloucestershire Tragedy' has apparently not survived but it could have been a ballad published in London under this title which showed:

> *How an old Miser, of a vast Estate, would have Married his Daughter to a covetous, rich Knight, whom she could not love; After which, he consented to a young gentleman to court her; but as soon as they were engaged to each other, he kept her from him, whereupon she denied him marriage without her Father's Consent; How he Poisoned himself, and afterwards his ghost appear'd to her with a burning Torch; How she was poison'd, which caus'd her Father to stab himself, etc.*

Another, even more sensational 'Gloucestershire Tragedy' appeared in 1703 as a prose narrative, headed:

> *Being a True, but very Dreadful Relation of one Mary Williams of Alvington near Glocester; who leading a wicked and lewd Life, was got with child by a Farmer's Son, who often had use of her Body. With the manner how her Mother's Ghost appear'd to them while they were in the very Act; and he thereupon forsaking her; she was afterwards brought to Bed of Two Sons; but he refusing to Marry her, she Drowned one of them in a Pond, and in a most Wretched and Barbarous manner Cut the other in Pieces, Bak'd it in a Pye and sent it to him fill'd with Blood, on the Day he was Married to another. With an Account of her Apprehension, Tryal, Conviction; and Confession at the Place of Execution.*

A successor of Harward's at Cheltenham was Thomas Willey (born 1794) who, in the 1830s, set up in part of the High Street 'never free of disease' where low lodging houses accommodated tramps. His billheads, one of which illustrates the modest press he used, advertise him as 'Plain and Ornamental letter-press and Copper-plate Printer, Stationer, &c'. On Willey's death in 1861 his daughter, Elizabeth, took over, to be succeeded within a few years by his nephew, former apprentice and foreman, Thomas Hailing. The Hailing firm continued in business - though not in ballads - until the 1950s. (It printed G.E. Rees's book on Bagendon which is listed in the Bibliography.)

Thomas Willey was involved in the Chartist land plan of 1847 which established smallholdings for subscribers chosen by lot at (among other places) Corse, Lowbands, and Staunton. In 1848 he published 'A Song for the Times; illustrative of Passing Events. Liberty or Bondage! or, A Voice from the Oppressed', a declamatory poem in 26 stanzas. A copy now preserved in the Home Office papers was sent to the local MP, G. Cornwall Lewis, by an anxious resident, J. McGacken of Corse Hill, with the comment: 'They [copies] were found in the cottage of a labourer and I understand they have been extensively circulated, which fact taking in conjunction with frequent meetings of Chartists from all quarters in this neighbourhood is making politicians of the agricultural labourers.'

Twenty or so of the ballads issued by Willey deal with political matters such as elections, the Reform Act of 1832, and the workings of the New Poor Law of

1834. As a counter-balance, ten or so include patriotic songs like 'Albion My Country', 'The British True Blue' and 'The King, God Bless Him'. The great majority of his sheets - some 150 of which have survived, bearing about 275 titles - consist of straightforward entertainment in the form of popular songs of the day and the past: 'Betsy Baker', 'The Blue-tailed Fly', 'Flora, the Lily of the West', 'The Garden Gate', 'Jim Crow', 'The Maid of Llangollen' and 'The Rose of Allendale'.

With an eye to local appeal Willey issued 'The Herefordshire Fox Chase' and 'The Cheltenham 'Prentice' (the latter a straight adaptation of 'The Sheffield Apprentice', with only the name changed). 'The Gloucestershire Colliers' - no doubt expected to sell well in the Forest of Dean - is a rewrite of 'Molly's Lamentation for her Sailor' (see above) with changes such as 'Of all the men in the world a sailor's the man for me' to 'Of all the lads in Gloucestershire a Collier for me'. In addition, Willey issued what seems to be the earliest extant version of an anthem of local pride, 'The Jovial Foresters', which probably dates from the 1790s. His text has several garbled words and phrases, which may show that it was taken down from a singer during a performance:

*I am a jovial Forester, my trade is getting Coal,*
*I never knew a Forester, but was a hearty soul,*
*It's what I like when at my work, some neighbour or some smoking trick,* [?Turk]
*But when I've done I'm ripe for fun, to dance or sing with any one.*
*For I'm a jovial Forester, &c.*

*Among mankind you know full well, there's miners of every degree,*
*But he who undermines his friend is more black than we;*
*He's black at heart, you need not doubt, he is black within and black without,*
*But we when free from work can be as smart and spruce as any one.*
*For I'm a jovial Forester, &c.*

*The countay* [courtier] *undermines the state; as for the doctor, he*
*The constitution undermines, for to prolong the fee.*
*The lawyer undermines your purse, none of them can work like us,*
*For I'm a jovial Forester, &c.*

*As for church it must be serv'd, to that we are no foes,*
*While we undermine the Deans we warm the bishop's nose,*

*In vain may Cloe turn the spit, nor would the cook yet fancy it*
*Nor for the mayor's feast yet prepare, if 'twas not for our tools* [toil] *and care.*
*For I'm a jovial Forester, &c.*

*To the Foresters lets drink success, wherever they may be,*
*For they are the boys that fear no noise, but delve on merrily,*
*May plenty thrive throughout our land, bread be always at command,*
*And this I think while we chink no collier will refuse to drink.*
*For we are the jovial Foresters, &c.*

The tune given here was noted from Richard Beach of Bream, a miner employed at Whitecroft Colliery, in 1925 - a time when the song was still widely known in the Forest. Now, though it features in concerts given by local choirs, it seems to have faded from oral tradition.

Crime featured strongly in the ballad printers' output, as it does in the popular newspapers of today. Thomas Willey issued 'The County Livery', a ballad dealing with the life of prisoners in the house of correction at Horsley, the reference being to the uniform of yellow and blue patchwork cap, jacket and trousers. A 'burster' (verse six) meant a spell on the treadmill. Horsley Gaol was demolished in the 1870s; a house called The Priory now stands on the site. Similar prisons can still be seen at Littledean and Northleach, the latter open to the public as part of a museum.

*There is a place in Horsley, I know it very well*
*There's such a place upon the earth, some call it little hell;*
*And to the place where I was sent for three long months tis true*
*To wear the County Livery, the yellow and the blue.*

*But when they got me to the place, pray what you think they*
*done*
*They put me on the treading mill some call it pretty fun*
*Which caus'd me for to puff & blow, & d—m swear 'tis true*
*And wear the county livery, the yellow and the blue.*

*They put me on a bed of straw, I thought it was no joke,*
*Which made my bones to snop and bounce, as if they had been*
*broke,*
*Instead of being a chamber pot a spitting dish 'tis true,*
*And wore the county livery, the yellow and the blue.*

*'Twas early the next morning, just by the break of day,*
*The turnkey he came up to me, and this to me did*
*say -*
*Arise my hearty fellow, to the mill you must go,*
*And you shall wear the county livery, the yellow and the blue.*

*I went down stairs and wash'd and comb'd my hair,*
*And then into the Chapel we did get seated there.*
*The governor read the prayers, just like a ramping Jew,*
*And I wore the county livery, the yellow and the blue.*

*And when the prayers it was o'er the governor he did crave*
*Stand round, you first class men, your burster for to have,*
*Then unto the mill we go and tread away 'tis true,*
*And wear the county livery, the yellow and the blue.*

*And then at night the bell does ring and off the mill we fall*
*And like a pack of hungry dogs come at the Tailor's call,*
*Our turnkey he does stamp and swear, like a madman I declare*
*'tis true*
*And wear the county livery, the yellow and the blue.*

# KIDD WAKE,

IN A SOLITARY CELL,

AND CLOATHED IN THE UNIFORM OF GLOCESTER PENITENTIARY HOUSE.

*FIVE years confinement, even in common goals, muſt ſurely be a very ſevere ſuffering; but if Judges or Juries would only reflect ſeriouſly on the horrors of ſolitary impriſonment, under penitentiary diſcipline! if they would allow their minds to dwell a little on what it is to be locked up, winter after winter, for ſixteen hours out of the twenty-four, in a ſmall brick cell—without company—without fire—without light—without employment—and ſcarcely to ſee a face but thoſe of criminals or turnkeys. No friend to converſe with when well; or to conſult with, or to complain to, when indiſpoſed! Above all—to be ſubjected to a thouſand inſults and vexations, almoſt impoſſible to be deſcribed, and therefore ſcarcely to be remedied; but by which continual torment may be, and often is, inflicted. If they would but conſider what an irreparable misfortune it is to have a conſiderable portion of life ſo weariſomely waſted, they would ſurely be more tender of dooming any man, for a long time, to ſuch wretchedneſs. It is a calamity beyond deſcription, more eaſily to be conceived than explained.*

LONDON: PRINTED AND SOLD BY KIDD WAKE, 66, OLD BAILEY; J. S. JORDAN, 19, LUDGATE HILL; AND AT BULLOCK'S BOOK REPOSITORY, GLOCESTER. *Price Sixpence.*

*Kidd Wake in Gloucester Gaol, c. 1799, wearing the parti-coloured suit known as the 'county livery'.*

Normally, crime ballads dealt with murders, the more gruesome (as we have seen) the better. Willey issued 'An Affecting Copy of Verses Written on the Body of Harriet Tarver, Who was Executed April 9th, 1836, at Gloucester, for Poisoning her Husband in the town of Camden.' He must have published many more sheets in a similar vein. W.E. Adams, born at Charlton Kings in 1832, and apprenticed at the age of fourteen as a printer on the *Cheltenham Journal*, wrote that Willey (whom he described as 'our local Catnach')

> *... was always ready with a 'last dying speech' for every criminal who was executed at Gloucester. It was generally the same speech, altered to suit the name and circumstances of the new culprit; and it was invariably adorned with a ghastly woodcut, showing the figure of the man or woman, as the case might be, dangling from a gallows. The passage leading to Willey's printing office (on High Street) was crowded on the morning of an execution with an astonishing collection of ragamuffins and tatterdemalions, greasy, grimy and verminous. Soon they were bawling their doleful wares all over town.*

Another glimpse of the ballad trade is provided by a letter written in 1889 to the *Gloucester Standard* by G. Armstrong Howitt:

> *At the time of which I write Barton street was a quiet neighbourhood, and had but few shops, and these were simply set out with a pint cup, in which were placed a few tallow candles for sale. The other part of the windows would be furnished with a display of legendary ballad poetry, songs, carols, last dying speeches, and broadsides, surmounted by a rude wood cut in as barbarous style of printing as we had the English bills printed for Dutch quack doctors. Some I have seen in the old black letter type, others printed by Catnach, of the Seven Dials, and his successors, and many by our old townsman and printer, Birt, who always kept a ballad poet who wrote out the dying speeches before the culprits were hung, so that the flying stationers should have a good start out into the country. Sometimes the individual in whose mouth was put one of these speeches was reprieved, but that was no matter, the speech was sold, and the travelling balladmonger was miles away before the fact would be known. Still, we owe much to these old printers, for many of these historical, traditional, and romantic ballads, but for them would have been lost for ever. We also see the old songs they circulated, with their jolly choruses of 'Sing tantar-ra-ra, rogues all! rogues all! Sing tantara-ra-ra, rogues a-a-a-all!' and 'Derry derry down, hey down, derry down, with a hey down, down a down down'.*

The Birt mentioned was in business in Westgate Street from 1816 to 1821 before moving to London, where he became very well known as a ballad printer. Miss

Jessie Howman (born 1894) of Stow-on-the-Wold, whom I interviewed in 1966, remembered her father's tales of itinerant vendors hawking at a penny a time murder ballads sung 'in a dolorous chant'. One of these concerned Charles Peace, hanged at Leeds in 1879; another, a crime closer to home:

*A young farmer's song the deed has done,*
*By jealousy and passion he was led.*
*At Arlington Miss Phipps was murdered;*
*Now she's in her lonely bed.*

## Songs for All Seasons

If Jessie Howman's father learned songs from broadsides, so did many other people. William Hands of Willersey, interviewed by James Carpenter in the 1930s, told how he heard 'Seventeen Come Sunday' from 'a ballet singer in Stratford, selling ballets', but it is not clear whether he acquired the song simply by listening, or bought a copy of the 'ballet' (the old country expression for a ballad sheet).

Several singers encountered some fifteen years earlier by Alfred Williams also mentioned ballad sheets. W. Merritt of Meysey Hampton possessed a copy of 'The Country Lass' bought at Cirencester Mop, and 'for many years this song was the first to be sung at the general harvest home.' Thomas Baughan of South Cerney sang 'Sweet Molly Mog', a favourite of his father's and grandfather's, 'who bought it on a broadside at Cirencester Mop, where it was sung at least as early as 1793.' The original words were by John Gay.

Such documented instances of songs learned from ballad sheets are rare, but there must have been many others which went unremarked. During the 17 years he was in business (from about 1820), W. Clift of Gosditch Street and later Dyer Street, Cirencester ('Travellers and Shops Supplied. - All Orders punctually attended to') issued 90 sheets bearing some 150 titles, of which roughly a third consisted of reprintings of traditional texts such as 'All Round my Hat', 'Banks of Sweet Dundee', 'Bonny Bunch of Roses', 'Claudy Banks', 'Dark-eyed Sailor', 'The Four Seasons', 'Lovely Joan', 'The Mermaid', 'The Mower', 'The Pretty Ploughboy', 'The Rambling Sailor', 'The Rambling Soldier', 'Streams of Lovely Nancy', 'Young Edwin' and 'Young Henry the Poacher'.

Other printers also helped to disseminate traditional songs in this way - though their motives were purely commercial. Some simply copied from the sheets of other printers; others obtained words from singers - see for example, 'The Jovial Foresters', above - and set them up in type for sale. Tunes were a different matter. For instance, of Clift's 150 ballads, only seven give the title of the air intended. People had to pick up tunes by ear, and this was often the case with words, too.

This did not prevent the acquisition of formidable repertoires, in some cases. 'Once started,' wrote Gibbs, 'there are very few Cotswold men who cannot sing a song of at least eighteen verses ... not only solos, but occasionally duets, harmoniously chanted in parts, and rendered with the utmost pathos ... Some of the old ballads, handed down from father to son by oral tradition, are very excellent.' He quotes three songs in full, 'George Ridler's Oven', 'Jim, the Carter's Lad' and 'Turmut Hoeing'.

There were many, many more. Between 1904 and 1921, Cecil Sharp noted several hundred songs in the county. During his busiest year, 1909, he visited Buckland, Chipping Campden, Ebrington, Ford, Snowshill and Winchcombe. The large number of songs he noted include versions of 'Beautiful Nancy', 'The Crafty Maid's Policy', 'The Derby Ram', 'General Wolfe', 'George Ridler's Oven', 'The Holly and the Ivy' (from Mary Clayton of Chipping Campden, whose tune has become nationally known as a consequence), 'Lord Bateman', 'The Oxford Murder' 'Shepherds are the best of men' and 'Wassail'.

Independently of Sharp, the composer Percy Grainger made three visits to the county in search of songs, some of which he recorded on wax cylinders which are still in existence. In 1907 he met three singers, Mrs Mary Hawker of Broad Campden, and two Stanton men, William Newman and John Collett, who between them sang ten songs including: 'The Drummer Boy', 'The Spotted Cow', 'Where Are You Going to, My Pretty Maid?', 'The Farmer's Boy', 'Jack Tar', 'Brisk Young Sailor' and 'Green Bushes'. The following year he stayed with Lady Elcho at Stanway and travelled round by car, spending three full days in the workhouse at Winchcombe, where he recorded 30 songs from five singers. One man alone, Archer 'Daddy' Lane, aged 83, of Alstone, sang 'The Lily-white boys', 'The Wraggle Taggle Gypsies', 'Susan's My Dear', 'The Valiant Monroe', 'Cloddy Banks', 'Died for Love', 'The Banks of Sweet Dundee', 'The Irish Girl', 'Shepherds are the best of Men', 'The Nightingale Sings' and 'High Germany':

*Oh, Polly, dear Polly, a rout has just begun*
*And we must march away by the beating of the drum.*
*Come dress yourself up in your best and come and go with me*
*An' I'll take you to the wars, love, in High Germany.*

*We'll call at every alehouse and drink when we're a-dry,*
*And sweetheart on the road, love, and marry by and by;*
*We will call at every alehouse and drink when we're a-dry,*
*And sweetheart on the road, love, and marry by and by.*

*Oh fiddle with you, Billy, oh mind what I do say;*
*My feet they are so tender I cannot march away.*
*Likewise, my dearest Billy, I am in child with thee;*
*I'm not fitting for the wars, love, in High Germany.*

*Oh cursed be those wars, would they never have begun.*
*And out of old Eng-a-land pressed many a brave son.*
*They took my Billy from me, likewise my brothers three,*
*And they send them to the wars, love, in High Germany.*

*But when my baby it is born, sits smiling on my knee,*
*I shall always think of Billy in High Germany;*
*But when my baby it is born and smiling on my knee,*
*I shall always think of Billy in High Germany.*

By the time of Grainger's third and final visit, in 1909, Archer Lane was dead but Mrs Wixey of Buckland gave him 'Georgy', 'Old Bonny Boy' and 'British Man o' War', greatly impressing him by her skilful variation of melody, her lively dialect speech and - at the age of ninety-three - her general spryness.

It so happened that Sharp had visited Mrs Wixey a few months earlier and had noted 'Georgy' and 'Rosetta and her Gay Ploughboy'. He apparently did not venture into Gibbs' territory of Alington, Arlington and Bibury, but his work inspired the song-hunting expeditions there of Alfred Williams.

Williams (1877-1930), born at South Marston in Wiltshire, was a self-taught intellectual who worked as a blacksmith in the railway works at Swindon until his health broke down in 1914. He then aquired a bicycle (also favoured by Sharp for collecting sorties) and set off on a series of trips on both sides of the Upper Thames which lasted in all weathers for two years and covered 13 000 miles. On different occasions Williams was taken for a tramp and a German spy (his health restored, he did join the army in 1916) but managed to acquire some eight hundred songs - though unfortunately not their tunes - of which about half were published in a weekly column he contributed to the *Wilts and Gloucestershire Standard*.

His brief notes on singers' sources underline the point Gibbs made about family transmission. The elderly Jane Wall of Driffield learned 'The Deserter' from her grandmother. 'Bunch of Nuts', sung by John Ockwell of Somerford Keynes, was 'one of his father's favourite pieces. The old man was a fine singer, and could beat all other local minstrels in the manner and quality of his songs.' John Pillinger's 'The Football Match' (about a game on Salisbury Plain) came from his father at Lechlade, seventy years previously, which means that the son, a one-legged veteran of the Crimean War, must have been well advanced in age. Some of his other songs may have been learned in the army. They include 'Paul Jones', 'The North American Rebels', 'Off to Flanders' and 'Love, Farewell'. James Midwinter of Aldsworth (a village 'famed for its song', said Williams) acquired 'Music and Wine' and 'How Happy is the Man' from his grandfather, fifty years earlier.

Williams had a disaster in Aldsworth. On the very day he was to have met seventy-seven-year-old James Mander, the last of the village's morris men, to take down some songs, Mander died in a threshing machine accident. Morris dancers at that time often seem also to have been singers. Robert Baxter, the last survivor of the Eastleach side, sang 'Good Company' for Williams. George Ash, a shepherd from Ampney Crucis, learned the hunting song, 'Here's Away to the Downs' from 'an aged morris dancer, near Cirencester'.

Among the villages which Williams singled out for the vigour of their singing tradition were Bibury, Coln St Aldwyns, Down Ampney, Eastleach, Poulton and Quenington. At Ablington he met William Mills, the gamekeeper who features in Gibbs' book as Tom Peregrine, 'the greatest character we ever possessed in the village.' Williams took down from him three songs, 'The Congreve Man', 'The Mice and the Crumbs' and 'The Genius', which were his regular party pieces at harvest homes.

A description of such a gathering is one of the set pieces of rural writing, and singing is almost invariably mentioned (see Chapter Eight). Other occasions for song which Williams covers are the 'parish gatherings' which took place every evening at Quenington, where James West learned 'Never cut your toenails on a Sunday' from an unnamed woman singer. He also mentions a singing competition at Kemble Flower Show, where in 1893 Robert Carpenter of Cerney Field won the prize with 'The Pretty Ploughing Boy'.

Gibbs instances the village feast or smoking concert as the kind of event where 'I have listened to as many as forty songs in an evening - some of them entertaining, others extremely dull.' He adds that 'The songs the labourer most delights in are those which are typical of the employment in which he happens to be engaged.' An account of the Chedworth Court Leet dinner given by Lord Eldon at the Foss Bridge Hotel in 1900 gives the choruses of two songs: 'With a yup, yup, yup, and a holler,' sung by Mr Belcher, the ox man, and 'A-rumplin' and a-crumplin' the muslin, O,' by James Millar, wheelwright, waggon maker and bellringer of 43 years standing. A choir supper at Westbury-on-Severn on New Year's Eve, 1888, was treated to 'Tobacco is an Indian Weed'. At Gretton in the 1920s an unnamed man sang for John Farmer 'When sh'll us get married?', which he had performed at village concerts. Farmer gives the full text, and elsewhere those of 'Jarge Riddler's Oven' and 'The Turmut 'Oer'.

As one might expect, songs were frequently sung in public houses - though details were seldom recorded, still less words or tunes. As a boy Harry Howell played by the Red Lion at Blockley before the First World War and heard the men inside singing such Boer War favourites as 'Dolly Gray', 'The Baby's Name is Kitchener' and 'The Song of the Thrush'. The last of these is remembered from the 1930s, together with 'The Barley Mow', at the Carpenter's Arms, Miserden, to the accompaniment of a fiddle:

*All away out in the wilds of Australia,*
*Out in the backwoods there once stood a camp.*
*Now the miners were made up of allsorts and classes*
*With many a scapegrace and many a scamp,*
*When into their midst came a young man from England,*
*And with him he brought a sweet thrush in a cage.*
*Now to hear the bird sing they would flock in their thousands*
*Until the sweet songster became all the rage.*
*There came a deep hush as the song of the thrush*
*Was heard by that motley throng.*
(Chorus)
*And many's the bold fellow's eyes grew dim*
*As the bird sang out clear and strong.*
*Eyes lighted up all of fond memories*
*As the bird trilled its sweet roundelay,*
*For it brought to their eyes dear old England home,*
*thousands of miles away.*

There must have been many more singing pubs, such as the Trout Inn at Lechlade, where Alfred Williams observed - unfortunately without taking down any words or even a title - 'The innkeeper's old grandfather was a rustic and a vigorous songster. One feat of his was to sing a song of his own making, the rendering of which took him no less than two hours and three-quarters.' The clientele must have been very tolerant.

When Williams published in 1923, in book form, a selection of the songs he had found by the Upper Thames he remarked 'Folk-song is dead.' Yet H.H. Albino went on noting songs until 1938 in such places as Bourton-on-the-Water,

Eastleach, Guiting Power, Lower Slaughter, Snowshill and Wyck Rissington. His manuscript collection is now in the Vaughan Williams Memorial Library at Cecil Sharp House.

As well as noting sea songs and shanties (see previous chapter) in Bristol in 1928, James M. Carpenter drove round Gloucestershire in the early 1930s in an Austin Seven car and used a dictaphone powered by a six-volt battery to make recordings on wax cylinders, many of which are now preserved in the Library of Congress (with copies at Cecil Sharp House). As well as making a fine collection of mumming play texts (see Chapter Ten), Carpenter turned up wassail songs at Avening, Cherington, Minchinhampton and Tetbury (see Chapter Eleven). His remarkable haul of singers stretched from Chedworth to Stow and Willersey, where William Hands sang a song he had learned forty-five years earlier from his father:

## An Outlandish Knight

*An outlandish knight came from the north lands,*
*An' he came a-wooing to me;*
*He promised he'd take me unto the northlands,*
*An' there he would marry me.*

*'Go fetch me some of your father's gold,*
*An' some of your mother's fee,*
*An' two of the best nags out of the stable*
*Where there stands thirty an' three.*

*She fetched him some of her father's gold,*
*An' some of her mother's fee,*
*An' two of the best nags out of the stable*
*Where there stood thirty an' three.*

*She mounted on her milk-white steed,*
*An' he rode on the dapple grey.*
*They rode till they came unto the seaside*
*Three hours before it was day.*

*'Pull off, pull off thy Holland smock,*
*An' deliver it unto me,*
*For I think it too rich an' costly*
*To rot all in the salt sea.*

*'Pull off, pull off thy silken gown,*
*An' deliver it unto me;*
*Methinks that's too rich an' costly*
*To rot all in the salt sea'.*

*'If I must pull off my silken gown,*
*Pray turn your back unto me,*
*For it's not fittin' that such a ruffian*
*A naked woman should see'.*

*He turned his back right unto her*
*An' gazed on the leaves so green;*
*She caught him round the middle so small*
*An' plunged him into the stream'.*

*He grooped high an' he grooped low*
*Until he came to the side.*
*'Catch hold of my hand, my pretty Polly,*
*An' I'll surely make thee my bride'.*

*'Lie there, lie there, you false-hearted knight,*
*Lie there instead of me,*
*For six pretty maidens though hast drowned here,*
*But the seventh hath drowned thee'.*

*She mounted on the milk-white steed*
*An' led the dapple grey;*
*She rode till she came to her own father's hall*
*Three hours before it was day.*

*The parrot being up in the window so high*
*An' hearing his lady did say:*
*'I fear that some ruffian hath led you astray,*
*That you tarry so long before day'.*

*Her father being up in his chamber so high,*
*An' hearing the parrot, did say:*
*'What ails you, what ails you, my pretty Polly,*
*That you prattle so long before day?'*

*'It's no laughing matter,' the parrot did say,*
*'So loudly I cry unto thee.*
*The cat has got up in the window so high,*
*An' I was afraid he would have me'.*

*'Well answered, well answered, my pretty Polly,*
*Well answered thou back for me.*
*Thy cage shall be made of the glittering gold*
*And the door of the best ivory'.*

With its mysterious knight, quick-witted lady and miraculous parrot, this is a compelling story. It is far from the only ancient ballad to survive in Gloucestershire until the 1930s. To cite one other example, Carpenter found 'Cold Blows the Wind' - which shows a belief in the corporeal return of ghosts and in the disturbance of the rest of the dead occasioned by excessive grief on the part of the living - to be known by at least four singers: Thomas Clappen of Driffield, Arthur Nightingale of Didbrook, Tom Tanner of Cherington and Mrs Sarah Phelps of Avening.

Mrs Phelps knew other songs, including 'Old woman tossed up', 'A fox went out one chilly night', 'Diamond Token' and 'The Wager', which is better known as 'Broomfield Hill':

*My master an' I a wager did lay,*
*Five hundred pounds unto the one,*
*That a maid she would go down to the bonny, bloomin' fields,*
*An' a maid she would never home return.*

*This maid she went down to the bonny bloomin' field,*
*An' found her true love lyin' fast asleep,*
*With his horse an' his hound an' his noble saddle bound,*
*An' his whipstick lay under his feet.*

*Three times she did walk to the crown of his head,*
*Three times to the sole of his feet;*
*Three times she did kiss of his sweet and rosy lips*
*As her true love lay there fast asleep.*

*Then when she had done all that she could do,*
*Softly she walked away,*
*An' hid herself all in a bonny bunch of broom*
*To hear what her true love would say.*

*An' when he woke right out of his sleep*
*An' found that his true love had been there,*
*He stamped an' he swore an' his own hair he tore,*
*Sayin', 'My true love has been here but she's gone'.*

*Then loudly he called to his little footman,*
*Who was covered all over in green,*
*Sayin, 'Where were you now that you did not waken me*
*When my true love had been here to be seen?'*

*'O, master,' he said, 'you should sleep more by night,*
*An' then you'd want to sleep less by day,*
*For if you'd been awake an' your true love had been here,*
*A maid she had never gone away.*

*'If I'd been awake an' my true love had been here*
*An' I could have had my own way,*
*All the pretty little birds in the bonny, bloomin' fields*
*Should have feasted on her body for their prey.'*

After the Second World War a further revival of interest in traditional songs brought more singers to light. In 1957 Peter Kennedy made recordings (later issued on cassette) of singers from Brockhampton, Longborough, Lower Swell and May Hill. In the 1960s, drawing partly on the repertoires of members of his own family, Richard Chidlaw noted an interesting collection of songs, including 'Buttercup Joe' from Uncle Joe Wytchard of North Nibley, 'The Shepherd's Song' (see Chapter Eight) from Granny Francom's father, William Chappell of Tresham, and 'Late Home Came I' from Granny Francom herself, who remarked: 'If you don't want that you burn it.'

*Late home came I one night, late home came I.*
*There upon the door another man's coat did lie.*
*'Whose coat is that, my love, or whose might it be?'*
*'My love, it is a blanket your mother sent to me.'*
*Thousand miles I travel, a thousand miles or more,*
*But never have seen a blanket with buttons down before.*

*Late home came I one night, late home came I.*
*There upon the floor another man's boots did lie.*
*'Whose boots is this, my love, or whose might it be?'*
*'My love, it is coal boxes your mother 'ave sent to me.'*
*Thousand miles I travel, a thousand miles or more,*
*But never have seen coal boxes with laceholes down before.*

*Late home came I one night, late home came I.*
*There upon the floor another man's hat did lie.*
*'Whose hat is that, my love, or whose might it be?'*
*'My love, it is a bowl your mother 'ave sent to me.'*
*Thousand miles I travel, a thousand miles or more,*
*But never 'ave seen a bowl with ribbon round before.*

*Late home came I one night, late home came I.*
*There upon the floor another man's stick did lie.*
*'Whose stick is that, my love, or whose might it be?'*
*'My love, it is a poker your mother 'as sent to me.'*
*Thousand miles I travel, a thousand miles or more,*
*But never 'ave seen a poker with notches down before.*

*Late home came I one night, late home came I.*
*There upon my bed another man did lie.*
*'What man is this, my love, or who might it be?'*
*'My love, it is a baby someone 'ave sent to me.'*
*Thousand miles I travel, a thousand miles or more,*
*But never have seen such a baby's face with whiskers round before.*

Chidlaw himself features as a singer with the song, 'Twelve Apostles' on *All Brought up on Cider*, a cassette selection from many songs assiduously gathered by Gwilym Davies of Charlton Kings between 1974 and 1987. With several folk groups - and latterly, Puzzlejug - Davies has made a series of records and cassettes featuring a wide range of traditional songs from Gloucestershire. Others have been recorded by Mike Yates.

It is now increasingly difficult to find such songs as people of the older generations disappear. The fate of traditional singing in the county now seems to lie with the civil servants, teachers, librarians, engineers, who appear at festivals and in folk clubs, but they will remain eternally indebted to the sailors and shepherds, miners and ploughmen, milkmaids and housewives, who cherished these songs and kept them alive.

10

# IN COMES I

Like the members of Thomas Hardy's Mellstock Quire, village musicians who played in church on Sundays made music for other occasions such as weddings and dances. Hardy treasured his father's violin and some of the carefully copied music for use in church which had been handed down in the family. He also preserved manuscript books of dance tunes and their steps which had been used at events such as parties and harvest suppers.

Similar practices prevailed in Gloucestershire. When musicians were displaced from the west galleries of churches (see also Chapter Four) some went on to join the village bands which played at secular events such as village feasts and club days. Informal dances often relied on a small number of musicians, and the morris men on one, who usually played a pipe and tabor - later a fiddle, concertina or melodeon. There is one instance, at Winchcombe, of a small ensemble.

While country dancing was mixed, morris dancing was male, though to the horror of some purists modern revivals have sometimes involved both sexes - and one side, that of England's Glory at Cheltenham, is made up solely of women. Revival was needed because morris was moribund or even dead, and the same applied to mumming, the performances by groups of local men - who 'might have been Bottom the Weaver and his hempen homespuns,' commented H.J. Massingham - in some seventy-five villages. In fact the number was much larger, because mummers from one village often performed in several others which did not have their own players.

There was an overlap between morris and mumming, both in the people involved and through the inclusion of dancing in some of the plays. Modern revivals can never reproduce exactly what went before but at least they provide some kind of link with the past. We know that some of the old morris dancers admired their revivalist successors, and the time-honoured words of 'In comes I' would still quicken the pulse of one of the King Georges or Turkish Knights if he could return to the scene.

## Noisy but Not Unskilled

Richard Clutterbuck of Rodborough, born in 1638, was still living sixty years later despite having started to go blind at the age of three. His hearing was so acute that he could detect when the sand in an hour-glass ran out. He constructed mills for oatmeal and pepper, and mended watches and musical instruments - violins, bass viols, citterns and a set of virginals - all of which he played himself. He 'taught music to a scale of his own devising,' wrote Rudder, and 'cut out his notes upon pieces of wood.'

Musicians like him played for dancing as well as for church services, until the old string and woodwind bands were replaced by organs. James Keen, a Blockley shoemaker, acted both as church organist and brass band organiser, and for good measure founded a choral society in 1906. Just a few years earlier, according to Gibbs, the Chedworth band - its players formerly church musicians - went the round of the villages once or twice or year.

Gibbs also mentions Isaac Sly, 'the last vestige of the old wandering minstrels of bygone days,' who played 'his inharmonious concertina in the hall of the manor house [at Ablington] regularly at Christmas and other festivals.' This reminds one that Charles Wheatstone (1802-75), who was born at Barnwood and baptised at St Mary de Lode, Gloucester, invented the concertina in 1827.

Brass bands flourished in small communities, their membership predominantly artisan. Early on musicians owned their instruments and played at events such as parades, club feasts and local dances. Later, bands tended to be bigger, with instruments collectively or institutionally owned, and performed increasingly at concerts and in contests. Early in the nineteenth century many musicians played by ear. As they learned to read music, parts were copied by hand until print took over in the 1840s with the advent of cheap editions of scores. Towards the end of the century printed music was paramount, though some musicians continued to play by ear on informal occasions such as pub sessions.

By this time instruments were almost entirely brass, though at Gotherington a concertina and tambourine were still played and Cresswell the Fiddler was a well known local figure. Even small villages had bands - Shipton Oliffe, and Upton St Leonards (until 1900), for example. At Tirley the band, organised by John Carter (who in 1932 made from scrap the clock still in the church), toured at Christmas in return for copious offerings of homemade cider. Lechlade boasted three bands: church lads, string and town. Of Bledington's two, one was temperance and the other, 'the boozers' band'. The first lasted longer, and continued playing at fetes and festivities in the neighbourhood until 1949. At Whiteshill the band, which owed its origin to the Parker family, was nicknamed the 'badger band' because (unknown to the members at the time) badger meat was served at one of its annual dinners.

Nailsworth's two bands (string, and drum and fife) were conducted by William Arundel Jones, who also managed to found (in 1859) and conduct the Minchinhampton Town Band. Jones could play flute, clarinet, cornet, oboe, cello and organ. By 1911 the Minchinhampton musicians included firemen, a stick-mill worker, a pin maker, a blacksmith, a poacher, the landlord of the Swan, the verger, a collector of rates and taxes, and even a professional musician. The band ceased to exist in the 1920s.

As in other mining communities, bands thrived in the Forest of Dean. Dennis Potter has written that the members of Berry Hill Silver Prize Band 'thought themselves possessors of a massive and enviable privilege'; they were constantly in demand for 'regular concerts, local concerts, marching for the chapel behind the tasselled admonitory banner, the rugby ground occasions, and coach trips to play in pub back-room or walled garden.' Members of the

Pillowell Band, founded in 1889, deciding to break away, said 'We're going onward,' and formed the Yorkley Onward Band. Cinderford's two bands, town and Excelsior, are now one, the Swanbrook, so called because it is sponsored by the coach firm of that name. The Meek family has been represented on its committee for a hundred years, and a sign of vitality is that a junior band was formed as recently as 1992.

Many bands have now disappeared but even tiny Tidenham still has one. So does Bream, and Lydney boasts two. On the other side of the Severn there are Cheltenham Silver, Gloucester Flowers, Marshfield, Nailsworth, Stinchcombe and Thornbury. The movement is lively enough for the *Citizen* newspaper to devote a weekly column to it.

Musicians (and dancers) do not please everyone. In 1826 Rev. F.E. Witts of Upper Slaughter tetchily recorded in his journal an occasion in Lord Wemyss' house at Stanway: 'A noisy but not unskilled band of music from Broadway played most of the evening in the hall, and a promiscuous dance among the gentry and domesticks was kicked up.' Others reacted only too enthusiastically. During a dance in the 'church-house' at Tortworth in 1602 the rector, John Wylmott, 'ledd the Cushin Dawnce with a Cushin on his sholder and kneeled downe as the order of the dawnce is, and kissed one goodwife Lickey.' To compound the offence he repeated the action with all the women present.

Informal dancing sessions often took place in the open. At Uley villagers turned out at Whitsuntide to dance in the street 'from the 'King's Head' to the turnpike, to the tune of "Haste to the Wedding" and many more.' Until the late nineteenth century the benefit club held its annual meeting in another public house, the Upper Crown. The men dined and the women went in afterwards to eat the leftovers. Then they all danced on the green. At times of full moon there was still more dancing in Fop Street.

Chedworth people also danced in the streets, to the music of concertina and tambourine. One of the items there, as at Lower Guiting, was the 'Butterfly Dance'. At Westbury-on-Severn, until about 1900, step-dancing competitions were held on boards put down on the green. One of the most skilful entrants, despite her sixteen stones, was Fanny Daunter. Music was provided by a fiddler.

On Club Day at Bledington, Edward Butler, a fiddler from Bampton, pitched a tent for dancing on the green. He stayed there for a whole week, charging twopence per session for dancers who flocked from villages for miles roundabout. 'They missed it terrible when he died,' said one of them. A fiddler played at Staverton for dances in Wilkins Barn. At Blockley dancing took place in the open at the Back Ends. A concertina player called Cotter sat on a stone stile to accompany sets of lancers and quadrilles. Another of the old Blockley musicians was William Lively, a blind fiddler who played for 'treats' in Northwick Park. Several places in the Forest of Dean acquired the name of 'dancing green' because of their use by local people.

In the 1950s Mrs Hannis of Cranham remembered when the hornpipe and the broomstick dance were performed outside the Black Horse, to the music of fiddle and banjo. At Birdlip Sam Heydon was well known during the First World War for his ability in the broomstick dance; and this was popular, too, at Brockweir:

> *Dancing was the chief enjoyment of all and a maypole was erected at the Cross. The maypole dance, to the music of a fiddler from the Forest and a melodeon, was very rural; a four-handed reel, now lost, was the favourite with the older people. Another feature was stepdancing on a flat board, raised with stones to get plenty of sound; some were quite expert at it. The besom jump was an entertaining dance by an old woman living near the Mackenzie Hall. She jumped to and fro over the broom handle with great agility, to the tune of a tin whistle.*

Such 'very rural' diversions declined with the rise of commercial entertainment; and new forms of dancing arose which a Cutsdean woman characterised to H.J. Massingham as 'waddling about like an old duck'. In their turn, these have now been superseded by disco dancing, to the extent that few people below the age of forty can do any form of 'joined-up dancing'.

The English Dance Society - formed in 1917 with Cecil Sharp as one of the prime movers - set about trying both to record and to revive traditional country dances. Oddly enough, one might think, many of its members were aristocratic, or at least monied. The first regional branch of the society, formed at Cirencester in 1912, had Lady Bathurst as its president. Activities were suspended during the First World War but resumed in the 1920s. Lavender Jones, sent by the society in 1923 to coach dancers for a festival to be held in Cirencester Park, writes:

> *Gloucestershire then was a feudal county: most of the large estates were still struggling on in the old way, with less than half the number of servants and farm labourers. The war had impoverished the landowners, deprived them of their sons - who lay dead in 'foreign fields', as did their able-bodied workmen, and their horses ... Some of the estates were being kept together by the widows of their former owners, with perhaps the help of a farm manager, until the teenage sons were old enough to take over. The houses were cold and dilapidated - I stayed in many of them - and in one case the big house was let to some people for the hunting season, while the owner retired to a cottage on the estate.*
>
> *The time when I was met at a small country station by a carriage reminded me of a film of highwaymen, for the coachman wore livery and a hat with a cockade, but it was all green with age and the coat of arms on the door was peeling off... One sad occasion was when I was to be driven to the station to catch a train to my next class. The old coachman had learnt to drive an ancient car, it would be a museum piece now, all brass fittings and huge lamps. The car refused to start and the old man ran round the front of the bonnet 'to give it a swing'*

*- he'd left the brake off and the car in gear and it went over him and killed him.*

Mrs Jones, equipped with a list of dances, two sets of morris sticks, eight wooden swords and sheaves of piano music, travelled round:

> *I taught the 'social' dances in every conceivable building - army huts converted to a parish hall, village schools with the tip-up benches pushed out of the way, in one place a large drawing room while the sad shell-shocked son of the house wandered aimlessly round the room and finally disappeared somewhere. Accompaniment was usually a piano of Victorian lineage, often the notes sticking, from the local church organist whose tempo was more suitable to the psalms. In one village the only musical instrument was an ancient harmonium.*

The participants were mainly women and children. The morris was represented by boys from Sapperton, coached by the wife of Ernest Gimson, the craftsman furniture maker (died 1919), on whom Norman Jewson comments:

> *He had a good baritone voice and enjoyed singing such songs as 'Turmut Hoeing', 'The Leather Bottel' and a curious old local song called 'Tom Ridler's Oven' as well as many from Gilbert and Sullivan operas. The old folk songs and country dances with their delightful airs delighted him, and every Saturday evening he joined the class of boys and girls at the village hall, learning the old dances, while Mrs Gimson played the piano. It pleased him when he found out that several of the dances had been popular in the neighbourhood within living memory, the postman remembering dancing some of them at Harvest Homes in his boyhood. The postman also knew the old Mummer's Play and brought the mummers round every Christmas.*

It was left to another revival of interest after the Second World War to return country dancing to adults, to bring it back from education into recreation. Currently, barn dances (or ceilidhs as they are sometimes called) are again held regularly, with music provided by amateur or semi-professional bands playing fiddle, guitar, concertina, accordion. Members of all sorts of organisations - parent-teacher associations, churches, young farmers, rambling groups, tennis and cricket clubs - once more meet in parish halls, schools, barns, pub room, and sometimes even in the open air, to enjoy again the dances of their ancestors.

## Morris On

The earliest references to morris dancing in the county are at Thornbury Castle in 1516, Bristol in 1530 and Gloucester in 1553. Over the centuries allusions occur from time to time in church documents, records of law suits, archives of great families such as the Duttons of Sherborne and the Cliffords of Frampton-on-Severn, private diaries and newspaper reports.

The first visual representation is a panoramic picture, dating from about 1730 and preserved in Cheltenham Museum and Art Gallery, which shows work in progress in the fields near Dixton Manor. Six morris dancers, preceded by two sword bearers, are also there, no doubt to encourage the efforts of the reapers. It is recorded that in July 1758 the Leigh family at Adlestrop paid one shilling to 'ye Morris Dancers at ye Mead Mowg', and perhaps a similar arrangement was made at Dixton.

During the eighteenth century the typical morris side consisted of ten men: seven dancers (six plus a spare), a fool, a collector and a musician. They did not always enjoy a good reputation. In 1772 William Keeling, a 'famous morrice-dancer' of Chipping Campden achieved notoriety by committing a murder; and in the same year at Newent an election mob, it was reported, went round extorting liquor 'after the manner of Morris-dancers'. In the nineteenth century fights took place between morris men from different villages. Some of these were no doubt caused by traditional rivalry between the *frères ennemis* of pairs of neighbouring places like Brockweir and Tintern, Blakeney and Lydney. Others were occasioned specifically by morris matters. In May 1836 the *Gloucester Chronicle* reported:

> *The Morris dancers of Monmouth, the Forest, and Lydbrooke, generally assemble at Cymon's [Symonds] Yatt, on the Wye, at Whitsuntide, to celebrate their annual 'revels' upon that commanding eminence. This year the parties contended for the possession of the post of honour, and a serious engagement took place which ended in several of the parties being carried off the field seriously injured.*

Again in the Forest, the Ruardean side was disbanded in the 1870s after a man was killed in a fight on Plump Hill.

When sides competed their rivalry on occasion became over keen. The honour of dancing at Dover's Games (see Chapter Seven) went to the side successful in an eliminatory competition, the last of which was Longborough. In the mid-nineteenth century a May Day competition at Withington attracted entries from Chedworth, Shipton and elsewhere. Eleanor Adlard describes how the Winchcombe side competed, 'notably doing their famous handkerchief dance', with those of neighbouring villages on the Abbey Terrace at Whitsun. Tension could also arise if one side danced in what another considered its territory, though there were instances of co-operation in jointly-organised tours.

The prime time for morris was Whitsun. From Easter until Whitsun the Rissington men put in two evenings a week of practice; the Longborough side worked 'night after night' in a quiet lane, possibly Banks Fee Lane. The men at Winchcombe practised at Cart House, one of a series of poor, damp dwellings in Silk Mill Lane:

*Brandy House and Lousy Row,*
*Cheese Press House and Cart House below.*

The pipe and tabor, once very widely used, were later superseded by other instruments such as fiddle or concertina. At one stage Winchcombe's music was supplied by James Major (melodeon), George Andrews (drum) and John Randall (triangle). William Edwards Davies (fiddle) and Albert Belcher White (concertina) played on other occasions. Most sides had only one musician at a given time, and some musicians played for more than one side. James Simpson - otherwise known as McDonald, and nicknamed 'Jim the Laddie' - played his pipe and tabor for Northleach, Sherborne and other sides until 1856 when, at the age of forty-five, while performing at Bourton-on-the-Water he became 'so Drunk that he Died from the Effects of it'. Thomas Pitts was a later pipe and tabor man at Sherborne, as well as being a dancer and singer.

Charles Benfield, an agricultural labourer from Bould in Oxfordshire, played the fiddle for Bledington, Longborough and other sides. Maud Karpeles tells how Cecil Sharp presented him with a new bow because he had been unable to play for some years since his own was broken:

*Charles Benfield (1841-1929) of Bould, Oxfordshire, fiddled for Bledington, Longborough and other morris sides.*

*The old man tuned up and played over a few tunes with his new bow, but the result did not please him. Thoughtfully he examined and fingered the bow, and said: 'It looks all right, and it seems a nice bow, but somehow it won't keep time with the other hand.'*

Nevertheless he was able to provide Sharp with several songs, and also many tunes, including 'Balancy Straw', 'Bonnets so Blue', 'Gallant Hussar', 'Glorisher', 'Maid of the Mill', 'Monk's March', 'Sherborne Jig', 'William and Nancy', 'Young Collins' and 'Saturday Night':

Each side had its requirement of tunes for the repertoire of stick, handkerchief, corner and set dances (for all six men) and jigs (for one or two). Among Bledington's preferences were 'Idbury Hill', 'Maid of the Mill', 'Bonnets so Blue', 'William and Nancy', 'General Monk's March', 'Constant Billy', 'Balance the Straw', 'My Lord Sherborne's Jig', 'Greensleeves' and 'Trunkles'. Longborough's repertoire included 'London Pride' (their name for 'Idbury Hill'), 'Swaggering Boney', 'Country Gardens', 'Old Woman tossed up' and 'Princess Royal'. Sherborne favoured 'Constant Billy', 'Orange and Blue', 'My

Lord Sherborne's Jig' and 'The Cuckoo's Nest'. Several dances were common to a number of villages.

There were many variations in style, steps and costume. Longborough - renowned for high stepping - wore caps or half-high hats. Their shirts, carefully made by their wives, had a straight pleat down the centre, with one inch frills and four or five narrow tucks on each side. They usually wore two shirts, the second 'to suck the sweat up'. They wore a crossed baldrick in blue braid and a band round the waist in red, various rosettes and ribbons, and pads of bells on their legs. Most wore trousers, though breeches with blue stockings were also considered correct. Handkerchiefs were tied on the middle finger. Harry Taylor, who always wore light nailed shoes, said: 'Must always have nails when you dance at Stow as stones be so cruel.'

The Sherborne garb in the nineteenth century was a white shirt, pleated front and back, with white knee-breeches and coloured stockings; billycock hat (square, high and black), trimmed with coloured ribbons; diagonal sash; pad of twenty-five bells strapped below the knees; a large handkerchief tied with a reef knot to the little finger; and the lightest shoes available.

Winchcombe men wore a 'faggoting' coat (that is, one with the skirts cut away in front), scarlet waistcoat, silk hat, one blue and one white stocking, tied with yellow ribbons, and bells below the knees. May Hill - to mention a side from the Forest of Dean - wore black trousers and white shirts covered back and front with four inch wide folds of bright ribbons and two sashes crossing diagonally and hanging down at the sides. They had high box hats trimmed with ribbons, and 'ruggles' (little bells) tied to the legs with yellow ribbons.

The May Hill side danced for a full week, starting on Whit Monday, during which they worked their way round neighbouring villages. One year they went to Gloucester (on foot), then down the east bank of the Severn; after crossing by ferry to Newnham (and spending the night there) they called at Northwood Green wake on the way home. Russell Wortley described them on the road:

> *There were six dancers in the set. As they marched from place to place the Foreman (or 'Flagman' as he was called) carried a large white flag three or four feet square embroidered with his initials and the name of the village or trimmed with rosettes; this, on a pole four or five feet long, he waved in time with the music. Alongside him, number 2 of the set carried a sword in each hand which he whirled round his head. The other four dancers followed behind in pairs and they had a Fool (with a tail on the end of a stick three or four feet long), a Bagman and a Fiddler.*

Longborough performed only in Whit week, and would walk to Shipston-on-Stour, Stow and Bourton to dance for the club celebrations, stopping at farms on the way and dancing for cider. Once a fierce dog confronted them. George Hathaway who played the part of the fool dived into the kennel, which consisted of half a barrel, barked, and made faces. The dog was 'never any good at housekeeping arter that.' The Longborough men might also walk ten miles in order to perform at Ascot-under-Wychwood.

The Rissington side was out for three weeks on and off, starting at Whitsun. Among their destinations would be Cheltenham, Cirencester and Burford (where they always returned in the last week of September for the fair). The Bledington men left home on Whit Monday and toured for a week. They also danced on May Day, and in June and July at club festivities on their own green and in other villages.

Sherborne started on Whit Tuesday and danced on and off for the next three weeks, including tours as far afield as Milton and Shipton-under-Wychwood. Such dancing was hard, physically tiring, and accompanied by serious drinking. The dancers, drawn from a tightly-knit group of families in each village, were predominantly agricultural labourers, as Keith Chandler has established by his painstaking trawls through census records. There were other farm workers (carter, farmer's boy, ploughboy, shepherd) and manual workers (carpenter, plumber, gardener, mason, sawyer, railwayman). The few other occupations represented include gamekeeper, farmer, grocer, postman, publican and storeman. Like Charles Benfield, many of the musicians were also agricultural labourers; other trades represented were parish clerk and sexton (William Edwards, Winchcombe, fiddle), master chimney sweep (Albert Belcher White, Winchcombe, concertina), land measurer (William Hooper, Sherborne, pipe and tabor). William Hathaway of Lower Swell was a shoemaker who exchanged a pair of boots, value 3s 6d, for one of the fiddles he played.

By the 1870s all fifteen sides in the Forest had gone. Some of the twenty-eight recorded in the Cotswolds lingered a little longer. Although Aldsworth, Guiting Power and Stow had disappeared in the 1860s, Oddington, Rissington and Sherborne survived for another twenty years. Bledington, in decline, seems to have made a final excursion in 1900 to Fifield, but gave up when stallholders at the village fair drowned their music with rattles. At Longborough there was hostility from the local gentry, with suggestions that the dancers were often drunk and disorderly, but the final blow was dealt by the vicar, Rev. Etches, 'whose wife strongly disapproved because the dancers, when chased by the fool, used to hide under the women's skirts.' The Whitsun dancing ended, but according to Margaret Shepard 'there is some evidence that the team went underground and joined up with the mummers at Christmas.' Campden disbanded in the 1850s but was revived in about 1896.

Though sides ceased to exist, dancers and musicians lived on; and when early this century Cecil Sharp sought to note the steps and tunes of the morris they were able to inform him. In 1909 he met Charles Benfield and in the following year set out to find Henry 'Harry' Taylor (born 1843) of Longborough, who as a boy risked a thrashing by playing truant from school so as to watch the morris. On 2 May Sharp travelled by train, probably to Moreton-in-the-Marsh, then cycled in pouring rain to Longborough, where he discovered that Taylor was working at Condicote. On Sharp went, and found his man pulling mangels by a hayrick. Soon the two were dancing, using wisps of hay as handkerchiefs. Taylor whistled the tunes. Sharp wrote in his notebook. In the middle of it all the farmer came through a gap in the hedge and subsided with amazement for although Taylor had worked for him for many years this was the first he had heard of any dancing - an indication of how the tradition had sunk into oblivion.

Sharp interviewed many other dancers, and also musicians. John Mason (born at Kingham in Oxfordshire), who played flute, clarinet, concertina and fiddle, provided Sharp at Stow with tunes for country dances and also morris, including 'Greensleeves', during the course of which, he said, 'The Squire of the Morris, that's the tom fool, used to run round and sing' some words (presumably to the second half of the tune). He added: 'You mustn't have a natural fool, but a man with his head screwed on, as I may say, for the Squire.'

*Green sleeves and yellow leaves* [lace]
*Boys and girls they work apace*
*They earn some money to buy some lace*
*To lace the lady's green sleeves.*

In 1910 Sharp met seventy-three-year-old Thomas Phelps of May Hill in the Forest of Dean, who had danced thirty years earlier, and Charles Baldwin, aged eighty-eight, an ex-charcoal burner, who had fiddled for Cliffords Mesne morris until it lapsed in about 1870. From Baldwin, who was living at the time in the almshouses at Newent, Sharp noted 'The Morris Call' (which summoned the men to dance), 'The Morris March' (a processional), 'The Wild Morris' ('always played 'em off the green to this tune') and 'The Gloucester Hornpipe':

When Russell Wortley visited the area in 1947 he met Baldwin's youngest son, Stephen, who was born in the early 1870s and died in 1955. He played the fiddle at Christmas for morris at Bromsberrow Heath (when he learned their stick dance), and ran his own side at Mitcheldean, where he then lived, for three years from 1900. Eight years after his first visit Wortley returned to make some recordings (later issued as an LP) which included 'The Gloucester Hornpipe' and 'The Coleford Jig'.

Wortley was a member of the Travelling Morrice, a group inspired by Sharp's work which learned dances and performed them in the villages from which they originated. A first expedition in 1924 took them on cycles to Charles Benfield at Bould, then to Sherborne, Stow and Longborough. In the last place the vicar and his wife, more tolerant than their predecessors, the Etches, invited them into the vicarage. They met Harry Taylor, who approved of their style, said they were 'lissom', and their first dance 'just quite right'. He could also be critical: 'Pardon me for larding it but thic-yer be a skew-carnered dance.' After lunch on the vicarage lawn the eighty-one-year-old Taylor - whom they had already nicknamed 'the generalissimo' - lined the visitors up and taught them 'Saturday Night', 'The Cuckoo's Nest', 'Trunkles' and 'The Old Woman tossed up'. 'Although Longborough is a very small and poor village,' said a note in the Travelling Morrice's records, 'yet even here 7s 4d taken in the collection.' Before the tour was over the news came of Sharp's death. There were further visits to Longborough, and memories of Harry Taylor's leaning on his stick in his black suit and white stock, joy in his eyes. He died in 1931 at the age of eighty-seven.

There were short-lived revivals at both Sapperton and Sherborne in the 1920s, and others after the Second World War. Currently there are only ten sides in Gloucestershire, of which only one - that of Chipping Campden - has any direct link with those of the past. The others are Forest of Dean, Lassington Oak (based at Highnam), Newent, Gloucestershire (Churchdown), Gloucestershire Old Spot (Cheltenham), Sherborne and two at Thornbury. The dancers here are all men, but Stroud performs with men or women or both. England's Glory of Cheltenham is an all-women's side.

To take one example, the Gloucestershire Morris can call on some thirty dancers and six musicians, some of whom also dance. Normally, only one musician plays at a time. The instruments available are melodeon, concertina, harmonica, jew's harp and, in an interesting reversion to earlier practice, the pipe and tabor.

The dancers practise weekly from September to March, and the side performs on at least forty occasions during the year, including bank holidays, folk festivals, fetes and galas. Joint tours with other sides - Stroud, Chipping Campden, Lassington Oak, Forest of Dean - often lead to performances in close proximity to public houses such as the Bell at Framilode, the Glasshouse at May Hill, the Coach and Horses at Longborough and the Fleet at Twyning.

The repertoire is drawn mainly from Bledington, Longborough, Oddington and Sherborne, so it is fitting that the side should visit such places, as well as Cheltenham and Gloucester. The morris men of the past would immediately recognise their successors. The main difference is that on the whole, though by no means exclusively, the new men are not agricultural labourers but computer operators and programmers, civil servants and teachers. Money raised in collections is donated to local charities. The dancing is still 'proper pretty', which is how Richard Bond, an old Bledington dancer, characterised what he saw of the Travelling Morrice. He added that he had hardly dared hope to see any more dancing before he died. He would surely have been pleased to know the morris retains a secure place in our calendar and our affections.

## Room to Rise

Folk drama has an even longer history in the county than morris. The earliest record dates from December 1283, when Edward I rewarded the young monks of Gloucester for their play on the miracles of St Nicholas and their ceremony of the boy bishop. Just under three hundred years later Bishop Latimer is said to have told the young Edward VI how one May Day, during the course of a journey from London to Worcester, he stopped at a village church in Gloucestershire intending to preach there. Finding the door 'fast locked', he 'tarried there half an hour or more,' after which the key was found, but 'one of the parish came to us and said, "Sir, this is a holiday with us, we cannot hear you, it is Robin Hood's day. The parish are gone abroad to gather for Robin Hood, I pray you, let [hinder] them not".' The people were probably watching a play about Robin Hood, and Latimer sensibly left them to it. The story is also attributed to places in both Leicestershire and Worcestershire.

Robin Hood turns up as a character in some of the more recent traditional or 'mumming' plays, including versions from Bibury, Chedworth, Coates and Minchinhampton. Some seventy-five towns and villages in Gloucestershire had such plays, though in several cases the text has survived in fragmentary fashion or not at all. The earliest to be recorded - in the first half of the nineteenth century - were at Chalford and Wotton-under-Edge in the south and Winchcombe in the north. The most recent to be noted was at Alveston in the 1950s from Mr W.G. Collins, an eighty-eight-year-old retired postman.

The characters - often as few as five or six but sometimes double that number - stand in a line, a semi-circle or a circle, stepping forward when the action demands, and speaking in declamatory fashion. The plot is very simple. There is a mock combat after which a quack doctor brings the casualty back to life. The play, lasting from fifteen minutes to half an hour depending on the version, usually concludes with a song or a dance, and always with a collection.

In many cases the action is introduced by Father Christmas, though one can also find Captain, Foreman, Foremost and Fust, Headman, Leading Man or Old Hindbefore. The character most commonly representing good is King, Prince or Saint George. Other champions might be Gallant or Valiant Soldier, Gallantine, John Bull Robin, Little Man John or, perhaps surprisingly, King of France. Bold Slasher and King of Egypt sometimes appear on the good side, sometimes the bad. The most usual figure in the adverse camp is Turkish Knight (sometimes garbled to Turkey Snipe), though Royal Prussian King (Royal Parochial King at Minchinhampton) often features and is, oddly, identified at Dumbleton as Duke Wellington. Other villains are King William, Bonaparte, Robin Wood, Speckleback, Black Knight and the Black Prince of Paradise. Bisley, Coates and Charlton Kings have a dragon.

The doctor, the only character who appears in every play, is sometimes called Dr Jones or Dr Jack Brown, and once Dr Phoenix (Marshfield). The assistant with whom he exchanges wordy by-play is Jack or John Finney or Vinney (sometimes two separate characters). Minor figures who may take part are Beelzebub (varied to Bells Abub or Belsey Bob), Old 'ooman (Aunt Sally, Old

Mother Magpie; and at Longhope an alternative name for the devil), Policeman, Tom Fool and Tenpenny Nit. The collector, aptly called Treasury Man at Highnam, can be Little Judy, Niddy Noddy, Dicky Toddy, Little Saucy Jack, Johnny Jack, Ragged Jack, Limping Jack or Humpbacked Jack. A singer or musician - Billy Wit, Fiddler Wit, Fiddler Crump, Father Scrump - may bring the proceedings to an end.

In several texts the tunes 'Ran tan tinder box', 'Cat in the fiddle bag' and 'Johnny up the orchard' are mentioned, but these may be cod titles. A three-handed reel was performed in the Weston-sub-Edge play, together with two other dances, but the only tune mentioned was 'Not for Joe', played by Cleverlegs on the mouth organ. The Icomb play ended with a step dance and a broomstick dance; Wickwar's, with all the characters dancing in a circle and singing 'To my high jig a jig, high jig a jig, high jig a jig canary./Come along my Christian boys for to be merry'. Several plays - those from Avening, Bibury, Chedworth, Eastleach, Sherborne and Yanworth - have verses such as 'Green sleeves, yellow lace,/My four boys dance apace', followed by a dance, presumably to the music of 'Greensleeves' (see above). At least one morris man, Alf Tufley of Longborough (died 1923), was also a mummer; and there would almost certainly have been other examples.

Some plays began (Wickwar) and others ended (Longborough) with this song (see also Chapter Eleven):

*We wish you a merry Christmas and a happy, bright New Year,*
*A pocket full of money and a cellar full of beer,*
*And a good fat pig to last you all the year.*

Many end with the words 'I'll sing you a song to please you all', after which the singer would perform his party piece - 'Darkies lead a happy life' (Snowshill, 1936); 'Every Inch a Sailor' (Bisley, 1935) - whether relevant to the play or no. Some versions had fragments of song inserted in passing: 'Robin Hood and the Tanner' (Coates and Kempsford), 'Rule Britannia' and 'The Mistloetoe Bough' (Bisley), 'Rosin the Beau' (Alderton), 'My father died the other night' (Chipping Campden), 'Jack Hall' and 'Good King Wenceslas' (Coates), 'My father is a barber' (Didbrook), 'Me aye ding dong' (Driffield), 'Once I was dead ' (Longborough), 'Old Mother Magpie' (Kempsford), and a version of 'Black, White, Yellow and Green' (Bibury). Marshfield finishes with 'The Valiant Welshman', which dates from the eighteenth century.

According to one of the performers Driffield 'sometimes' finished with what one might have thought an obvious choice, 'The Waysailing Bowl' (see also Chapter Eleven):

*Waysail, waysail, all over the town,*
*Our bread it is white and our ale it is brown.*
*Our ale it is made of the best of barley,*
*To my waysailing bowl we'll drink unto thee.*

*Drink unto thee, drink unto thee,*
*Wi' our waysailing bowl we'll drink unto thee.*

*If thou wilt fill me a bowl of the best,*
*I hope your soul in heaven may rest;*
*But if you fill me a bowl of the small,*
*Then devil take butler, bowl and all.*

Sherborne and Yanworth also ended with a seasonal song (see below).

Costumes were regarded as important. Charles Dowdeswell of Arlington Row paid six shillings for the materials for his in the 1880s. The older tradition favoured anonymity, and this persisted to the extent that all the actors at Bibury, Chipping Campden, Kempsford, Longborough, Oddington and Sherborne blacked their faces. In some cases only certain characters blacked up: Fiddler Wit, Turkey Snipe and Beelzebub (who usually carried a frying pan or ladle and a club, sometimes wore a dress and was known as Old 'ooman). At Marshfield all the characters dressed alike, their smocks and head-dresses festooned with

*The Marshfield 'paperboys' shortly after their revival in the 1930s (taken from a drawing in* The Gloucester Countryside ). *Today, hundreds of spectators watch their Boxing Day play.*

tiny strips of paper giving them the nickname of Paper Boys. Something similar, with strips either of paper or cloth, was done at Chedworth, Lower Swell (where the characters also wore masks of cardboard), Newent, Oddington, Minchinhampton and Yanworth. Elsewhere dress was more or less appropriate to the characters, with the Turkish Knight sporting a turban, King George a red coat, the doctor, black top hat, long-tailed coat and black bag. Jack Finney/Vinney usually dressed as a groom. Father Christmas wore the familiar red robe and cap. Rev. G.E. Rees wrote in 1932:

> *Fifty years ago the Mummers used to come to the [Bagendon] Rectory at Christmas. They were dressed in white shirts dotted with large, coloured paper stars, and white paper caps similarly trimmed. One had a big head-dress, like a Jack-in-the-Green. The two champions, Christian and Turk, each had a shield, one with St George's cross. Father Christmas had a white beard, and hobbled on a stick; the doctor was in black, and the devil had horns.*

When in 1934-35 James M. Carpenter was making his fine collection of play texts, from some thirty Gloucestershire villages, he also enquired about costumes, times of performance, and how parts were learned. On the last point, the overwhelming response was that they were learned from old mummers, forty or fifty years earlier. James Larner of Sherborne obviously benefitted from a workmate, for he learned when he first went to plough. In the same village Thomas Saunders learned from his brothers, father and grandfather. Riley Wall at Driffield and the Gorton brothers at Oddington also learned from their fathers. Several old men had learned at a very young age: Job Ind of Avening at six; Frederick Norman of Chedworth at ten or twelve; George Newman of Cherington at fifteen.

Eber Wright of Weston-sub-Edge learned in 1883-84, both from people and from a printed copy. This could have been the version taken down in about 1864 by the village schoolmistress on the instructions of Canon Bourne (though it was not published until 1933). There is a report that Bourne later paid George Hands a shilling to write out the play once more, and that he coached some of the mummers in the rectory. He does not seem to have interfered further (by contrast with his efforts over Dover's Games - see Chapter Seven). According to several performers at Bisley, a Miss Gamble in 1906 or 1907, introduced fools and a dragon's part to their play, and also seems to have tinkered with the text in general. The same thing may have happened to the Coates version written down in about 1914 by a Mrs Swannick.

In several places the actors themselves intervened. For example, Mr A. Nightingale of Didbrook acquired his text from Fred Coltam of Todenham Park and Joe Fry of Laverton. Eli Gardner of Condicote learned from John and George Finch of Lower Guiting and 'Longborough people'. Warren Eskins, Horace Appley and Jim Cox of Minchinhampton were taught by 'Old' John Shaylor (aged eighty-two), who in turn learned his version as a youth of fourteen or fifteen at Kirkbridge, near Witney in Oxfordshire. This process explains some of the variations in text from village to village, and even within one village.

The Minchinhampton men performed in all the public houses and the big farm houses. They must have been confronted by scoffers at times, for they all carried sticks with which they 'laid out' any who interfered. Public houses were favoured venues; two especially mentioned are the Crown at Blockley and the Mill at Withington. Houses of the well-to-do might merit two performances, one for the gentry in the great hall, another for the servants in the kitchen. At Woolstone and Gotherington, barns were brought into service.

At Newent, performances started three weeks before Christmas. Dursley began a week earlier still, and continued till New Year's Eve. Like the morris dancers, mummers went on short tours: the Alderton men to Charlton Kings; Didbrook to Winchcombe ('where people filled the streets to hear the play'), Willersey and Sedgeberrow; Snowshill, travelling by bicycle, to Broadway, Buckland, Stanton and Stanway.

Performances of many village plays petered out in the late nineteenth or early twentieth century. As with so many other things, the First World War proved a watershed. In the 1920s, however, as some village plays were finishing, at Longborough for example, another was being revived at Snowshill. A group of ex-servicemen - J. Coppinger, George Diston (a mason) and William Hodge (gardener to Charles Wade of Snowshill Manor) - learned the play from W. Wiggins of Blockley. Their performance was authentic enough to please H.J. Massingham, who wrote in the 1930s: 'It was from Snowshill that I obtained the oldest version of the Mummers' Play that, to the best of my knowledge, exists over the entire area of the Cotswolds..., certainly one of the very oldest versions in England, and still acted every Christmas.' Performances, suspended during the Second World War but resumed afterwards, did not end until 1970.

The only play still traditionally performed is at Marshfield. Even here the continuity was broken. In 1930 the vicar, Rev. C.S.L. Alford, heard his gardener, a Mr Harding, reciting some verses while he was working. The picture of parson bent over a sermon in his study while his attention is distracted (or attracted) by unusual words floating from the garden through an open window is arresting. The vicar contacted his sister, the folklorist Violet Alford, who immediately recognised part of a play text. Meetings were convened at the rectory of the oldest men of Marshfield, who between them recalled the whole play. In 1931 it was revived after a lapse of forty years, with three of the cast having taken part in the early 1890s.

Every year at 11 a.m. on Boxing Day a crowd of a few hundred people turns up to see the play, of which several performances are given in the streets of Marshfield during the next hour. There is a quiet dignity in the occasion which is deeply impressive, with the actors seeming to respond to a kind of compulsion. The event is in the hands of members of a few local families, which is another of the hallmarks of the tradition.

Recent revivals elsewhere are more extrovert, with ad libbing, fantastic costumes and properties, and an emphasis on the plays' knockabout aspects. Gloucester and Stroud both have such revivals but the pioneers were the Waterley Bottom Mummers who have performed every year since 1969. Their text is based on one from Dursley taken down by the local vicar in 1883, and they have introduced a wassail song from Tresham. They perform in and around Dursley and Wotton every Christmas, and donate their takings to charity.

Contrasting traditional texts from the Carpenter Collection, previously unpublished, now follow, from Oddington and Yanworth.

## ODDINGTON

From A. Gorton and H. Gorton; learned from their father, who died six years earlier. Handed down for generations - never saw in print. Other mummers: George Hale, William Gardner. Went last in 1911. Black faces. Cut paper ribbons all over clothes. Similar versions: Coln St Aldwyns, Sapperton.

*Hind Before*
*In comes I, old Hind before.*
*I comes fust to open the door;*
*I comes fust to kick up a dust.*
*As I was walking down a narrow, dirty, clane lane -*
*He wusn't very dirty nor he wusn't very clane -*
*I come to an iron house thatched with brass candlesticks.*
*I knocked at the maid and the door came out.*
*She ast me if I'd have a bit o' her home-brewed ale*
*An' a drop o' her home-brewed cheese.*
*I said 'Yes, thankee', an' meant 'No, please'.*
*There was a big iron pur treet stood near by;*
*I ask her for one an' she gave me one*
*As big an' as hard as a blacksmith's anvil.*
*So a room, a room, I do presume.*
*Within my gallant hall*
*There's room to rise an' room to fall.*
*If you don't believe me, walk in, King George, an' show 'em all.*

*King George*
*In comes I, King George, this noble knight,*
*To shed man's blood for England's right;*
*For England's right an' England's reign,*
*All the glory I maintain.*
*I am the royal Proosian king;*
*Many a battle have I fought in,*
*More than one, two, or three,*
*But always gained the victory.*
*Is there a man that dare before me stand?*
*I'd knock him down with my gracious hand,*
*Hick 'im, hack 'im, small as flies,*
*Send 'im to the cookshop to make mince pies;*
*Mince pies hot, mince pies cold,*
*I'd send him to the devil before he was nine days old.*
*Who's that comin' over yonder's hill?*

*Hind Before*
*Bold Slasher, comin' to fight thee in thy field.*
*Walk in, Bold Slasher.*

*Bold Slasher*
*In comes I, Bold Slasher.*
*Bold Slasher is my name.*
*With brass buckles at my side*
*I mean to win this game.*
*Where is that man that bid me stand,*
*Said he'd knock me down with his gracious hand?*
*Hick me, hack me, small as flies,*
*Send me to the cookshop to make mince pies,*
*Mince pies hot, mince pies cold,*
*Said he'd send me to the devil before I's nine days old?*
*I'd send him.*

*King George*
*Nay, nay, my little fellow,*
*Thou talkest very bold;*
*But if thy blood's so very hot,*
*I'll quickly turn it cold.*
*Guard thy hits an' guard thy blows,*
*And face all foes.*

*(They fight. Bold Slasher falls.)*

*King George*
*Is yure a good old noble doctor to be found?*

*Doctor*
*Ah, an' a good un he is too.*

*King George*
*I'll give him ten pound if he will but come.*

*Doctor*
*Shan't come for no sich money.*

*King George*
*I'll give him five pound if he will but come.*

*Doctor*
*Shan't come for no sich money.*

*King George*
*I'll give him four good old rusty farthings if he will but come.*

*Doctor*
*I'll come and glad o' that money. Bring my hoss, Jack.*

*Jack*
*Fetch 'n theeself.*

*Doctor*
*What's that?*

*Jack*
*Comin' as fast as 'e can, sir.*

*(Jack leads in one of the other mummers as a horse, the doctor mounted on his back. He falls off beside the wounded man).*

*King George*
*That's a fine way to come to a man half jud.*

*Doctor*
*I only done it to liven his nerves.*
*Take my horse back, Jack.*

*Jack*
*Take 'n back theeself.*

*Doctor*
*What's that?*

*Jack*
*Goin' as fast as 'e can, sir.*

*Doctor*
*An' when thee get 'n back, wipe 'n down with a wet snowball, give 'n a bucket of lukewarm ashes to drink. That's the way to do to a hoss, Jack. An' mind he don't kick thu.*

*(Doctor pretends to examine man).*

*King George*
*D'ye know what's the matter with this man?*

*Doctor*
*Looks as if he wants a tuth drawd.*

*King George*
*Could you draw it?*

*Doctor*
*I'll have a try. Bring me my snuffbox, pill box an' pliers, Jack.*

*Jack*
*Fetch 'n theeself.*

*Doctor*
*What's that?*

*Jack*
*Comin' as fast as 'e can, sir.*

*(Brings them in and throws them on floor).*

*Doctor*
*What'st want to throw 'n down there for?*

*Jack*
*For thee to pick up.*

*Doctor*
*What's that?*

*Jack*
*For me to pick up.*

*Hind Before*
*Come in, Jack Finney.*

*Jack Finney*
*My name's not Jack Finney.*
*My name's Mr Finney, a man of great fortune.*
*I can cure this man or any other man that's lame.*

*Hind Before*
*What can'st thee do, then?*

*Jack Finney*
*Draw a tuth.*

*Hind Before*
*What else can'st thee do?*

*Jack Finney*
*Cure a magpie with the tuthache.*

*Hind Before*
*How dost do that, then?*

*Jack Finney*
*Cut off his yud an' throw his body in a ditch.*

*Doctor*
*Well, what's the matter with this man?*

*Jack Finney*
*Looks as if he wants a tuth drawed.*

*Doctor*
*Canst thee draw 'n?*

*Jack Finney*
*I'll have a try.*

*(Goes to the man's boot; draws nail out).*

*Doctor*
*That yunt the way. Give me the tack, an' get behind an' pull.*

*(All mummers line up in a chain for pulling; they pull).*

*Jack Finney*
*Got 'n, sir?*

*Doctor*
*No.*

*(They pull again).*

*Jack Finney*
*Got 'n, sir?*

*Doctor*
*No.*

*(They try a third time.)*

*Jack Finney*
*Got 'n, sir?*

*(They all fall backwards, with doctor's arms held up stiff with pliers in hand, and in them a large horse's tooth).*

*Doctor*
*I should think I have. Look yure. More like a elephant's tuth not a Christian's. Hold a*

*bag o' beer a oneside and a glass o' bread an' cheese the t'other.*

*All*
*That's a warm un.*

*(Doctor gets his pliers; offers man a pill).*

*Doctor*
*Now, my man, take this pill to cure all ill,*
*The itch, the stitch, the mulligrubs,*
*Ting tang tillarums; all sorts of diseases my pills pleases.*
*After thee'st been led jed seven an' twenty yurs*
*It's about time to rise up an' sing.*
*Let's help the poor chap up.*

*(All mummers help him up. He sings).*

*Bold Slasher*
*Once I was jud but now I'm alive,*
*God bless the old doctor that made me revive.*

*Hind Before*
*Come in, Ole Beelzebub.*

*Ole Beelzebub*
*In comes I, Old Beelzebub.*
*On my shoulder I car's me club,*
*In me hand the drippin' pan.*
*Don't ye think I'm a jolly ole man?*

*Little Wit*
*In comes I as an't bin yit,*
*With my big yd an' little wit.*
*Me yud's so big, me wit's so small;*
*I'll play you a tune that'll plase ye all.*

*Hind Before*
*Come in, Little Judy.*

*Little Judy*
*In comes I, Little Judy,*
*An' Little Judy is my name.*
*If you've anything for Little Judy,*
*Please to pop it in.*

*Little Devil Out*

*In comes I, Little Devil Out.*
*If ye don't give me some money*
*I'll kick ye all out.*
*For money I want, an' money I crave;*
*If ye don't give me some money*
*I'll kick ye to your grave.*

*(All sing).*

YANWORTH

From John Philips, William Paish. Learned 40 years earlier from old mummers, Jack Griffin, Jim Griffin and William Legg. Wore top coats covered with plaited strips of rag and a pointed hat, up to 18 inches high, similarly treated. Jack Finney has a black beard and a false black face. Old 'ooman wears a white sun bonnet and assumes a high-pitched voice. Doctor wears a tall hat, breeches and gaiters.

*Father Christmas*
*In comes I, old Father Christmas.*
*Welcome in or welcome not,*
*I hope that old Father Christmas*
*Will never be forgot.*
*I brought my bisom to sweep up your house,*
*I brought my bisom to kick up a douse.*
*I pray good master an' good missus,*
*I hope you're both within,*
*For I'm come yure this merry Christmas time*
*To show you cleft [?kith] an' kin.*
*A room, a room for me an' my brave gallants so brave,*
*Room to show you activity,*
*Activity of youth, activity of age,*
*Activity as never been acted afore upon a common stage.*
*As I walked out one summer's morn*
*Down by a shady grove,*
*There an' I saw a red deer.*
*I waved my staff, he flew away.*
*My staff is in length five foot three and a half,*
*So I warrant if he'd knock down a calf he'd knock down thee.*
*So I can neither whistle nor sing,*
*Walk in the Royal o' Proosia King.*

*Royal o' Proosia King*
*I am the Royal o' Proosia King.*
*Many a long battle have I been in,*
*Fightin' for St George our king.*

*If this is not true I am mistaken,*
*Or why should I wear this red waven?*
*I vally no man,*
*Neither French, Spanish nor Turk.*
*There's not a man in this room*
*Could do me any hurt.*
*I'd hack 'n and hew 'n as small as flies,*
*Send 'n to Saatan to make mince pies;*
*Mince pies hot, mince pies cold,*
*Mince pies in the pot nine days old.*
*Rise a row, rise and sing,*
*I am the Royal o' Proosia King.*

*Father Christmas*
*If this is not true, I have been told,*
*Walk in the Valiant Sailor Bold.*

*Valiant Sailor Bold*
*I am the Valiant Sailor Bold,*
*Bold Slasher is my name.*
*Sword and buckle by my side,*
*I long to win this game.*
*French officer, French officer am I,*
*Many a long time I've drove these fields to fly.*
*Now I think I have a right to try.*
*Where is the man that bid me stand,*
*An' swore he'd kill me, sword in hand?*
*I'd hack 'n an' hew 'n as small as flies,*
*Send 'n to Saatan to make mince pies.*
*Mince pies hot, mince pies cold,*
*Mince pies in the pot nine days old.*
*So mind thee face an' guard thee brow.*
*There'll be a battle betwixt thee and I*
*To see which on the ground shall lie.*

*Royal o' Proosia King*
*Thy face also.*

*(They fight. King falls. In runs Old 'ooman).*

*Old 'ooman*
*Get away, boys. Get away, boys.*

*(Falls on top of King).*

*Father Christmas*

*Hello, ye old bitch. Been an' kilt one o' my best sons.*

*Old 'ooman*
*Plenty more about. Plenty more about.*

*Father Christmas*
*Doctor, doctor, come an' see.*
*King George is 'ounded in the knee.*
*Doctor, doctor, do thy part.*
*King George is 'ounded to the heart.*
*Five pound 'ould I give for a good doctor if a wus but yure.*
*So, doctor.*

*Doctor*
*I shan't come for that.*

*Father Christmas*
*Ten pound 'ould I give for a good doctor if a wus but yure.*
*So, doctor.*

*Doctor*
*All right, my lard. 'Old my 'oss, Jack.*

*Jack Vinney*
*'Old 'n theeself.*

*Doctor*
*What's that , Jack?*

*Jack*
*Comin' as fast's 'e can.*

*Doctor*
*Dost know 'ow to do a 'oss, Jack?*

*Jack*
*No.*

*Doctor*
*Gie 'n two oats an' a byun, scrub 'n down wi' a fiz faggot.*
*Tie's taiyl t'the manger an' tell 'n to get fat.*
*Hast got 'n?*

*Jack*
*Tight be the kick as he shaun tail.*

*Doctor*
*In comes I, old Doctor Aero,*
*Very well known at home an' abroad;*
*Travelled all over the country*
*But never been far from home.*
*I 'ave some pills - they are the best,*
*North, south, east an' west.*
*I 'ave some pills, they are but few,*
*They'll search the body an' stomach through.*
*So yure, bold fellow, yure's one for you.*
*If this pill has not cured this man,*
*If this man is not quite dead,*
*Rise up, bold fellow, rise up thy head.*

*(Gives King a pill).*

*Father Christmas*
*What else canst thee cure?*

*Doctor*
*All sarts o' diseases,*
*Just which my little pills pleases,*
*And carns, soft carns, all bruises an' sprains,*
*All shuppick stails [pitchfork handles] without any grains,*
*The itch, the stitch, the pips and the plain,*
*The palsy an' the gout,*
*All pains within an' all pains without.*
*Bring an auld dead 'oman to me, ninety-nine yurs of age,*
*Ninety-nine yurs 'ave 'er been laid in her grave,*
*Her's able to raise an' crack one o' my golden pills,*
*Bound for her life to save.*
*All over maintain, break's neck and set 'n again.*
*Ald John Bacca Chops, open's mouth an' in thu pops,*
*Thee's knows he's well's I do.*

*Father Christmas*
*What else canst thee cure?*

*Doctor*
*Magpie with tuthache.*

*Father Christmas*
*How's do that?*

*Doctor*
*Cuts off his yud an 'is wing an' lets 's live body swim down a dry ditch.*

*Father Christmas*
*All through this battle, this man got slain.*
*Rise up, bold fellow, an' round again.*

*(King rises and goes round after Father Christmas. Old 'ooman follows doctor).*

*Doctor*
*What canst thee cure?*

*Father Christmas*
*I can neither cure 'orses, bulls, nor pigs worth 'alf a guinea.*
*Please to walk in Jack Finney.*

*Jack Finney*
*In comes I as ain't been yit,*
*Wi' my great yud an' little wit.*
*Me yud's so big, me wit's so small,*
*I'll play you a tune to plaze ye all.*
*My face is black, my beard is long,*
*Me 'at's tied on with leatheren throng.*
*My father's a broken-down shopkeeper,*
*That you can plainly see.*
*He gave me this old tin canister*
*To make me this hurdy gurdy.*

*(Sings).*

*Green sleeves, yellow leaves,*
*You five fools dance a piece.*

*(They dance).*

*To me aye ding, to me aye ding, to me aye ding, to me derry.*
*We all come yure this Christmas time,*
*We all come yur to be merry.*

*(Father Christmas hits Old 'ooman across the legs with his besom; she falls down and groans.)*

*Father Christmas*
*Hello, Old 'ooman. That's the matter with thu?*

*Old 'ooman*
*Got the tuthache.*

*Father Christmas*

*Ult have 'n out?*

*Old 'ooman*
*Yes.*

*Father Christmas*
*Suppose thee's ave 'n out if 'e takes thee yud off.*

*Old 'ooman*
*Yes.*

*Father Christmas*
*Doctor, come 'an pull me old 'ooman's tuth out.*
*Says 'er 'ave 'n out if 'e 'as 'er yud 'alf off.*

*Doctor*
*Fetch my implements, Jack.*

*Jack*
*Fetch 'n theeself.*

*Doctor*
*Wha's that, Jack?*

*Jack*
*Comin' fast as I can.*

*(Doctor kneels down by Old 'ooman, with a big bone from a sheep's head and a pair of pliers. The others form a chain.)*

*Jack Vinney*
*All you men's can't pull this old 'ooman's tuth out afore I count to ten, stand a one side.*

*(They pull tooth. Doctor rises).*

*Doctor*
*Ladies 'an gentlemen, call this a human bein's tuth? More like a elephant's tuth nor a human bein's.*

*(Old 'ooman gets up and goes round in a circle behind Father Christmas. As she gets up he falls down.)*

*Old 'ooman*
*Hello, old man, wha's the matter wi' thee?*

*Father Christmas*

*Got the bellyache.*

*Old 'ooman*
*Think a drop o' physic'd do thee good?*

*Father Christmas*
*I should think so.*

*(Old 'ooman bumps him in the belly with a bladder tied to a broomstick).*

*Old 'ooman*
*Physic, O, physic, O, broomstick. Physic, O, physic, O, broomstick.*
*Think a drop more'd do thee good?*

*Father Christmas*
*I should think so.*

*Old 'ooman*
*(Hitting with bladder) Physic, O, physic, O, broomstick. Physic, O, physic, O, broomstick. 'St think a pill'd do thu good?*

*Father Christmas*
*I should think so.*

*Old 'ooman*
*Doctor, come an' gie my ole man a pill. Min', not gie 'n but one.*

*(Doctor gives him a pill.)*

*Old 'ooman*
*'Ow many's 'st gien 'n?*

*Father Christmas*
*Twelve, an' one for thee. Spet 'n out.*

*Old 'ooman*
*In comes I, Old Mother Jack,*
*With me family at me back.*
*Me family's big an' I am small,*
*Few coppers in the box'll plaze us all.*
*Roast beef an' plum pie,*
*Who likes that better nor Old Father Christmas and I?*

*Father Christmas*
*Nobody at all.*
*Demand, demand to what I say.*

*Couch your swords an' sing away.*

*(All get up and go round in ring. Jack Vinney goes last. Sings).*

*Jack Vinney*
*Yure we all stand all in a row,*
*The finest young fellow that ever you saw.*
*Victuals not money we'll never deny,*
*A glass of good beer for we're all very dry.*
*Singing fal the ro raddie, sing the ro raddie,*
*Sing fal the ro raddie I O.*

*If you want any matches you'll buy them off me,*
*They are the best matches that ever you see;*
*For lightin' the candle or lightin' the fire,*
*They are the best matches that you can desire.*

*Go down in your cellar an' see what you'll find,*
*Your barrels are not empty if you will provide*
*For a glass of good wine or a glass of good beer*
*We won't come yur until the next yure.*

*[Pray master an' missus both sit by the fire,*
*Put your hands in your pockets and pray and desire.]*
*Put your hand in your pocket and pull out your purse,*
*An' give us a little an' think it no worse.*

11

# A CALENDAR OF CUSTOMS

At midsummer and midwinter, the longest and shortest days are natural and inexorable turning points in the year which have served as a focus for a wide variety of seasonal customs. Some of these, though very much worthy of interest, are long gone - Jack-in-the-Green in May and wassailing in December, for example. Others - Oak Apple Day, gooding, buff blowing - survive in memory rather than in observance.

Fortunately, Gloucestershire remains relatively rich in calendar customs (some of which have been considered in earlier chapters), such as various May Day celebrations, Bisley well dressing, Randwick Wap, Cooper's Hill Wake, Scuttlebrook Wake and the Marshfield play. None of these events has an unbroken history save for Cooper's Hill Wake, yet they are all very much alive.

In the late twentieth century they attract fascinated audiences, drawn by the deep need for ritual, the thrill of a special occasion, the enjoyment of colour, movement and music. Both participants and spectators experience, consciously or otherwise, a sense of roots, of continuity, of community, which is otherwise often lacking in a confused and fragmented society.

## January, February

The people of several villages including Minchinhampton and Winchcombe believed that the first person to enter a house on New Year's Day should be dark. At Charlton Kings until the 1930s 'the boy visitor' would call in the morning. He entered by the back door and left by the front, both of which were left ajar for the purpose. If there were no back door the boy would climb in the back window, using a ladder if necessary. A silver coin, usually a two shilling piece, would be left for him. He would stand in the hallway and shout: 'Old Year out, New Year in. Coo-ee.' A variation on the custom was for groups of young children to go round, shout the same words through the letterbox, and knock. The door would open wide enough for a hand to proffer a silver coin. If the coin were not silver or if any words were exchanged with the visitors, who also had to be unknown to the household, the expected good luck would not follow.

Washing clothes on New Year's Day was considered unlucky at Tewkesbury, lest 'you wash a child away'. At St Briavels they took down and burned the Christmas holly, contrary to the normal rule which forbade the burning of holly on the fire. Until the 1950s people took their friends a New Year's gift consisting of an apple mounted on three short, slender legs of holly wood, and trimmed with a sprig of box, holly or yew festooned with nuts. The apple stood for sweetness; the box or yew, long life; the nuts, fruitfulness. When the 'calend egg' (from the Welsh *calennig*, New Year's gift) had been presented, the gift had to be renamed every year until the donor or recipient died.

At Upton St Leonards near Gloucester, and Gotherington and Woolstone near Cheltenham, children went from house to house with baskets on their arms and sang:

*Blow well and bud well and bear well,*
*God send you fare well.*
*Every sprig and every spray,*
*A bushel of apples to be given away*
*On New Year's Day in the morning.*

They were rewarded with apples and cakes. The ceremony - which they called 'bud-welling' - was known in Charlton Kings, where it lingered until the 1940s as 'buff blowing':

*Buff blow, God send fare well.*
*Every sprig and every spray,*
*A bushel of apples to give away*
*On New Year's Day in the morning.*
(Spoken) *Shoo-ee.*
*Buff blow, fare well,*
*God send you e'er well.*
*Apples to roast, nuts to crack,*
*A barrel of cider ready to tap*
*On New Year's Day in the morning.*
(Spoken) *Shoo-ee.*
*The old year's out, the new year's in.*
*Please open the door and let us in*
*On New Year's Day in the morning.*
*Shoo-ee.*

Boys would sing this between 4.30 and 6 a.m., then hammer on the door to receive money, mince pies or apples. The older ones might be given wine or cider. The song may be a relic of the wassailing of apple trees once carried out on Twelfth Night, January 6th.

In the Forest of Dean this was celebrated as Old Christmas, in disregard of the change of calendar of 1752 which removed eleven days and moved everything forward. A further day subtracted later added to the gap. At midnight on Old Christmas Eve Foresters believed that oxen knelt and the rosemary bloomed as tokens that Christ was born at that hour. T.A. Ryder who was brought up near Westbury-on-Severn wrote:

> *My father used to tell me that when he was a small boy ... - that would have been in the late 1870s - his father kept up Christmas on that day [6 January] and that December 25th was regarded as a Sunday, with only the minimum of work being done, and no festivities.*

In some of the areas which did accept 6 January as Twelfth Day a ceremony was held on its eve which the historian, Fosbrooke, described in 1807:

> *In the parish of Pauntley, and the surrounding neighbourhood, the servants of each farmer formerly assembled together in one of the fields that had been sown with wheat. At the end of twelve lands, they made twelve fires in a row with straw, around one of which, much larger than the rest, they drank a cheerful glass of cider to their master's health, and success to the future harvest; then, returning home, they feasted on cakes soaked in cider, which they claimed as a reward for their past labours in sowing the grain.*

Until much more recent times (see Chapter Eight) Plough Sunday and Monday celebrations took place on the first Sunday and Monday after Twelfth Night.

The textile workers of the Cotswolds honoured their patron saint, Bishop Blaise, on 3 February with elaborate processions and also copious drinking (see Chapter Five). Shrove Tuesday, depending on the date of Easter, falls between early February and early March. The day before is Collop Monday, so called because the last meat of the season in the form of collops of mutton or bacon was eaten then. Shrove Tuesday is still the day for eating pancakes, though the bells which once signalled the meal (Chapter Four) are now silent.

On the following day, Ash Wednesday, the traditional dish at Minchinhampton was pease pudding. In the same village one's Valentine was the first person of the appropriate sex (and presumably age) seen on 14 February, which must have produced a good deal of careful manoeuvring. As far back as 1620 people in Berkeley Vale said: 'On St Valentine's Day/Cast beans in clay'. Elsewhere children went round collecting, as this entry in the Broadwell school log for 1871 shows: 'Opened school at ten o'clock this morning as the children were gone round the village for Valentines. Usual progress not made as too much excitement prevailed.' In the 1950s Miss A.

Smith of Great Rissington recalled how seventy years earlier she had gone round with tiny flowers and a chant:

*Good morrow to you, Valentine,*
*I'll be yours if you'll be mine.*
*Give us a penny and save us all.*
*One for Peter and one for Paul,*
*And one for the little boy over the wall.*

## March, April

Mother's Day as we know it is an American institution, invented in 1906. Mothering Sunday, the fourth in Lent, is much more ancient, moving with Easter and normally falling in March, occasionally in April. A letter written from Bristol in 1827 explains that 'the day is scrupulously observed in this city and neighbourhood.' The writer adds:

*All who consider themselves dutiful children, or who wish to be so considered by others, on this day make presents to their mother. The family all assemble; and, if the day prove fine, proceed, after church to the neighbouring village to eat frumenty. The higher classes partake of it at their own houses, and in the evening come the cake and wine.*

Frumenty is hulled wheat boiled in milk, seasoned with cinnamon and sweetened with sugar. The cake may be the simnel mentioned in connection with Gloucestershire by the poet Herrick:

*I'le to thee a simnell bring*
*'Gainst thou go'st a mothering;*
*So that when she blesseth thee*
*Half that blessing thou'lt give me.*

Mothering Sunday was kept up in the old way until the First World War. Chine of pork found particular favour for the family meal, though at Haresfield veal was preferred. Servant girls round Minchinhampton and Stroud would be given the day off to go home, taking a cake with them. At the Swan Inn and elsewhere at Wotton-under-Edge servants were treated to cake and wine, and also encouraged to invite their friends and sweethearts.

Palm Sunday, a week before Easter, comes in March or April. T.A. Ryder (born in 1904) remembered how as a small boy he and his sisters 'would spend days before Palm Sunday picking wild flowers. These were then tied in small bunches and taken to Westbury-on-Severn churchyard, where we placed them in circular or cross-shaped containers on our godparents' graves.' He adds that it was not thought fitting to use 'boughten' flowers for the purpose. Round

Dymock the famous wild daffodils were used both to flower the graves on Palm Sunday and to present to mothers on Mothering Sunday.

On the Thursday before Easter the children of Doynton in the deep south of the county went from house to house saying 'they had come gooding and expecting some largesse.' Elsewhere in Gloucestershire 21 December was the date for this (see below).

It was customary for crowds of people from Leckhampton to spend Good Friday on the hill, which they claimed had been given to the parish by William the Conqueror. When, late in the nineteenth century, the legal owners tried to exclude visitors, villagers responded by breaking fences, setting fire to the furze, and parading with the rough music of tins, cans, pots and kettles. In 1897 a cottage considered to be encroaching on the hill was burnt down, and nine years later another, thought to be built over a public footpath, was broken into. As a result, the Riot Act was read and eight men subsequently served terms of imprisonment for their part in the action. Respectable opinion was very much behind such protests, and in 1928 the hill was bought by Cheltenham Town Council.

On Good Friday the men of Uley held their marbles championship finals in the street, to the accompaniment of music supplied by the village band. After attending church in the morning young people from Wotton-under-Edge climbed Nibley Knoll in the afternoon for a session of games. Vendors provided hot-cross buns and gingerbeer. For the Dursley congregation - often numbering a hundred - the custom was to spend Good Friday afternoon hunting squirrels in the wooded parts of Stinchcombe Hill. A quieter activity at Great Rissington was the gathering of primroses in Bush Woods.

Villagers of all ages from Minchinhampton preferred Easter Monday for games in the street and in the park formerly attached to the Manor House. 'Jumping Bushes' and 'Crooked Mustard' were for girls; 'A Bundle of Matches' and 'Thread the Needle' were open to all.

For eight centuries off and on, starting with Henry I, the kings and queens of England were presented on 23 April with a pie made in Gloucester from lampreys caught in the Severn. Latterly they were cooked at Fisher's Restaurant, between St John's Lane and the Cross, and before being despatched to London they were displayed for a time in the window. They were therefore probably inedible when they arrived, but the Lamprey Pie custom was nevertheless a source of pride to the city of Gloucester. It ended in 1917, with the exception of a special pie sent to Queen Elizabeth II in honour of her coronation.

## May, June

May Day and Whitsuntide (seven weeks after Easter) were times for celebration and dancing, fairs and frolics. On May Eve people travelled six miles from Newent to Payford Bridge and gathered wood to make fires. They sat round the fires till dawn, then warmed some spring water and, 'Having drunk a number of horns full of it, they used to run round a field in the shape of a figure of eight, until the desired result was obtained.' This form of internal spring cleaning came to an end early this century because of farmers' protest about damage to hedges.

May dew was thought good for the complexion, and in 1667 and 1669, Samuel Pepys mentions his wife's gathering it - 'the only thing in the world to wash her face with'. A Gloucestershire rhyme says:

> *I wash my face in water which has never rained nor run;*
> *I wipe my face with a napkin* [?leaves] *which was never wove nor spun.*

On the other side of Newent from Payford Bridge is May Hill (see also Chapter Two), of which Rudder wrote:

> *Annually, on the first day of May, there is a custom of assembling in bodies on the top of that hill, from the several parishes, to fight for possession of it... What gave rise to this custom I cannot with any certainty learn; but some are of opinion that it is a relick of the ancient Campus Martius, which was an annual assembly of the people upon May-day, when they confederated together to defend the kingdom against all foreigners and enemies, as mentioned in the laws of Edward the Confessor.*

Some might find this rather fanciful. Fosbrooke's comment, written roughly 30 years later, seems more credible:

> *There is, or was, a custom here, for the youth to meet on Yartledon-Hill, on May-day (from which, probably, came the name of May-Hill), and contend, in a mock-battle, for the possession of it ... The youth divided into troops; the one in winter livery, the other in the gay habit of spring. The mock-battle was always fought booty [in modern parlance, was fixed]: the spring was sure to obtain the victory, which they celebrated, by carrying triumphantly green branches, with May-flowers, proclaiming and singing the song of Joy, of which the burthen* [chorus] *was in these, or equivalent terms - 'We have brought the summer home.'*

It is most gratifying that every year since 1979 morris men have turned out at dawn on May Day to dance on May Hill, and then gone on to Newent, once more bringing the summer home.

The latter part of the old May Hill ritual is remarkably similar to the 'May walking' described by Vincent Perkins (died 1921) at Wotton-under-Edge:

> *It was the custom for everyone [on May Day] to go to the woods Maying, starting out at 5.00 and returning about 7.00 principally to get young beech boughs with young leaves to decorate the town, and*

*place them in shop windows before business opened. It was considered most unlucky if beech leaves were not brought into the house before breakfast. Schools had a whole or half-holiday, and every boy or girl wore a leaf in their jacket or frock: those who did not were scoffed with an epithet I cannot remember, but which implied slug-a-beds not entitled to join in games. I remember we used to implore our mother to let us sit up the night before so that we might be among the first to start away. It is many years now since our streets were decorated with 'May boughs'.*

The gathering of beech boughs continued in Westridge Wood until the outbreak of the Second World War. A similar custom came to an end in Minchinhampton thirty years earlier because of opposition from landowners but on the Sunday after May Day villagers continued to walk through the lanes and over the common to Rodborough and back before breakfast. At Avening there was an element of mischief in the proceedings, with the removal of garden gates. Back in Minchinhampton, on Old May Day (13 May) children sported beech leaves, but only till noon - after which time they would have been called May Fools. At Nailsworth a spray of beech leaves would be presented to a friend as a luck-bringer on May Day. May walking continues at Cam, though since early this century - on the initiative of a Congregationalist minister, Rev. D.G. Truss - the climb to the top of Cam Peak on the first Sunday of May has been a religious exercise, followed by a service.

Some villages erected a new maypole every year. Cherington's was set up in time for its fair on 6 May. Dursley had the same date, which was also favoured for setting kidney beans. Bourton-on-the-Water's fairs were on the first Fridays in May and June. At Hallwood Green, near Dymock, a maypole was set up. Jack Gibbons played his concertina, and there was a plentiful supply of cider to quench the dancers' thirst since in that hamlet there were five cidermakers.

Alderton's pole, fifty feet high and festooned with flowers and bunting, was set in a hole on the last Sunday in May every year until 1939. The villagers flocked to a fair with roundabouts and barrel organ but the main attraction was a contest for a leg of mutton. Blindfolded competitors struck at a joint with a sword as it swung on a line stretched between two posts. One year the meat remained intact but a bystander's ear was sliced off.

Other places had a permanent maypole. At Paganhill, near Stroud, the great larch spar was taken down before every Whitsuntide to be repainted and freshly decked with streamers. Old Hookey, a musician who played for the dancing there, once served a term in gaol for stealing a tree for a new pole from Penn Wood, near Selsley Common. Bledington's pole went in 1924; Bream's, two years later.

The entry for 9 March 1864 in Withington school's log reads: 'Children absent owing to the erection of a new maypole in the centre of the village.' This (or perhaps a later pole) was replaced in 1931 and again in the 1950s. By then a full-bloodied adult celebration had become a children's event, with sedate dances and genteel songs.

Paxford celebrated on 12 May. 'We spent the morning going around singing our May Day song,' wrote Mrs E.M. Prosser in 1984, 'while the older children carried a flower-bedecked maypole. After tea we all went down to a field and had races, before being entertained by Mr Bennett and his Morris Dancers.' The reference is to Sam Bennett of Ilmington, Warwickshire, who died in 1951. The maypole was probably similar to the one used at neighbouring Draycott, made of two large children's hoops attached to a broomstail and covered with cowslips, bluebells, ladysmock, primroses and violets. A Mrs Digweed of Draycott remembered the May song:

*All around the maypole, trit, trit, trot,*
*See what a pretty maypole we have got.*
*Fine and gay, skip away,*
*Happy is our new May Day.*
*Gentlemen and ladies, we wish you a happy day.*
*We have only come to tell you*
*It is the first of May.*

*Garlands above, garlands below,*
*See what a pretty maypole we can show.*
*Children come, children go*
*In a merry, pretty row.*
*The birds will sing*
*And we'll dance in a ring,*
*And bow to the Queen of May.*

*Merry little gypsies are we,*
*With hearts so light and steps so free.*
*We dance together hand in hand,*
*A gay and happy little band.*
*Tra la la la la.*

*Now I'm queen of the gypsies all,*
*Each must answer when I call.*
*I love the earth and sky above,*
*And rule my subjects all with love.*
*Tra la la la la.*

On 1 May children from Bussage Primary School near Stroud, led by their headmaster, go into Frith Wood and tap on the trees with this injunction: 'Bud well, bear well, and wake up in the morning.' They also have a May Queen, elected by fellow pupils.

In the 1890s Emma Dent wrote of the Winchcombe schoolchildren:

*What added greatly to the fun and merriment of the youngsters was Jack in the Green, with his clowns fantastically dressed in tall hats, and streamers of varied and bright coloured ribbons. Jack himself was hidden in his frame of hoops covered with evergreens, to which were suspended bells, jingling as he danced about, and capered round and round, eliciting screams of delight from the lookers on.*

From much the same time comes a detailed account of May Day revels in Cheltenham:

*The dancers are the chimney-sweeps of the town, two of whom, dressed in ordinary clothes, but with faces blackened, play on a fiddle and a tin-whistle for the dancing. The centre of the group is formed by a large bush: on a framework of wood leaves are fastened, so as to make a thick cone of them, about six feet high, topped with a crown made out of two hoops of wood covered with flowers, fastened crosswise. The mass of leaves is only broken at one place ... through which peers the face of Jack-i'-the-Green, or the Bush-carrier. Jack advances halfway down the street, and then sets down the bush. Three young men of the party ... now begin to dance round it. Their faces are blackened; they are crowned with complete caps (not garlands) made of all manner of leaves and flowers...*

*The rest of the party are two boys and two men, most fantastically dressed ... The leader of the whole procession - the Clown - wears a tall hat, whose crown has been cut almost round, and turned back, like the lid of a meat-tin ... The second man wears a red fool's-cap, with a tassel, all stuck with flowers. On the right and left breast of his white pinafore are stuck or painted white figures, meant for human beings; and behind, a large black pattern in the shape of a gridiron, with a red bar crossing it diagonally.*

*The two boys have white pinafores, with similar figures, or stars...Most or all of these last five carried in the left hand an iron ladle or spoon ... which they held out for contributions; in the right they had a stick, with some kind of bladder hung on the end. Whirling this, they ran about, and tried to strike the passers-by, who scampered off, shrieking, as hard as they could go. They sometimes danced, sometimes roared, and pretended to bite any child who ventured too near. Their faces, like their leaders', were painted in divers colours, fearful and wonderful to behold.*

Similar processions, which also took place in Bristol, were held in Cheltenham until perhaps the First World War. Alfred Noyes gave an account of one in his poem, 'The Cheltenham Chimney-sweeps', written in 1919:

*When hawthorn buds are creaming white,*
*And the red foolscap all stuck with may,*
*Then lasses walk with eyes alight,*
*And it's chimney-sweepers' dancing day.*

*For the chimney-sweeps of Cheltenham town,*
*Sooty of face as a swallow of wing,*
*Come whistling, fiddling, dancing down*
*With white teeth flashing as they sing.*

*And Jack in the green, by a clown in blue,*
*Walks like a two-legged bush of may,*
*With the little wee lads that wriggled up the flue*
*Ere Cheltenham town cried 'dancing day'.*

On the first Sunday in May cheeses are carried to Randwick Church and rolled three times widdershins (anti-clockwise) round it. This is a preliminary to the celebrated Randwick (or Runnick) Wap held the following Saturday.

As early as 1779 Ryder mentioned the wap's 'irregularity and intemperance'. Five years later a full account came from a contributor to the *Gentleman's Magazine*:

> *As I was last year [1783] passing through the village of Randwick, near Stroud, in Gloucestershire, my attention was attracted by a crowd of people assembled round an horsepond, in which I observed a man, on whom I imagined the country people were doing justice in that summary way for which an English mob is so famous, though I was at the same time surprised to hear them singing, as I thought, a psalm since I never knew that to be a part of such judicial proceedings. I soon, however, was informed of my error, and learned that it being the second Monday after Easter, the people of the parish were assembled, according to an annual custom (the origin of which no one could tell me), to keep a revel. One of the parish is, it seems, on the above-mentioned day, elected mayor, and carried with great state, colours flying, drums beating, men, women, and children shouting, to a particular horsepond, in which his worship is placed, seated in an arm-chair; a song is then given out line by line by the clerk, and sung with great gravity by the surrounding crowd.*
>
> *When Archelus began to spin,*
> *And 'Pollo wrought upon a loom;*
> *Our trade to flourish did begin,*
> *Tho' Conscience went to selling broom.*
>
> *Had Helen then sat carding wool,*
> *Whose beauteous face did cause such strife,*
> *She had not sure broke through that rule*
> *Which caus'd so many to lose their lives.*
>
> *Had too Helen's wanton love*
> *Eaten his food with sweet content,*

*He had not then disturb'd the peace,*
*When he to Greece a wooing went.*

*When princes' sons kept sheep in field,*
*And queens made cake with oaten flour,*
*And men to lucre did not yield,*
*Which brought good cheer to every bower.*

*But when the giants huge and high,*
*Did fight with spears like weavers' beams;*
*And men in iron beds did lie,*
*Which brought the poor to hard extremes:*

*When cedar trees were grown so rife,*
*And pretty birds did sing on high;*
*The weavers liv'd more void of strife,*
*Than princes of great dignity.*

*Then David with a sling and stone,*
*Not fearing great Goliath's strength,*
*He pierc'd his brains, and broke his bones,*
*Tho' he was nine feet and a span in length.*

Chorus
*Let love and friendship still agree*
*To hold the bonds of amity.*

*The instant it is finished the mayor breaks the peace by throwing water in the face of his attendants. Upon this much confusion ensues; his worship's person is however considered as sacred, and he is generally the only man who escapes being thoroughly soused. The rest of that day, and often of the week, is devoted to riot and drunkenness. The county magistrates have endeavoured, but in vain, to put a stop to this practice.*

The anonymous writer's request for information on the origins of the ceremony seems to have gone unanswered. It has elements of a church wake, and local tradition held that one of the original builders of the fourteenth century church, a hod carrier, was ducked in a nearby pool by his workmates for being drunk. Some have seen traces of a manorial ceremony or a Feast of Fools. The theme of a world turned upside down to favour the humbler sort is certainly present in the weavers' song. Others claim a Saxon origin, suggesting that Wap derives from 'wappenshaw' (weapon show), a muster of men under arms.

The event formerly began on Low Saturday (the first after Easter) with the crying of candidates' names for the mayoralty. On the Sunday a church service drew many visitors. Local people sold cider (which they advertised by hanging out a green bough), hot mutton pies, shortcakes and 'wiput' (whitepot).

Proceedings started in earnest on the Monday with the voting, which took place orally at the High Cross by the stocks (now the war memorial). Male 'freeholders' - those who opted to pay a small fee to be enrolled - had one vote each; former mayors (known as 'old lords'), two. A high sheriff, sword-bearer and mopman were also elected. Then, fortified with wiput and beer, a procession set off for the pool, close to the church. As well as the officials there were musicians and four boys with white wands, bedecked with ribbons. Once the song had been sung (to the tune of the 'Old Hundredth') by the poolside the mayor was carefully carried in his chair and set down in the middle. The mopman then began liberally to sprinkle bystanders, paying special attention to any strangers present. Finally, the mayor having been solemnly borne back to the cross, the rest of the day was devoted to merry-making and dancing.

People spent so much money that the day after the Wap a man was sent up Randwick Hill to watch for smoke from chimneys to see who could still afford a fire, only for some householders to mislead him by lighting a bundle of straw in the hearth. On the Wednesday after the Wap a party of men, led by a band, marched round the parish to claim the customary annual allowance of cider from the farmers.

There was tremendous local affection for these ceremonies. One old Wapper - a parish clerk called Danny Bassett - insisted that he should be buried just inside the churchyard wall: 'Then I shall hear the mayor go to town.' Sadly for him the Wap ceased after 1892. Problems with rowdiness had arisen, and the church's support was withdrawn.

The story might well have ended there; but it did not, for the Wap was revived in 1972 by Rev. Niall Morrison, vicar of Randwick. It has continued every year since, with the support of enthusiastic crowds. The first woman to wield a mop (at least in this context) was Jean Wilkes, elected in 1989. Other innovations are May princesses, a Wap Queen and cheese bearers. Dummy cheeses are rolled down Well Leaze, a steep and narrow slope adjacent to the churchyard. The song (without verses two and three) is now sung to the tune of 'Greensleeves'. Archelus in the first line has become Hercules, though Achilles was probably intended since his mother hid him among her maidens and set him to spin to avoid the death fated for him (Hecuba is probably intended for Helen in line five). The words 'bonds of amity' in the chorus have been garbled to 'banns of amity'. A new window in the church's Wesley Room in honour of the late Niall Morrison includes a bright vignette of his beloved Wap.

Few of the events previously associated with Whitsuntide now remain, though this too, was a time for vigorous celebration, as we see from a complaint about the people of Bisley and their parson, Christopher Windle:

> *At Whitsontide in Anno Domini: 1610 there was a maye pole sett upp neare unto the parish church of Biesleye & pipeing & Daunceing at the same pole by the youth of the parish there & all of the same*

*was Done as this Deponent hath very credibley heard at the appointement & abettings of mr Christophre Windle ye viccar there & ... Uppon the Munday in the same Whitson weeks ... Did in a sermon that he preached before the congregacion most prophanely & erroniously Defend averre and affirme that pipeing & Daunceinge at a Maye poule & keepinge of Somerale was as lawfull as used & keepte by the people as it was lawfull for them to here the word of god smierely preached.*

The outcome is unclear, but Windle was later imprisoned for debt, and in 1618 wrote from Gloucester Gaol to King James.

Dover's Games, Scuttlebrook Wake and Cooper's Hill Wake have all moved from Whitsun to take place on or near the new Spring Bank Holiday (last Monday in May). The Bread and Cheese Dole at St Briavels has stayed faithful to its tradition, and after evening service on Whit Sunday small cubes of bread and cheese are thrown to the waiting crowd from Pound wall. The event is said to date from the time of Milo, Earl of Hereford, in the twelfth century, but the earliest record is Rudder's account, published in 1779:

*They have a custom of distributing yearly upon Whitsunday, after divine service, pieces of bread and cheese to the congregation at church, to defray the expense of which, every household in the parish pays a penny to the churchwardens; and this is said to be for the liberty of cutting and taking the wood in Hudnolls. The tradition is, that the privilege was obtained of some earl of Hereford, then lord of the Forest of Dean, at the instance of his lady, upon the same terms that lady Godiva obtained the privileges for the citizens of Coventry.*

If anything, the ceremony became too popular for some. The bread and cheese were thrown from a gallery inside the church 'among the congregation, who have a grand scramble for them ... This is as great a tumult and uproar as the amusement of a village wake,' so wrote a correspondent in the *Gentleman's Magazine* of 1816. Some of the food was used as pellets, 'the parson coming in for his share as he left the pulpit.' Most, though, was carefully preserved for a year, for luck. Miners and quarrymen carried pieces as charms against accidents. Others slept with pieces under their pillows, to dream of the future.

Rev. W. Taprell Allen, vicar of St Briavels, made these comments in the 1890s:

*About 1857, or perhaps a year or so later, the unseemly custom was transferred from the church to the churchyard, the bread and cheese being thrown down from the church tower. Later on it was transferred to the road outside the church gates. It now lasts but a few minutes. A few years ago all the roughs of the Forest used to come over, and there was much drinking and fighting; but now it is very different. The custom has, in fact, been dying out.*

If this is so, it has been a long time a-dying since it still exists, thanks in good measure to members of the Creswick family who have been closely involved for two hundred years. James Thompson of Bream wrote this affectionate verse in the 1930s:

*It's a pleasure to go to St Briavels,*
*Where you meet with more angels than devils.*
*As everyone knows every Forester goes*
*To the Whitsuntide bread and cheese revels.*

During the Second World War when cheese was rationed a special permit was granted so that the ceremony could continue. In 1992 the boundary commission proposed to transfer part of St Briavels parish on the bank of the Wye to Hewelsfield, causing consternation to residents there, who feared they might lose their right (dating from 1282) of picking up wood from the Hudnalls. In 1994 people were still collecting pieces of the bread and cheese for good luck. The ritual - now quiet and sedate - produces a sense of wonderment and delight. The Creswick family's commitment is unshakeable, tinged only by regret that no jackdaws now fly down from the castle walls to feast on any unwanted scraps of bread and cheese: they have fallen prey to pesticides used on the crops.

Cockshoot Fair, a 'disreputable revel' held in Westridge Wood near Wotton-under-Edge, was suppressed through the efforts of Rev. Rowland Hill. Rodborough's 'original Prince Albert' - a kind of mock mayor elected and paraded round at Whitsuntide - has now gone. So has the men's traditional swim in the brook from the Rooksmoor end of the parish to Woodchester.

The Whitsuntide club festivals are no more, the need for provision for sickness and burial having been assumed by the welfare state. Many villages had their own little benefit societies which organised an annual celebration for members and their families. Blockley Friendly Society's revel, held on Whit Monday, included a greasy pole climbing competition. At Avening there were parades on both the Monday and Tuesday, and local pubs sold rice pudding at a penny a slice. St Mary's Sick and Burial Society (known as the Cock and Hen Club) at St Briavels was open to men and women, on payment of an annual subscription of ten shillings. On its Feast Day members assembled at the school and marched to the church for a service. There was a small fair at which green peas and faggots were sold. In the same village the Oddfellows, based on the Old Crown Inn, was a rival club. Neither survived the Lloyd George Insurance Act of 1912.

On Whit Wednesday at Stinchcombe men marched through the village behind a band. They carried iron frames (known as garlands) covered with flowers and a banner with the device: 'Unity is Strength'. The procession halted in a field in front of the manor house where roundabouts, coconut shies and side shows were set up. Members ate dinner in a tent. Remarkably, the Stinchcombe club survived until the 1950s. Ebrington's, discontinued at the outbreak of the First World War, did not restart afterwards.

On the Thursday, after a church service people marched with banners and band through the village. Men dressed in their best suits bore wooden poles topped with ornate brass knobs. When a man died his staff would be broken, and the pieces put into his coffin. Women and children in their best white dresses followed the men. The men's dinner of roast beef, plum pudding, bread and cheese, beer and cider, was provided at the Ebrington Arms. Wives and children had to be content with a tea party, and there was another for visiting friends and relations. Swings and roundabouts were installed on the village green, together with stalls selling cakes and sweets. In the evening people danced to the music of fiddle and melodeon.

At Chipping Campden they also favoured Whit Thursday. Men went round and tied oak boughs to all the inns and beer houses, and also to the houses of 'the most important residents'. Later they did the rounds of the places decorated to receive the refreshment traditionally due. The Campden historian, Percy Rushen, wryly commented: 'One can easily understand that this custom died from the latter-day reluctance of persons to reward unasked attention.'

The Lechlade Friendly Society carried oak boughs in its procession, a practice which might have been influenced by Oak Apple Day (29 May) which celebrated the restoration of the monarchy in 1660. Until the end of the nineteenth century, adults at Minchinhampton gathered oak boughs, gilded them, and decorated houses with them. W.E. Adams (born 1832) writes that in Cheltenham on May 29th:

> *Innkeepers adorned their premises with oak boughs, and the inhabitants, especially the lads, carried oak apples or oak leaves in their buttonholes. The lad who failed to adorn himself in this manner was an object of derision to the rest, who saluted him with cries of 'Shick-shack'. The precise meaning of this contumelious expression I never knew.*

Whatever its significance, the expression produced the alternative name of Shick-shack or Jick-jack Day for 29 May. Children would call after adults not wearing a sprig of oak (preferably complete with oak-apple): 'Shick-shack, no oak in your hat.' Later this became largely a children's custom, with stinging nettles being applied to the bare legs of anyone failing to sport the talismanic sprig of oak. By the late 1940s even this residue of the custom had gone.

The modern Spring Bank Holiday is Tetbury's Woolsack Day, when competitors race up and down Gumstool Hill carrying a 65lb bale of wool. The event was originally intended to allow men to display their strength, but there are now races for women, too. Among many other events on the same day, Coleford Carnival takes place. A carnival princess leads a procession in streets closed to traffic. Six local teams compete at tug-of-war, and in 1993 a Forest of Dean cycle race attracted sixty riders from all over the country.

Many fairs (see Chapter Seven) were held in June, which is now the month of the Three Counties' Show. This once rotated round Gloucester, Hereford and Worcester but is now held on a permanent site at Malvern. On Midsummer Eve

(23 June; also known as St John's Eve) bonfires were once lit in Gloucestershire villages to mark the middle of summer just as they did the same for winter later. The last Friday in the month was Bourton-on-the-Water's club day, with festivities at the New Inn.

## July, August

These months were not widely favoured for traditional celebrations since work on the land would be at its height. Even so, the modern Tewkesbury Carnival takes place on the first Saturday in July. On St Margaret's Day (20 July) at Nympsfield the traditional dish was dumplings with wild plums (hegpegs) which gave the villagers their nickname.

Cranham Feast, revived in 1951 after a lapse of many years, now takes place on the second Monday in August. Events include maypole dancing, races, a tug-of-war, and deer roasting, which is thought originally to have been an assertion of villagers' right of access to common land. A similar feast with deer from the Berkeley estate features in the Frampton-on-Severn feast which was relaunched in 1965.

## September, October

Uley Feast was held on St Giles' Day (1 September) until the 1980s. Painswick Church Clipping (see Chapter Four) continues every year on the Sunday on or after 19 September. September is also the month for Barton Fair at Gloucester (Chapter Seven). Mop Fairs survive in October - though no longer for hiring workers - at Cirencester (first Monday), Tewkesbury (first Friday and Saturday) and Stow (fourth Saturday). A strange sport lingered until perhaps the 1950s in this month at Cam - that of 'bird batting'. Several men equipped with lantern, cow bell, net and stick went out at dusk. The bat man beat ricks, bushes and the thatch of barns. Confused by the light of the lantern and the noise of the bell the birds emerged, to be caught in the nets. They were mainly sparrows but the occasional pheasant went into the bag 'by mistake'. The resulting pie was known as sparrow pudding.

## November, December

As well as having a fire and fireworks at the Cross on Bonfire Night (5 November ), 'the populace' at Stroud rolled 'flaming pitch and tar barrels down High-street, to the great annoyance and terror of the inhabitants.' In 1824 the same 'inhabitants' hired a piece of ground where Trinity Church now stands and provided wood for a bonfire there, but the 'rabble' insisted on moving some of the materials to the traditional site, and gave a beating to those who tried to interfere. Several of the men responsible were imprisoned for three months, and there were no more bonfires at the Cross or blazing tar barrels rolled down the High Street. It is ironic to reflect that if the ceremony had persisted (as at Ottery St Mary in Devon, for example) it by now would have been considered a splendid attraction for tourists and others, and a source of civic pride.

A century after the end of Stroud's event Algernon Gissing described similarly tough behaviour at Willersey:

> *At odd times during the day of November 5th the village boys would be seen preparing heavy stakes, one of which must be in the hands of each boy who joined the group that went from door to door to beg fuel for the bonfire ... All the boys together beat time on the pavement with a solemn rhythmic thud at each word as they delivered their recitative, ending up with a hurried repetition of the last word accompanied by a thunderous roll of all the stakes rapidly beaten on the ground together, with a vigour which sometimes even broke the blue lias flagstones of the farm courtyard.*
>
> *The words thus chanted were these:*
>
> *Remember, remember, the fifth of November,*
> *Gunpowder, treason and plot.*
> *It shall never be forgot.*
> *A stick and a stake for King Gearge's sake,*
> *Pray, master, give us a faggit.*
> *If you wunt give us one we'll take two,*
> *The better for we and the wuss for you, you, you, you.*

Continuing in the same spirit, within living memory boys in the Forest of Dean asked for halfpence or cider (for which they carried a suitable tin). If they received nothing they would remove the garden gate from its hinges.

Many villages had communal bonfires in a field or on a green. At Boxwell, where the fire was lit near the Fox Inn, a local saying ran: 'Dark bonfire, light Christmas'.

In November Northleach's High Bailiff was elected to preside over parish meetings, and a Court Leet dinner took place in the 'Wheatsheaf'. During the meal children trooped into the courtyard and 'kicked up a hullabaloo on tin trays' until they were given a traditional gift of a small sum of money. One of the duties of the Court Leet was to oversee the 'doling of the downs' - the yearly allocation of a strip of land to householders with common rights.

An important occasion for the old, the poor and the children was St Thomas's Day (21 December), when those normally too respectable to beg had licence to do so. In the north of the county the custom was called thomasing. At Winchcombe old people and children who went round would be given small sums of money. By the 1920s at Willersey only children were involved, and they supported their plea with this rhyme:

> *Please to remember St Thomas's Day,*
> *St Thomas's Day is the shortest day.*

*Up the stocking and down the shoe,*
*If you an't got no apples money'll do.*
*Up the ladder and down the wall,*
*A peck o' apples'll serve us all.*

At 6 a.m. a bell rang and all the schoolchildren went to the White House to receive an apple, an orange and a sugar mouse or clock.

Hylda King-Ross lived as a child at Beckford Hall, near Tewkesbury, in the early years of this century. She remembered how the wives, mothers and children of all the estate workers would call on 21 December. The butler would answer the door, then her father would go out with a leather bag from which he gave 'a sixpenny piece to each person to help in buying Christmas fare'. Then the recipients, some forty in number, went round to the back door to be given 'a steaming cup of hot coffee, and plenty of bread, spread thickly with lovely farm butter.'

Avening, Minchinhampton and Slimbridge were among the places where the collecting was known as 'mumping'. the term of 'gooding' was preferred in villages as far apart as Todenham, near Moreton-in-the-Marsh, and Tidenham in the Forest of Dean (where children were given money, cakes and sweets). Corn for frumenty was donated at Aston Blank (Cold Aston), and to be ground for flour at St Briavels (where the ritual request was: 'Please to give against a good day'). The school log at Bitton for 21 December 1876 reads: 'Only 25 children present this morning, the rest collecting gifts on St Thomas' Day according to an old custom.' There until the early twentieth century children went round saying:

*Please, I've come a-gooding*
*To buy m' mother a Christmas pudding.*

Some charities chose St Thomas' Day for their doles. For example, residents in part of Chipping Campden called Leasebourne received a St Thomas' loaf every year.

On Christmas Eve houses were decorated with holly and mistletoe - to have done this earlier would have been considered unlucky. (A sprig of the mistletoe was kept for a year for good luck.) At Winchcombe raffles for geese were traditionally held in public houses on 24 December. Before going to bed Yorkley villagers made up the kitchen fire and put a bowl of water before it so that the fairies could have their annual bath. Neglecting to provide in this way would have brought bad luck through the year.

At midnight the rosemary burst into flower and the oxen knelt in their stalls. At Hill Pill a holy thorn which blooms at Christmas came from the staff which Joseph of Arimathea stuck into the ground as he preached there. Brian Waters says that more likely the tree was planted by the priest of the nearby medieval chapel (now known as Chapel Cottages) which also served as a mark for Severn navigators. Many attempts have been made to propagate from the tree by means of cuttings but all have failed.

Willersey people believed that any work done on Christmas Eve would prosper. Cloth woven would last longer, bread baked would be better flavoured. On the other hand it was unlucky to work on Christmas Day. Bread would be tasteless and heavy. If any clothes put on were found to have holes they would be in rags before the next Christmas, yet on no account should they be mended since this would bring poverty to the family.

Still at Willersey, the Christmas Day Yule Log was often in fact a bundle of sticks. While it burnt no one with bare feet or a squint (the one more remediable than the other) would be allowed in the room lest bad luck ensue for the house and its inmates. If the log or faggot were poked as it burned all the good fortune which would otherwise accrue would be poked away. The burning wood was sprinkled with corn and cider. A piece was carefully preserved, to bring good luck and plenty of food during the ensuing year.

At Cheltenham it was customary for children's Christmas stockings to be furnished with three newly-minted pennies and a tiny pudding in its own basin which was later cooked with the family pudding. On Christmas morning the Wickwar handbell ringers toured the village and outlying farms. They called the names of householders and wished 'A happy uprising'. In return suitable refreshment was offered. Ringers at Alveston were given sandwiches and cider in farm kitchens in exchange for the carols and hymns they played.

Boxing Day - still the occasion for an annual cricket match at Newent and a meeting of the Berkeley Hunt at Thornbury - was a time for rabbiting (Haresfield), squirrel hunting (Uley) and the shooting of pigeons, sparrows and starlings (Winchcombe). The famous Paper Boys perform at Marshfield (Chapter Ten). Morris dancers and mummers appear outside Gloucester Cathedral, where (later in the day) carols are sung inside. At Winchcombe the Haslum family was renowned for carol singing.

Writing of his early years in Cheltenham, W.E. Adams makes the point that even then carol singing was mainly done by children, with items like 'The Joys of Mary' drawn from the traditional repertoire. He adds:

> *As a rule, the carol-singers closed their serenades with an appeal:*
>
> *God bless the master of this house,*
> *Likewise the mistress too,*
> *And all the little children*
> *Who about the house do go,*
> *With money in their pockets*
> *And silver in their purse.*
> *Please, ma'am, to give us a ha'penny,*
> *And you'll be none the worse.*
> *H-o-o-p!*
>
> *[What the 'h-o-o-p' meant was unknown to us; but we always ended the appeal with the shout].*

'While children were so engaged,' says Adams, 'some among their elders organised parties of mummers' and many others mention the traditional Christmas play which is described in Chapter Ten.

J. Arthur Gibbs, writing from Ablington Manor in the late nineteenth century, tells how 'during this last Christmas ... we received visits from carol singers and musicians of all kinds to the number of seventy-two ... So from villages three and four miles away came bands of children to sing the old, old songs. The brass band, including old grey-haired men who fifty years ago with strings and woodwind led the psalmody at Chedworth Church, come too, and play inside the hall.'

The quintessential account of carol singing in Gloucestershire must be the one given by Laurie Lee (who was born at Slad in 1914) in *Cider with Rosie*, beginning, 'The week before Christmas, when snow seemed to lie thickest, was the moment for carol-singing'. He mentions 'Wild Shepherds' - a corruption by the boys singing (mainly from Slad Church choir) of 'While Shepherds' - and gives the traditional appeal which followed:

*Knock on the knocker! Ring on the bell!*
*Give us a penny for singing so well.*

Adults continued to sing some of the 'old, old songs', though not necessarily from door to door, and traditional carols found in Gloucestershire include 'The Bitter Withy' (Snowshill), 'The Holly and Ivy' (Chipping Campden), 'The Holy Day' (Mitcheldean), 'The Joys of Mary' (Old Sodbury), 'On Christmas Night' (Buckland), 'The Twelve Apostles' (Yate) and 'The Virgin Unspotted' (Tewkesbury). Mrs Jane Ockwell of Poulton sang:

*God sent for us the Sunday;*
*All with his holy hand*
*He made the sun fair and the moon,*
*The waters and dry land.*

*There are six good days in the week,*
*All for a labouring man,*
*The seventh day to serve the Lord,*
*The Father and the Son.*

*Now when you go to church, dear man,*
*Down on your knees you fall,*
*And pay your worship to the Lord,*
*And on his mercy call.*

*For the saving of your soul, dear man,*
*Christ died upon the cross;*
*For the saving of your soul, dear man,*
*Christ's precious blood was lost.*

*Three drops of our sweet saviour's blood*
*Were shed and spilt for me;*

*We shall never do for our sweet saviour*
*As he has done for we.*

*My song is done, we must begone,*
*We stay no longer here;*
*So I wish you all a merry, merry Christmas*
*And a happy New Year.*

Alongside this religious tradition was the secular wassailing (sometimes called waysailing or walsailing) widely carried on from Maisemore and Shurdington in the north to Little Sodbury and Badminton in the south of the county. The 'Gloucestershire Wassail' is now nationally known, thanks to the version published in *The Oxford Book of Carols* (1928) by Ralph Vaughan Williams. However, this is in a sense an artificial text assembled from several sources, and in the past many villages had their own versions both of words and tunes. The earliest recorded text - noted by Samuel Lysons, probably at Rodmarton - was printed in 1813. The first tune to be published appeared in William Chappell's *English National Airs* of 1838.

Wassailers carried a large bowl which could be replenished with quantities of drink and, in the south, a sort of imitation bull known as the Broad. At Leighterton, for example:

*They used to have a big swede, hollowed out with eyes, nose, mouth and ears, wi' a candle inside, decked in ribbons and set on a pole. When they did knock at the door they did shove it in quick. They did have a walsail bowl which was small and made of wood and they did hope to get lots of drink in it.*

Vincent Perkins comments that, very sensibly, the wassailers visited the largest houses where they might expect the greatest reward. At Newark Park the Tresham men sang in the servants' hall. Their great wooden bowl with iron hoops arching over and decorations of evergreen and ribbons would be refilled with beer or cider. Uley had a similar bowl and a Broad with 'sad face and large horns'.

The bowl at Rodley, near Westbury-on-Severn, was made of sycamore. At Minchinhampton some small wooden dolls also featured. The bowl was kept by a man known as the king of the wassailers. There were once twenty or so who went out on Christmas Eve but these dwindled to three or four, considered 'rather low and rough'. The Old Broad is mentioned in the Minchinhampton song which the admirable James Carpenter noted in the 1930s from T.J. Tranter (who had learnt it twenty years earlier from William Evans). Robert Wilkins, of 73 West Street, Tetbury, from whom Carpenter obtained another version, told him that it was 'handed down in the family for a hundred and fifty years; sung a fortnight at Christmas and right straight on through; formerly eight to twelve went round; dressed in Romney coats [coats provided by a charity founded by Sir William Romney in the seventeenth century]... One man carried bull's head, the same bull's head handed down for hundred and fifty years; other carries wassailing bowl ... decorated with Christmas tree and ribbons; put money in bowl. People give singers beer, Christmas good things. People asked for revival after war. Went to old houses: Chavenage House, Oliver Cromwell House.'

Carpenter noted this text, and recorded the melody on a wax cylinder, from George Herbert of High Street, Avening, who learnt it forty years earlier from older singers. The second couplet of each verse is repeated.

*Wassail, wassail all over the town,*
*Our toast it is white an' our ale it is brown.*
*Our bowl is made of some map-a-lin tree,*
*With the wassailing bowl we'll drink unto thee.*

*Here's to Broad an' to his long harn,*
*Pray God send our master a good crop of carn.*
*A good crop of carn, that may we all see,*
*With the wassailing bowl I'll drink to thee.*

*Yure's to Broad an' to his right eye,*
*Pray God send our mistress a good Christmas pie.*

*A good Christmas pie as we may all see,*
*With the wassailing bowl I'll drink to thee.*

*Here's to Broad an' to his right ear,*
*Pray God send our master a happy New Year.*
*A happy New Year, that may we all see,*
*With the wassailing bowl I'll drink to thee.*

*Here's to old Broad n' to his right hoof,*
*Pray God send our master a good crop of roots.*
*A good crop of roots an' another of hay,*
*To help the cold stormy winter away.*

*Yure's to Whitefoot an' to her long tail,*
*Pray God send our master 'ave n'er a 'oss fail,*
*But a bowl of strong beer to begin the New Year,*
*An' then you shall hear our jolly wassail.*

*Come butler, come fill us a bowl of your best,*
*I 'ope your soul in heaven may rest;*
*But if you do fill us a bowl of your small,*
*Then down falls butler, bowl an' all.*

*If there's any fair maid, which we hope there's some,*
*Pray never let the young men stand on the cold stone;*
*But step to the door and draw back the pin,*
*An' the fairest maid in the house, let us all in.*

*(The men say:) Yes, let us all in and see how we do.*
*(The maid says:) Yes, merry boys all, an' welcome, too.*

Broadly speaking, wassailing east of the Severn ended with the First World War. Yet in some Forest of Dean villages - such as Clearwell and Bream - it continued perhaps until the 1960s. At neighbouring Sling a few people would set off with lantern and bowl, calling on others who would join in after offering drinks. Eventually, most villagers would end the evening at the Orepool Inn or Miner's Arms with a general singsong. On both sides of the Severn wassail songs are still remembered in some families. Long may they continue to be sung.

# BIBLIOGRAPHY

ooks listed are published in London, unless otherwise stated. These abbreviations have been used: GC: Gloucestershire Collection in Gloucester Library; GR: ucestershire Record Office; MS: manuscript; n.d.: no date of publication given; n.p.: no ce of publication given; TBGAS: *Transactions of the Bristol and Gloucestershire chaeological Society*; TS: typescript.


ams, W.E. *Memoirs of a Social Atom*, (2 vols, 1903).
lard, Eleanor, *Winchcombe Cavalcade* (1939).
ino, H.H. 'Folklore in Gloucestershire', *Gloucestershire Countryside*, 3 (1937-40),422-3.
'Gloucestershire Crafts. The Cotswold Stone Tile "Quars"', *Gloucestershire Countryside*, 3 (1937-40), 384-5.
'The Snowshill Mummers', *Folklore*, 50 (1939), 83-8.
'Stow Fair', *Gloucestershire Countryside*, 3 (1937-40), 490-1.
xander, Diana. *The Story of Coberley, Gloucestershire* (? Coberley, 1980).
en, A.J. *Cotswold Stories* (? Cheltenham, n.d.).
*More Cotswold Stories* (? Gloucester, ? 1957).
en, M. (ed.) 'The Story of our Village, Iron Acton', MS (? 1957) in GC.
drews, William, (ed.) *The Church Treasury of History, Custom, Folklore* (1898)
on. 'A Gloucestershire Dialect Song', *The Cheltenham Looker-on*, (28 December 1912), 13.
on. 'Medical Recipes, Charms and Spells', MS (1770 96) in GR.
on. 'Racing in Gloucestershire', *The Cheltenham Looker-on*, (9 March 1912), 9-10.
on. *Strange and True Newes from Gloucester* (1660).
on. *Vox Stellarum; or, A Loyal Almanack* (Gloucester 1826).
stis, Ralph. *The Story of Parkend* (Coleford, 1982).
kell, B.A., et al. 'The Story of Our Village within Living Memory, 1850-1957. Minsterworth', TS ? 1957) in GC.
hbee, C.R. *The Last Records of a Cotswold Community: being the Weston Subedge Field Account Book* Chipping Campden, 1904).
hby, M.K. *The Changing English Village. A History of Bledington, 1066-1914* (Kineton, 1974)
man, R.J. 'History of Brockworth in the Last 100 Years', TS (1958) in GC.
kin, Malcolm and Laughlin, Wayne. *Gloucester and the Civil War* (Stroud, 1992).
yns, Robert. *The Ancient and Present State of Glostershire* (1712).
k, W.N.R.J. *A History of Woodchester* (Stroud, 1972).
ddeley, Welbore St Clair. *A Cotteswold Manor, being the History of Painswick* (Gloucester and London, 1907).
'The Holy Blood of Hayles', TBGAS, 23 (1900), 276-84.
'The Severn-God and Lydney', TBGAS, 50 (1928), 103-22.
ker, M. Lloyd. *The Story of Uley* (? Dursley, n.d.).
nard, E.A.B. 'The Church and Rectory at Buckland', TBGAS 45 (1923), 71-85.
'Some Cotswold Tales', *Notes and Queries concerning Evesham and the Four Shires*, 1 (1911) 161-6.
Stanton and Snowshill, Gloucestershire (Cambridge, 1927).
y. F.W. 'Custom and Superstition', *Gloucestershire Countryside*, 5 (1943-6),56-7.
'The Devil in Gloucestershire', *Gloucestershire Countryside*, 8, no. 2 (Jan. - Mar. 1953), 29,47.
'Forest of Dean' (1952).
'Free Miner', *Gloucestershire Countryside*, 9 (1955-8), 38, 48.
*In Gloucestershire But Out of this World* (priv. pub., Longhope, ? 1980).
'A Village Band', *Gloucestershire Countryside*, 9 (1955-8), 53
dley, Christopher. 'Gloucestershire Crafts: Roofing with Cotswold Stone Tiles', *Gloucestershire*

*Countryside*, 3 (1937-40), 416-18.
Bazeley, Canon. 'The Battle of Tewkesbury, 1471', TBGAS, 26 (1903), 173-99.
Beckinsale, R.P. *Companion into Gloucestershire* (1939).
Beddington, Harry. *Forest Humour* (Coleford, 1977).
Beecham, K.J. *History of Cirencester* (Dursley, 1978; orig. 1887).
Belcher, Ernest. *Rambles among the Cotswolds* (Evesham, 1892).
Bellows, John. 'Relics of Ancient British Forest Life', TBGAS, 6 (1881-2), 222-29.
Bellows, John and Holland, Major. *A Week's Holiday in the Forest of Dean* (Gloucester, 1880).
Benjamin, Marion. 'An A to Z of Folklore, Legend, Custom and Superstition in Gloucestershire ar Avon', *Gloucestershire and Avon Life*, Jan. 1976 - Sept. 1978.
Bick, David. 'The Enigma of Crocket's Holes, Newent', *The New Regard*, no. 5 (1989), 62-5.
Biggs, Mary (ed.) 'The Story of our Village within Living Memory, 1850-1957. Willersey', MS (? 195 GC.
Blewitt, E. 'The Story of Our Village Within Living Memory, 1850-1957. Lechlade', TS (1957) in GC.
Bliss, Mary and Sharpe, Frederick. *The Church Bells of Gloucestershire* (Gloucester, 1986).
Blunt, John Henry. *Dursley and Its Neighbourhood; being historical Memorials of Dursley, Beverston, Ca and Uley* (London and Dursley, 1877; repr. Dursley, 1975).
Bowers, Brian. *Sir Charles Wheatstone, 1802-1875* (1975).
Braine, A. *The History of Kingswood Forest* (London and Bristol, 1891).
Branch, Henry. *Cotswold and Vale* (Cheltenham, 1905; 2nd imp.).
Briggs, Katherine M. *A Dictionary of British Folk-tales*, 4 vols (1970-1).
— *The Folklore of the Cotswolds* (1974).
Bright, L. (ed.) 'The Story of Coleford', TS (?1957) in GC.
Brill, Edith. *Cotswold Ways* (1985).
— *Life and Tradition on the Cotswolds* (1973).
Brinton, Mary (ed.) 'Oldbury-on-Severn. Village History, 1850-1958', TS (? 1958), GC.
Brooks, J.A. *Ghosts and Witches of the Cotswolds* (Norwich, 1986).
Bryant, Richard. 'Excavations at St Mary de Lode, Gloucester, 1978-1979', *Glevensis*, 14 (1980), 4-12.
Buckingham, E.R. (ed.) 'Our Village, 1850-1958. Hucclecote', TS (? 1958), GC.
Buckley, Mrs. 'Marshfield. A History of the last Hundred Years, to 1957', TS (1957), GC.
[Buckman, S.S.] *John Darke's Sojourn in the Cotteswolds and Elsewhere* (1890).
Burns, Francis. *Heigh for Cotswold. A History of Robert Dover's Olimpick Games* (Chipping Campde 1981).
Burton, R. Jowett. 'Folklore Notes', TBGAS, 53 (1932), 255-60.
Bush Henry and Fox, Francis F. *History of the Gloucestershire Society*, (Bristol, 1899)
Bushaway, Bob. By Rite. *Custom and Community in England, 1700-1880* (1982).
Butler, Mrs., et al. 'Lower Swell. The Story of Our Village, 1850-1957', TS (? 1957), GC.
Butterworth, George. *Deerhurst. A Parish in the Vale of Gloucester* (Tewkesbury and London, 1890, 2n ed.).
Byng, John. *The Torrington Diaries*, ed. C. Bryn Andrews (1954).
Byrne, William. *The Legends of Cheltenham and Gloucestershire* (Cheltenham, 1871).
Cam Women's Institute members. 'Our Village, Cam, 1858-1958', TS (1958) inGC.
Camm, W.A. *Bream through the Ages* (Bream, 1979).
Carlton, Charles. *Going to the Wars. The Experience of the British Civil Wars, 1638-1651* (1992).
Carver, Anne. *The Story of Daglingworth* (n.p. 1968).
— *The Story of Duntisbourne Abbots* (n.p. 1966).
Cash, J. Allan. *History, People and Places in The Cotswolds* (Bourne End, 1975).
Caton, A. Gertrude. 'Kempsford in Story and Legend', TS (n.d.) in GC.
Cave, Ivor M. *Under the Cherry Trees. The Autobiography of a Gloucestershire Lad* (Lewes, 1992).
Cawte, E.C. *Ritual Animal Disguise. A Historical and Geographical Study of Animal Disguise in the Britis Isles* (Cambridge and Ipswich, 1978).
Cawte, E.C., Helm, Alex and Peacock, N. *English Ritual Drama. A Geographical Index*, (1967).
Chambers, Edmund. *The English Folk Play* (Oxford, 1969; orig. 1933).
Chandler, Keith. *An Interim Checklist of References to Morris Dancing in Local Newspapers* (Eynshan 1985).
— *'Ribbons, Bells and Squeaking Fiddles.' The Social History of Morris Dancing in the English Sout*

Midlands, 1660-1900 (Enfield Lock, 1993).
*Morris Dancing in the English South Midlands, 1660-1900: A Chronological Gazetteer* (Enfield Lock, 1993).
aappell, K. (ed.) 'North Nibley. The Story of our Village within Living Memory', TS (?1957) in GC.
hidlaw], R.P. (ed.) *A Gloucestershire Entertainer* (priv. pub., Dursley, 1975).
'Some Folklore of Wotton-under-Edge', pp. 14-21 in G.B. Masefield (ed.), *Wotton-under-Edge. A Century of Change* (Gloucester, 1980).
aidlaw, Richard. 'The Gloucestershire Wassail', *Folkwrite*, no.6 (1979), 3-5.
ark, George. *The Campden Wonder* (1959).
ark, Leonard. *Green Wood. A Gloucestershire Childhood* (1978; orig. 1962).
*A Fool in the Forest* (1965).
ark, Oscar W. 'The Misereres in Gloucester Cathedral', TBGAS, 28 (1905),61-85.
arke, L.B. (ed.) 'The Village of Leckhampton', TS (? 1957) in GC.
ifford, Harry. *History of Bourton-on-the-Water*, (Stow-on-the-Wold, 1916).
leman, S. Jackson. *Gloucestershire Lore* (Douglas, Isle of Man, 1954).
llett, Mrs. (ed.) 'Upper Slaughter', TS (? 1957) in GC.
llins, Abdy B. *The Cheltenham Ghost* (1948).
nder, Edward. 'Some Notes of the Purlieus of the Forest of Dean', TBGAS, 29 (1906), 293-302.
nway-Jones, Hugh (ed.) *Working Life on Severn & Canal. Reminiscences of Working Boatmen* (Gloucester, 1990).
oke, Arthur O. *The Forest of Dean* (1913).
oke, G.K. and Murgatroyd, V. 'A History of the Parish of Redmarley', TS (? 1957) in GC.
oke, Kenneth. 'Painswick Hauntings', TS (1962) in GR.
oper, E.L. and England, J. (eds.) 'The Story of the Village within Living Memory, 1850-1957. Shipton Oliffe', TS (? 1957) in GC.
oper, H.A. (ed.) 'The Story of our Village within Living Memory. Tidenham', TS (? 1957) in GC.
ote, Mark. 'Cotswold Ghosts', *Cotswold Life*, Nov. 1975 - Mar. 1976.
rbet, John. *An Historical Relation of the Military Government of Gloucester* (1645).
x, W.L. and Meredith, R.D. *Haunted Cheltenham* (Gloucester, 1982).
awford, O.G.S. *The Long Barrows of the Cotswolds* (Gloucester, 1925).
awford, Phyllis. *In England Still* (Bristol, 1938).
eswick, W.G. *Where I was bred* [St Briavels]. *The Thoughts and Reminiscences of William G. Creswick* (priv. pub., n.d.).
oker, T.F. Dillon. 'Cotswold and its Popular Customs', *Journal of the British Archaeological Association*, 25 (1869), 113-119.
osher, G.R. *Along the Cotswold Ways* (1976).
unnington, C. (ed.) 'Alveston. Our Village in Living Memory', 2 vols, TS (1957) in GC.
ttino, G.P. and Lyman, Thomas W. 'Where is Edward II?' *Speculum*, 53(1978), 522-544.
arvill, M. (ed.) *I Remember. The Day's Work in Gloucestershire Villages, 1850-1950* (Gloucester, 1977).
arvill, Marguerite (ed.) *The Story of our Village [Mickleton] 1850-1957* (Mickleton, 1981; orig. 1961).
aube], D[avid]. 'Nursery Rhymes and History - II. Humpty Dumpty', *Oxford Magazine*, 16 Feb. 1956.
avies, Gwilym. 'Charlton Kings Play', *Charlton Kings Local History Society Research Bulletin*, no. 10 (Autumn 1983).
'A Gloucestershire New Year Custom', *Folkwrite*, no. 6 (1979), 10-11.
'John Mason, Cotswold Fiddler', *Folkwrite*, no. 7 (1979), 6-9.
'Percy Grainger's Folk Music Research in Gloucestershire, Worcestershire and Warwickshire, 1907-1909', *Folk Music Journal*, 6, no. 3 (1992), 339-358.
avies, W.H. 'A Cotswold Village', in Massingham (ed.), *English Country* (qv).
avies, W.H. Silvester. 'Notes on Chavenage', TBGAS, 22 (1899), 128-135.
avis, Mollie. *The History of Winson* (Stroud, 1992).
eane, Diana. 'A Little Cotswold Town' [Stow], *Gloucestershire Countryside*, (Jan. - Mar. 1949), 200-204.
elderfield, Eric R. *The Cotswold Countryside and its Characters* (Newton Abbot, 1967).
*The Cotswolds* (Exmouth, 1977; orig. 1961).
ent, Emma. *Annals of Winchcombe and Sudeley*, (1877).
Articles on superstitions, beliefs and customs in *The Winchcombe and Sudeley Record*, Jul. 1891 - Oct.

1892.
Devas, E.H. et al. 'The Story of Our Village Within Living Memory, 1857-1958. Broad Campden', TS 1958) in GC.
Dodd, Arthur and Moss, Philip. *Gloucester Alehouses* (n.p., 1985).
Douglas, Audrey and Greenfield, Peter. *Records of Early English Drama: Cumberland, Westmorland Gloucestershire* (Toronto, Buffalo and London, 1986).
Ditchfield, P.H. (ed.) *Memorials of Old Gloucestershire* (1911).
Drew, Catherine. *A Collection of Poems on the Forest of Dean* (Coleford, 1841).
Drinkwater, John. *Cotswold Characters* (New Haven, USA, 1921).
Duggan, Elizabeth. 'Plough Monday', *Gloucestershire Life*, (Jan. 1975), 61.
Ekwall, Eilert. *The Concise Oxford Dictionary of English Place-names*, repr. of 4th ed.(Oxford, 1991).
Ellacombe, H.T. *Church Bells in Gloucestershire* (Exeter, 1881).
Edmunds, D. (ed.) 'Our Village. Brockweir', TS (? 1975) in GC.
Evans, H.A. *Highways and Byways in Oxford and the Cotswolds* (1905).
Evans, Vivien (ed.) 'Our Village. A History of Woolstone and Gotherington in Living Memory', (1958) in GC.
Exell, A.W. (ed.) *A Blockley Miscellany* (Blockley, 1981).
— *Five Centuries of Blockley Verse* (Blockley, 1980).
Eyre, L.M[argaret]. 'Folklore Notes from St Briavel's', *Folklore*, 13 (1902), 170-7.
—'Folklore of the Wye Valley', *Folklore*, 16 (1905), 162-179.
Farley, Jack. *The Misericords of Gloucester Cathedral* (Gloucester, 1981).
Farmer, David Hugh. *The Oxford Dictionary of Saints* (Oxford, 1987).
Farmer, John A. *Memories of Home in a Cotswold Village*, [Siddington] (Cheltenham, 1925).
— *A Wanderer's Gleanings: Round about Gloucestershire* (Cheltenham and London, 1927).
Farr, Grahame. 'Severn Navigation and the Trow', *Mariner's Mirror*, 32, no. 2 (April 1946), 66-95.
Fawcett, William. 'Fred Archer: the Greatest of all Jockeys', *Gloucestershire Countryside*, 3 (1937-4 406-7.
Fees, Craig. 'Cecil Sharp in Chipping Campden', *Folk Song Research*, 6, no. 3 (Jul. 1988),58-61.
— 'Sources for the Mumming in Chipping Campden, Gloucestershire, 1860-1900', *Roomer*, 8, no (1991), 10-12.
Fennemore, E. *History of Randwick* (Stroud, 1893).
Field, Dick. *Up and Down the Valley* (Barnsley, 1985).
Field, John. *English Field Names. A Dictionary* (Gloucester, 1989; orig. 1972).
Fielding, L.M. et al. 'The Story of Upton St Leonards Within Living Memory, 1850-1957', TS (1957) GC.
Fiennes, Celia. *Journeys*, ed. John Hillaby (n.d.).
Finberg, H.P.R. (ed.) *Gloucestershire Studies* (Leicester, 1957).
Finch, M. (ed.) 'The Story of Chedworth', TS (1957) in GC.
Fisher, Chris. *Custom, Work and Market Capitalism. The Forest of Dean Colliers, 1788-1888* (1981).
Fisher, Paul Hawkins. *Notes and Recollections of Stroud* (London and Stroud, 1891).
FitzRandolph, M. (ed.) *I Remember. Social Life in Gloucestershire Villages, 1850-1950* (Gloucester, 1965).
Fletcher, H.L.V. *The Wye Valley* (1968).
Fletcher, Ronald. *The Woodchester Mosaic Decoded* (Cheltenham, 1990).
Foley, Winifred. *A Child in the Forest* (1974).
Foot, David. 'The Versatile Vicar of Cam' [T.A. Ryder], *Gloucestershire Life*, (Feb. 1970), 25.
Forman, Joan. *Haunted Royal Houses* (1987).
Forrest, John. Morris and Matachin. *A Study in Comparative Choreography* (London and Sheffie 1984).
Fosbrooke, Thomas Dudley. *Abstracts of Records and Manuscripts respecting the County of Gloucest formed into a History* (Gloucester, 1807).
— *An Original History of the City of Gloucester* (1819).
Fox, Francis F. *The History of the Parishes of Old Sodbury and of Little Sodbury, and of the Town of Chippi Sodbury* (Bristol 1907).
Frith, Brian. 'Some Gloucester Ghosts', *The Citizen*, Dec. 27th 1954.
Fry, Eileen. *Strange and Ghostly Tales of Historic Gloucester* (Stroud, 1989).
Gambier-Parry, Major. *The Spirit of the Old Folk* (1913).

mmon, Vic. and Sheila. 'From "Repeat and Twiddle" to "Precision and Snap": The Musical Revolution of the Mid-nineteenth Century', chap. 4 in Trevor Herbert (ed.) *Bands: The Brass Band Movement in the 19th and 20th Centuries* (Milton Keynes, 1991).
unt, Peter. *The Cromwellian Gazetteer* (Gloucester, 1987).
thyn-Jones, J.E. *Dymock down the Ages* (n.p. 1985; 2nd ed.).
bbs, J. Arthur. *A Cotswold Village. Or, Country Life and Pursuits in Gloucestershire* (1934;orig. 1898).
les, Granville H. *Bygone Years. The Forest of Dean Miners* (n.p. 1981; 2nd ed.).
ssing, Algernon. *The Footpath Way in Gloucestershire* (1924).
oucestershire Federation of Women's Institutes. *The Gloucestershire Village Book* (Newbury and Gloucester, 1987).
ucestershire Notes and Queries*, ed. Beaver H. Blacker, vols 1-4 (1881-90); W.P.W. Phillimore, vols 5-7 (1896-1901); and Sidney J. Madge, vol. 9 (1902).
ant, R. 'Ampney Crucis, 1886-1896. A Walk through the Village with the Squire's Daughter', TS (? 1957) in GC.
aves, Richard. *The Spiritual Quixote* (3 vols 1774, 2nd ed.; orig, 1772)
eat Rissington Women's Institute Members. 'A History of the Village within Living Memory, 1857-1957', TS (? 1957) in GC.
eaves, Ralph. *Foxhunting in Gloucestershire* (n.d.).
*A Short History of the Berkeley Hunt* (1951, 2nd ed.).
een, Russ. *May Hill. A Short History* (n.p., 1987).
eenfield, Peter Henry. 'Medieval and Renaissance Drama in Gloucestershire', PhD thesis, Washington University, 1981 (copy in GR).
eenhill, Basil. 'Severn Trows: A Vanished Craft', *Gloucestershire Countryside*, 3 (1937-40), 446-7.
ale, C.H. *Graves of Our Fathers* (1858).
all, A.A. (ed.) 'The History of Yate', TS (? 1957) in GC.
all, George Edmund. *William Wurkman's Wit and Wisdom* (Stroud, 1910).
ancox, Avery S. *A Country Collection of Random Recollections (Stratford and the Cotswolds)* (Shipston-on-Stour, 1988).
annam-Clark, Theodore. *Drama in Gloucestershire* (1928).
are, Kenneth. *Gloucestershire* [1949].
arrowven, Jean. *Origins of Rhymes, Songs and Sayings* (1977).
art, Cyril. *Coleford. The History of a West Gloucestershire Town* (Gloucester, 1983).
*The Industrial History of Dean* (Newton Abbot, 1971).
artland, Ethel M. 'Barton Fair', a collection of papers in GC.
artland, E.S. *County Folk-lore: Gloucestershire* (1892).
'Deerhurst Church and the Battle of Tewkesbury', *Transactions of the Woolhope Naturalist Field Club*, (1921-3), 49-53.
'The Deerhurst Dragon', *The Antiquary*, 38 (1902), 140-5.
'The Legend of St Kenelm', TBGAS, 39 (1916), 13-65.
'Notes on the Folk-lore of Gloucestershire', MS (c.1892) in GC.
'On an Inscribed Leaden Tablet found at Dymock', *Reliquary and Illustrated Archaeologist*, (July 1897).
'The Whitsuntide Rite at St Briavels', TBGAS, 18 (1893-4), 82-93.
ayes, H.W. and Walter, J.E. *The Parish Church of St Mary the Virgin, Marshfield. A Short History and Guide* (Marshfield, 1992).
aygarth, E.G. *Cirencester Society in London* (Cirencester, 1905).
eaney, Michael. 'The Dean Forest Traditions', *The Morris Dancer*, 12 (1982),11-16.
eaney, Michael and Forrest, John. *Annals of Early Morris* (Sheffield, 1991).
edges, Kathleen and Randall, Eileen. 'A History of the Village of Stinchcombe, 1857-1957', TS (? 1957) in GC.
eighway, Carolyn. *Gloucester. A History and Guide* (Gloucester, 1985).
erbert, Henry. *Autobiography of Henry Herbert, a Gloucestershire Shoemaker, and Native of Fairford* (Gloucester, 1985).
inde, Thomas. *Forests of Britain* (1985).
inder, M.C. 'The History of the Village of Avening', MS (? 1957) in GC.
odgson, Eric. *A History of Tetbury* (Dursley, 1976).

Hole, Christina. *Witchcraft in England* (1977).
Holloway, John (ed.) *The Oxford Book of Local Verses* (Oxford, 1987).
Holmes, A. Dorothy. *Severn, Wye and Forest of Dean* (Shrewsbury, 1946).
Hopkins, Harry. *The Long Affray. The Poaching Wars in Britain* (1985).
Hopkins, Leslie (ed.) *Uley. A Cotswold Village* (Uley, 1983).
Hughes, Thomas. *The Scouring of the White Horse* (1856).
Huntley, R.W. *Chavenage. A Tale of the Cotswolds* (1845).
Huntley, Richard Webster. *A Glossary of the Cotswold* (Gloucestershire) Dialect (1868).
Hutton, Edward. *Highways and Byways in Gloucestershire*, (1932).
Hutton, William Holden. *By Thames and Cotswold: Sketches of the Country* (1903).
Hyett, F.A. *Glimpses of the History of Painswick* (Gloucester, 1928).
— 'Notes on the First Bristol and Gloucestershire Printers', TBGAS, 20 (1895-7), 38-52.
Hyett, Francis Adams and Bazeley, William. *The Biographer's Manual of Gloucestershire Literature*, 3 vo (Gloucester, 1895-7).
Icely, H.E.M. *Blockley through Twelve Centuries. Annals of a Cotswold Parish* (Bungay, 1984).
Jewson, Norman. *By Chance I Did Rove* (n.p., 1973; 2nd ed.).
Jobbins, M.E. (ed.) 'The History of Pucklechurch, 1850-1957', TS (? 1957) in GC.
Johnson, Joan. *The Gloucestershire Gentry* (Gloucester, 1989).
— *Stow-on-the-Wold* (Gloucester, 1980).
Jones, Arthur Emlyn. *Our Parish: Mangotsfield, including Downend* (Bristol, 1899).
Jones, D.M. (ed.) 'The Story of Our Village [Churchdown] within Living Memory, 1850-1957', TS 1957) in GC.
Jones, John. *Notes on Certain Superstitions Prevalent in the Vale of Gloucester* (Gloucester,? 1854).
Jones-Baker, Doris. 'The Graffiti of Folk Motifs in Cotswold Churches', *Folklore*, 92, ii(1981), 160-7.
Judge, Roy. *Jack-in-the-Green. A May Day Custom* (Cambridge and Ipswich,1979).
Karpeles, Maud. *Cecil Sharp. His Life and Work* (1967).
Kear, Bernard. *Scenes of Childhood. A Forest of Dean Childhood Remembered* (Gloucester, 1992).
Keates, Jonathan. *The Companion Guide to the Shakespeare Country* (1979).
Keogh, M.C. 'Throwing the Bread and Cheese. A Dean Forest Custom',*Gloucestershire Countryside*, (1946-9), 187-8.
Kerr, Russell J. 'The Customs of the Forest of Dean', TBGAS, 43 (1921), 63-78.
King-Ross, Hylda. 'Going a-thomasing', *Gloucestershire and Avon Life*, (Dec. 1972), 44.
Knight, Sid. *Cotswold Lad* (1960).
Law, Sue. *Ghosts of the Forest of Dean* (Coleford, 1982).
Lee, Alfred T. *The History of the Town and Parish of Tetbury* (1857).
Lee, Laurie. *Cider with Rosie* (1959).
Lees, Hilary. *Hallowed Ground. Churchyards of Gloucestershire and the Cotswolds* (Cheltenham, 1993).
Lewis, June. 'A Cotswold Village Alphabet. Poulton', *Cotswold Life* (Jul. 1974), 24-5.
— 'Gloucestershire's most haunted village? Kempsford: Bubbles, a Knight and two Lady Mauds *Gloucestershire and Avon Life*, (Dec. 1985).
Lilley, H.T. *A History of Standish, Gloucestershire* (Portsmouth, 1932).
Lindley, E.S. *Wotton-under-Edge* (1962).
Lindley, Kenneth. *Of Graves and Epitaphs* (1965).
Lloyd, W. Wynn. 'Bromesberrow', TBGAS, 45 (1923), 95-153
Long, George. 'Some Gloucestershire Spectres', *Gloucestershire Countryside*, (1949-52), 371.
Longhurst, Sybil, Tufnell, Walter and Tufnell, Alice. *Sherborne. A Cotswold Village* (Stroud, 1992).
'Lycidas'. 'The Grey Geese of Addlestrop Hill', *Gentleman's Magazine* (Apr. 1808), 341-3.
Lysons, Samuel. *Claudia and Pudens; or The Early Christians in Gloucestershire* (London and Gloucester 1861).
*Mabinogion, The*, trans. Jeffrey Gantz (Harmondsworth, 1976).
MacArthur, Wilson. *The River Windrush* (1946).
Madden, D.H. *The Diary of Master William Silence. A Study of Shakespeare and of Elizabethan Sport* (190? orig. 1897).
Malcolmson, Robert W. Popular *Recreations in English Society, 1700-1850* (Cambridge, 1973).
Mann J. de L. *The Cloth Industry in the West of England from 1640 to 1880* (Gloucester, 1987; orig. 1971).
Mason, Carolyn. *Snowshill. A Gloucestershire Village* (Cheltenham, 1987).

ason, Edmund J. *The Wye Valley* (1987).
ason, F.J. and Hart, L.C. 'Staunton', TS (? 1957) in GC.
assingham, H.J. *Cotswold Country* (1946; orig. 1937).
- *The Curious Traveller* (1950).
- (ed.) *English Country: Fifteen Essays by Different Authors* (1934).
- *The English Countryman* (1942)
- 'The Mummers' Play', *Out of Doors*, 13, no. 9 (Dec. 1951), 27-31.
- *Remembrance: An Autobiography* (1942).
- *Shepherd's Country* (1938).
- *Wold Without End* (1932).
cWhirr, Alan. *Roman Gloucestershire* (Gloucester, 1981).
ee, Arthur. *The King's England. Gloucestershire* (1966 ed.).
enefee, Samuel Pyeatt. *Wives for Sale. An Ethnographic Study of British Popular Divorce* (Oxford, 1981).
iller, Celia H. 'Farming, Farm Work and Farm Workers in Victorian Gloucestershire', PhD thesis, Bristol University, 1980 (copy in GR).
inchinton, W.E. 'The Beginnings of Trade Unionism in the Gloucestershire Woollen Industry', TBGAS, 70 (1951), 126-141.
onk, William J. *Northleach and Around. A History of the Town*, (Cheltenham and London, 1935).
- *Tales that are Told on the Cotswolds* (Oxford, 1927).
oore, John, *The Season of the Year* (1954).
- *The Welsh Marches* (1933).
orris. A.S. *The Story of Avening* (Stroud, 1911).
orris, Chris. *Gloucestershire Folk Lore* (Gloucester, 1988).
orris, Richard. *Churches in the Landscape* (1989).
oss, H. 'Our Village within Living Memory. Westbury-on-Severn', TS (1959) in GC.
ountjoy, Timothy]. *The Life, Labours and Deliverances of a Forest of Dean Collier* (n.p. 1887).
ylius, Miss. 'The Story of Poole Keynes within Living Memory, 1850-1957', TS (? 1957) in GC.
ynors, A.B. 'Kempsford', TBGAS 57 (1935), 192-233.
ettel, Reginald. *Folk-Dancing* (1962).
- *A Social History of Traditional Song* (1969).
ewhouse, Clare and Dennis, Mildred. 'Christmas Mummers' Play from Bisley, Glos.', *Folklore*, 46 (1935), 361-5.
iblett, H. Morton. *A Short History of Redmarley d'Abitot* (Redmarley, 1990; orig. 1928).
icholls, H.G. *The Forest of Dean; an Historical and Descriptive Account* (1858).
orthall, G.F. *English Folk-rhymes* (1892).
akey, John A. *Reminiscences of Winchcombe*, (Winchcombe, 1936).
ldacre, Susan (ed.) *The Blacksmith's Daughter* (Gloucester, 1985).
pie, Iona and Peter. (eds.) *The Oxford Dictionary of Nursery Rhymes* (Oxford, 1977 ed.).
pie, Iona and Tatem, Moira. (eds.) *A Dictionary of Superstitions* (Oxford, 1989).
rgan, D. (ed.) 'Stone', MS (? 1957) in GC.
acker, T.H. 'Some Gloucestershire Songs and Old Time and Present Day Christmas Customs', *The Cheltenham Looker-on*, Christmas Supplement (Dec. 21st 1912).
aget, Mary. (ed.) *A History of Charlton Kings* (Charlton Kings, 1988).
aine, Alfred E.W. 'Gloucestershire Words, Expressions and Superstitions', TBGAS, 53 (1932), 260-4.
almer, Roy. *Britain's Living Folklore*, (Newton Abbot, 1991).
- *The Folklore of Hereford and Worcester* (Almeley, 1992).
- 'George Ridler's Oven', *Folkwrite*, no. 30 (1988).
- 'Street Ballads in Gloucestershire', *Gloucestershire History*, no. 4 (1990), 6 - 10.
- (ed.) *Songs of the Midlands* (East Ardsley, 1972).
artridge, J.B. 'Cotswold Place-lore and Customs', *Folklore*, 23 (1912), 332-42; 443-57; and (note by E.S. Hartland) 482-5.
ercival, D.K. 'History of Bream', TS (1958) in GC.
erkins, Vincent R. 'Random Recollections of Old Customs', TS (Wotton-under-Edge, c. 1920) in GR.
errett, D.M. (ed.) 'Bitton. The Story of Our Village within Living Memory, 1850-1957', TS (? 1957) in GC.

[Peter, F.] *Our River: the Little Avon in Berkeley Vale* (Gloucester, 1949).
Phelps, Humphrey. 'The Essence of H.J. Massingham', *Gloucestershire County Magazine*, (Feb. 1989 20-1.
— *The Forest of Dean. A Personal View* (Gloucester, 1983).
Phelps, Muriel. 'May Day Memories at Whiteway', *Cotswold Life* (May 1984), 41.
Phythian-Adams, Henry. 'Three Winchcombe Ghosts', *Cotswold Life*, (Oct. 1983), 38-39.
Picken, Trevor G. *The History of Minchinhampton Town Band* (Minchinhampton,1977).
Pickford, Ron. *Country Days. A Childhood Remembered* (Gloucester, 1984).
Pilbeam, M.M. (ed.) 'The Story of Our Village within Living Memory. Aylburton', TS (1957) in GC.
Pinnell, Pat et al. *Village Camera* [Sapperton] (Stroud, 1990).
— *Village Heritage* [Sapperton] (Gloucester, 1986).
Piper, G.H. 'On Crockett's Hole, and Horne, the Newent Martyr', *Transactions of the Woolhop Naturalist Field Club*, (1886), 89-92.
Playne, Arthur Twisden. *A History of the Parishes of Minchinhampton and Avening* (n.p.1978; orig Gloucester, 1915).
Playne, G.F. 'On the Ancient Camps of Gloucestershire', *Proceedings of the Cotteswold Naturalists' Field Club*, 6 (1877), 202-46.
Pool, John. *Country Astrology* (1650).
Potter, Beatrix. *The Tailor of Gloucester from the Original Manuscript* (1969).
Potter, Dennis. *The Changing Forest. Life in the Forest of Dean Today* (1962).
Powell, K.H. (ed.) 'Our Village within Living Memory. Haresfield', TS (? 1957) in GC.
Prance, Margaret H. (ed.) 'The History of Toddington Village', TS (? 1957) in GC.
Price, Douglas F. 'Gloucester Diocese under Bishop Hooper', TBGAS, 60 (1938), 51-151.
Price, Merlin. *Folktales and Legends of Gloucestershire* (Peterborough, 1984).
Price, Michael David Kean. *Songs, Stories and a Mummers' Play from Gloucestershire* (Gloucester, 1972).
Purefoy, Brian. *The Pictorial History of Tewkesbury Abbey*, (1958; repr. 1967).
Radford, E. and M.A. *Encyclopaedia of Superstitions* (?1947).
Raikes, Robert. Letter on Painswick Feast, *Gentleman's Magazine*, 62 (1787), 73-4.
Randall, Adrian. 'The Industrial Moral Economy of the GloucestershireWeavers in the Eighteenth Century', in John G. Rule (ed.) *British Trade Unionism, 1750-1850* (1988).
Rees, George Edward. *The History of Bagendon* (Bagendon, 1932).
Rendell, Brian and Childs, Keith (eds.) *Wyntours of the White Cross* (Lydney, 1986).
Reeves, Mrs. *History of Little Marcle and Preston*, (Preston, 1972).
Rhys, Jon. 'The Nine Witches of Gloucester', p.p. 285-93 in *Anthropological Essays presented to Edwar Burnett Tylor* (Oxford, 1907).
Richards, Mark. *The Cotswold Way* (1984).
Richards, W.A. 'A Day at Stow Fair', *Cotswold Life*, (May 1984), 39.
Ruck, Grace. *Preston, Gloucestershire. A Guide and History* (priv. pub., 1953).
Rudd, Mary A. *Historical Records of Bisley* (Dursley, 1977; orig. 1937).
Rudder, Samuel. *A New History of Gloucestershire* (Dursley, 1977; orig. Cirencester, 1779).
Rushen, Percy C. *The History and Antiquities of Chipping Campden* (1911).
Rushton, Miss (ed.) 'Our Village, Box', TS (? 1957) in GC.
Ryder T.A. A *Gloucestershire Miscellany* (n.p. 1951).
— *Gloucestershire through the Ages* (Worcester, 1950).
— 'Lore and Legend of Gloucestershire', TS (1969-76) in GC.
— 'May Day Customs', *Cotswold Life*, (May 1973), 30.
— *A Portrait of Gloucestershire*, (1972, 3rd ed.; orig. 1966).
— "Twixt Severn and Wye', TS (n.d.) in GC.
Sale, Richard. *The Visitor's Guide to the Cotswolds* (Ashbourne, 1991, 3rd ed.).
Scobell, Edward C. *Letters from Upton St Leonards* (1907).
— *Parish Gleanings in Upton St Leonards, Gloucestershire* (n.p. 1905).
Scotland, Nigel. *Agricultural Trade Unionism in Gloucestershire, 1872-1950* (Cheltenham, 1991).
Sessions, Frederick. *Beating the Bounds* (Gloucester, 1894).
Sharp, Cecil. *Cecil Sharp's Collection of English Folk Songs*, ed. Maud Karpeles, 2 vols (1974)
Sharp P.M. (ed.) 'Wotton-under-Edge', TS (? 1957) in GC.
Shaw, John (ed.) *Alongside Bristol Quay* (n.p., n.d.).

ıepard, Margaret. 'Harry Taylor and the Longborough Morris', in Stapleton (ed.), q.v., 36-39.
hipway-Blackwell, Nancy. *The Sporting Farmer* (Lewes, 1989).
impson, Jacqueline. *The Folklore of the Welsh Border* (1976).
mith, Betty. *Tales of Old Gloucestershire* (Newbury, 1987).
mith, Brian S. *The Cotswolds* (1976).
– 'The Dymock Curse', TBGAS, 93 (1974), 185-6.
mith, Ethel. *Box as I Remember* (n.p., n.d.).
nell, S. (ed.) 'The Story of Our Village [Cranham] within Living Memory, 1938-1958', TS (1959) in GC.
ollars, Margaret. *Hidden Gloucestershire* (Newbury, 1988).
tagg, R.S. (comp.) 'Reminiscences of Severn Boatmen', MS D4764/4/16 (c. 1926) in GR.
tapleton, Guy (ed.) *Four Shire Memories* (Moreton, 1992).
tayt, Robin and Gibson, Patricia. *Royal Lamprey Pie of Gloucester: The History of a Custom* (Gloucester, 1953).
tawell, Jessica. *The History of Burford and Bibury Racecourses* (Burford, 1980).
terry, Frank W. 'H.Y.J.T.' *A Brief Biographical Sketch of the Life of Henry Yates Jones Taylor* (Gloucester, 1909).
teynor, R. Leslie. *Bromesberrow Church* (Bromsberrow, 1984).
tourton, Michael. *The Mill Inn and Withington Village, Gloucestershire* (n.p. 1983)
ullivan D.P. *Old Stones of Gloucestershire* (Cheltenham, 1991).
utton, Alan. *The Cotswolds of One Hundred Years Ago* (Stroud, 1990).
– (ed.) *Cotswold Tales* (Stroud, 1992).
wift, William T. *Some Account of the History of Churchdown* (Gloucester, 1905).
winford, George. *The Jubilee Boy. The Life and Recollections of George Swinford of Filkins*, ed. Judith Fay and Richard Martin (Filkins, 1987).
ait, Margaret and Isabella. *Wotton-under-Edge, What to See and How to See It* (Wotton-under-Edge, 1897, 2nd ed.)
aylor, C.S. 'Aust, the Place of Meetings', TBGAS, 24 (1901), 159-171.
aylor, H.Y.J. Letters and articles contributed to the Gloucester newspapers, file (c. 1886-99) in GC.
– *The Pig that Saved the City. A Story of the Siege of Gloucester* (Tewkesbury, n.d.).
– *Saint Harold the Martyr. The Red Well at Matson. Two Local Legends* (Gloucester, 1866).
– 'The Three Old Men of Painswick', *Notes and Queries*, 4 Ser., 10 (1872), 162.
aylor, Judy (ed.) *Letters to Children from Beatrix Potter* (1992).
homas, Keith. *Religion and the Decline of Magic* (Harmondsworth, 1973).
hompson, E.P. *Customs in Common* (1991).
hursby, D. 'A History of Broadwell in the Last 100 Years', TS (? 1957) in GC.
iddy, R.J.E. *The Mummer's Play* (Oxford, 1923).
od, D.A.N. 'Christmas Mummers' Plays from Bisley, Dursley, Gloucester, Minchinhampton, Wickwar', *Folklore*, 46 (1935), 365-75.
odd, David. 'The Mummers' Play', *Gloucestershire Countryside*, 2 (1934-7), 62-4.
ongue, Ruth (ed.) *Forgotten Folk-tales of the English Counties* (1970).
onkinson, T.S. *Elkstone: its Manors, Church and Registers* (Cheltenham, 1919).
urner, J.S. Lovett (ed.) 'Withington. A Survey of a Village, 1857-1957', TS, 2 vols (? 1957) in GC.
yack, George S. *Lore and Legend of the English Church* (1899).
/aux, J. Edward. *Church Folk Lore* (1902, 2nd ed.; orig. 1894).
/erey, David. *Cotswold Churches* (1976).
– *The Buildings of England. Gloucestershire: The Cotswolds* (Harmondsworth, 1986).
– *The Buildings of England. Gloucestershire: The Vale and the Forest of Dean* (1988).
/yvyan, E.R. *Cotswold Games. Annalia Dubrensia* (Cheltenham, 1878).
Vakefield, D.L. (ed.) 'South Cerney. Our Village in Living Memory', MS (? 1957) in GC.
Valters R.C.S. *The Ancient Wells, Springs and Holy Wells of Gloucestershire. Their Legends, History and Topography* (Bristol, 1928).
Varren, A.S. *A Life in Gloucestershire and Somerset* (Gloucester, 1973).
Varren, C. Henry. *A Cotswold Year* (1936).
– 'A Valley in the Cotswolds', *The Lady*, (June 12th 1958), 824-5.
Vashbourne, John (ed.) *Bibliotheca Gloucestrensis* (1825).
Vaters, Brian. *The Forest of Dean* (1951).

— *Severn Tide* (1947).
Waters, Ivor. *Folklore and Dialect in the Lower Wye Valley* (Chepstow, 1973).
Watkins, Baden. *The Story of Flaxley Abbey* (Flaxley, 1985).
Welander, David. *The History, Art and Architecture of Gloucester Cathedral* (Stroud, 1991).
Welcome, John. *Fred Archer. His Life and Times* (1967).
Westwood, Jennifer. Albion. *A Guide to Legendary Britain* (1987).
Wherry, Beatrix Albinia. 'Wizardry on the Welsh Border', *Folklore*, 15 (1904),75-86.
White, Henry. *Record of My Life* (Cheltenham, 1889).
Whitfield, Christopher. *History of Chipping Campden* (Eton and Windsor, 1958).
— (ed.) *Robert Dover and the Çotswold Games. Annalia Dubrensia* (London and New York, 1962).
— 'Robert Dover and William Shakespeare', *Transactions of the Worcestershire Archaeological Societ*y new ser., 38 (1961), 9-19.
Whittington, Michael. *The Whittington Story. From the Three Counties to the City* (Cirencester, 1988).
Whitlock, Ralph. *Here be Dragons* (1983).
Wickenden, W.S. 'Customs of the Forest of Dean', *Gentleman's Magazine*, 92 (1822), 602-3.
Wilkins, N. (ed.) 'A Village History. Staverton, Gloucestershire, 1857-1957', TS (? 1957) in GC.
Williams, Adin. *Lays and Legends of Gloucestershire* [1879].
— *Lechlade; being the History of the Town* (Cirencester, 1888).
— *Legends, Tales and Songs, in the Dialect of the Peasantry of Gloucestershire* [1876].
— (ed.) *Roger Plowman's Garland of Merry Tales* (London, Cirencester and Gloucester, 1879).
Williams, Alfred. 'Folk Songs from the Upper Thames', articles in the *Wilts and Gloucestershir Standard*, Oct. 2nd 1915 - Sept. 2nd 1916.
— (ed.) *Folk Songs of the Upper Thames* (1923).
— *Round About the Upper Thames* (1922).
Williams, Tudor. 'Gloucestershire's Most Haunted Village? Prestbury: Bumps, the Black Abbot - an an old bike', *Gloucestershire and Avon Life* (Dec. 1985).
Williamson, Hugh Ross. *Historical Enigmas* (1974).
— *The Silver Bowl* (1948).
Willis Bund, J.W. 'Legends of the Severn', *Transactions of the Birmingham Archaeological Society*, 4 (1917), 87-107.
Wilshire, Lewis. 'Fairies in Gloucestershire', *Gloucestershire Countryside*, 8 (1952-55), 107-8.
— *The Vale of Berkeley* (1954).
Winnington-Ingram, A.R. 'On the Origin of Names of Places with special Reference t Gloucestershire, its Folk-lore and Traditions', *Proceedings of the Cotteswold Naturalists' Field Club*, (1895), 21-39.
Witts, F.E. *The Diary of a Cotswold Parson*, ed. David Verey (Dursley, 1978).
Women's Institute Members. 'The Story of France Lynch and Chalford Hill from the mid-19t Century', TS (1957) in GC.
Woods, Mabel K. *Newnham-on-Severn. A Retrospect* (Gloucester, 1962; orig. 1912).
Wortley, Russell. 'Bledington Morris: Stages in the Recovery of a Dance Tradition', *English Dance an Song*, 38, no. 3 (1976), 94; 39, no. 1 (1977), 18.
—'The Morris of the Dean Forest. Glimpses of an Extinct Tradition', *English Dance and Song*, 42, no. (1980), 16-17.
Wright, Brian. 'Maytime on the Cotswolds', *Cotswold Life* (May 1984), 40.
Wright, Geoffrey N. *Discovering Epitaphs* (Aylesbury, 1972).
Wright, Ray. *Secret Forest* (Coleford, 1980).
Wright, Ray and Young, Bob. *The Royal Forest of Dean Free Miners' Association* (Cinderford, 1974).
Wyatt, I. 'The Cock Road Gang', *Gloucestershire Historical Studies*, 4 (1970), 37-46.
— 'Some Transportees from Gloucestershire', *Gloucestershire Historical Studies*, 3 (1969),17-25.
Wyatt, J.W. 'The Gloucestershire Poacher, 1734-1862', *Gloucestershire Historical Studies*, 4 (1970), 24-31.
Wyatt-Smith, Mrs. 'The Story of Minchinhampton, 1850-1957', TS (1957) in GC.
Wynne-Jones, Davina. *Bibury. A History and Guide* (Cirencester, 1987).

# iscography

Many of these items are now unavailable, though some may be found in libraries. *Indicates that ocks remain.

**ong-playing records**

*otswold Characters*, Saydisc CSDL 222, 1972
*otswold Craftsmen*, Saydisc CSDL 247, 1973
*otswold Music*, Green Willow Band, Sweet Folk & Country SFA 115, 1980
*otswold Voices*, Saydisc SDL 267, 1975
*ongs of Ceremony*, Topic 12T197, 1971
*he Songwainers*, Argo ZFB 31, 1971
*tephen Baldwin, English Village Fiddler*, Leader LED 2068, 1976

**assettes**

*All Brought Up On Cider. Gloucestershire Songs, Customs and Tunes*, Folktracks 60-416, 1987
*All Our Own Work*, Puzzlejug, 1987
*Blossom in Slaughter*, Puzzlejug PJ 001, 1991
*Carol Barking*, Puzzlejug PJ 002, 1992
*The Horkey Load* (two cassettes), Veteran Tapes VT 108/9, 1988
*The Old Stable Jacket. Customs and Dialect of Gloucestershire*, Folktracks 45-415, 1978
*West Country Christmas*, Johnny Coppin, Red Sky Records RSKC 111, 1990 (also CD)

hese items are not recordings of traditional songs, but settings of Gloucestershire poems:
*English Morning*, Johnny Coppin, Red Sky Records RSKC 107, 1987
*Forest, Vale and High Blue Hill*, Johnny Coppin, Red Sky Records RSKC 015,1983

# INDEX